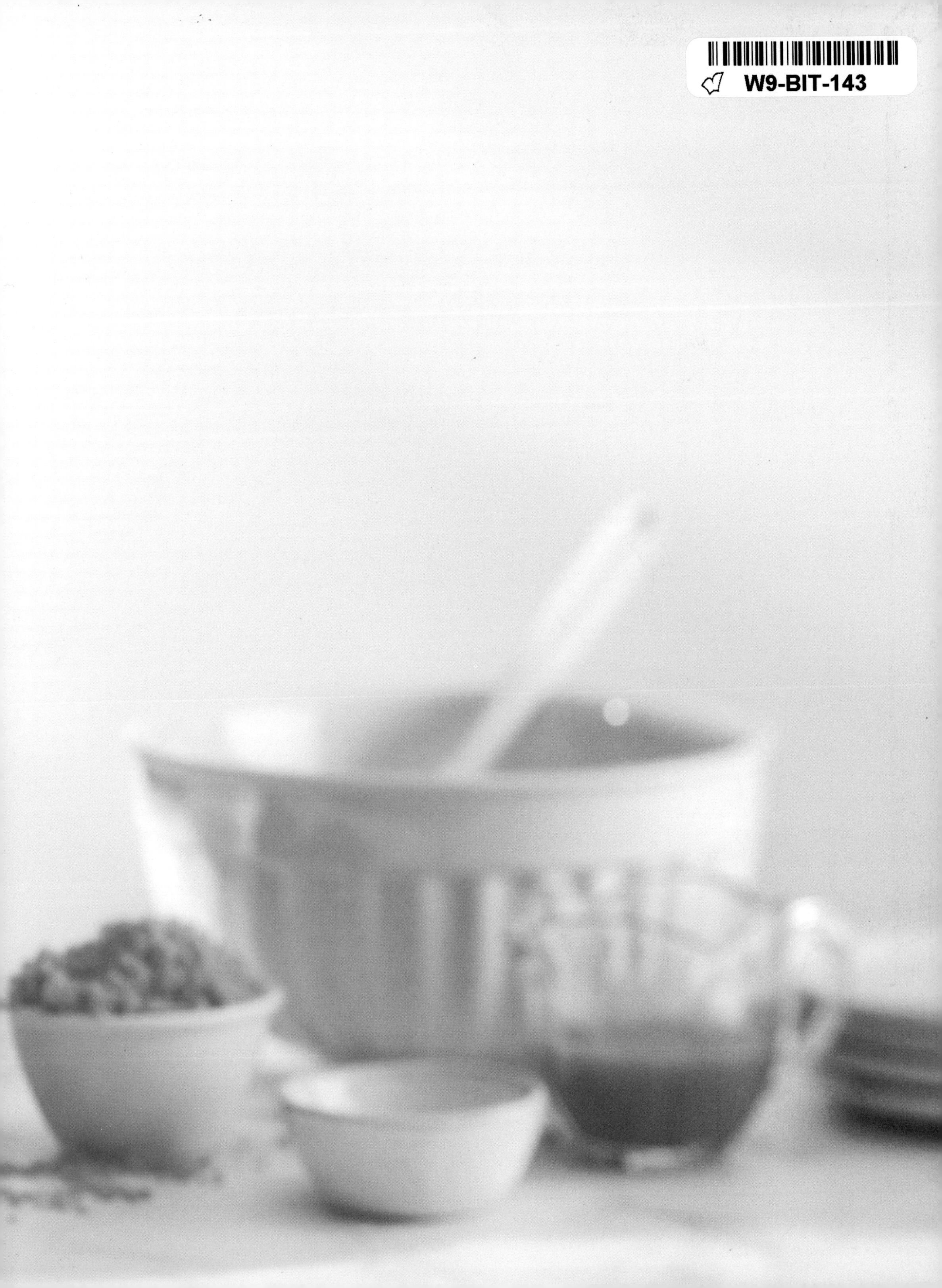

VOLUME FOUR

bake

FROM SCRATCH®

ARTISAN RECIPES
FOR THE HOME BAKER

Brian Hart Hoffman

PRESS®

83 Press
1900 International Park Drive, Suite 50
Birmingham, Alabama 35243
www.83press.com

ISBN: 978-1-940772-72-1
Printed in China

VOLUME FOUR

bake

FROM SCRATCH®

ARTISAN RECIPES FOR THE HOME BAKER

Brian Hart Hoffman

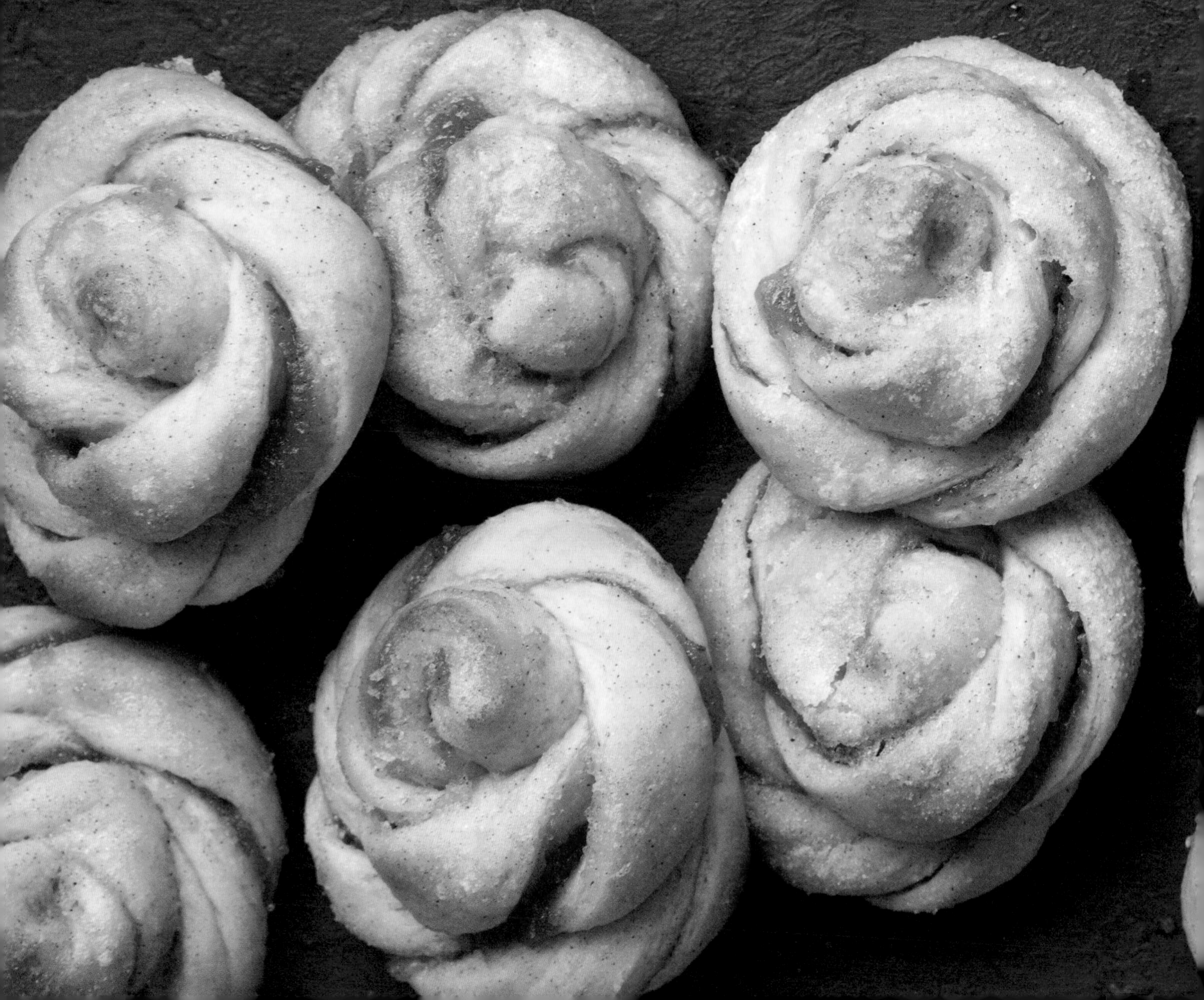

table of contents

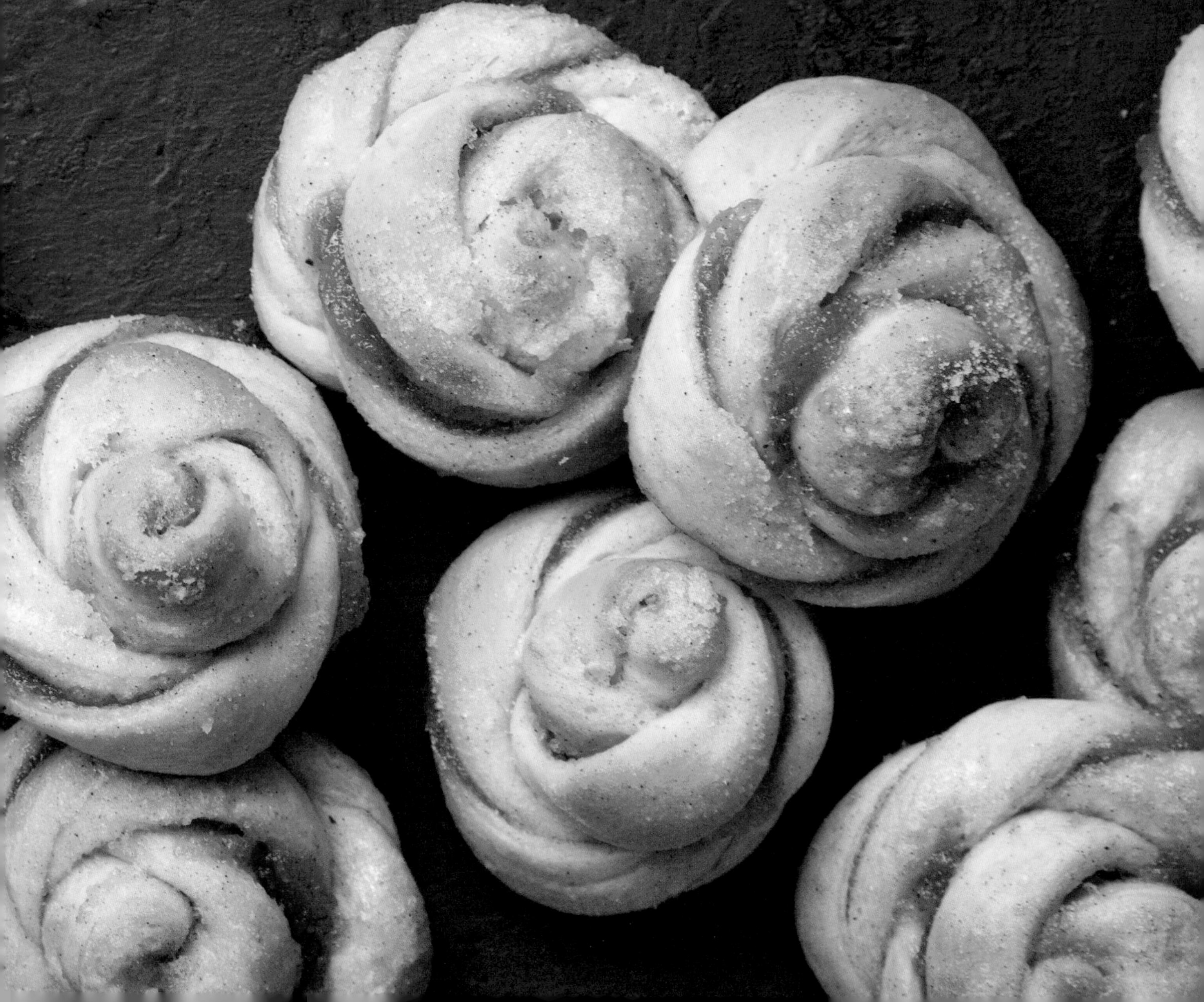

CREATE. BAKE. EAT. REPEAT.

FOUR YEARS INTO *BAKE FROM SCRATCH*, AND THINGS ARE ONLY GETTING SWEETER. AS FELLOW HOME BAKERS, WE KNOW YOU'RE LOOKING FOR RECIPES YOU CAN TRUST, DETAILED AND HELPFUL TECHNIQUES, AND BEAUTIFUL PHOTOGRAPHY TO INSPIRE YOU. THIS COOKBOOK HAS YOUR BACK, TAKING THE GUESSWORK OUT OF ARTISAN BAKING AND BREATHING SOME NEW LIFE INTO YOUR FAVORITE PASTIME.

In our bread chapter, you can expect a recipe for everything from our fuss-free dinner rolls to involved and elaborate babka. Nothing brings the family together like a well-stocked bread basket, so give one of our many cheesy, herbaceous rolls, buns, and biscuits a go. If breakfast is the order of the day, one of our quick bread muffins or scones stuffed with peak seasonal produce, from pears to pumpkin to persimmons, should do the trick. Try your hand at our versatile doughs, like our master sourdough recipe or our tomato-studded shortcut focaccia.

For those searching for a master class in pastry, you can select from dozens of time-honored, diligently tested recipes, from French pâte à choux to expertly laminated morning buns. In fact, if butter-rich pastry is on your mind, look no further than our flaky crusted pies and tarts. From sunny tropical pies to an epic tarte Tatin blowout, we've got you covered.

Plus, we've got cookie recipes galore for each season. Holiday cookie classics, like gingerbread and delicately iced sugar cookies, share space with summery thumbprints filled with everything from cherry buttercream to pineapple jam. Then skip over to an instant fall favorite, like our Pumpkin Spice Whoopie Pies and Chai Crescent Cookies.

And what would a baking cookbook be without cake? Whether layered, frosted, filled, or swirled, each one of these tender-crumbed recipes will fit the bill for a celebratory occasion. For a taste of the tropics, try one of our rum-soaked cakes, like the Rum Swizzle Cake or Banana Rum Coffee Cake. Then you can go traditional with one of the towering American layer cakes, highlighting red velvet, Italian cream, and more. If you're looking for a cake to ring in the holidays, look no further than our two bûches de Noël, seminal roulades that bring high class and decadent flavor to the yule season. Or if simplicity is the thing you crave most, try one of our stir-together cakes that come together in a flash, from a chocolate-rich olive oil cake to a peanut butter and golden syrup stunner.

Create. Bake. Eat. Repeat.

CAKES

LAYER
CAKES

Frosted with velvety buttercream, filled with rich ganache,
or covered in caramel, these layer cakes are just as
indulgent as they are centerpiece-worthy

TIRAMISÙ LAYER CAKE

Makes 1 (9-inch) cake

For this take on the Italian classic, we kept our favorite familiar elements—Mascarpone Filling and coffee syrup—and added a few new surprises, like a thick cap of Coffee Ganache and white chocolate-filled Mascarpone Frosting.

1 cup (227 grams) unsalted butter, softened
2 cups (400 grams) granulated sugar
4 large eggs (200 grams), room temperature
2 teaspoons (8 grams) vanilla extract
3 cups (375 grams) cake flour
1 tablespoon (15 grams) baking powder
¼ teaspoon kosher salt
1 cup (240 grams) whole milk, room temperature
Coffee Simple Syrup (recipe follows)
Mascarpone Filling (recipe follows)
Mascarpone Frosting (recipe follows)
Coffee Ganache (recipe follows)

1. Preheat oven to 350°F (180°C). Butter and flour 2 (9-inch) round cake pans. Line bottom of pans with parchment paper.
2. In the bowl of a stand mixer fitted with the paddle attachment, beat butter and sugar at medium speed until fluffy, 3 to 4 minutes, stopping to scrape sides of bowl. Add eggs, one at a time, beating well after each addition. Beat in vanilla.
3. In a medium bowl, whisk together flour, baking powder, and salt. With mixer on low speed, gradually add flour mixture to butter mixture alternately with milk, beginning and ending with flour mixture, beating just until combined after each addition. Divide batter between prepared pans, smoothing tops with an offset spatula.
4. Bake until a wooden pick inserted in center comes out clean, 30 to 35 minutes. Let cool in pans for 15 minutes. Invert onto parchment paper-lined wire racks, and let cool completely.
5. Using a serrated knife, remove any rounded tops from cake layers. Cut each layer in half horizontally. To assemble, place a bottom-sided cake layer, cut side up, on a serving plate or cardboard round; brush with ½ cup Coffee Simple Syrup. Using an offset spatula, spread about 1 cup Mascarpone

Filling onto cake layer. Repeat layers twice; top with remaining bottom-sided cake layer, and brush with ½ cup Coffee Simple Syrup.
6. Spread a thin layer of Mascarpone Frosting on top and sides of cake to create a crumb coat. Freeze cake for 30 minutes; refrigerate remaining frosting until ready to use.
7. Place cake on a turntable. If desired, re-beat remaining frosting for 15 seconds for a smoother consistency. Spread remaining frosting on top and sides of cake. Rotating turntable, use a large offset spatula or bench scraper to smooth sides and create straight edges. Freeze for 30 minutes.
8. Spoon Coffee Ganache on top of cake; spread to edges. To create spiral design, position the tip of a small offset spatula at center of cake. While pressing down lightly at tip, spin turntable and pull spatula gradually toward edge of cake. Refrigerate for at least 4 hours (preferably overnight) before serving. Refrigerate for up to 5 days.

COFFEE SIMPLE SYRUP
Makes about 2½ cups

1 cup (200 grams) turbinado sugar
1 cup (240 grams) water
1 cup (240 grams) cold brew coffee concentrate

1. In a small saucepan, bring turbinado sugar and 1 cup (240 grams) water to a boil over medium-high heat; cook for 1 minute. Remove from heat; stir in coffee concentrate. Let cool completely.

MASCARPONE FILLING
Makes 3¼ cups

24 ounces (680 grams) mascarpone cheese, room temperature
1 cup (120 grams) confectioners' sugar
½ teaspoon (1.5 grams) kosher salt

1. In the bowl of a stand mixer fitted with the paddle attachment, beat all ingredients at medium speed just until smooth, about 15 seconds. (Do not overbeat.) Use immediately.

MASCARPONE FROSTING
Makes about 4 cups

8 ounces (225 grams) mascarpone cheese, room temperature
½ cup (113 grams) unsalted butter, softened
4 ounces (115 grams) chopped white chocolate, melted and cooled to 85°F (29°C) to 90°F (32°C)
1 teaspoon (4 grams) vanilla extract
½ teaspoon (1.5 grams) kosher salt
4 cups (480 grams) confectioners' sugar

1. In the bowl of a stand mixer fitted with the paddle attachment, beat mascarpone and butter at medium speed until smooth, about 1 minute. Add melted white chocolate, vanilla, and salt; beat at low speed just until combined, about 30 seconds. Add confectioners' sugar, 1 cup (120 grams) at a time, beating well after each addition. Increase mixer speed to medium; beat for 1 minute. Use immediately.

COFFEE GANACHE
Makes 1 cup

1 cup (170 grams) 60% cacao dark chocolate chips
⅛ teaspoon kosher salt
¼ cup (60 grams) heavy whipping cream
3 tablespoons (45 grams) cold brew coffee concentrate
2 tablespoons (42 grams) light corn syrup

1. In a small heatproof bowl, place chocolate chips and salt.
2. In a small saucepan, heat cream, coffee concentrate, and corn syrup over medium heat, stirring frequently, just until bubbles form around edges of pan. (Do not boil.) Pour hot cream mixture over chocolate; let stand for 1 minute. Whisk until smooth. Let cool for 30 minutes before using.

GOLDEN PEANUT BUTTER CAKE

Makes 1 (8-inch) cake

Melding the smooth, nutty flavor of peanut butter with the warm butterscotch notes of golden syrup, this cake combines the ease of the stir-together formula with the elegance of a layer cake. Enrobed in a silky Swiss meringue buttercream and a cap of Golden Caramel, it looks like a masterpiece as well.

1   cup (220 grams) firmly packed light brown sugar
⅔   cup (150 grams) unsalted butter, melted
½   cup (128 grams) creamy peanut butter
¼   cup (85 grams) golden syrup
3   large eggs (150 grams), room temperature
1½   teaspoons (6 grams) vanilla extract
2¼   cups (281 grams) all-purpose flour
1   tablespoon (15 grams) baking powder
1   teaspoon (5 grams) baking soda
1   teaspoon (3 grams) kosher salt
1½   cups (360 grams) whole buttermilk, room temperature
      Golden Meringue Buttercream (recipe follows)
¾   cup (234 grams) Golden Caramel (recipe follows)

1. Preheat oven to 350°F (180°C). Butter and flour 2 (8-inch) round cake pans.
2. In a large bowl, stir together brown sugar, melted butter, peanut butter, and golden syrup until combined and creamy. Add eggs and vanilla, stirring just until combined.
3. In a medium bowl, sift together flour, baking powder, baking soda, and salt. Gradually add flour mixture to sugar mixture alternately with buttermilk, beginning and ending with flour mixture, stirring just until combined after each addition. Divide batter between prepared pans.
4. Bake until a wooden pick inserted in center comes out clean, 30 to 35 minutes. Let cool in pans for 10 minutes. Remove from pans, and let cool completely on wire racks. Spread Golden Meringue Buttercream between layers and on top and sides of cake. Refrigerate until set, about 30 minutes.
5. Pour Golden Caramel over cake, letting it drip down sides. Refrigerate until ready to serve.

GOLDEN MERINGUE BUTTERCREAM
Makes about 5½ cups

4   large egg whites (120 grams), room temperature
1½   cups (300 grams) granulated sugar
1¾   cups (397 grams) unsalted butter, softened
½   cup (156 grams) Golden Caramel (recipe follows)
2   tablespoons (42 grams) golden syrup

1. In the bowl of a stand mixer, whisk together egg whites and sugar by hand. Place bowl over a saucepan of simmering water. Cook, whisking occasionally, until an instant-read thermometer registers 155°F (68°C) to 160°F (71°C).
2. Carefully return bowl to stand mixer. Using the whisk attachment, beat at high speed until stiff peaks form and bowl is cool to the touch, about 8 minutes. Add butter, 2 tablespoons (28 grams) at a time, beating until combined. (If buttercream breaks, beat for 2 to 3 minutes more, and the emulsion will come back together.) Gradually add Golden Caramel and golden syrup, beating until combined. Use immediately.

GOLDEN CARAMEL
Makes about 1¼ cups

5   tablespoons (70 grams) unsalted butter
¾   cup (165 grams) firmly packed light brown sugar
3   tablespoons (63 grams) golden syrup
1½   teaspoons (6 grams) vanilla extract
1   teaspoon (3 grams) kosher salt
6   tablespoons (90 grams) heavy whipping cream

1. In a small saucepan, melt butter over medium heat. Add brown sugar, golden syrup, vanilla, and salt, whisking until dissolved. Add cream, and bring to a boil; cook for 3 minutes. Transfer to a small bowl. Let cool to room temperature before using.

> **PRO TIP**
> If the Golden Caramel is too thick to pour, heat it in the microwave in 10-second intervals until pourable. You don't want it hot, though, because it will melt your buttercream. All you are looking for is a slow pour.

VANILLA MALTED MILK CAKE

Makes 1 (8-inch) cake

A throwback to the malted milkshakes of the 1950s, this layer cake combines the rich notes of malted milk with warm vanilla.

1   cup (227 grams) unsalted butter, softened
1   cup (200 grams) vanilla sugar
1   cup (200 grams) granulated sugar
4   large eggs (200 grams)
2   teaspoons (8 grams) vanilla extract
3   cups (375 grams) cake flour
¼   cup (31 grams) malted milk powder
1   tablespoon (15 grams) baking powder
1   teaspoon (3 grams) kosher salt
1   cup (240 grams) whole milk
Vanilla Malted Milk Icing (recipe follows)
Garnish: vanilla sugar

1. Preheat oven to 350°F (180°C). Butter and flour 3 (8-inch) round cake pans.
2. In the bowl of a stand mixer fitted with the paddle attachment, beat butter, vanilla sugar, and granulated sugar at medium speed until fluffy, 3 to 4 minutes, stopping to scrape sides of bowl. Add eggs, one at a time, beating well after each addition. Beat in vanilla extract.
3. In a medium bowl, whisk together flour, malted milk powder, baking powder, and salt. With mixer on low speed, gradually add flour mixture to butter mixture alternately with milk, beginning and ending with flour mixture, beating just until combined after each addition. Divide batter among prepared pans.
4. Bake until a wooden pick inserted in center comes out clean, about 25 minutes. Let cool in pans for 10 minutes. Remove from pans, and let cool completely on wire racks. Spread Vanilla Malted Milk Icing between layers and on top and sides of cake. Garnish with vanilla sugar, if desired.

VANILLA MALTED MILK ICING
Makes about 5 cups

1½   cups (340 grams) unsalted butter, softened
1   cup (124 grams) malted milk powder
½   teaspoon (1.5 grams) kosher salt
1½   tablespoons (27 grams) vanilla bean paste
2   teaspoons (8 grams) vanilla extract
8   cups (960 grams) confectioners' sugar
3 to 4 tablespoons (45 to 60 grams) whole milk

1. In the bowl of a stand mixer fitted with the paddle attachment, beat butter, malted milk powder, and salt at medium speed until creamy, about 4 minutes. Beat in vanilla bean paste and vanilla extract. Gradually add confectioners' sugar alternately with milk, beating until smooth. Use immediately.

RUM SWIZZLE CAKE

Makes 1 (8-inch) cake

Our take on Bermuda's signature cocktail, the Rum Swizzle, lets you have your beachside drink and eat it, too. We filled the cake with pineapple, orange zest, and gold and dark rums as a nod to the cocktail and then whipped up a Rum Swizzle to soak the layers in after baking. Generous swoops of Orange Buttercream give it a zesty summertime finish.

1   cup (227 grams) unsalted butter*, softened
1½ cups (300 grams) granulated sugar
4   large eggs (200 grams), room temperature
1   tablespoon (15 grams) gold rum*
1   tablespoon (15 grams) dark rum*
3   cups (375 grams) all-purpose flour
1   tablespoon (15 grams) baking powder
1   teaspoon (3 grams) kosher salt
½   cup (100 grams) finely diced fresh pineapple
½   cup (120 grams) whole buttermilk
Rum Swizzle (recipe follows)
Orange Buttercream (recipe follows)

1. Preheat oven to 350°F (180°C). Butter and flour 2 (8-inch) tall-sided round cake pans. Line bottom of pans with parchment paper.
2. In the bowl of a stand mixer fitted with the paddle attachment, beat butter and sugar at medium speed until fluffy, 3 to 4 minutes, stopping to scrape sides of bowl. Add eggs, one at a time, beating well after each addition. Beat in rums.
3. In a medium bowl, whisk together flour, baking powder, and salt. In a small bowl, stir together pineapple and buttermilk. With mixer on low speed, add flour mixture to butter mixture alternately with pineapple mixture, beginning and ending with flour mixture, beating just until combined after each addition. Divide batter between prepared pans.
4. Bake until a wooden pick inserted in center comes out clean, 30 to 35 minutes. Let cool in pans for 10 minutes. Remove from pans, and let cool completely on wire racks.
5. Place 1 cake layer on a serving platter. Brush with half of Rum Swizzle. Top with half of Orange Buttercream. Top with

remaining cake layer. Brush with remaining Rum Swizzle, and top with remaining Orange Buttercream. Using a bench scraper, smooth buttercream, leaving sides of cake exposed. Cover and refrigerate for up to 3 days.

We used Président Butter, Mount Gay Eclipse Gold Rum, and Gosling's Black Seal Rum.

RUM SWIZZLE
Makes about ⅓ cup

1½ tablespoons (22.5 grams) gold rum
1½ tablespoons (22.5 grams) dark rum
1½ tablespoons (22.5 grams) fresh pineapple juice
1½ tablespoons (22.5 grams) fresh orange juice
½   tablespoon (8 grams) falernum*
2   dashes Angostura bitters

1. In a small bowl, whisk together all ingredients until combined. Refrigerate until ready to use.

Falernum is a Caribbean syrup liqueur often used in tropical drinks. Find it at your local liquor store or online.

ORANGE BUTTERCREAM
Makes about 5 cups

1   cup (227 grams) unsalted butter, softened
½   cup (112 grams) cream cheese, softened
2   tablespoons (6 grams) orange zest
7½ cups (900 grams) confectioners' sugar
3   tablespoons (45 grams) fresh orange juice

1. In the bowl of a stand mixer fitted with the paddle attachment, beat butter at medium speed until creamy, about 3 minutes. Add cream cheese, and beat until smooth. Beat in orange zest. Gradually add confectioners' sugar alternately with orange juice, beating at low speed until smooth.

PRO TIP

This buttercream is nice and thick, but it can be a little soft. Before using, refrigerate the buttercream for 15 minutes, folding every 5 minutes, to stiffen it, if necessary.

PUMPKIN SPICE LAYER CAKE

Makes 1 (8-inch) cake

Studded with walnuts and coated in a pumpkin spice-speckled buttercream, this layer cake will be the crowning glory of your autumn meals.

1   (15-ounce) can (425 grams) pumpkin
1½ cups (330 grams) firmly packed light brown sugar
1   cup (224 grams) vegetable oil
3   large eggs (150 grams)
3   cups (375 grams) all-purpose flour
1½ tablespoons (9 grams) Pumpkin Spice (recipe follows)
1   tablespoon (15 grams) baking powder
1   teaspoon (5 grams) baking soda
1   teaspoon (3 grams) kosher salt
1   cup (113 grams) chopped walnuts
Pumpkin Spice Frosting (recipe follows)

1. Preheat oven to 350°F (180°C). Line bottoms of 3 (8-inch) round cake pans with parchment paper; lightly butter and flour sides of pans.
2. In the bowl of a stand mixer fitted with the paddle attachment, beat pumpkin, brown sugar, oil, and eggs at medium speed until well combined, about 1 minute.

3. In a medium bowl, whisk together flour, pumpkin spice, baking powder, baking soda, and salt. With mixer on low speed, gradually add flour mixture to pumpkin mixture, beating until well combined. Fold in walnuts. Divide batter among prepared pans.
4. Bake until a wooden pick inserted in center comes out clean, 28 to 30 minutes. Let cool in pans for 10 minutes. Remove from pans, and let cool completely on wire racks. Spread 1 cup Pumpkin Spice Frosting between each layer and on top of cake. Lightly spread Pumpkin Spice Frosting on sides of cake. Refrigerate for 30 minutes.
5. Place half of remaining Pumpkin Spice Frosting in a piping bag fitted with a Wilton 4B star tip. Place remaining Pumpkin Spice Frosting in a piping bag fitted with a Wilton 2A round tip. Pipe frosting on top of cake as desired. Serve immediately. Store, covered, in refrigerator for up to 3 days.

PUMPKIN SPICE
Makes about ½ cup

¼   cup (24 grams) ground cinnamon
1   tablespoon (6 grams) ground ginger
1   tablespoon (6 grams) ground nutmeg
1½ teaspoons (3 grams) ground allspice
1½ teaspoons (3 grams) ground cloves

1. In a small bowl, whisk together all ingredients. Store in an airtight container for up to 6 months.

PUMPKIN SPICE FROSTING
Makes 4½ cups

1½ cups (340 grams) unsalted butter, softened
4   cups (480 grams) confectioners' sugar
⅓   cup (80 grams) heavy whipping cream
½   teaspoon (1 gram) Pumpkin Spice (recipe precedes)
¼   teaspoon kosher salt

1. In the bowl of a stand mixer fitted with the paddle attachment, beat butter at medium speed until smooth, about 2 minutes. Add confectioners' sugar, 1 cup (120 grams) at a time, beating well after each addition and stopping to scrape sides of bowl. Beat in cream. Add pumpkin spice and salt, beating until smooth. Use immediately.

OPERA CAKE

Makes 1 (6-inch) cake

Recipe by Frank Barron and Jennifer Drew

The traditional opera cake has layers of almond sponge cake soaked in coffee syrup and finished off with a shiny ganache. This version has a luxurious chocolate cake base and a layer of Coffee Buttercream for a subtle kick.

2½ cups (313 grams) all-purpose flour
2   cups (400 grams) granulated sugar
½   cup (43 grams) Dutch process cocoa powder
2   teaspoons (10 grams) baking powder
2   teaspoons (10 grams) baking soda
½   teaspoon (1.5 grams) kosher salt
1   cup (240 grams) whole buttermilk
1   cup (240 grams) strong-brewed hot coffee
½   cup (112 grams) sunflower or vegetable oil
2   large eggs (100 grams)
1   teaspoon (4 grams) vanilla extract
Coffee Syrup (recipe follows)
Chocolate Buttercream (recipe follows)
Coffee Buttercream (recipe follows)
Almond Buttercream (recipe follows)
6   ounces (175 grams) dark chocolate, chopped
Dark Chocolate Ganache (recipe follows)
Garnish: edible gold leaf

1. Preheat oven to 350°F (180°C). Butter and flour 4 (6-inch) round cake pans*; line bottom of pans with parchment paper.
2. In a large bowl, whisk together flour, sugar, cocoa, baking powder, baking soda, and salt. Add buttermilk, hot coffee, and oil, and stir until combined. Add eggs, one at a time, stirring well after each addition. Stir in vanilla. Divide batter among prepared pans.
3. Bake until a wooden pick inserted in center comes out clean, 35 to 40 minutes. Let cool in pans for 10 minutes. Remove from pans, and let cool completely on wire racks.
4. Using a serrated knife, level top of cake layers. Using a pastry brush, brush each layer

with Coffee Syrup. Place 1 cake layer on a cake plate, and top with a few dollops of Chocolate Buttercream. Spread Chocolate Buttercream in an even layer, and top with second cake layer. Dollop with a few spoonfuls of Coffee Buttercream, and spread in an even layer. Top with third cake layer, and spread Almond Buttercream on top. Add remaining cake layer, and spread a thin layer of Chocolate Buttercream on top and sides of cake to create a crumb coat. Refrigerate for 20 minutes.
5. In the top of a double boiler, heat dark chocolate over simmering water until melted. (Alternatively, place chocolate in microwave-safe bowl. Heat on high in 30-second intervals, stirring between each, until melted.) Place melted chocolate in a piping bag. Pipe quarter-size circles onto a sheet of parchment paper. Using a palette knife, bring each circle down to form a petal. Drape parchment paper over a rolling pin or inside a tuile pan, and refrigerate until hardened, about 1 hour.
6. Spread Dark Chocolate Ganache on top and sides of cake. Top cake with dark chocolate petals, and garnish with gold leaf, if desired.

We used Fat Daddio's Alluminum 6-inch round cake pans, available at amazon.com.

COFFEE SYRUP
Makes ⅔ cup

½   cup (120 grams) water
¼   cup (50 grams) granulated sugar
1½   tablespoons (9 grams) instant coffee powder

1. In a small saucepan, combine ½ cup (60 grams) water, sugar, and coffee powder. Cook over medium heat, stirring occasionally, just until bubbles form around edges of pan. (Do not boil.) Remove from heat; let cool completely.

CHOCOLATE BUTTERCREAM
Makes about 3 cups

⅔   cup (133 grams) granulated sugar
2   tablespoons (30 grams) water
2   large egg whites (60 grams)
1¼   cups (284 grams) unsalted butter, softened
3.75 ounces (105 grams) 60% cacao chocolate, melted
1   teaspoon (4 grams) vanilla extract

1. In a small saucepan, bring sugar and 2 tablespoons (30 grams) water to a boil over medium heat, stirring occasionally. Cook until an instant-read thermometer registers 238°F (114°C).
2. Meanwhile, in the bowl of a stand mixer fitted with the whisk attachment, beat egg whites at high speed until soft peaks form.
3. With mixer on medium speed, add sugar syrup to egg whites in a slow, steady stream until combined. Increase mixer speed to high, and beat until bowl is cooled to room temperature. Switch to the paddle attachment. Add butter, a few tablespoons at a time beating until combined after each addition. Add melted chocolate and vanilla, and beat until smooth. Use immediately.

COFFEE BUTTERCREAM
Makes about 1½ cups

½   cup (100 grams) granulated sugar
2   tablespoons (30 grams) water
3   large egg yolks (56 grams)
⅔   cup (150 grams) unsalted butter, cubed and softened
1½   tablespoons (22.5 grams) hot water
1   teaspoon (2 grams) instant coffee powder
1   teaspoon (4 grams) vanilla extract

1. In a small saucepan, bring sugar and 2 tablespoons (30 grams) water to a boil over medium heat, stirring occasionally. Cook until an instant-read thermometer registers 238°F (114°C).
2. Meanwhile, in the bowl of a stand mixer fitted with the whisk attachment, beat egg yolks at high speed until pale and doubled in volume.

3. With mixer on low speed, add sugar syrup to egg yolks in a slow, steady stream. Increase mixer speed to high, and beat until bowl is cooled to room temperature. Switch to the paddle attachment. With mixer on low speed, add butter, 1 tablespoon (14 grams) at a time, beating until combined after each addition.
4. In a small bowl, stir together 1½ tablespoons (22.5 grams) hot water and coffee powder. With mixer on high speed, add coffee mixture and vanilla, and beat until smooth and creamy. Use immediately.

ALMOND BUTTERCREAM
Makes about 1 cup

½	cup (113 grams) unsalted butter, softened
1½	cups (180 grams) confectioners' sugar
½	teaspoon (2 grams) almond extract
¼	teaspoon (1 gram) vanilla extract
⅛	teaspoon kosher salt
1	tablespoon (15 grams) heavy whipping cream or whole milk

1. In the bowl of a stand mixer fitted with the paddle attachment, beat butter at medium speed until creamy. Add confectioners' sugar, ½ cup (60 grams) at a time, beating until combined after each addition. Add extracts and salt, and beat until combined, about 3 minutes. Add cream or milk in small increments until desired consistency is reached. Use immediately.

DARK CHOCOLATE GANACHE
Makes about 3 cups

12	ounces (340 grams) 60% cacao chocolate, chopped
1	cup (240 grams) heavy whipping cream

1. In a heatproof bowl, place chocolate.
2. In a small saucepan, heat cream over medium heat, stirring frequently, just until bubbles form around edges of pan. (Do not boil.) Remove from heat. Pour hot cream over chocolate. Let stand for 1 minute; whisk until combined. Let cool to room temperature before using.

Photo by Joann Pai

CITRON CAKE

Makes 1 (6-inch) cake

Recipe by Frank Barron and Jennifer Drew

This layer cake version of tarte au citron plays up the original with lemon cake layers, Meringue Buttercream, and a tart Lemon Curd center.

1 cup (227 grams) unsalted butter, softened
2 cups (200 grams) granulated sugar
4 large eggs (200 grams), lightly beaten
3 cups (375 grams) sifted all-purpose flour
1 tablespoon (15 grams) baking powder
1 teaspoon (5 grams) baking soda
1 teaspoon (3 grams) kosher salt
1¼ cups (300 grams) whole buttermilk
6 tablespoons (18 grams) lemon zest (about 2 lemons)
1 teaspoon (4 grams) vanilla extract
Meringue Buttercream (recipe follows)
Lemon Curd (recipe follows)
Italian Meringue (recipe follows)

1. Preheat oven to 350°F (180°C). Butter and flour 3 (6-inch) round cake pans; line bottom of pans with parchment paper.
2. In the bowl of a stand mixer fitted with the paddle attachment, beat butter and sugar at medium speed until fluffy, 3 to 4 minutes, stopping to scrape sides of bowl. Add beaten eggs in small increments, beating well after each addition.
3. In a medium bowl, sift together flour, baking powder, baking soda, and salt. With mixer on low speed, gradually add flour mixture to butter mixture alternately with buttermilk, beginning and ending with flour mixture, beating just until combined after each addition. Beat in zest and vanilla. Divide batter among prepared pans.
4. Bake until a wooden pick inserted in center comes out clean, 25 to 30 minutes. Let cool in pans for 10 minutes. Remove from pans, and let cool completely on wire racks.
5. Using a serrated knife, level top of cake layers. Place 1 cake layer on a cake plate. Place Meringue Buttercream in a piping bag fitted with a round piping tip. Pipe a ring of Meringue Buttercream around top edge of cake layer. Spoon Lemon Curd inside ring. Top with second cake layer, and repeat with Meringue Buttercream and Lemon Curd. Add remaining cake layer, and spread a thin layer of Meringue Buttercream on top and sides of cake to create a crumb coat. Refrigerate for 20 minutes.
6. Spread remaining Meringue Buttercream on top and sides of cake. Place Italian Meringue in a piping bag fitted with a round piping tip. Pipe dollops of Italian Meringue in varying sizes on top of cake. Using a kitchen torch, brown Italian Meringue. Place remaining Lemon Curd in a piping bag fitted with a small round piping tip. Pipe tiny droplets of Lemon Curd at base of Italian Meringue.

MERINGUE BUTTERCREAM
Makes about 3 cups

½ cup (100 grams) granulated sugar
2 tablespoons (30 grams) water
2 large egg whites (60 grams)
1 cup (227 grams) unsalted butter, softened
1½ teaspoons (6 grams) vanilla extract

1. In a small saucepan, bring sugar and 2 tablespoons (30 grams) water to a boil over medium heat, stirring occasionally. Cook until an instant-read thermometer registers 238°F (114°C).
2. Meanwhile, in the bowl of a stand mixer fitted with the whisk attachment, beat egg whites at high speed until soft peaks form.
3. With mixer on low speed, add sugar syrup to egg whites in a slow, steady stream until combined. Increase mixer speed to high, and beat until bowl is cooled to room temperature. With mixer on medium speed, add butter, 1 tablespoon (14 grams) at a time, beating until combined after each addition. Add vanilla, and increase mixer speed to high; beat until smooth. Use immediately.

LEMON CURD
Makes about 1¼ cups

⅓ cup (67 grams) granulated sugar
¼ cup (32 grams) cornstarch
1½ teaspoons (1.5 grams) lemon zest
¼ cup (60 grams) fresh lemon juice (about 1½ lemons)
1 large egg (50 grams)
1 large egg yolk (19 grams)
1 tablespoon (15 grams) heavy whipping cream
¼ cup (57 grams) unsalted butter, softened

1. In the top of a double boiler, whisk together sugar, cornstarch, lemon zest and juice, egg, egg yolk, and cream. Cook over simmering water, whisking constantly, until thickened, 10 to 15 minutes.
2. Strain mixture through a fine-mesh sieve into a medium bowl. Add butter, 1 tablespoon (14 grams) at a time, whisking until combined after each addition. Transfer to a Mason jar to let cool; refrigerate until set.

ITALIAN MERINGUE
Makes 1½ cups

½ cup (100 grams) castor sugar
1 tablespoon plus 2 teaspoons (25 grams) water
¼ cup (50 grams) egg whites

1. In a small saucepan, bring castor sugar and 1 tablespoon plus 2 teaspoons (25 grams) water to a boil over medium heat, stirring occasionally. Cook until a candy thermometer registers 250°F (121°C).
2. Meanwhile, in the bowl of a stand mixer fitted with the whisk attachment, beat egg whites at high speed until soft peaks form.
3. With mixer on medium speed, add sugar syrup to egg whites in a slow, steady stream until combined. Increase mixer speed to high, and beat until bowl is cooled to room temperature. Use immediately.

Photo by Joann Pai

FRAISIER LAYER CAKE

Makes 1 (8-inch) cake

Recipe by Frank Barron and Jennifer Drew

This cake is inspired by the fraisier, an elegant cake featuring kirsch-soaked genoise, strawberries, crème patissière, and marzipan. In this transatlantic version, all-American white cake is layered with alternating rings of Strawberry Pastry Cream and Italian Meringue Buttercream.

- 1¼ cups (284 grams) unsalted butter, softened
- 1½ cups (300 grams) castor sugar
- 6 large egg whites (180 grams), room temperature
- 2 teaspoons (8 grams) almond extract
- 1 teaspoon (4 grams) vanilla extract
- 3½ cups (438 grams) all-purpose flour
- 4 teaspoons (20 grams) baking powder
- ½ teaspoon (1.5 grams) kosher salt
- 1½ cups (360 grams) whole milk
- Italian Meringue Buttercream (recipe follows)
- Strawberry Pastry Cream (recipe follows)
- ⅓ cup (107 grams) seedless strawberry jam
- 1 cup (125 grams) (¼-inch-thick) sliced fresh strawberries
- Pink food coloring
- Garnish: fresh strawberries

1. Preheat oven to 350°F (180°C). Butter and flour 2 (8-inch) round cake pans; line bottom of pans with parchment paper.
2. In the bowl of a stand mixer fitted with the paddle attachment, beat butter at medium speed until creamy, 3 to 4 minutes. With mixer on medium-high speed, gradually add castor sugar, beating until fluffy, about 5 minutes. With mixer on low speed, add egg whites, one at a time, beating well after each addition. Beat in extracts. Scrape sides of bowl.
3. In a medium bowl, sift together flour, baking powder, and salt. Gradually add flour mixture to butter mixture alternately with milk, beginning and ending with flour mixture, beating just until combined after each addition. (Do not overbeat.) Divide batter between prepared pans.
4. Bake until a wooden pick inserted in center comes out clean, 30 to 40 minutes. Let cool in pans for 15 minutes. Remove from pans, and let cool completely on wire racks.

5. Using a serrated knife, level top of cake layers, and cut layers in half horizontally. Place 1 cake layer on a cake stand. Place Italian Meringue Buttercream in a piping bag fitted with a round piping tip. Place Strawberry Pastry Cream in another piping bag fitted with a round piping tip. Pipe a ring of Italian Meringue Buttercream around top edge of cake layer. Pipe a ring of Strawberry Pastry Cream inside ring of buttercream. Continue alternating rings of Italian Meringue Buttercream and Strawberry Pastry Cream until you reach center of cake. Top with second cake layer, and pipe a ring of Italian Meringue Buttercream. Spread jam inside buttercream ring. Top with strawberry slices. Add third cake layer, and repeat Italian Meringue Buttercream and Strawberry Pastry Cream rings. Add remaining cake layer, and spread a thin layer of Italian Meringue Buttercream on top and sides of cake to create a crumb coat. Refrigerate for 20 minutes.
6. Place half of remaining Italian Meringue Buttercream in a small bowl. Dip tip of a wooden pick in food coloring, and gently dip tip into buttercream. (A little food coloring goes a long way.) Place pink buttercream in a piping bag fitted with a round piping tip. Pipe a ring of pink buttercream around bottom of cake. Pipe a ring of white buttercream around cake above pink buttercream. Repeat until you reach top of cake. Hold an offset palette knife or cake scraper against side of cake as you turn cake completely around, smoothing out striped frosting as you go. Spread remaining white buttercream on top of cake to meet sides. Garnish with strawberries, if desired.

ITALIAN MERINGUE BUTTERCREAM
Makes about 5 cups

- 1 cup (200 grams) granulated sugar
- ¼ cup (60 grams) water
- 4 large egg whites (120 grams)
- 2 cups (454 grams) unsalted butter, softened
- 1 tablespoon (13 grams) vanilla extract

1. In a small saucepan, bring sugar and ¼ cup (60 grams) water to a boil over medium heat, stirring occasionally. Cook

until an instant-read thermometer registers 238°F (114°C).
2. Meanwhile, in the bowl of a stand mixer fitted with the whisk attachment, beat egg whites at high speed until soft peaks form.
3. With mixer on medium speed, add sugar syrup to egg whites in a slow, steady stream until combined. Increase mixer speed to high, and beat until bowl is cooled to room temperature. With mixer on medium speed, add butter, a few tablespoons at a time, beating until combined after each addition. Add vanilla, and increase mixer speed to high; beat until well combined. Use immediately.

STRAWBERRY PASTRY CREAM
Makes about 3 cups

- 2 cups (480 grams) half-and-half
- ⅓ cup (67 grams) plus ¼ cup (50 grams) granulated sugar, divided
- ⅛ teaspoon kosher salt
- 5 large egg yolks (93 grams)
- ⅓ cup (64 grams) cornstarch
- ⅓ cup (107 grams) seedless strawberry jam
- ¼ cup (57 grams) unsalted butter
- 2 teaspoons (8 grams) vanilla extract

1. In a medium saucepan, cook half-and-half, ⅓ cup (67 grams) sugar, and salt over medium heat, stirring occasionally, just until bubbles form around edges of pan. (Do not boil.)
2. In a medium bowl, whisk together egg yolks, cornstarch, and remaining ¼ cup (50 grams) sugar for about 45 seconds. Slowly add half of hot half-and-half mixture to egg yolk mixture, whisking constantly. Return mixture to saucepan, whisking to combine. Reduce heat to medium; cook, whisking vigorously, until mixture is thickened, about 45 seconds. Remove from heat; let cool for 1 minute. Whisk in jam, butter, and vanilla.
3. Transfer pastry cream to a bowl; cover with a piece of plastic wrap, pressing wrap directly onto surface of cream to prevent a skin from forming. Refrigerate until set, about 4 hours.

Photo by Joann Pai

GRASSHOPPER DRIP CAKE

Makes 1 (8-inch) cake

Recipe by Jessie Sheehan

Named for its minty hue, the traditional grasshopper dessert is green and topped with chocolate fudge and whipped cream. Mayonnaise makes this rendition of the cake especially fudgy. It's deeply dark (thanks to black cocoa powder) and not too sweet. The fluffy American buttercream is flavored in two ways: milk chocolate on the inside of the cake and minty green on the outside.

2   cups (480 grams) hot water (212°F/100°C)
⅔   cup (57 grams) black cocoa powder*
⅓   cup (28 grams) Dutch process cocoa powder
1   tablespoon (4 grams) instant espresso powder
1½   cups (315 grams) full-fat mayonnaise*
1   cup (200 grams) granulated sugar
1   cup (220 grams) firmly packed light brown sugar
2   large eggs (100 grams)
1   teaspoon (4 grams) peppermint extract
½   teaspoon (2 grams) vanilla extract
3   cups (375 grams) all-purpose flour
2   teaspoons (10 grams) baking powder
1   teaspoon (6 grams) table salt
¼   teaspoon (1.25 grams) baking soda
Milk Chocolate and Minty Green Buttercreams (recipe follows)
Dark Chocolate Mint Ganache (recipe follows)

1. Preheat oven to 350°F (180°C). Butter 3 (8-inch) round cake pans; line bottom of pans with parchment paper.
2. In a small bowl, whisk together 2 cups (480 grams) hot water, cocoas, and espresso powder until smooth. Let cool slightly.
3. In the bowl of a stand mixer fitted with the paddle attachment, beat mayonnaise and sugars at medium speed until smooth, about 2 minutes. Reduce mixer speed to low. Add eggs, one at a time, beating well after each addition. Beat in extracts.
4. In a medium bowl, whisk together flour, baking powder, salt, and baking soda. Gradually add flour mixture to mayonnaise mixture alternately with cocoa mixture,

beginning and ending with flour mixture, beating just until combined and stopping to scrape sides of bowl after each addition. Divide batter among prepared pans.
5. Bake until a wooden pick inserted in center comes out with a moist crumb or two, 18 to 22 minutes, rotating pans halfway through baking. Let cool in pans for 10 minutes. Remove from pans, and let cool completely on wire racks. Trim and level domed cake layers.
6. Place 1 cake layer on desired cake plate. Spread half of Milk Chocolate Buttercream onto cake layer, and top with second cake layer. Spread remaining Milk Chocolate Buttercream onto second cake layer, and top with remaining cake layer, pressing gently to adhere. Spread a thin layer of Minty Green Buttercream on top and sides of cake to create a crumb coat, and refrigerate for 15 minutes. Spread remaining Minty Green Buttercream on top and sides of cake. Refrigerate for 30 minutes.
7. To create a drip effect, use a spoon to scoop up a bit of Dark Chocolate Mint Ganache, and beginning very close to edge of top of cake, let it drip off spoon in a stream down side of cake. (If drip speeds along and pools at bottom, it is not ready and needs to cool a bit more before you continue.) To cover entire cake in drips, slowly move around top of cake with your spoon, pouring tiny streams of chocolate as you go. You can pour more or less Dark Chocolate Mint Ganache from spoon, depending on if you want longer drips or shorter ones. Once you have completed all drips, using a small offset spatula, cover top of cake with remaining Dark Chocolate Mint Ganache. Refrigerate before serving.

*We used King Arthur Flour Black Cocoa Powder and Hellman's Real Mayonnaise.

MILK CHOCOLATE AND MINTY GREEN BUTTERCREAMS

Makes about 6 cups (about 2 cups Milk Chocolate Buttercream and about 4 cups Minty Green Buttercream)

¼   cup (43 grams) milk chocolate chips
1½   cups (340 grams) unsalted butter, room temperature
Scant ½ teaspoon (2.5 grams) table salt
4   cups (480 grams) confectioners' sugar
⅓   cup (80 grams) heavy whipping cream
½   teaspoon (2 grams) vanilla extract
1½   teaspoons (6 grams) peppermint extract
3   drops liquid green food coloring

1. In a small microwave-safe bowl, place chocolate chips. Heat on high in 30-second intervals, stirring between each, until melted and smooth. Let cool.
2. In the bowl of a stand mixer fitted with the paddle attachment, beat butter and salt at low speed until smooth. Add confectioners' sugar, 1 cup (120 grams) at a time, alternately with cream, about 1 tablespoon (15 grams) at a time, beating until smooth after each addition. Increase mixer speed to medium, and beat for 5 minutes. Add vanilla, and beat to combine.
3. In a small bowl, place 2 cups frosting. Add cooled melted chocolate, and whisk to combine. Set aside.
4. Add peppermint extract and food coloring to remaining frosting, and beat at medium speed until combined. Use immediately.

DARK CHOCOLATE MINT GANACHE

Makes about ¾ cup

½   cup (85 grams) 63% cacao extra-dark chocolate chips
½   cup (120 grams) heavy whipping cream
⅛   teaspoon peppermint extract

1. In the top of a double boiler, combine chocolate chips and cream. Cook over simmering water, whisking until smooth. Remove from heat, and whisk until mixture just begins to thicken, 20 to 30 seconds. Whisk in peppermint extract. Use immediately.

GREEK NUT CAKE

Makes 1 (8-inch) cake

Recipe by Miro Uskokovic

New York City's Gramercy Tavern pastry chef Miro Uskokovic put a slight twist on his mother's Greek cake. While the original was five layers cut from a sheet pan and made with walnuts, this version is a four-layer cake calling for a homemade pecan meal. What hasn't changed? The egg yolk-rich and candy bar-packed frosting that makes this cake so special.

2   cups (250 grams) bleached cake flour
2   cups (283 grams) whole toasted pecans
12   large egg whites (360 grams)
½   teaspoon (1.5 grams) kosher salt
¼   teaspoon cream of tartar
1½   cups (300 grams) granulated sugar, divided
1   teaspoon (5 grams) baking powder
1   cup (227 grams) unsalted butter, melted
3   tablespoons (63 grams) golden syrup*
Crunchy German Buttercream (recipe follows)
Garnish: chopped crisped rice milk chocolate candy bars*

1. Preheat oven to 350°F (180°C). Lightly spray bottoms of 2 (8-inch) tall-sided round cake pans with cooking spray; line bottoms with parchment paper.
2. In the work bowl of a food processor, place flour and pecans; process until combined and pecans are finely ground. Set aside.
3. In the bowl of a stand mixer fitted with the whisk attachment, beat egg whites, salt, and cream of tartar at medium-low speed until foamy, about 1 minute. Gradually add ¾ cup (150 grams) sugar. Increase mixer speed to medium, and beat for 2 to 3 minutes. Gradually add remaining ¾ cup (150 grams) sugar, and beat until glossy, medium-firm peaks form, 10 to 15 minutes. Add baking powder, and beat for 30 seconds.
4. In a small bowl, whisk together warm melted butter and golden syrup. With mixer on low speed, add butter mixture to egg white mixture in a slow, steady stream, beating just until combined. (Don't overmix—the fat will deflate the egg whites.) Using a whisk, fold in flour mixture, scraping bottom and sides of bowl. Divide batter between prepared pans.
5. Bake until a wooden pick inserted in center comes out clean and cakes bounce back when lightly touched, 25 to 35 minutes. Let cool completely in pans on wire racks. Remove from pans, and wrap in plastic wrap; refrigerate overnight. (Refrigerating overnight is not essential—just make sure the layers are cold, which makes for easier cutting.)
6. Cut each cake layer in half horizontally. Place 1 layer on a cake turntable or flat plate. Using an offset spatula, spread about 2 cups Crunchy German Buttercream on top. Repeat layers twice. Place remaining cake layer, flat side up, on top of buttercream. Refrigerate for 30 minutes.
7. Spread remaining Crunchy German Buttercream on top and sides of cake. Garnish with chopped candy bars. For the best flavor, make the cake the day before, cover, and let stand overnight.

We used Lyle's Golden Syrup and Crunch Bars.

CRUNCHY GERMAN BUTTERCREAM
Makes about 8 cups

13   large egg yolks (240 grams)
¼   cup (31 grams) all-purpose flour
1   tablespoon plus ¾ teaspoon (10 grams) cornstarch
2½   cups (600 grams) whole milk
½   cup plus 1 tablespoon (112 grams) granulated sugar
1½   teaspoons (4.5 grams) kosher salt
1   teaspoon (6 grams) vanilla bean paste
2   cups (454 grams) unsalted butter, softened
¾   cup plus 1 tablespoon (97 grams) confectioners' sugar
6.5 ounces (182 grams) chopped crisped rice milk chocolate candy bars (about 4 bars)
⅔   cup plus 2 tablespoons (97 grams) whole toasted pecans, chopped

1. In a medium bowl, whisk together egg yolks, flour, and cornstarch until smooth and well combined.
2. In a medium saucepan, heat milk, granulated sugar, and ½ teaspoon (1.5 grams) salt over medium heat just until bubbles form around edges of pan. (Do not boil.) Slowly pour about 1 cup warm milk mixture into egg yolk mixture, whisking constantly. Return mixture to saucepan, whisking constantly. Bring to a boil over medium heat, whisking constantly. Reduce heat to low, and cook, whisking constantly, for 4 to 5 minutes. Remove from heat, and stir in vanilla bean paste. Strain mixture through a fine-mesh sieve into a medium bowl. Cover with a piece of plastic wrap, pressing wrap directly onto surface of pastry cream to prevent a skin from forming. Refrigerate until an instant-read thermometer registers 65°F (18°C) to 70°F (21°C), 2½ to 3 hours.
3. In the bowl of a stand mixer fitted with the paddle attachment, beat butter at medium speed until smooth and creamy, about 1 minute. Add confectioners' sugar and remaining 1 teaspoon (3 grams) salt, beating until light and creamy.
4. Switch to the whisk attachment. Add pastry cream; beat at medium speed until smooth, fluffy, and pale yellow. Using a silicone spatula, gently fold in candy bars and pecans. Use immediately.

Photo by Dave Katz

SPICED FRUITCAKE

Makes 1 (9-inch) cake

Lightly spiced with ginger, cinnamon, nutmeg, and cloves, our Spiced Fruitcake is at once tender and aromatic. For our boozy Fruit Filling, brandy-soaked dried figs, cranberries, cherries, and apricots combine with crunchy slivered almonds for a triumph of texture and taste. To top it off, we enrobed our cake in the ultimate vanilla-scented American buttercream.

1   cup (227 grams) unsalted butter, softened
1   cup (200 grams) granulated sugar
1   cup (220 grams) firmly packed light brown sugar
4   large eggs (200 grams)
2   teaspoons (8 grams) vanilla extract
3   cups (375 grams) all-purpose flour
2   teaspoons (4 grams) ground cinnamon
1½ teaspoons (3 grams) ground ginger
1   teaspoon (5 grams) baking powder
1   teaspoon (5 grams) baking soda
1   teaspoon (1 gram) ground nutmeg
¾   teaspoon (2.25 grams) kosher salt
¼   teaspoon ground cloves
1   cup (240 grams) whole buttermilk
Brandy Simple Syrup (recipe follows)
Vanilla Buttercream (recipe follows)
Fruit Filling (recipe follows)

1. Preheat oven to 350°F (180°C). Butter and flour 2 (9-inch) round cake pans.
2. In the bowl of a stand mixer fitted with the paddle attachment, beat butter and sugars at medium speed until fluffy, 3 to 4 minutes, stopping to scrape sides of bowl. Add eggs, one at a time, beating well after each addition. Beat in vanilla.
3. In a medium bowl, whisk together flour, cinnamon, ginger, baking powder, baking soda, nutmeg, salt, and cloves. With mixer on low speed, gradually add flour mixture to butter mixture alternately with buttermilk, beginning and ending with flour mixture, beating just until combined after each addition. Divide batter between prepared pans, smoothing tops with an offset spatula.
4. Bake until a wooden pick inserted in center comes out clean, about 40 minutes. Let cool in pans for 10 minutes. Remove from pans, and place on wire racks. Brush warm cake layers with Brandy Simple Syrup. Let cool completely.
5. Place 2 cups Vanilla Buttercream in a piping bag, and cut a ½-inch opening. Pipe a thick border around edge of 1 cake layer. Using an offset spatula, spread chilled Fruit Filling inside piped border. Top with remaining cake layer, and spread remaining Vanilla Buttercream on top and sides of cake. Store in an airtight container in the refrigerator.

BRANDY SIMPLE SYRUP
Makes about 1 cup

⅔   cup (133 grams) granulated sugar
⅓   cup (80 grams) water
⅓   cup (80 grams) brandy

1. In a small saucepan, bring sugar and ⅓ cup (80 grams) water to a boil over medium-high heat. Cook, stirring occasionally, until sugar is dissolved. Remove from heat, and stir in brandy. Let cool completely. Store in an airtight container in the refrigerator for up to 2 weeks.

VANILLA BUTTERCREAM
Makes about 6 cups

2   cups (454 grams) unsalted butter, softened
2   teaspoons (12 grams) vanilla bean paste
½   teaspoon (1.5 grams) kosher salt
7½   cups (900 grams) confectioners' sugar
½   cup (120 grams) heavy whipping cream

1. In the bowl of a stand mixer fitted with the paddle attachment, beat butter, vanilla bean paste, and salt at low speed until smooth. Add confectioners' sugar, about 1 cup (120 grams) at a time, alternately with cream, about 1 tablespoon (15 grams) at a time, beating just until combined after each addition. Increase mixer speed to medium, and beat until smooth and fluffy, 2 to 3 minutes.

FRUIT FILLING
Makes about 2 cups

¼   cup (57 grams) unsalted butter
⅔   cup (133 grams) granulated sugar
4   large egg yolks (76 grams)
¾   cup (85 grams) chopped slivered almonds
¼   cup (32 grams) dried cranberries
¼   cup (32 grams) dried cherries
¼   cup (32 grams) chopped dried figs
¼   cup (32 grams) chopped dried apricots
3   tablespoons (45 grams) brandy

1. In a medium saucepan, melt butter over medium heat. Stir in sugar until combined. Whisk in egg yolks until well combined; cook, stirring occasionally, until mixture is very thick, 4 to 5 minutes. Remove from heat; stir in almonds and all remaining ingredients. Cover with plastic wrap, pressing wrap directly onto surface of filling. Refrigerate until completely cool.

ITALIAN CREAM CAKE

Makes 1 (8-inch) cake

Studded with chopped pecans and sweet coconut flakes, this cake batter is kept light with the addition of whipped cream. A heavy coat of Cream Cheese Frosting—appropriately adorned with more pecans and toasted coconut—brings the fluffy cake back down to earth.

1   cup (227 grams) unsalted butter, softened
1½ cups (300 grams) granulated sugar
½   cup (110 grams) firmly packed light brown sugar
4   large eggs (200 grams)
2   teaspoons (8 grams) vanilla extract
2½ cups (313 grams) all-purpose flour
1   teaspoon (5 grams) baking soda
½   teaspoon (1.5 grams) kosher salt
1   cup (240 grams) whole buttermilk
½   cup (120 grams) heavy whipping cream, room temperature
1¼ cups (126 grams) packed sweetened flaked coconut
¾   cup (85 grams) chopped pecan pieces
Cream Cheese Frosting (recipe follows)
Garnish: toasted coconut, chopped pecans

1. Preheat oven to 350°F (180°C). Butter and flour 2 (8-inch) round cake pans.
2. In the bowl of a stand mixer fitted with the paddle attachment, beat butter and sugars at medium speed until fluffy, 3 to 4 minutes, stopping to scrape sides of bowl. Add eggs, one at a time, beating well after each addition. Beat in vanilla.
3. In a medium bowl, whisk together flour, baking soda, and salt. With mixer on low speed, gradually add flour mixture to butter mixture alternately with buttermilk, beginning and ending with flour mixture, beating just until combined after each addition.
4. In another medium bowl, whisk cream by hand until soft peaks form. Using a rubber spatula, fold whipped cream into batter in two additions. Fold in sweetened coconut and pecans. Divide batter between prepared pans, smoothing tops with an offset spatula.
5. Bake until a wooden pick inserted in center comes out clean, 45 to 50 minutes. Let cool in pans for 10 minutes. Remove from pans, and let cool completely on wire racks. Spread Cream Cheese Frosting between layers and on top and sides of cake. Garnish sides with toasted coconut and pecans, if desired. Store in an airtight container in the refrigerator.

CREAM CHEESE FROSTING
Makes about 6 cups

16 ounces (455 grams) cream cheese, softened
1   cup (227 grams) unsalted butter, softened
2   teaspoons (8 grams) vanilla extract
½   teaspoon (1.5 grams) kosher salt
7½ cups (900 grams) confectioners' sugar

1. In the bowl of a stand mixer fitted with the paddle attachment, beat cream cheese and butter at medium-low speed until smooth and creamy, about 1 minute. Add vanilla and salt, beating until combined. With mixer on low speed, gradually add confectioners' sugar, beating until combined. Increase mixer speed to medium, and beat until fluffy, about 1 minute.

GERMAN CHOCOLATE CAKE

Makes 1 (9-inch) cake

Our German Chocolate Cake has melted chocolate folded right into the batter. We decided there's plenty of room for both the Creamy Chocolate Frosting and the Coconut Pecan Filling. Piping a thick border of frosting on the top allows our coconut-pecan custard to pool without overflowing.

1	cup (227 grams) unsalted butter, softened
1	cup (200 grams) granulated sugar
1	cup (220 grams) firmly packed light brown sugar
4	large eggs (200 grams)
1	teaspoon (4 grams) vanilla extract
2½	cups (313 grams) all-purpose flour
¼	cup (21 grams) unsweetened cocoa powder
½	teaspoon (2.5 grams) baking powder
½	teaspoon (2.5 grams) baking soda
½	teaspoon (1.5 grams) kosher salt
1½	cups (360 grams) whole buttermilk
6	ounces (175 grams) sweet baking chocolate, melted and cooled

Creamy Chocolate Frosting (recipe follows)
Coconut Pecan Filling (recipe follows)
Garnish: flaked coconut, chopped pecans

1. Preheat oven to 350°F (180°C). Butter and flour 2 (9-inch) round cake pans.
2. In the bowl of a stand mixer fitted with the paddle attachment, beat butter and sugars at medium speed until fluffy, 3 to 4 minutes, stopping to scrape sides of bowl. Add eggs, one at a time, beating well after each addition. Beat in vanilla.
3. In a medium bowl, whisk together flour, cocoa, baking powder, baking soda, and salt. With mixer on low speed, gradually add flour mixture to butter mixture alternately with buttermilk, beginning and ending with flour mixture, beating just until combined after each addition. Stir in melted chocolate until combined. Divide batter between prepared pans, smoothing tops with an offset spatula.
4. Bake until a wooden pick inserted in center comes out clean, 40 to 45 minutes. Let cool in pans for 10 minutes. Remove from pans, and let cool completely on wire racks.
5. Place 2 cups Creamy Chocolate Frosting in a piping bag fitted with a medium open star tip (Wilton No. 4B). Pipe a thick border around top edge of 1 cake layer. Using an offset spatula, spread half of chilled Coconut Pecan Filling inside piped border. Top with remaining cake layer. Pipe Creamy Chocolate Frosting in a swirl pattern around top edge of cake layer, and spread remaining Coconut Pecan Filling inside border. Spread remaining Creamy Chocolate Frosting on sides of cake. Garnish with coconut and pecans, if desired.

CREAMY CHOCOLATE FROSTING
Makes about 4 cups

1	cup (227 grams) unsalted butter, softened
¼	cup (21 grams) unsweetened cocoa powder
⅔	cup (160 grams) sour cream
5	cups (600 grams) confectioners' sugar

1. In the bowl of stand mixer fitted with the paddle attachment, beat butter at medium speed until smooth and creamy, about 2 minutes. Add cocoa, and beat at low speed until combined. Beat in sour cream until smooth. With mixer on low speed, gradually add confectioners' sugar, beating until smooth and creamy.

COCONUT PECAN FILLING
Makes about 4 cups

1	cup (200 grams) granulated sugar
1	cup (247 grams) evaporated milk
½	cup (113 grams) unsalted butter, softened
3	large egg yolks (57 grams)
¼	teaspoon kosher salt
1½	cups (180 grams) packed sweetened flaked coconut
1	cup (113 grams) chopped pecans
2	teaspoons (8 grams) vanilla extract

1. In a medium saucepan, whisk together sugar, evaporated milk, butter, egg yolks, and salt until smooth. Cook over medium heat, whisking frequently, until mixture is thickened and coats the back of a spoon, 10 to 12 minutes. Remove from heat, and stir in coconut, pecans, and vanilla. Cover and refrigerate for at least 2 hours or up to 3 days.

RED VELVET CAKE

Makes 1 (8-inch) cake

Rich, tender, and deeply red, our Red Velvet Cake comes equipped with the luxurious crumb and tangy taste you've grown accustomed to. We opted for the more traditional Ermine Icing, a frosting with a cooked roux base and an infinitely smooth finish.

- 1   cup (227 grams) unsalted butter, softened
- 2   cups (400 grams) granulated sugar
- 4   large eggs (200 grams), room temperature
- 2½   cups (313 grams) all-purpose flour
- ½   cup (43 grams) unsweetened cocoa powder
- 1   teaspoon (5 grams) baking soda
- ½   teaspoon (1.5 grams) kosher salt
- 1   cup (240 grams) whole buttermilk
- 1   (1-ounce) bottle (30 grams) liquid red food coloring
- 1   tablespoon (15 grams) distilled white vinegar
- 2   teaspoons (8 grams) vanilla extract
- Ermine Icing (recipe follows)

1. Preheat oven to 350°F (180°C). Butter and flour 3 (8-inch) round cake pans.

2. In the bowl of a stand mixer fitted with the paddle attachment, beat butter and sugar at medium speed until fluffy, 3 to 4 minutes, stopping to scrape sides of bowl. Add eggs, one at a time, beating well after each addition.

3. In a medium bowl, whisk together flour, cocoa, baking soda, and salt. With mixer on low speed, gradually add flour mixture to butter mixture alternately with buttermilk, beginning and ending with flour mixture, beating just until combined after each addition. Stir in food coloring, vinegar, and vanilla. Divide batter among prepared pans, smoothing tops with an offset spatula.

4. Bake until a wooden pick inserted in center comes out clean, 28 to 30 minutes. Let cool in pans for 10 minutes. Remove from pans, and let cool completely on wire racks.

5. Trim each cake layer flat; reserve trimmings for garnish. Spread Ermine Icing between layers and on top of cake. Spread a thin layer of Ermine Icing on sides of cake; using a bench scraper, smooth icing, leaving sides of cake exposed. Crumble reserved cake trimmings on top of cake. Store in an airtight container.

ERMINE ICING
Makes about 3 cups

- 1   cup (240 grams) cold whole milk
- 5   tablespoons (40 grams) all-purpose flour
- 2   teaspoons (8 grams) vanilla extract
- ¼   teaspoon kosher salt
- 1   cup (227 grams) unsalted butter, softened
- 1   cup (200 grams) granulated sugar

1. In a small saucepan, cook cold milk and flour over medium heat, whisking constantly, until thickened and pudding-like and an instant-read thermometer registers 170°F (77°C), 4 to 5 minutes. Remove from heat, and whisk in vanilla and salt. Pour into a small bowl; cover with a piece of plastic wrap, pressing wrap directly onto surface to prevent a skin from forming. Refrigerate until completely cool, about 1 hour.

2. In the bowl of a stand mixer fitted with paddle attachment, beat butter until creamy and smooth, about 2 minutes. With mixer on medium speed, slowly add sugar, and beat until smooth and fluffy, 6 to 7 minutes. Slowly add cooled milk mixture to butter mixture, beating until light and fluffy. (It should look like whipped cream.) Use immediately.

BURNT SUGAR CAKE

Makes 1 (8-inch) cake

Our cake is nothing without the essential Burnt Sugar Syrup, a simple caramel syrup that will remind you sugar can offer complex flavor all on its own. With a further nod toward tradition, we covered the tender cake layers in silky waves of Penuche Icing.

1   cup (227 grams) unsalted butter, softened
1   cup (200 grams) granulated sugar
¾   cup (165 grams) firmly packed dark brown sugar
4   large eggs (200 grams)
2   teaspoons (8 grams) vanilla extract
3½   cups (437 grams) cake flour
1   tablespoon (15 grams) baking powder
1   teaspoon (3 grams) kosher salt
1   cup (240 grams) whole milk
Burnt Sugar Syrup (recipe follows)
Penuche Icing (recipe follows)

1. Preheat oven to 350°F (180°C). Butter and flour 2 (8-inch) round cake pans.
2. In the bowl of a stand mixer fitted with the paddle attachment, beat butter and sugars at medium speed until fluffy, 3 to 4 minutes, stopping to scrape sides of bowl. Add eggs, one at a time, beating well after each addition. Beat in vanilla.
3. In a medium bowl, whisk together flour, baking powder, and salt. In a small bowl, combine milk and Burnt Sugar Syrup. With mixer on low speed, gradually add flour mixture to butter mixture alternately with milk mixture, beginning and ending with flour mixture, beating just until combined after each addition. Divide batter between prepared pans, smoothing tops with an offset spatula.
4. Bake until a wooden pick inserted in center comes out clean, 35 to 40 minutes. Let cool in pans for 10 minutes. Remove from pans, and let cool completely on wire racks. Spread Penuche Icing between layers and on top and sides of cake. Store in an airtight container.

BURNT SUGAR SYRUP
Makes about ½ cup

½   cup (100 grams) granulated sugar
½   cup (120 grams) boiling water

1. In a small heavy-bottomed saucepan, spread sugar; cook over medium-low heat until sugar begins to melt. (Do not stir.) Using a silicone spatula, gently drag melted sugar to center of pan so sugar melts evenly. Cook until melted sugar turns a light amber color. (Do not stir.) Remove from heat, and slowly add ½ cup (120 grams) boiling water. (Be careful—it will steam, and it can splatter.) Cook over medium-low heat, stirring constantly, until smooth and mixture looks like maple syrup, about 5 minutes. Remove from heat, and let cool for 15 minutes.

PENUCHE ICING
Makes 4½ cups

1½   cups (340 grams) unsalted butter, softened and divided
1½   cups (330 grams) firmly packed dark brown sugar
½   cup (120 grams) heavy whipping cream
½   teaspoon (1.5 grams) kosher salt
4½   cups (540 grams) confectioners' sugar, sifted

1. In a small saucepan, melt ¾ cup (170 grams) butter over medium heat. Pour into the bowl of a stand mixer fitted with the paddle attachment. Let cool slightly.
2. In same saucepan, whisk together brown sugar, cream, and salt. Cook over medium heat, stirring occasionally, until sugar is melted and mixture starts to boil. Add to melted butter. Add half of confectioners' sugar, and beat until smooth. Add remaining confectioners' sugar, beating until combined. With the mixer on medium speed, slowly add remaining ½ cup (170 grams) butter, 1 tablespoon (14 grams) at a time, beating until smooth and combined. Cover and let stand until icing has reached a spreadable consistency, 10 to 30 minutes.

CLASSIC BÛCHE DE NOËL

Makes 1 bûche de Noël

Our bûche de Noël is a proper holiday centerpiece. With a stiff buttercream filling and moist syrup-soaked genoise, it can be stored in the refrigerator a day before decorating.

¼   cup (21 grams) Dutch process cocoa powder, plus more for dusting
¼   cup (60 grams) hot water
3   ounces (86 grams) 60% cacao bittersweet chocolate, melted
5   large eggs (250 grams)
½   cup (100 grams) granulated sugar
2   large egg yolks (37 grams)
¾   cup (94 grams) cake flour
½   teaspoon (1.5 grams) kosher salt
3   tablespoons (42 grams) unsalted butter, melted
Cold Brew Simple Syrup (recipe follows)
Vanilla Bean Buttercream (recipe follows)
Chocolate Buttercream (recipe follows)
Meringue Mushrooms (recipe follows)
Garnish: ground pistachios, confectioners' sugar

1. Preheat oven to 350°F (180°C). Spray an 18x13-inch rimmed baking sheet with cooking spray; line pan with parchment paper, and spray pan again.
2. In a small bowl, whisk together cocoa and ¼ cup (60 grams) hot water until dissolved. Add melted chocolate, and whisk until smooth.
3. In the bowl of a stand mixer, whisk together eggs, granulated sugar, and egg yolks by hand. Place bowl over a saucepan of simmering water. Cook, whisking occasionally, until an instant-read thermometer registers 110°F (43°F), about 5 minutes. Return bowl to stand mixer fitted with the whisk attachment, and beat at high speed until thick and tripled in volume, about 5 minutes.
4. In a medium bowl, place about 2 cups egg mixture. Fold in warm chocolate mixture. Set aside.
5. In a small bowl, sift together flour and salt. Using a large balloon whisk, gently fold flour mixture into remaining egg mixture in two additions just until combined. Fold in chocolate mixture. Fold in warm melted butter in two additions. Using an offset spatula, quickly and gently spread batter evenly in prepared pan.
6. Bake until cake starts to pull away from sides of pan, 10 to 12 minutes. Loosen cake from sides of pan, if needed. Invert onto a tea towel dusted with cocoa. Gently peel off parchment. Starting with one long side, roll up cake and towel together. Let cool completely on a wire rack.
7. Carefully unroll cake, and brush with Cold Brew Simple Syrup. Spread with Vanilla Bean Buttercream. Reroll cake without towel, and place, seam side down, on a baking sheet, using towel as a sling. Cover with towel, and refrigerate until firm, about 1 hour.
8. Trim ends of cake flat. Trim 3 to 4 inches diagonally from one end; set aside. Trim a ¾-inch slice from same end; set aside.

Place large cut piece at an angle off side of cake, and attach with Chocolate Buttercream. Place small cut piece, angle cut side up, on top, and attach with Chocolate Buttercream. Spread remaining Chocolate Buttercream on outside of cake, leaving ends exposed. Use an offset spatula to create detailed bark ridges. Decorate with Meringue Mushrooms; garnish with ground pistachios and confectioners' sugar, if desired.

COLD BREW SIMPLE SYRUP
Makes about ⅔ cup

¼   cup (50 grams) granulated sugar
¼   cup (60 grams) water
¼   cup (60 grams) cold brew coffee

1. In a small saucepan, bring sugar and ¼ cup (60 grams) water to a boil over medium-high heat, stirring occasionally, until sugar is dissolved. Remove from heat, and stir in coffee. Let cool completely. Refrigerate in an airtight container for up to 1 week.

VANILLA BEAN BUTTERCREAM
Makes about 3 cups

3   large egg whites (90 grams), room temperature
1   cup (200 grams) granulated sugar
1   vanilla bean, split lengthwise, seeds scraped and reserved
1¼   cups (284 grams) unsalted butter, cubed and softened
¼   teaspoon kosher salt

1. In the bowl of a stand mixer, whisk together egg whites, sugar, and reserved vanilla bean seeds by hand. Place bowl over a saucepan of simmering water. Cook, whisking occasionally, until an instant-read thermometer registers 155°F (68°C) to 160°F (71°C).
2. Carefully return bowl to stand mixer fitted with the whisk attachment, and beat on high until bowl is cool to the touch, about 8 minutes. Add butter, 2 tablespoons (28 grams) at a time, beating until combined after each addition. Beat in salt. Use immediately, or refrigerate in an airtight container for up to 3 days. If refrigerating, let stand at room temperature for 2 hours and rewhip until smooth before using.

CHOCOLATE BUTTERCREAM
Makes 2 cups

½   cup (113 grams) unsalted butter, softened
3   tablespoons (15 grams) Dutch process cocoa powder
⅓   cup (80 grams) sour cream
2½   cups (300 grams) confectioners' sugar

1. In the bowl of a stand mixer fitted with the paddle attachment, beat butter at medium speed until smooth and creamy, about 2 minutes. Add cocoa, beating until combined. Beat in sour cream until smooth. Gradually add confectioners' sugar, beating until smooth and creamy. Use immediately, or refrigerate in an airtight container for up to 3 days. If refrigerating, let stand at room temperature for 2 hours before using.

MERINGUE MUSHROOMS
Makes about 24 mushrooms

2	large egg whites (60 grams)
¼	teaspoon cream of tartar
⅛	teaspoon kosher salt
½	cup (100 grams) granulated sugar
¼	cup (40 grams) dark chocolate melting wafers, melted according to package directions and cooled slightly

Cocoa powder, for dusting

1. Preheat oven to 275°F (140°C). Line a rimmed baking sheet with parchment paper.

2. In the bowl of a stand mixer fitted with the whisk attachment, beat egg whites, cream of tartar, and salt at low speed until foamy. Increase mixer speed to high, and add sugar in a slow, steady stream, beating until stiff peaks form.

3. Place meringue in a large piping bag fitted with a ½-inch round tip. Holding tip perpendicular to parchment paper, pipe half of meringue as mushroom tops, ¾ to 1¼ inches across. (Use a wet finger to press down any points.) Pipe remaining meringue as large kisses with ½-inch wide base. (It is OK if the kisses don't have smooth tips.)

4. Bake until meringues look dry and have started to brown slightly, 30 to 40 minutes. Let cool completely.

5. Using a wooden pick, poke a small hole in bottom of each mushroom top. Dip or brush melted chocolate on bottom of each mushroom top, and insert pointed stem end. Let stand until chocolate is set, about 5 minutes. Lightly dust with cocoa before serving. Best served the same day.

GINGERBREAD BÛCHE DE NOËL

Makes 1 bûche de Noël

Our gingerbread Yule log—or stump, if you will—is a well-spiced, vertical take on the original, with a toasty Brown Sugar Buttercream coating the interior and exterior. Our final touch? Panels of edible birch bark, a delicious and realistic final touch to our epic cake.

3 tablespoons (42 grams) unsalted butter
¼ cup (85 grams) molasses
1 teaspoon (5 grams) grated fresh ginger
1 teaspoon (4 grams) vanilla extract
5 large eggs (250 grams)
½ cup (110 grams) firmly packed dark brown sugar
1 large egg yolk (19 grams)
¾ cup (94 grams) cake flour
3 tablespoons (24 grams) cornstarch
1 teaspoon (2 grams) ground ginger
1 teaspoon (2 grams) ground cinnamon
¼ teaspoon kosher salt
¼ teaspoon ground nutmeg
¼ teaspoon ground cloves
Molasses Simple Syrup (recipe follows)
Brown Sugar Buttercream (recipe follows)
White Chocolate Bark (recipe follows)

1. Preheat oven to 350°F (180°C). Spray an 18x13-inch rimmed baking sheet with cooking spray; line pan with parchment paper, and spray pan again.
2. In a small saucepan, melt butter over medium heat. Remove from heat, and stir in molasses, grated ginger, and vanilla. Set aside.
3. In the bowl of a stand mixer, whisk together eggs, brown sugar, and egg yolk by hand. Place bowl over a saucepan of simmering water. Cook, whisking occasionally, until an instant-read thermometer registers 110°F (43°C), about 5 minutes. Return bowl to stand mixer fitted with the whisk attachment, and beat at high speed until thick and tripled in volume, about 5 minutes.
4. In a medium bowl, place about 1 cup egg mixture. Fold in warm butter mixture. Set aside.
5. In a small bowl, sift together flour, cornstarch, ground ginger, cinnamon, salt, nutmeg, and cloves. Using a large balloon whisk, gently fold flour mixture into remaining egg mixture in two additions just until combined. Fold in butter mixture. Using an offset spatula, quickly and gently

spread batter evenly in prepared pan.
6. Bake until cake starts to pull away from sides of pan, 12 to 15 minutes. Let cool completely in pan.
7. Loosen cake from sides of pan, if needed. Using a serrated knife, cut into 4 (12x4-inch) rectangles. (You will have some cake edges left over.) (Be sure to cut through the parchment paper as well; use scissors if needed). Lift each piece, with parchment attached, out of pan. Brush with Molasses Simple Syrup. Spread ⅔ cup Brown Sugar Buttercream on each rectangle.
8. Roll up 1 rectangle, jelly roll style, and place in center of a cake plate. Remove parchment. Carefully wrap a second rectangle around center roll, using parchment to help. Remove parchment, and repeat with remaining rectangles, creating a spiral. Using a serrated knife, trim end of final piece at an angle to make it flush with outer edge of cake.
9. Spread remaining Brown Sugar Buttercream on outside of cake. Without adding additional buttercream, lightly spread buttercream that peeks through the layers on top. Place White Chocolate Bark vertically on sides of cake, overlapping slightly and pressing into buttercream to hold in place. Cover and refrigerate for at least 2 hours or overnight. Let stand at room temperature for 1 hour before serving.

MOLASSES SIMPLE SYRUP
Makes about ½ cup

⅓ cup (67 grams) granulated sugar
⅓ cup (80 grams) water
1 tablespoon (21 grams) molasses

1. In a small saucepan, bring sugar and ⅓ cup (80 grams) water to a boil over medium-high heat, stirring occasionally, until sugar is dissolved. Remove from heat, and stir in molasses. Let cool completely. Refrigerate in an airtight container for up to 1 week.

BROWN SUGAR BUTTERCREAM
Makes about 4 cups

4 large egg whites (120 grams), room temperature

1 cup (220 grams) firmly packed light brown sugar
½ cup (100 grams) granulated sugar
1¾ cups (397 grams) unsalted butter, cubed and softened
1 teaspoon (4 grams) vanilla extract
¼ teaspoon kosher salt

1. In the bowl of a stand mixer, whisk together egg whites and sugars by hand. Place bowl over a saucepan of simmering water. Cook, whisking occasionally, until an instant-read thermometer registers 155°F (68°C) to 160°F (71°C).
2. Carefully return bowl to stand mixer fitted with the whisk attachment, and beat at high speed until bowl is cool to the touch, about 8 minutes. Add butter, 2 tablespoons (28 grams) at a time, beating until combined after each addition. Beat in vanilla and salt. Use immediately, or refrigerate in an airtight container for up to 3 days. If refrigerating, let stand at room temperature for 2 hours and rewhip until smooth before using.

WHITE CHOCOLATE BARK
Makes 2 (14x5-inch) rectangles of chocolate bark

¼ cup (40 grams) dark chocolate melting wafers, melted according to package directions and cooled slightly
2 cups (320 grams) white chocolate melting wafers, melted according to package directions and cooled slightly

1. Using a permanent marker, draw a 14x5-inch rectangle on each of 2 sheets of parchment paper. Turn parchment over, and place on 2 rimmed baking sheets.
2. Using a fine-point, food-safe brush, brush melted dark chocolate inside each rectangle. Refrigerate until set, about 5 minutes.
3. Pour half of melted white chocolate on a rectangle. Using an offset spatula, spread white chocolate evenly, using the rectangle as a guide. Repeat procedure with remaining white chocolate. Refrigerate until set, 10 to 15 minutes. Break into small rectangles, about 5x1½ inches. (They do not have to be perfect.)

BUNDT & TUBE
CAKES

With ridges and grooves in all the right places, the emblematic Bundt pan and timeless tube pan are the perfect canvases for everything from an ombré strawberry pound cake to a rum-soaked gâteau

BOSTON CREAM CAKE

Makes 1 (10-inch) tube cake

With a rich ganache, pillowy yellow cake, and luscious vanilla cream cheese filling, our tube pan twist on Boston's most famous dessert literally turns this classic upside-down. We flipped the cake as it cooled, creating a flat top for our shiny ganache glaze.

1	cup (227 grams) unsalted butter, softened
1½	cups (300 grams) granulated sugar
2	large eggs (100 grams), room temperature
3	large egg yolks (56 grams), room temperature
1	tablespoon (13 grams) vanilla extract
2¾	cups (344 grams) all-purpose flour
2	teaspoons (10 grams) baking powder
1	teaspoon (3 grams) kosher salt
1	cup (240 grams) whole buttermilk, room temperature

Vanilla Filling (recipe follows)
Ganache (recipe follows)

1. Preheat oven to 350°F (180°C). Butter and flour a 10-inch tube pan.

2. In the bowl of a stand mixer fitted with the paddle attachment, beat butter and sugar at medium speed until fluffy, 3 to 4 minutes, stopping to scrape sides of bowl. Add eggs and egg yolks, one at a time, beating well after each addition. Beat in vanilla.

3. In a medium bowl, whisk together flour, baking powder, and salt. With mixer on low speed, gradually add flour mixture to butter mixture alternately with buttermilk, beginning and ending with flour mixture, beating just until combined after each addition. Spoon two-thirds of batter (about 3¼ cups [765 grams]) into prepared pan, smoothing top. Spoon Vanilla Filling on top of batter, spreading evenly but ensuring filling does not touch sides of pan. Top with remaining batter, smoothing top.

4. Bake until a wooden pick inserted near center comes out clean, about 55 minutes. Let cool in pan for 20 minutes. Invert cake onto a wire rack, and let cool completely. Just before serving, top with Ganache.

VANILLA FILLING

Makes 1¼ cups

4	ounces (115 grams) cream cheese, softened
½	cup (100 grams) granulated sugar
¼	cup (57 grams) unsalted butter, softened
1	tablespoon (18 grams) vanilla bean paste
1	teaspoon (4 grams) vanilla extract
2	tablespoons (16 grams) all-purpose flour
¼	teaspoon kosher salt

1. In the bowl of a stand mixer fitted with the paddle attachment, beat cream cheese, sugar, butter, vanilla bean paste, and vanilla extract at medium speed until smooth. Add flour and salt, and beat until combined. Use immediately.

GANACHE

Makes 1½ cups

8	ounces (225 grams) 60% cacao bittersweet chocolate, chopped
¾	cup (180 grams) heavy whipping cream
1	tablespoon (14 grams) unsalted butter, softened
1	teaspoon (4 grams) vanilla extract

1. In a large heatproof bowl, place chocolate.

2. In a small saucepan, bring cream to a boil over medium-low heat. Pour half of hot cream over chocolate; let stand for 30 seconds. Starting in center of bowl, slowly stir with a rubber spatula until well combined. Add remaining hot cream, and slowly stir to combine. Add butter and vanilla, and stir until well combined. Use immediately.

PAIN D'ÉPICE

Makes 1 (10-cup) cake

Recipe by Marjorie Taylor and
Kendall Smith Franchini

*Pain d'épice, or spice bread, is a classic
Burgundian favorite. Traditionally, it is
baked in a loaf pan, but Marjorie Taylor and
Kendall Smith Franchini, founders of The
Cook's Atelier in Burgundy, France, like to
make theirs a bit more festive by baking it in
a fluted cake pan.*

2   large eggs (100 grams)
¾   cup (180 grams) water
1   cup (336 grams) honey
½   cup (110 grams) firmly packed light
     brown sugar

2   cups (250 grams) unbleached
     all-purpose flour, divided
1½   teaspoons (7.5 grams) baking powder
½   teaspoon (2.5 grams) baking soda
1   teaspoon (2 grams) ground cinnamon
1   teaspoon (2 grams) ground nutmeg
1   teaspoon (2 grams) ground ginger
1   teaspoon (2 grams) ground coriander
1   teaspoon (2 grams) ground aniseed
½   teaspoon (1 gram) ground cloves
¼   teaspoon ground black pepper
Pinch fleur de sel
1   tablespoon (3 grams) lemon zest
1   tablespoon (3 grams) orange zest

1. Preheat the oven to 350°F (180°C).
Butter the inside of a 10-cup cake mold.
2. Whisk the eggs in a large bowl.

3. In a large saucepan, place ¾ cup
(180 grams) water, honey, and the brown
sugar and bring it to a boil. Once it comes to
a boil, remove from the heat and sift 1 cup
(125 grams) of the all-purpose flour into the
mixture, whisking vigorously.
4. Sift the remaining 1 cup (125 grams) flour
with the baking powder, baking soda, and
ground spices. Add the fleur de sel, lemon
zest, and orange zest.
5. Slowly add the honey mixture to the eggs,
whisking constantly.
6. Add the flour and spice mixture a little
at a time to the honey and egg mixture,
whisking constantly to avoid any lumps. Pour
the batter into the prepared pan.
7. Bake until firm to the touch, 35 to
40 minutes.

Photo by Joann Pai

BROWN SUGAR PECAN POUND CAKE

Makes 1 (10-inch) tube cake

Recipe by Dolester Miles

Dolester Miles is the undisputable queen of pound cake. The James Beard Award-winning pastry chef leads the dessert programs for three Birmingham, Alabama, institutions opened by restauranteur Frank Stitt, but this cake isn't offered on the menu at any of them. It's a special Miles family recipe that Dolester grew up making with her mother and aunt. Zesty orange juice brightens up the brown sugar-loaded batter, and toasted pecans lend a lovely crunch to every bite.

1   cup (227 grams) unsalted butter, softened
½   cup (113 grams) shortening*
2   cups plus 1 tablespoon (454 grams) firmly packed light brown sugar
½   cup (100 grams) granulated sugar
6   large eggs (300 grams), room temperature
1   teaspoon (4 grams) vanilla extract
3   cups (375 grams) all-purpose flour
½   teaspoon (2.5 grams) baking powder
¼   teaspoon kosher salt
1   cup (240 grams) whole milk, room temperature
1   cup (113 grams) toasted pecan pieces
2¼ cups (270 grams) sifted confectioners' sugar
¼   cup (60 grams) fresh orange juice

1. Preheat oven to 325°F (170°C). Butter and flour a 10-inch tube pan.
2. In the bowl of a stand mixer fitted with the whisk attachment, beat butter, shortening, brown sugar, and granulated sugar at medium speed until fluffy, 4 to 5 minutes, stopping to scrape sides of bowl. Reduce mixer speed to low. Add eggs, one at a time, beating well after each addition. Beat in vanilla.
3. In a medium bowl, sift together flour, baking powder, and salt. Gradually add flour mixture to butter mixture alternately with milk, beginning and ending with flour mixture, beating just until combined after each addition. Fold in pecans. Pour batter into pan.
4. Bake until a wooden pick inserted near center comes out clean, about 1 hour and 15 minutes. Let cool in pan for 15 to 20 minutes. Invert cake onto a wire rack, and let cool completely.
5. In a small bowl, stir together confectioners' sugar and orange juice. Spoon glaze onto cooled cake, allowing it to drizzle down sides. Serve immediately.

You can also use ½ cup (113 grams) softened unsalted butter.

TRIPLE-LAYER STRAWBERRY POUND CAKE

Makes 1 (10-inch) tube cake

Slice into this unassuming pound cake to find a surprise berry-brilliant interior. In sweet shades of strawberry and vanilla ombré, this velvet cake is the epitome of the colors and flavors of spring.

2	cups (454 grams)	unsalted butter, softened
3	cups (600 grams)	granulated sugar
1	teaspoon (3 grams)	kosher salt
7	large eggs (350 grams), room temperature	
2	teaspoons (8 grams)	vanilla extract
3½	cups (438 grams)	all-purpose flour, divided
⅓	cup (80 grams)	sour cream
½	cup (160 grams)	strawberry preserves, divided
16	drops liquid red food coloring*, divided	
1½	cups (30 grams)	freeze-dried strawberries
Strawberry Glaze (recipe follows)		

1. Preheat oven to 300°F (150°C). Butter and flour a 10-inch tube pan. Wrap pan with foil, shiny side out. (See Note.)
2. In the bowl of a stand mixer fitted with the paddle attachment, beat butter, sugar, and salt at medium speed until fluffy, 6 to 7 minutes, stopping to scrape sides of bowl. Add eggs, one at a time, beating well after each addition. Beat in vanilla. Divide batter among 3 bowls (460 grams each).
3. In first bowl, fold in 1¼ cups (156 grams) flour alternately with sour cream, beginning and ending with flour, just until combined. Set aside.
4. In second bowl, fold in 1 cup plus 2 tablespoons (141 grams) flour alternately with ¼ cup (80 grams) strawberry preserves and 6 drops food coloring, beginning and ending with flour, just until combined. Set aside.
5. In the container of a blender, blend freeze-dried strawberries to a fine powder.

6. In a small bowl, whisk together ¼ cup (21 grams) freeze-dried strawberry powder and remaining 1 cup plus 2 tablespoons (141 grams) flour. Fold flour mixture into remaining batter alternately with remaining ¼ cup (80 grams) strawberry preserves and remaining 10 drops food coloring, beginning and ending with flour mixture, just until combined.
7. Spoon plain vanilla batter into prepared pan, smoothing top. Gently spoon light pink batter on top, smoothing top. Gently spoon dark pink batter on top, smoothing top.
8. Bake until a wooden pick inserted near center comes out clean and an instant-read thermometer inserted near center registers 205°F (96°C) to 210°F (99°C), 2 hours to 2 hours and 10 minutes, loosely covering top of pan with foil after 1 hour and 15 minutes of baking to prevent excess browning, if necessary. Let cool in pan for 15 minutes. Invert cake onto a wire rack, and let cool completely. Top with Strawberry Glaze.

*We used McCormick Red Food Color. You can also use gel food coloring, but the color will not be as vibrant.

Note: *Because this cake has a long bake time, we wrapped the pan in foil to prevent the crust from becoming too dark. The foil shield also helps the cake rise and bake evenly throughout.*

STRAWBERRY GLAZE
Makes ¾ cup

1½	cups (180 grams)	confectioners' sugar
¼	cup plus 2 tablespoons (120 grams) strawberry preserves	
½	tablespoon (7.5 grams)	whole milk

1. In a medium bowl, whisk together all ingredients until smooth. Use immediately.

ANGEL FOOD CAKE

Makes 1 (10-inch) tube cake

As fine and fluffy as cotton, this ring-shaped sponge cake is a recipe for the ages. The ideal pillowy bed for macerated fruit and cream, it's the epitome of sweet, understated perfection.

1½   cups (188 grams) bleached cake flour
2   cups (400 grams) granulated sugar, divided
2   cups (480 grams) egg whites, room temperature (from about 14 large eggs)
1   teaspoon (3 grams) cream of tartar
½   teaspoon (1.5 grams) kosher salt
2   teaspoons (8 grams) vanilla extract

1. Preheat oven to 350°F (180°C).
2. In a medium bowl, sift together flour and 1 cup (200 grams) sugar. Set aside.
3. In the bowl of a stand mixer fitted with the whisk attachment, beat egg whites at medium-high speed until foamy, about 1 minute. Slowly add remaining 1 cup (200 grams) sugar. Increase mixer speed to high; immediately add cream of tartar and salt. Add vanilla, and beat until soft peaks form, about 2 minutes.
4. Transfer egg white mixture to a large bowl. Using a large balloon whisk, fold in flour mixture in four additions just until combined. Gently spread batter into an ungreased 10-inch removable-bottom tube pan. Run a knife through batter to release any air bubbles, and smooth top.
5. Bake until firm to the touch and an instant-read thermometer inserted near center registers 205°F (96°C) to 210°F (99°C), about 40 minutes. Immediately invert pan (onto a bottle if needed; see Note), and let cool completely. Using an offset spatula, loosen cake from sides and bottom of pan. Invert onto a cake plate.

Note: *If your pan doesn't have prongs to support it, rest it on the narrow neck of a full glass bottle, like a wine bottle. You turn the pan upside down to ensure that your freshly baked cake doesn't sink when cooling.*

PRO TIP
To keep from squishing down your cake during slicing, be sure to use a serrated knife to cut through cleanly without compressing.

CITRUS VARIATION
Try this with a bright kiss of citrus. Substitute **1 tablespoon (15 grams) fresh lemon juice** for vanilla extract. Fold in **2 tablespoons (6 grams) lemon zest** (about 2 lemons) with last addition of flour mixture.

MINI CHOCOLATE ANGEL FOOD CAKES

Makes 6 mini tube cakes

When nothing will do but the rich notes of cocoa, turn to these mini chocolate cakes baked into perfect individual portions. We like to serve these almond-accented treats with Peach Compote and Coconut Whipped Cream (recipes on page 50).

½ cup (63 grams) bleached cake flour
1 cup (200 grams) granulated sugar, divided
⅓ cup plus 1 tablespoon (30 grams) Dutch process cocoa powder
1 cup (240 grams) egg whites, room temperature (from about 7 large eggs)

1 teaspoon (3 grams) cream of tartar
¼ teaspoon kosher salt
1 teaspoon (4 grams) vanilla extract
½ teaspoon (2 grams) almond extract

1. Preheat oven to 350°F (180°C).
2. In a medium bowl, sift together flour, ½ cup (100 grams) sugar, and cocoa. Set aside.
3. In the bowl of a stand mixer fitted with the whisk attachment, beat egg whites at medium-high speed until foamy, about 30 seconds. Slowly add remaining ½ cup (100 grams) sugar. Increase mixer speed to high; immediately add cream of tartar and salt. Add extracts, and beat until soft peaks form, about 1 minute.

4. Transfer egg white mixture to a large bowl. Using a large balloon whisk, fold in flour mixture in four additions just until combined. Divide batter among the ungreased wells of a 6-well mini tube pan*, smoothing tops.
5. Bake until firm to the touch, about 15 minutes. Immediately invert pan (onto bottles if needed), and let cool completely. Using an offset spatula, loosen cakes from sides of wells, and invert onto a serving platter.

We used Nordic Ware Mini Angel Food Cake Pan.

ANGEL FOOD CAKE ACCOMPANIMENTS

VANILLA MACERATED STRAWBERRIES

Makes about 3 cups

The classic fruit complement to Angel Food Cake (recipe on page 48). What more could you want?

3   cups (441 grams) hulled and sliced
    fresh strawberries
2   tablespoons (24 grams) granulated sugar
2   teaspoons (12 grams) vanilla bean paste
1   teaspoon (4 grams) vanilla extract

1. In a medium bowl, toss together all ingredients. Let stand, stirring occasionally, until sugar is dissolved and a syrup is created, about 20 minutes.

BLUEBERRY BALSAMIC COULIS

Makes about 2¼ cups

In this jammy accompaniment, plump fresh blueberries are tempered by the acidic sweetness of balsamic vinegar.

2⅔   cups (452 grams) fresh blueberries
½   cup (100 grams) granulated sugar
1   tablespoon (15 grams) fresh lemon juice
2   tablespoons (30 grams) balsamic vinegar

1. In a medium saucepan, stir together blueberries, sugar, and lemon juice. Cook over medium heat, stirring occasionally, until sugar is dissolved. Gently mash blueberries. Stir in vinegar, and bring to a boil. Remove from heat, and let cool slightly. Transfer to the container of a blender, and blend on low speed until smooth.

PEACH COMPOTE

Makes about 2½ cups

Boozy, nutty, and fruity, this stone fruit stunner will become your new favorite use for amaretto.

3⅔   cups (824 grams) sliced fresh peaches
     (about 6 medium peaches)
⅔   cup (133 grams) granulated sugar
¼   teaspoon kosher salt
¼   cup (60 grams) water
3   tablespoons (45 grams) amaretto
2   tablespoons (30 grams) fresh lemon
     juice

1. In a large saucepan, fold together peaches, sugar, and salt until peaches are evenly coated. Add ¼ cup (60 grams) water, amaretto, and lemon juice, stirring to combine. Cook over medium heat, stirring frequently, until sugar is dissolved and mixture starts to boil. Cook until liquid is reduced and mixture is thickened to desired consistency, about 18 minutes.

VANILLA CHANTILLY CRÈME

Makes about 2 cups

For old-school finesse, finish off your Angel Food Cake (recipe on page 48) with generous scoops of this cloud-like, vanilla-scented cream.

1   cup (240 grams) cold heavy whipping
    cream
1   teaspoon (6 grams) vanilla bean paste
1   teaspoon (4 grams) vanilla extract
3   tablespoons (21 grams) confectioners'
    sugar

1. In the bowl of a stand mixer fitted with the whisk attachment, combine cold cream, vanilla bean paste, and vanilla extract. With mixer on high speed, slowly add confectioners' sugar, beating until stiff peaks form. Cover and refrigerate until ready to serve.

LEMON CURD

Makes about 2½ cups

If you're looking to up the sunshine level of any dessert, look no further than this velvety citrus curd.

4   large eggs (200 grams)
4   large egg yolks (74 grams)
1   cup (200 grams) granulated sugar
2   tablespoons (6 grams) lemon zest
1   cup (240 grams) fresh lemon juice
½   teaspoon (1.5 grams) kosher salt
½   cup (113 grams) unsalted butter, cubed

1. Place a fine-mesh sieve over a medium bowl; set aside. In another medium bowl, whisk together eggs and egg yolks until well combined; set aside.

2. In a medium saucepan, whisk together sugar, lemon zest and juice, and salt. Cook over medium-low heat until sugar is dissolved and mixture begins to steam. (Do not boil.) Pour lemon mixture into egg mixture in a slow, steady stream, whisking constantly. Return mixture to saucepan. Cook, stirring slowly and constantly in a figure eight motion with a silicone spatula, until curd is thickened and can coat the back of a spoon and an instant-read thermometer registers 175°F (79°C) to 180°F (82°C), 10 to 12 minutes.

3. Press curd through prepared sieve into bowl, discarding solids. Add butter, 1 to 2 cubes at a time, stirring until melted after each addition. Cover with a piece of plastic wrap, pressing wrap directly onto surface of curd to prevent a skin from forming. Refrigerate until well chilled and set, at least 2 hours.

COCONUT WHIPPED CREAM

Makes about 2¾ cups

The rich upper cream of full-fat coconut milk becomes the fluffy base of this tropical topper.

1   (13.5-ounce) can (400 grams) full-fat
    coconut milk
¼   cup (30 grams) confectioners' sugar
1   cup (240 grams) cold heavy whipping
    cream

1. Place unshaken coconut milk can in refrigerator overnight.

2. Open can of coconut milk, and skim solid fat from top and bottom into a small bowl; discard thin coconut liquid.

3. In the bowl of a stand mixer fitted with the whisk attachment, beat coconut cream and confectioners' sugar at high speed until smooth and light, about 2 minutes. Transfer to a small bowl; set aside.

4. In mixer bowl, beat heavy cream at high speed until soft peaks form. Add whipped coconut cream, and beat until stiff peaks form. Cover and refrigerate until ready to use.

MINI COCONUT-PEPPER JELLY CAKES

Makes 6 mini Bundt cakes

These nectarine-studded cakes get sweet heat with a double dose of pepper jelly mixed into the batter and the spiced rum glaze.

½   cup (113 grams) unsalted butter, softened
⅔   cup (133 grams) granulated sugar
3   tablespoons (60 grams) hot pepper jelly
1   large egg (50 grams), room temperature
1   tablespoon (15 grams) spiced rum*
1½   cups (188 grams) cake flour
½   teaspoon (2.5 grams) baking powder
½   teaspoon (2.5 grams) baking soda
½   teaspoon (1.5 grams) kosher salt
¼   cup (60 grams) full-fat coconut milk
¼   cup (60 grams) whole buttermilk, room temperature
¾   cup (120 grams) diced peeled nectarines
½   cup (60 grams) packed sweetened shredded coconut
Rum Pepper Jelly Glaze (recipe follows)

1. Preheat oven to 350°F (180°C).
2. In the bowl of a stand mixer fitted with the paddle attachment, beat butter and sugar at medium speed until fluffy, 3 to 4 minutes, stopping to scrape sides of bowl. Beat in pepper jelly. Add egg, beating well. Beat in rum.
3. In a medium bowl, whisk together flour, baking powder, baking soda, and salt. In a small bowl, stir together coconut milk and buttermilk. With mixer on low speed, gradually add flour mixture to butter mixture alternately with coconut milk mixture, beginning and ending with flour mixture, beating just until combined after each addition. Fold in nectarines and coconut.
4. Spray a 6-well mini Bundt pan* with baking spray with flour. Divide batter among prepared wells.
5. Bake until a wooden pick inserted near center comes out clean, about 20 minutes. Let cool in pan for 10 minutes. Invert cakes onto a wire rack, and let cool completely. Place wire rack over a rimmed baking sheet, and brush cakes with warm Rum Pepper Jelly Glaze. Serve immediately.

We used Pusser's Spiced Rum and Nordic Ware Brilliance Cakelet Pan. Bake time may vary when using a different pan.

RUM PEPPER JELLY GLAZE

Makes ½ cup

¼   cup (80 grams) hot pepper jelly
¼   cup (60 grams) spiced rum

1. In a small saucepan, melt pepper jelly over medium-low heat. Remove from heat; stir in rum. Use immediately.

SPICED MULLED WINE PEAR CAKE

Makes 1 (10-inch) tube cake

With whole poached pears rising up like regal statues, this cake is a conversation starter. It may seem like an artistic feat, but with some simple engineering, the look is easy to accomplish. A blend of pear juice and homemade mulled wine enhances the pears' flavor and dyes them that gorgeous hue. Buttermilk and sour cream in the batter tone down the spice and zingy citrus and give the cake a super-tender texture.

2   cups (400 grams) granulated sugar
1   cup (224 grams) canola oil
3   large eggs (150 grams)
½   cup (120 grams) sour cream
2   tablespoons (6 grams) orange zest
2   teaspoons (8 grams) vanilla extract
3   cups (375 grams) all-purpose flour
2   teaspoons (10 grams) baking powder
1½   teaspoons (4.5 grams) kosher salt
1   teaspoon (2 grams) ground cinnamon
½   teaspoon (1 gram) ground allspice
¼   teaspoon ground cloves
¼   teaspoon ground star anise
1   cup (240 grams) whole buttermilk
5   (12-inch) metal or wooden skewers
Mulled Wine-Poached Pears (recipe follows)
Mulled Wine Glaze (recipe follows)

1. Position oven rack in bottom third of oven, and preheat oven to 350°F (180°C). Wrap a 10-inch removable-bottom tube pan with foil, shiny side out. Spray pan with baking spray with flour.
2. In a large bowl, whisk together sugar, oil, eggs, sour cream, orange zest, and vanilla. In a medium bowl, whisk together flour, baking powder, salt, cinnamon, allspice, cloves, and star anise. Gradually add flour mixture to sugar mixture alternately with buttermilk, beginning and ending with flour mixture, whisking until combined after each addition. Spoon batter into prepared pan, smoothing top with an offset spatula.
3. Spray skewers with cooking spray. Drain Mulled Wine-Poached Pears, reserving 2 tablespoons (30 grams) poaching liquid for Mulled Wine Glaze. Insert prepared skewers horizontally through pears ½ inch below stem. Place pears in batter, not letting them touch bottom of pan; let skewers rest on sides of pan. (Skewers will suspend the pears in the batter.)
4. Bake until a wooden pick inserted near center comes out clean, 1 hour and 35 minutes to 1 hour and 45 minutes, covering with foil after 1 hour of baking to prevent excess browning. Let cool for 10 minutes. Gently twist skewers, and remove from pears. Let cake cool completely in pan.
5. Lift cake out of pan using center tube. Using 2 spatulas, lift cake off bottom of pan. Top with Mulled Wine Glaze. Serve immediately.

MULLED WINE-POACHED PEARS
Makes 5 poached pears

5   medium Bosc or Anjou pears (1,010 grams)
1   cup (240 grams) pear juice*
½   cup (110 grams) firmly packed light brown sugar
½   cup (170 grams) clover honey
½   cup (120 grams) brandy
1   (750-ml) bottle full-bodied red wine, such as Merlot
7   (1-inch-wide) strips orange zest (28 grams)
½   cup (120 grams) fresh orange juice
1   vanilla bean, split lengthwise, seeds scraped and reserved
2   cinnamon sticks
5   whole allspice
3   whole star anise
4   whole cloves

1. Peel pears, leaving stems intact. Using a melon baller, core pears from bottom.
2. In a large saucepan, cook pear juice, brown sugar, honey, and brandy over medium-high heat until sugar is dissolved and mixture starts to boil. Add wine, orange zest and juice, vanilla bean and reserved seeds, cinnamon sticks, allspice, star anise, and cloves; return to a boil. Add pears; reduce heat to medium-low. Shape a small sheet of foil into a circle. Place on top of pears to keep them fully submerged in poaching liquid. Simmer until pears are fork-tender, 30 to 35 minutes.
3. Transfer pears to a bowl. Pour poaching liquid over pears, and let cool to room temperature. Cover and refrigerate until ready to use, up to 1 week.

*We used R.W. Knudsen Organic Pear Juice.

MULLED WINE GLAZE
Makes about ½ cup

1⅓   cups (160 grams) confectioners' sugar
2   tablespoons (30 grams) reserved poaching liquid from Mulled Wine-Poached Pears (recipe precedes)

1. In a small bowl, whisk together confectioners' sugar and reserved poaching liquid until smooth. Use immediately.

PRO TIP
Slightly underripe pears are best for poaching. The longer the pears soak in the poaching liquid, the more intense the flavor will be. We recommend refrigerating them in the poaching liquid overnight.

DARK 'N STORMY BUNDT CAKE

Makes 1 (15-cup) Bundt cake

Inspired by renowned rum company Gosling's signature Dark 'n Stormy cocktail, we gave classic pound cake an island update by mixing dark rum and crystallized ginger into the batter. A luxurious soak in a rum-spiked glaze ensures that the sugar spirit permeates every bite.

1½ cups (340 grams) unsalted butter, softened
2¾ cups (550 grams) granulated sugar
7 large eggs (350 grams), room temperature
1 tablespoon (3 grams) lime zest
3½ cups (438 grams) all-purpose flour
1 teaspoon (3 grams) kosher salt
¾ cup (180 grams) whole buttermilk
½ cup (120 grams) dark rum*
½ cup (88 grams) chopped crystallized ginger
Dark Rum Glaze (recipe follows)

1. Preheat oven to 300°F (150°C).
2. In the bowl of a stand mixer fitted with the paddle attachment, beat butter and sugar at medium speed until fluffy, 6 to 7 minutes, stopping to scrape sides of bowl. Add eggs, one at a time, beating well after each addition. Beat in lime zest.
3. In a medium bowl, sift together flour and salt. In a small bowl, combine buttermilk and rum. With mixer on low speed, gradually add flour mixture to butter mixture alternately with buttermilk mixture, beginning and ending with flour mixture, beating just until combined after each addition. Fold in ginger.
4. Spray a 15-cup Bundt pan* with baking spray with flour. Spoon batter into prepared pan.
5. Bake for 1 hour. Loosely cover with foil, and bake until a wooden pick inserted near center comes out clean, 45 to 55 minutes more. Let cool in pan for 10 minutes. Invert cake onto a wire rack, and let cool completely. Place wire rack over a rimmed baking sheet, and pour Dark Rum Glaze over cake. Let glaze dry before serving.

We used Gosling's Black Seal Rum and Nordic Ware Anniversary Pan.

DARK RUM GLAZE
Makes about 1 cup

2¼ cups (270 grams) confectioners' sugar
⅓ cup (80 grams) dark rum

1. In a small bowl, whisk together confectioners' sugar and rum until smooth. Use immediately.

CLASSIC VANILLA POUND CAKE

Makes 1 (10-cup) Bundt cake

You can choose your flavor with this incredibly simple, perfectly sweet pound cake. Go almond, lemon, or vanilla. (See Flavor Variations.)

1½ cups (340 grams) unsalted butter, softened
2 cups (400 grams) granulated sugar
6 large eggs (300 grams), room temperature
1 tablespoon (13 grams) vanilla extract
3 cups (375 grams) all-purpose flour
1 teaspoon (3 grams) kosher salt
½ teaspoon (2.5 grams) baking powder
1 cup (240 grams) whole milk, room temperature

1. Preheat oven to 350°F (180°C).
2. In the bowl of a stand mixer fitted with the paddle attachment, beat butter and sugar at medium speed until fluffy, 5 to 7 minutes, stopping to scrape sides of bowl. Reduce mixer speed to low. Add eggs, one at a time, beating well after each addition. Beat in vanilla.
3. In a medium bowl, whisk together flour, salt, and baking powder. Gradually add flour mixture to butter mixture alternately with milk, beginning and ending with flour mixture, beating just until combined after each addition.
4. Spray a 10-cup Bundt pan* with baking spray with flour. Pour batter into prepared pan. Firmly tap pan on counter to settle batter.
5. Bake until a wooden pick inserted near center comes out clean, about 1 hour. Let cool in pan for 10 minutes. Invert cake onto a wire rack, and let cool completely.

We used Nordic Ware Brilliance Bundt Pan.

FLAVOR VARIATIONS:

Lemon Pound Cake: Substitute 1 tablespoon (3 grams) lemon zest for vanilla extract; add lemon zest with butter and sugar.

Almond Pound Cake: Substitute 1½ teaspoons (6 grams) almond extract for vanilla extract.

TWO-TIER ORANGE-GINGER POUND CAKE

Makes 1 (10-cup) and 1 (6-cup) Bundt cake

This glimmering holiday beauty gives a whole new meaning to the term "layer cake." Nordic Ware's Heritage Bundt Pan, which comes in two perfectly stackable sizes, provides the ideal shape for a plethora of garnishes. A luscious Vanilla Glaze and a light dusting of confectioners' sugar cascade down the concentric edges, and a smattering of metallic sprinkles rests in the sloping channels. With orange zest and both freshly grated and ground ginger in the batter, this two-tier masterpiece tastes as incredible as it looks.

2	cups (454 grams) unsalted butter, softened
3	cups (600 grams) granulated sugar
1	tablespoon (9 grams) packed orange zest
4	large eggs (200 grams), room temperature
4	cups (500 grams) all-purpose flour
1¾	teaspoons (5.25 grams) kosher salt
1½	teaspoons (3 grams) ground ginger
¼	teaspoon (1.25 grams) baking soda
1	cup (240 grams) whole milk, room temperature
2	tablespoons (30 grams) grated fresh ginger
2	teaspoons (8 grams) vanilla extract

Vanilla Glaze (recipe follows)
Assorted gold sprinkles (optional)
3- to 3½-inch star-shaped sugar cookie*, for topping
Confectioners' sugar, for dusting

1. Preheat oven to 325°F (170°C).
2. In the bowl of a stand mixer fitted with the paddle attachment, beat butter, granulated sugar, and orange zest at medium speed until fluffy, 3 to 4 minutes, stopping to scrape sides of bowl. Add eggs, one at a time, beating until well combined after each addition.
3. In a medium bowl, whisk together flour, salt, ground ginger, and baking soda. In a medium bowl, whisk together milk, grated ginger, and vanilla. With mixer on low speed, add flour mixture to butter mixture alternately with milk mixture, beginning and ending with flour mixture, beating just until combined after each addition.
4. Spray a 10-cup and a 6-cup Nordic Ware Heritage Bundt Pan with baking spray with flour. Spoon 5¼ cups (about 1,236 grams) batter into prepared 10-cup pan; spoon remaining batter (about 788 grams) into prepared 6-cup pan. Tap pans on counter several times to spread batter into grooves and release any air bubbles.
5. Bake until a wooden pick inserted near center comes out clean, 45 to 50 minutes for the 6-cup pan and 55 minutes to 1 hour for the 10-cup pan. Let cool in pans for 10 minutes. Gently loosen center and edges from pans using a small offset spatula. Invert cakes onto wire racks; let cool completely.
6. Transfer 10-cup Bundt cake to desired serving plate. Place Vanilla Glaze in a large piping bag fitted with a ¼-inch round piping tip (Wilton No. 12). Carefully pipe glaze into and over grooves of cake. Once glaze stops dripping, decorate with sprinkles (if using). On a separate plate or cake board, repeat glazing process with 6-cup Bundt cake, and decorate with sprinkles (if using); stack on top of 10-cup Bundt cake. Trace over ridges of cakes with glaze, pausing briefly at various points to create a drip effect. Top 6-cup cake with sugar cookie (see PRO TIP), and dust with confectioners' sugar.

*See Iced Eggnog Shortbread Cookie Trees on page 340.

Vanilla Glaze

Makes 1¾ cups

5	cups (600 grams) confectioners' sugar
⅓	cup (80 grams) whole milk
2	tablespoons (30 grams) fresh orange juice
1	teaspoon (4 grams) vanilla extract*
¼	teaspoon kosher salt

1. In a medium bowl, whisk together all ingredients until smooth. Use immediately.

We used Heilala.

PRO TIP
To help keep the star cookie upright, stick a wooden skewer through the cake and lean the cookie against the skewer. Remove before serving.

BLUEBERRY MUFFIN LOAF

Makes 1 (10-inch) tube cake

To all the blueberry muffin fans, this one's for you. This quick bread-like cake takes the concept of a jumbo muffin one step further. Tangy yogurt highlights the bright flavor of the blueberries while a shower of turbinado and sparkling sugars creates that shimmering, crunchy topcoat signature to a bakery-style muffin.

- 1½ cups (188 grams) plus 1 tablespoon (8 grams) all-purpose flour, divided
- 1½ cups (187 grams) cake flour
- 1½ teaspoons (4.5 grams) kosher salt
- 1 teaspoon (5 grams) baking powder
- 1 teaspoon (5 grams) baking soda
- ¾ cup (170 grams) unsalted butter, melted
- ½ cup (110 grams) firmly packed light brown sugar
- ½ cup (100 grams) granulated sugar
- ½ cup (170 grams) maple syrup
- 3 large eggs (150 grams)
- 1 vanilla bean, split lengthwise, seeds scraped and reserved
- 1 tablespoon (3 grams) lemon zest (about 1 lemon)
- ½ cup (120 grams) Greek yogurt*
- 1 cup (170 grams) fresh blueberries
- 2 tablespoons (24 grams) turbinado sugar
- 2 tablespoons (24 grams) sparkling sugar

1. Preheat oven to 350°F (180°C). Butter and flour a 10-inch tube pan.

2. In a medium bowl, whisk together 1½ cups (188 grams) all-purpose flour, cake flour, salt, baking powder, and baking soda. Set aside.

3. In a large bowl, whisk together melted butter, brown sugar, granulated sugar, maple syrup, eggs, reserved vanilla bean seeds, and zest. Whisk in yogurt. Add flour mixture, and whisk just until dry ingredients are moistened.

4. In a small bowl, toss together blueberries and remaining 1 tablespoon (8 grams) all-purpose flour. Fold blueberries into batter. Spoon batter into prepared pan. Top with turbinado sugar and sparkling sugar.

5. Bake until a wooden pick inserted near center comes out clean, 50 to 55 minutes, covering with foil halfway through baking to prevent excess browning. Let cool in pan for 15 minutes. Serve warm or at room temperature.

We used Fage Total 5% Greek Yogurt.

VANILLA SAVARIN

Makes 1 (10-cup) Bundt cake

This Old-World French dessert is a delicious fusion of buttery cake and yeasted bread. Though it's traditionally soaked in orange liqueur, we soaked our cake in a blend of vanilla syrup and spiced rum and piled the center high with Spiced Vanilla Chantilly Crème for an island twist.

¼   cup (50 grams) granulated sugar
1   vanilla bean, split lengthwise, seeds scraped and reserved
2⅔ cups (333 grams) all-purpose flour
1   tablespoon (9 grams) instant yeast
4   large eggs (200 grams), room temperature
¼   cup (60 grams) warm whole milk (105°F/41°C to 110°F/43°C)
1½ teaspoons (6 grams) vanilla extract
1   teaspoon (3 grams) kosher salt
¾   cup (170 grams) unsalted butter, room temperature (see Note)
Vanilla Rum Syrup (recipe follows)
Spiced Vanilla Chantilly Crème (recipe follows)
Garnish: sliced fresh strawberries

1. In a spice grinder or the work bowl of a small food processor, place sugar and reserved vanilla bean seeds; pulse until combined. Transfer vanilla sugar to a medium bowl; add flour and yeast, stirring to combine.
2. In the bowl of a stand mixer fitted with the paddle attachment, whisk together eggs, warm milk, vanilla extract, and salt by hand. With mixer on medium speed, gradually add flour mixture, beating until a thick, sticky batter forms, about 1 minute. Gradually add butter, beating until combined. Increase mixer speed to high, and beat until dough is smooth and elastic and pulls away from sides of bowl but not bottom, about 4 minutes. Cover and let rise in a warm, draft-free place (75°F/24°C) until doubled in size, about 1 hour.
3. Brush a 10-cup Bundt pan* with melted butter. Gently punch down dough, and place in prepared pan. Using floured hands, press dough until it is even and fills ridges of pan. (The dough will feel very thick and sticky.) Tap pan on counter several times to release air bubbles. Cover and let rise until pan is three-fourths full, about 30 minutes.
4. Preheat oven to 350°F (180°C).
5. Bake until golden and an instant-read thermometer inserted near center registers 190°F (88°C), about 25 minutes. Let cool in pan for 10 minutes. Trim cake to level, if necessary. Invert cake onto a wire rack. Pour half of Vanilla Rum Syrup into pan, and place cake back in pan. Pour remaining Vanilla Rum Syrup over cake; let stand for 5 minutes. Invert cake onto a rimmed dish, letting excess syrup drain. Transfer cake to a serving dish. Pipe Spiced Vanilla Chantilly Crème into center of cake. Garnish with strawberries, if desired.

We used Nordic Ware Heritage Bundt Pan.

Note: *It is important for butter to be room temperature, not just softened, so it can be incorporated into the dough faster. If you need to get your butter to room temperature quickly, microwave it in 5-second intervals until it reaches the proper consistency. Try not to melt it.*

VANILLA RUM SYRUP
Makes about 2¾ cups

1   cup (200 grams) granulated sugar
½   cup (120 grams) water
1⅓ cups (400 grams) vanilla syrup
¼   cup plus 3 tablespoons (105 grams) spiced rum

1. In a small saucepan, bring sugar and ½ cup (120 grams) water to a boil over medium-high heat, stirring occasionally, until sugar is dissolved. Remove from heat; stir in vanilla syrup and rum. Let cool slightly.

SPICED VANILLA CHANTILLY CRÈME
Makes about 3 cups

1½ cups (360 grams) cold heavy whipping cream
2   teaspoons (10 grams) spiced rum
½   vanilla bean, split lengthwise, seeds scraped and reserved
¼   cup plus 1 tablespoon (37 grams) confectioners' sugar

1. In the bowl of a stand mixer fitted with the paddle attachment, combine cold cream, rum, and reserved vanilla bean seeds. With mixer on high speed, gradually add confectioners' sugar, beating until stiff peaks form. Cover and refrigerate until ready to serve.

ONE-LAYER
CAKES

Small in size but big on flavor, these one-layer cakes run the
gamut from a decadent dark chocolate marvel to a creamy
ricotta cheesecake and more

COFFEE TRES LECHES CAKES

Makes 3 (5½x3½-inch) cakes

In this coffee-laced take on a Latin American favorite, luscious mini pound cakes get soaked in the classic trinity of milks, with shots of espresso and coffee liqueur added in for good measure. Topped with meringue and a sticky coffee syrup drizzle, this cake offers custard-like texture with oodles of coffee flavor.

5   large eggs (250 grams), room temperature
¾   cup (150 grams) granulated sugar
1   teaspoon (4 grams) vanilla extract
½   cup (113 grams) unsalted butter, melted and cooled
1½ cups (188 grams) all-purpose flour
1   teaspoon (5 grams) baking powder
½   teaspoon (1.5 grams) kosher salt
½   cup (120 grams) sweetened condensed milk
½   cup (120 grams) evaporated milk
¼   cup (60 grams) heavy whipping cream
¼   cup (60 grams) brewed espresso, chilled
3   tablespoons (45 grams) coffee liqueur*
Meringue Topping (recipe follows)
Coffee syrup**

1. Preheat oven to 350°F (180°C). Butter and flour
3 (5½x3½-inch) loaf pans. (See Note.)
2. In the bowl of a stand mixer fitted with the whisk attachment, beat eggs, sugar, and vanilla at medium-high speed until thick, pale, and doubled in volume, about 5 minutes. Reduce mixer speed to medium. Add melted butter in a slow, steady stream until combined. (It's important to add the butter very slowly. If added quickly, the air whipped into the egg mixture will deflate.)
3. In a medium bowl, whisk together flour, baking powder, and salt. With mixer on low speed, gradually add flour mixture to egg mixture, beating just until combined. Divide batter among prepared pans.
4. Bake until a wooden pick inserted in center comes out clean, 25 to 30 minutes.
5. Meanwhile, in a liquid-measuring cup, whisk together condensed milk, evaporated milk, cream, espresso, and liqueur until well combined.
6. Remove cakes from oven; using a wooden skewer, immediately poke holes about ¼ inch apart into cakes, piercing through to bottom. Immediately pour ¼ cup milk mixture over each cake, allowing mixture to soak into cakes. Divide remaining milk mixture

among cakes. Let cool in pans for 1 hour. Wrap pans in plastic wrap, and refrigerate until ready to serve.
7. Just before serving, use a small offset spatula to loosen cakes from sides of pans; remove from pans. Using a serrated knife, remove rounded tops from cakes. Place Meringue Topping in a piping bag fitted with a jumbo rose tip. (See Note.) Starting at short end of cake, hold piping bag vertically, and pipe in a zigzag motion down length of cake. Using a kitchen torch, lightly brown Meringue Topping. Drizzle with coffee syrup.

*We used Kahlúa.

**We like Dave's Coffee Syrup in Vanilla. To make your own coffee syrup, prepare Coffee Simple Syrup (recipe on page 14) using a heavy-bottomed saucepan. After adding coffee concentrate, bring mixture to a rolling boil over medium heat, and cook until reduced to ¾ cup, about 45 minutes.

Note: *We used Williams Sonoma Goldtouch Nonstick Mini Loaf Pans, available at williams-sonoma.com, and Wilton No. 127D Giant Rose Petal Decorating Tip, available at amazon.com.*

MERINGUE TOPPING
Makes about 3 cups

½   cup (100 grams) granulated sugar
¼   cup (60 grams) water
2   large egg whites (60 grams), room temperature
¼   teaspoon cream of tartar
½   teaspoon (1.5 grams) kosher salt
½   teaspoon (2 grams) vanilla extract
½   teaspoon (2 grams) coffee extract

1. In a small saucepan, bring sugar and ¼ cup (60 grams) water to a boil over medium-high heat, stirring until sugar is dissolved. Cook until a candy thermometer registers 248°F (120°C).
2. Meanwhile, in the bowl of a stand mixer fitted with the whisk attachment, beat egg whites and cream of tartar at medium speed until soft peaks form.
3. With mixer on high speed, add hot sugar syrup to egg white mixture in a slow, steady stream, being careful not to hit sides of bowl. Beat until smooth, glossy peaks form, about 3 minutes. Fold in salt and extracts. Use immediately.

IRISH COFFEE COFFEE CAKE

Makes 1 (9-inch) cake

Behold: a nightcap coffee cake. Buzzing with espresso, topped with a sprinkling of espresso sugar, and packed with two layers of crumbly whiskey-spiked streusel, this cake is a tender delicacy you'll enjoy to the last crumb.

½   cup (113 grams) unsalted butter, softened
1   cup (200 grams) granulated sugar
2   large eggs (100 grams), room temperature
2   cups (250 grams) all-purpose flour
1¼ teaspoons (6.25 grams) baking powder
½   teaspoon (2.5 grams) baking soda
½   teaspoon (1.5 grams) kosher salt
⅔   cup (160 grams) whole buttermilk
⅓   cup (80 grams) Irish whiskey
3   tablespoons (18 grams) espresso powder, divided
1   teaspoon (4 grams) vanilla extract
½   teaspoon (2 grams) coffee extract
Irish Whiskey Streusel (recipe follows)
Garnish: espresso sugar (see Note)

1. Preheat oven to 350°F (180°C). Spray a 9-inch square baking pan with cooking spray. Line pan with parchment paper, letting excess extend over sides of pan.
2. In the bowl of a stand mixer fitted with the paddle attachment, beat butter and granulated sugar at medium speed until fluffy, about 2 minutes, stopping to scrape sides of bowl. Add eggs, one at a time, beating well after each addition.
3. In a medium bowl, whisk together flour, baking powder, baking soda, and salt. In a liquid-measuring cup, whisk together buttermilk, whiskey, 2 tablespoons (12 grams) espresso powder, and extracts until espresso is dissolved. With mixer on low speed, gradually add flour mixture to butter mixture alternately with

buttermilk mixture, beginning and ending with flour mixture, beating just until combined after each addition.
4. Spoon half of batter into prepared pan, spreading with an offset spatula. Sprinkle with half of Irish Whiskey Streusel and remaining 1 tablespoon (6 grams) espresso powder. Top with remaining batter, spreading gently with an offset spatula, being careful that streusel doesn't blend with batter too much. Crumble remaining Irish Whiskey Streusel over batter, squeezing to form larger clumps.
5. Bake until a wooden pick inserted in center comes out clean, 40 to 45 minutes. Let cool completely in pan. Garnish with espresso sugar, if desired. Store in an airtight container for up to 3 days.

Note: *To make espresso sugar, in the work bowl of a food processor, place 1 cup (200 grams) granulated sugar and 1 tablespoon (6 grams) espresso powder. Process until combined and uniform in color.*

IRISH WHISKEY STREUSEL
Makes 3 cups

1¾ cups (219 grams) all-purpose flour
1   cup (220 grams) firmly packed light brown sugar
2   teaspoons (4 grams) espresso powder
1¼ teaspoons (2.5 grams) ground cinnamon
½   teaspoon (1.5 grams) kosher salt
½   cup plus 2 tablespoons (141 grams) cold unsalted butter, cubed
1   tablespoon (15 grams) Irish whiskey

1. In the work bowl of a food processor, place flour, brown sugar, espresso powder, cinnamon, and salt; pulse until combined. Add cold butter and whiskey; pulse until pea-size clumps form, about 10 pulses. Refrigerate until ready to use.

TWICE-BAKED MERINGUE CAKE

Makes 1 (9-inch) cake

A textural masterpiece, this twice-baked treat combines white cake with an airy Vanilla Meringue. The moist cake and crunchy meringue need to be baked separately due to different baking times, so we baked the cake first, topped it with meringue, and baked a second time. Our Brown Sugar Rum Sauce poured over the meringue after baking brings buttery, boozy flavor to round out the dessert.

½   cup (113 grams) unsalted butter, softened
1   cup plus 2 tablespoons (224 grams) granulated sugar
1¾   cups (219 grams) cake flour
2   teaspoons (10 grams) baking powder
½   teaspoon (1.5 grams) kosher salt
½   cup (120 grams) whole milk, room temperature
3   tablespoons (45 grams) dark spiced rum
4   large egg whites (120 grams), room temperature
Vanilla Meringue (recipe follows)
Brown Sugar Rum Sauce (recipe follows)

1. Preheat oven to 350°F (180°C). Butter and flour a 9-inch springform pan. (See PRO TIP.)
2. In the bowl of a stand mixer fitted with the paddle attachment, beat butter and sugar at medium speed until fluffy, 3 to 4 minutes, stopping to scrape sides of bowl.
3. In a medium bowl, sift together flour, baking powder, and salt. In a small bowl, combine milk and rum. With mixer on low speed, gradually add flour mixture to butter mixture alternately with milk mixture, beginning and ending with flour mixture, beating just until combined after each addition. Transfer batter to a large bowl; set aside.
4. Clean bowl of stand mixer. Using the whisk attachment, beat egg whites at high speed until stiff peaks form, about 2 minutes. Gently fold half of egg whites into batter. Fold in remaining egg whites.

Pour batter into prepared pan, smoothing top if necessary.
5. Bake until a wooden pick inserted in center comes out clean, 25 to 30 minutes. Let cool in pan for 15 minutes. (You do not want the cake to cool completely. If completely cool, it will affect the bake time for the meringue.) Run a knife around edges of pan. Open pan, and place strips of parchment paper around cake, letting an excess of 2½ inches extend up sides. Close pan back around cake.
6. Spoon about one-third of Vanilla Meringue on top of cake. (You want to handle the meringue as little as possible, so this does not need to be a measured amount.) Spread into an even layer, leaving about a ¼-inch border between meringue layer and cake pan. (If there is too much meringue pushed to outside edge, the meringue may collapse when out of the oven.) Spoon remaining Vanilla Meringue in center of cake, and gently spread around center of cake so there is less meringue on outside edge. Loosely cover with foil.
7. Return cake to oven, and immediately reduce oven temperature to 325°F (170°C). Bake for 15 minutes. Reduce oven temperature to 300°F (150°C), and bake until meringue is dry to the touch, 30 to 35 minutes more. Let cool completely in pan. Serve with Brown Sugar Rum Sauce.

PRO TIP
To ensure our cake came out perfectly flat, we insulated the outside of the cake pan with oven-safe cake strips, available in the baking aisle of your local grocery store or online. (We used Wilton Bake-Even Strips, available at *amazon.com*.) Soak strips in a bowl of ice water for 5 minutes and then remove excess water but do not wring it out. Wrap strips around pan. We used 2 strips to cover height of pan. This is not necessary for the recipe to work, but it makes a prettier final product.

VANILLA MERINGUE
Makes about 3 cups

3   large egg whites (90 grams), room temperature
¾   cup (150 grams) granulated sugar
¾   teaspoon (3.75 grams) apple cider vinegar
¼   teaspoon (1 gram) vanilla extract
2   teaspoons (6 grams) cornstarch

1. In the bowl of a stand mixer fitted with the whisk attachment, beat egg whites at high speed until stiff peaks form, about 2 minutes. Add sugar, 1 tablespoon (12 grams) at a time, beating for 30 seconds after each addition; scrape sides of bowl. Beat until sugar is dissolved, 7 to 8 minutes. (To test meringue for doneness, rub a small amount between two fingers; if you feel any sugar granules, it is not ready. It should feel completely smooth.) Add vinegar and vanilla, beating until combined. Sift cornstarch over meringue mixture, and beat until combined. Use immediately.

BROWN SUGAR RUM SAUCE
Makes about ¾ cup

¼   cup (57 grams) unsalted butter
½   cup (110 grams) firmly packed light brown sugar
¼   teaspoon kosher salt
¼   cup (60 grams) heavy whipping cream
1   tablespoon (15 grams) dark spiced rum
1   teaspoon (4 grams) vanilla extract

1. In a small saucepan, melt butter over medium heat. Whisk in brown sugar and salt. Add cream, rum, and vanilla, and bring to a boil. Cook, stirring constantly, for 3 minutes. Remove from heat, and let cool to room temperature.

APPLE CRUMB CAKE WITH CRÈME FRAÎCHE GLAZE

Makes 1 (8-inch) cake

Filled with layers of roasted apples and topped off with an Orange-Cinnamon Streusel and tangy glaze, this crumb cake is sweet to the core. We used Honeycrisp apples for their sweet-tart flavor, but if you can't find Honeycrisps, any other bright baking apple, like Granny Smith or Braeburn, will do.

3   cups (300 grams) thinly sliced
    Honeycrisp apples
1   cup (200 grams) plus 2 tablespoons
    (24 grams) granulated sugar, divided
1½ teaspoons (3 grams) ground cinnamon
1½ cups (188 grams) all-purpose flour
1½ teaspoons (7.5 grams) baking powder
¾   teaspoon (2.25 grams) kosher salt
½   cup (113 grams) unsalted butter, melted
2   large eggs (100 grams), room
    temperature
¼   cup (60 grams) crème fraîche, room
    temperature
1½ teaspoons (6 grams) vanilla extract
⅛   teaspoon almond extract
Orange-Cinnamon Streusel (recipe follows)
Crème Fraîche Glaze (recipe follows)

1. Preheat oven to 400°F (200°C). Line a rimmed baking sheet with parchment paper. Spray an 8-inch light-colored springform pan with cooking spray; line bottom and sides of pan with parchment paper.
2. In a large bowl, toss together apples, 2 tablespoons (24 grams) sugar, and cinnamon. Let stand for 20 minutes. Pat apples dry; reserve 23 slices. Cut remaining slices crosswise into ½-inch pieces; spread on prepared baking sheet.
3. Bake apple pieces until tender, 10 to 12 minutes. Let cool on pan for 20 minutes. Reduce oven temperature to 350°F (180°C).
4. In a large bowl, whisk together flour, baking powder, salt, and remaining 1 cup (200 grams) sugar. Make a well in center of flour mixture; add melted butter, eggs, crème fraîche, and extracts, whisking just until combined, stopping to scrape sides of bowl.

5. Spread half of batter in prepared pan. Arrange roasted apple pieces on batter, leaving a ¼-inch border. Spread remaining batter on top of apples. Arrange reserved 23 apple slices in fans of 3 or 4 on batter as desired. Top with Orange-Cinnamon Streusel, letting apples peek through.
6. Bake until golden brown and a wooden pick inserted in center comes out with just a few moist crumbs, 55 minutes to 1 hour and 5 minutes, covering with foil after 30 minutes of baking to prevent excess browning. Let cool in pan for 5 minutes. Run a knife around edges of cake. Remove from pan, and let cool completely on a wire rack. Drizzle Crème Fraîche Glaze onto cooled cake before serving.

ORANGE-CINNAMON STREUSEL
Makes ⅔ cup

3   tablespoons (42 grams) firmly packed
    light brown sugar
2   tablespoons (24 grams) granulated
    sugar
½   teaspoon orange zest
¼   teaspoon kosher salt
¼   teaspoon ground cinnamon
¼   cup (57 grams) unsalted butter, melted
⅔   cup (83 grams) all-purpose flour

1. In a medium bowl, whisk together sugars, orange zest, salt, and cinnamon. Stir in melted butter, and fold in flour just until combined. Use immediately, or refrigerate for up to 5 days.

CRÈME FRAÎCHE GLAZE
Makes ½ cup

1   cup (120 grams) confectioners' sugar
2   tablespoons (30 grams) crème fraîche
1   tablespoon (15 grams) fresh orange
    juice

1. In a small bowl, stir together all ingredients until smooth. Use immediately.

BLOOD ORANGE MARMALADE BABY CAKES

Makes 12 (3½-inch) cakes

Recipe by Marian Cooper Cairns

Baked in brioche pans, these baby cakes pack a zesty center of homemade Blood Orange Marmalade. In order to thicken properly, the marmalade needs to chill overnight before being added to the baby cakes, so make it the day before.

½   cup (113 grams) unsalted butter, softened
¾   cup (150 grams) granulated sugar
2   large eggs (100 grams)
2   teaspoons (8 grams) rose water
1½   teaspoons (6 grams) vanilla extract
1½   cups (188 grams) all-purpose flour
1   teaspoon (5 grams) baking powder
¼   teaspoon kosher salt
½   cup (120 grams) whole milk
⅓   cup (80 grams) sour cream
Blood Orange Marmalade (recipe follows)
Garnish: confectioners' sugar

1. Preheat oven to 350°F (180°C). Butter and flour 12 (3½-inch) brioche pans.
2. In the bowl of a stand mixer fitted with the paddle attachment, beat butter and granulated sugar at medium speed until fluffy, about 2 minutes, stopping to scrape sides of bowl. Add eggs, one at a time, beating well after each addition. Stir in rose water and vanilla.
3. In a medium bowl, whisk together flour, baking powder, and salt. In a small bowl, whisk together milk and sour cream until smooth. With mixer on low speed, gradually add flour mixture to butter mixture alternately with milk mixture, beginning and ending with flour mixture, beating just until combined after each addition. Spoon 3 tablespoons (39 grams) batter in each prepared pan. Place 1 teaspoon (6 grams) Blood Orange Marmalade in center of batter, and top with 1 tablespoon (13 grams) batter.
4. Bake until golden around edges, 20 to 24 minutes. Let cool in pans for 5 minutes. Remove from pans, and let cool completely on a wire rack. Garnish with confectioners' sugar, if desired.

BLOOD ORANGE MARMALADE
Makes about 1¼ cups

2   small blood oranges (262 grams)
1   cup (200 grams) granulated sugar
1   cup (240 grams) water
3   tablespoons (45 grams) fresh lemon juice

1. Wash blood oranges well. Thinly slice oranges, discarding seeds. Cut slices into bite-size pieces.
2. In a small saucepan, stir together oranges, sugar, 1 cup (240 grams) water, and lemon juice. Bring to a boil over medium heat; reduce heat to low, and simmer until a candy thermometer registers 220°F (104°C) to 225°F (107°C) , about 1 hour.
3. Remove from heat, and let cool completely. Cover and refrigerate overnight before using. Refrigerate for up to 2 weeks.

Photo by Matt Armendariz

BRÛLÉED BLOOD ORANGE RICOTTA CHEESECAKE

Makes 1 (9-inch) cake

Recipe by Marian Cooper Cairns

This extra-creamy, silky-smooth cheesecake packs a double dose of our favorite red citrus. Blood orange juice lends tangy berry notes to the ricotta filling, and brûléed blood oranges on top create a smoky caramelized flavor.

24   gingersnap cookies (173 grams)
1   cup (121 grams) roasted salted shelled pistachios
½   teaspoon (1.5 grams) kosher salt
6   tablespoons (84 grams) unsalted butter, melted
16   ounces (455 grams) cream cheese, room temperature
1   cup (200 grams) granulated sugar
3   tablespoons (24 grams) cornstarch
1   (12-ounce) package (340 grams) ricotta cheese, room temperature
⅓   cup (80 grams) heavy whipping cream, room temperature
1   tablespoon (3 grams) blood orange zest
1   tablespoon (15 grams) fresh blood orange juice
1½   teaspoons (6 grams) vanilla extract
4   large eggs (200 grams), room temperature
1   large egg yolk (19 grams), room temperature
3 to 4 small blood oranges (393 to 524 grams)
¼   cup (50 grams) turbinado sugar

1. Preheat oven to 350°F (180°C). Lightly butter the bottom of a 9-inch springform pan.
2. In the work bowl of a food processor, place gingersnaps, pistachios, and salt; process until finely ground. Add melted butter, pulsing until combined. Press crumb mixture into bottom and halfway up sides of prepared pan.
3. Bake until set, about 8 minutes. Let cool for 15 minutes. Reduce oven temperature to 325°F (170°C).
4. In the bowl of a stand mixer fitted with the paddle attachment, beat cream cheese at medium-low speed until very creamy and smooth, stopping to scrape sides of bowl.
5. In a small bowl, whisk together granulated sugar and cornstarch. Add sugar mixture and ricotta to cream cheese, beating until smooth. Beat in cream, blood orange zest and juice, and vanilla. Add eggs and egg yolk, one at a time, beating just until combined and yellow disappears after each addition, stopping to scrape sides of bowl. Pour filling into prepared crust.
6. Bake until set around edges but slightly jiggly in center, 55 minutes to 1 hour. Turn oven off, and leave cheesecake in oven with door closed until completely cool, 3 to 4 hours. Remove from oven, and refrigerate overnight.
7. Using a sharp paring knife, slice off ends of blood oranges. Stand oranges upright, and remove just the peel, cutting from top to bottom. Slice oranges into ¼- to ½-inch rounds. Arrange on a baking sheet. Cover and refrigerate.
8. Just before serving, sprinkle orange rounds with turbinado sugar. Using a kitchen torch, melt sugar until caramelized and browned in spots. Arrange on cheesecake, and serve immediately.

PRO TIPS

Two secrets to a crack-free cheesecake: First, have all your ingredients at room temperature. Second, don't rush to chill your cheesecake; let it cool slowly and completely before placing in the refrigerator. A chilled cheesecake can be frozen for up to 1 month, if desired.

Photo by Matt Armendariz

FRENCH YOGURT CAKE WITH MARMALADE GLAZE

Makes 8 servings

Recipe by Dorie Greenspan

It's rare to be invited to a French person's house for dinner and have a baked-at-home dessert. Most French people don't bake because they don't have to—no matter where you are, a pâtisserie with wonderful cakes is just minutes away. But I don't think there's a home cook in France who doesn't make this moist yogurt cake, a delightful cross between pound cake and sponge cake. The primary reason the French make this cake is that it's delicious, absolutely foolproof, and shamelessly easy.

1   cup (125 grams) all-purpose flour
½   cup (52 grams) ground almonds (or, if you'd prefer, omit the almonds and use another ½ cup [63 grams] all-purpose flour)
2   teaspoons (10 grams) baking powder
Pinch salt
1   cup (200 grams) granulated sugar
1   tablespoon (3 grams) lemon zest (about 1 lemon)

½   cup (120 grams) plain yogurt
3   large eggs (150 grams)
¼   teaspoon (1 gram) vanilla extract
½   cup (112 grams) flavorless oil, such as canola or safflower

For the glaze
½   cup (160 grams) lemon marmalade, strained
1   teaspoon (5 grams) water

1. Center a rack in the oven and preheat the oven to 350°F (180°C). Generously butter an 8½x4½-inch loaf pan and place the pan on a baking sheet.
2. Whisk together the flour, ground almonds (if using), baking powder, and salt.
3. Put the sugar and zest in a medium bowl and, with your fingertips, rub the zest into the sugar until the sugar is moist and aromatic. Add the yogurt, eggs, and vanilla and whisk vigorously until the mixture is very well blended. Still whisking, add the dry ingredients, then switch to a large rubber spatula and fold in the oil. You'll have a thick, smooth batter with a slight sheen. Scrape the batter into the pan and smooth the top.

4. Bake for 50 to 55 minutes, or until the cake begins to come away from the sides of the pan; it should be golden brown and a thin knife inserted into the center will come out clean. (Please note that sometimes the cake domes, but most of the time it doesn't, a quirk that seems to be attributable to the whims of ovens and the difference between French and American baking ingredients. Either way, it's delicious.) Transfer the pan to a rack and cool for 5 minutes, then run a blunt knife between the cake and the sides of the pan. Unmold, and cool to room temperature right side up on the rack. Wrapped well, the cake keeps at room temperature for at least 4 days. If you do not glaze the cake, you can wrap it airtight and freeze it for up to 2 months; it's best not to freeze the glazed cake. Glaze before serving.
5. To make the glaze, put the marmalade in a small saucepan or a microwave-safe bowl, stir in 1 teaspoon (5 grams) water, and heat until the jelly is hot and liquefied.
6. Using a pastry brush, gently brush the cake with the glaze.

Photo by Joann Pai

BANANA RUM COFFEE CAKE

Makes 1 (9-inch) cake

Cream cheese, chunks of mashed banana, and gold rum lend a mellow bite to this lightly boozy coffee cake twist on banana nut bread.

8   ounces (225 grams) cream cheese, softened
½   cup (113 grams) unsalted butter, softened
1¼ cups (275 grams) firmly packed light brown sugar
1   large egg (50 grams)
3   tablespoons (45 grams) gold rum
2½ cups (313 grams) all-purpose flour
2   teaspoons (10 grams) baking powder
½   teaspoon (1.5 grams) kosher salt
¾   cup (171 grams) mashed banana
Pecan Streusel (recipe follows)

1. Preheat oven to 350°F (180°C). Line a 9-inch square baking pan with parchment paper.

2. In the bowl of a stand mixer fitted with the paddle attachment, beat cream cheese and butter at medium speed until combined. Add brown sugar, and beat until fluffy, 3 to 4 minutes, stopping to scrape sides of bowl. Add egg, beating well. Beat in rum.

3. In a medium bowl, whisk together flour, baking powder, and salt. With mixer on low speed, gradually add flour mixture to cream cheese mixture alternately with mashed banana, beginning and ending with flour mixture, beating just until combined after each addition. Spoon batter into prepared pan, smoothing top. Top with Pecan Streusel.

4. Bake until a wooden pick inserted in center comes out clean, about 55 minutes, loosely covering with foil during last 15 minutes of baking to prevent excess browning, if necessary. Let cool in pan for 10 minutes. Remove from pan, and let cool completely on a wire rack.

PECAN STREUSEL

Makes about 1¼ cups

½   cup (63 grams) all-purpose flour
¼   cup (55 grams) firmly packed light brown sugar
2   tablespoons (24 grams) granulated sugar
½   teaspoon (1 gram) ground cinnamon
¼   teaspoon kosher salt
2   tablespoons (28 grams) unsalted butter, softened
1   tablespoon (15 grams) gold rum
½   cup (57 grams) chopped pecans

1. In a medium bowl, whisk together flour, sugars, cinnamon, and salt. Add butter and rum, and using your fingertips, mix until crumbly and desired consistency is reached. Mix in pecans. Refrigerate until ready to use.

ST. LOUIS GOOEY BUTTER CAKE

Makes 1 (13x9-inch) cake

For this butter cake, we opted for a yeasted base (as a nod to its German kuchen beginnings) and butter-rich filling (because we're staunchly pro butter). For a twist and a boost of warm nutty flavor, we added browned butter to the mix.

¾   cup (170 grams) plus 6 tablespoons (84 grams) unsalted butter, softened and divided
5   tablespoons (75 grams) warm whole milk (105°F/41°C to 110°F/43°C)
2   teaspoons (6 grams) active dry yeast
1½   cups (300 grams) plus 3 tablespoons (36 grams) plus ¼ teaspoon (1 gram) granulated sugar, divided
1½   teaspoons (4.5 grams) kosher salt, divided
3   cups (375 grams) all-purpose flour, divided
2   large eggs (100 grams), room temperature and divided
3½   teaspoons (14 grams) vanilla extract, divided
3   tablespoons (63 grams) light corn syrup
2   tablespoons (30 grams) water
Garnish: confectioners' sugar

1. In a medium stainless steel skillet, heat ¾ cup (170 grams) butter over medium heat. Cook until butter turns a medium-brown color and has a nutty aroma, 7 to 11 minutes. Transfer to a medium bowl; refrigerate just until firm, 1 to 1½ hours. Let stand at room temperature until ready to use.

2. Butter a 13x9-inch baking pan; line pan with parchment paper, letting excess extend over sides of pan.

3. In a small bowl, stir together warm milk, yeast, and ¼ teaspoon (1 gram) granulated sugar. Let stand until mixture is foamy, about 5 minutes.

4. In the bowl of a stand mixer fitted with the paddle attachment, beat 3 tablespoons (36 grams) granulated sugar, 1 teaspoon (3 grams) salt, and remaining 6 tablespoons (84 grams) butter at medium speed until creamy, 3 to 4 minutes, stopping to scrape sides of bowl. Add yeast mixture, 1¾ cups (219 grams) flour, 1 egg (50 grams), and ½ teaspoon (2 grams) vanilla; beat at low speed just until combined, 30 seconds to 1 minute, stopping to scrape sides of bowl. Increase mixer speed to medium, and beat until dough is well combined and elastic, 4 to 5 minutes, stopping to scrape sides of bowl. (Dough will be tacky but should not stick to hands.) Press dough into prepared pan in a thin layer. Cover loosely with plastic wrap, and let rise in a warm, draft-free place (75°F/24°C) until doubled in size, about 2 hours.

5. Preheat oven to 350°F (180°C).

6. Clean bowl of stand mixer and paddle attachment. Add browned butter, remaining 1½ cups (300 grams) granulated sugar, and remaining ½ teaspoon (1.5 grams) salt; beat at low speed just until combined. Increase mixer speed to medium, and beat until fluffy, 4 to 5 minutes, stopping to scrape sides of bowl. Beat in remaining 1 egg (50 grams); scrape sides of bowl.

7. In a small bowl, whisk together corn syrup, 2 tablespoons (30 grams) water, and remaining 3 teaspoons (12 grams) vanilla. With mixer on low speed, gradually add remaining 1¼ cups (156 grams) flour to butter mixture alternately with corn syrup mixture, beginning and ending with flour mixture, beating just until combined after each addition and stopping to scrape sides of bowl. Spread batter on dough in pan.

8. Bake until top is set and edges are golden brown, 25 to 35 minutes. (Center should still seem soft and jiggly and look lighter than golden-brown edges.) Let cool completely in pan. Using excess parchment as handles, remove from pan; garnish with confectioners' sugar, if desired.

CARIBBEAN BLACK LOAVES

Makes 2 (8½x4½-inch) cakes

Fair warning: this cake is potent. Similar to molasses-rich British pudding, black cake is a dense loaf cake filled with rum-soaked dried fruit. Traditionally served during the holidays or weddings in the Caribbean, this cake gets its robust flavor from molasses and dark rum and its bold, boozy notes from a generous pour of dark rum icing.

1 cup (128 grams) chopped dates
1 cup (128 grams) chopped dried cherries
1 cup (128 grams) golden raisins
1 cup (128 grams) dried currants
1 cup (240 grams) plus 2 tablespoons (30 grams) dark rum, divided
½ cup (120 grams) cherry brandy
1 cup (227 grams) unsalted butter, softened
1¼ cups (275 grams) firmly packed dark brown sugar
½ cup (170 grams) molasses
4 large eggs (200 grams), room temperature
1 tablespoon (3 grams) orange zest
1 tablespoon (3 grams) lemon zest
1 tablespoon (3 grams) lime zest
1 teaspoon (4 grams) vanilla extract
¼ teaspoon (1 gram) aromatic bitters*
2 cups (250 grams) all-purpose flour
2 teaspoons (10 grams) baking powder
1 teaspoon (2 grams) ground cinnamon
½ teaspoon (1 gram) ground nutmeg
¼ teaspoon ground cloves
Rum Glaze (recipe follows)

1. In a medium bowl, toss together dates, cherries, raisins, and currants. Pour 1 cup (240 grams) rum and brandy over fruit. Cover and let stand overnight or for up to 3 days. (The longer it stands, the stronger the flavor.)
2. Preheat oven to 300°F (150°C). Line 2 (8½x4½-inch) loaf pans with parchment paper.

3. In the bowl of a stand mixer fitted with the paddle attachment, beat butter and brown sugar at medium speed until fluffy, 3 to 4 minutes, stopping to scrape sides of bowl. Beat in molasses until well combined. Add eggs, one at a time, beating well after each addition. Beat in zests, vanilla, and bitters. Add dried fruit and any remaining liquid in bowl (about ½ cup [120 grams]).
4. In another medium bowl, whisk together flour, baking powder, cinnamon, nutmeg, and cloves. With mixer on low speed, gradually add flour mixture to butter mixture, beating just until combined. Divide batter between prepared pans.
5. Bake for 1 hour. Cover with foil, and bake until a wooden pick inserted in center comes out clean, about 50 minutes more. Let cool in pans for 10 minutes. Remove from pans, and let cool completely on wire racks. Brush loaves with remaining 2 tablespoons (30 grams) rum. Top with Rum Glaze. Store in an airtight container for up to 2 weeks.

Because it is traditionally used in Caribbean black cake, we used Angostura aromatic bitters, available at local grocery stores or online.

> **PRO TIP**
> To make sure the rum fully saturates your dried fruit, start soaking the fruit the night before you plan to bake, if not sooner.

RUM GLAZE

Makes 1 cup

2½ cups (300 grams) confectioners' sugar
5½ tablespoons (82 grams) dark rum

1. In a small bowl, whisk together confectioners' sugar and rum until smooth. Use immediately.

CHOCOLATE PEAR CLAFOUTIS

Makes 1 (9½-inch) cake

Dark chocolate takes the time-honored clafoutis to a new level of decadence. With their slender necks and firm skins, Bosc pears have an elegant appearance and do not soften too much during poaching. We poached the pears in spices and Chablis, a dry white burgundy wine from Chablis in eastern France.

1   cup (240 grams) warm heavy whipping cream
3   large eggs (150 grams)
½   cup (63 grams) all-purpose flour
½   cup (85 grams) 63% cacao dark chocolate chips, melted
⅓   cup (67 grams) granulated sugar
1   teaspoon (4 grams) almond extract
⅛   teaspoon kosher salt
Poached Pears (recipe follows)
Garnish: confectioners' sugar

1. Preheat oven to 350°F (180°C). Lightly spray a 9½-inch enamel-coated cast-iron skillet or baking dish with cooking spray.
2. In a large bowl, whisk together warm cream, eggs, flour, melted chocolate, granulated sugar, almond extract, and salt. Let stand for 10 minutes.
3. Pour half of batter (about 1½ cups) into prepared skillet.
4. Bake for 10 minutes. Pour remaining batter into skillet, and top with 3 fanned Poached Pear halves, letting stems join in center. (You will have 1 pear half left over.) Bake until soft and set in center, about 30 minutes more. Let cool for 20 minutes before serving. Dust with confectioners' sugar, if desired.

POACHED PEARS
Makes 4 halves

2   cups (480 grams) Chablis*
1   cinnamon stick
5   whole cloves
1   teaspoon (4 grams) almond extract
⅛   teaspoon kosher salt
⅛   teaspoon ground cardamom
2   medium Bosc pears* (500 grams), halved and cored

1. In a large saucepan, combine wine, cinnamon stick, cloves, almond extract, salt, and cardamom. Add pears. If pears are not covered with poaching liquid, add enough water to cover. Cook over medium heat until pears are tender, about 1 hour. Strain pears from liquid; let cool before using.
2. To slice pears, cut diagonally from bottom to halfway up neck in ¼-inch slices. Fan slices out before placing in batter.

*We used Chablis, but any dry white wine can be used. Because they have nice stems, we used Bosc pears, but any kind of pear will work.

GINGERBREAD

Makes 1 (13x9-inch) cake

Though you may associate this dense, spice-packed cake with the holidays, Bermudian bakeries and gas stations sell it by the slice year-round. We like ours the old-school way, topped with homemade Whipped Cream, but it's flavorful enough to enjoy on its own.

½   cup (120 grams) boiling water
1½ teaspoons (7.5 grams) baking soda
1   cup (336 grams) molasses
1   cup (227 grams) unsalted butter, softened
1   cup (200 grams) granulated sugar
2   large eggs (100 grams), room temperature
2½ cups (313 grams) all-purpose flour
1½ teaspoons (3 grams) ground ginger
1   teaspoon (2 grams) ground cinnamon
½   teaspoon (1.5 grams) kosher salt
½   teaspoon (1 gram) ground cloves
¼   cup (60 grams) spiced rum

3   tablespoons (45 grams) sour cream, room temperature
Whipped Cream (recipe follows)
Garnish: ground cinnamon

1. Preheat oven to 325°F (170°C). Lightly spray a 13x9-inch baking pan with cooking spray; line pan with parchment paper, letting excess extend over sides of pan.
2. In a small heatproof bowl, stir together ½ cup (120 grams) boiling water and baking soda until dissolved. Stir in molasses; set aside.
3. In the bowl of a stand mixer fitted with the paddle attachment, beat butter and sugar at medium speed until creamy, 3 to 4 minutes, stopping to scrape sides of bowl. Add eggs, one at a time, beating just until combined after each addition.
4. In a medium bowl, whisk together flour, ginger, cinnamon, salt, and cloves. With mixer on low speed, gradually add flour mixture to butter mixture alternately with molasses mixture, beginning and ending with flour mixture, beating just until combined

after each addition. Stir in rum and sour cream. Pour batter into prepared pan.
5. Bake until a wooden pick inserted in center comes out clean, 45 to 50 minutes. Let cool in pan on a wire rack. Serve warm or at room temperature with Whipped Cream. Garnish with cinnamon, if desired. Store in an airtight container for up to 1 week.

WHIPPED CREAM
Makes 2 cups

1   cup (240 grams) cold heavy whipping cream
3   tablespoons (21 grams) confectioners' sugar
¼   teaspoon kosher salt

1. In the bowl of a stand mixer fitted with the whisk attachment, beat cold cream at medium speed until it begins to thicken, 3 to 5 minutes. Add confectioners' sugar and salt; beat until soft peaks form. Use immediately.

REINE DE SABA CAKE WITH GRAND MARNIER WHIPPED CREAM

Makes 1 (8½- or 9-inch) cake

One of Julia Child's favorite desserts, this cake has a biblical namesake, the Queen of Sheba, but is often called "fallen soufflé cake." We infused ours with espresso powder and topped it with clouds of Grand Marnier Whipped Cream.

⅓   cup (80 grams) heavy whipping cream
2½   teaspoons (5 grams) espresso powder
8   ounces (225 grams) 70% cacao bittersweet chocolate, chopped (about 1⅓ cups)
1   cup (227 grams) unsalted butter, cubed and softened
1   tablespoon (3 grams) orange zest
1   teaspoon (3 grams) kosher salt
¼   teaspoon (1 gram) almond extract
1¼   cups (250 grams) plus 2 tablespoons (24 grams) granulated sugar, divided
6   large eggs (300 grams), separated and room temperature
½   cup (48 grams) very finely ground almond flour
⅓   cup (42 grams) all-purpose flour
¼   cup (21 grams) Dutch process cocoa powder (see PRO TIPS)
¼   teaspoon cream of tartar
Grand Marnier Whipped Cream (recipe follows)
Garnish: toasted sliced almonds, bittersweet chocolate shavings (see Note)

1. Preheat oven to 350°F (180°C). Butter an 8½-inch round copper cake pan*. Line bottom of pan with parchment paper; flour sides of pan.
2. In the top of a double boiler, stir together cream and espresso powder until mostly dissolved. Add chocolate and butter; cook over simmering water, stirring frequently, until melted and smooth, 8 to 12 minutes. Remove from heat; whisk in orange zest, salt, and almond extract.
3. In a large bowl, whisk together 1¼ cups (250 grams) sugar and egg yolks until pale and well combined, 1 to 2 minutes. Gradually whisk in chocolate mixture; scrape sides of bowl.
4. In a medium bowl, whisk together flours and cocoa. Sift flour mixture over chocolate mixture; fold just until combined. (Mixture will be thick.)
5. In the bowl of a stand mixer fitted with the whisk attachment, beat egg whites and cream of tartar at high speed until soft peaks

form, 1 to 2 minutes. Gradually add remaining 2 tablespoons (24 grams) sugar, beating until stiff peaks form, 6 to 8 minutes. Fold egg white mixture into chocolate mixture in four additions until well combined. Gently spoon batter into prepared pan; using a small silicone or nylon offset spatula, spread in an even layer.
6. Bake until risen and a wooden pick inserted about 2½ inches from edge comes out with just a few moist crumbs, 35 to 45 minutes. (A wooden pick inserted in center will still come out wet.) Let cool completely in pan. Run a thin nylon offset spatula around edges of pan to loosen.
7. Using a large offset spatula, decoratively swirl Grand Marnier Whipped Cream on top of cake, leaving a ½-inch border. Garnish with almonds and chocolate shavings, if desired. Serve using a nylon or silicone cake server.

This recipe can also be made in a light-colored 9-inch springform pan.

Note: *To create chocolate shavings, briefly microwave chocolate bar in 5-second intervals. Use a Y-shaped vegetable peeler to create shavings.*

Grand Marnier Whipped Cream

Makes about 5 cups

2½   cups (600 grams) cold heavy whipping cream
2½   tablespoons (30 grams) granulated sugar
2½   tablespoons (37.5 grams) Grand Marnier

1. In the bowl of a stand mixer fitted with the whisk attachment, beat all ingredients at high speed until medium peaks form. Cover and refrigerate until ready to use.

PRO TIPS

Dutch process cocoa powder can look and act differently in baked goods compared to other cocoa varieties. Pay close attention to labels to ensure you pick up the right one.

When removing your baked goods from copper pans, use silicone spatulas or wooden spoons. Using sharp metal utensils will scratch through the tin lining and into your lovely copper.

FRENCH APPLE CAKE

Makes 1 (9-inch) cake

Layer upon layer of apple slices meld with a custardy cake batter spiked with dark rum in this dessert inspired by the classic Normandy Apple Cake.

7	cups (714 grams) ¼-inch-thick sliced unpeeled Honeycrisp apples
5	cups (520 grams) ¼-inch-thick sliced unpeeled Pink Lady apples
16	tablespoons (192 grams) granulated sugar, divided
4½	teaspoons (22.5 grams) dark rum, divided
1	teaspoon (5 grams) fresh lemon juice
3	large eggs (150 grams), room temperature
1½	teaspoons (6 grams) vanilla extract
1	cup (125 grams) all-purpose flour
1½	teaspoons (7.5 grams) baking powder
1	teaspoon (3 grams) kosher salt
¾	cup (170 grams) unsalted butter, melted and cooled
1	tablespoon (14 grams) sparkling sugar

Confectioners' sugar, for dusting (optional)
Crème fraîche, to serve

1. Preheat oven to 400°F (200°C). Line 2 rimmed baking sheets with parchment paper. Butter a 9-inch round copper cake pan*. Line bottom of pan with parchment paper; flour sides of pan.

2. In a large bowl, toss together apple slices, 2 tablespoons (24 grams) granulated sugar, 3 teaspoons (15 grams) rum, and lemon juice. Let stand for 15 minutes. Place on prepared pans.

3. Bake until apples have softened and released significant moisture, 20 to 30 minutes, stirring halfway through baking. (Apples will be slightly reduced in size but should retain their shape.) Let cool on pans for 20 minutes. Reduce oven temperature to 350°F (180°C).

4. In a large bowl, whisk eggs until pale and foamy, about 2 minutes. Add vanilla, remaining 14 tablespoons (168 grams) granulated sugar, and remaining 1½ teaspoons (7.5 grams) rum; whisk until well combined.

5. In a medium bowl, whisk together flour, baking powder, and salt. Gradually add flour mixture to egg mixture alternately with melted butter, beginning and ending with flour mixture, whisking just until combined after each addition.

6. Reserve 14 apple slices; using a large silicone spatula, fold remaining apple slices into batter. Using a small offset spatula, spread batter in prepared pan, pressing down to distribute batter between apples and into edges of pan; smooth into an even layer. Arrange reserved 14 apple slices on top as desired; sprinkle with sparkling sugar.

7. Bake until golden brown and set, 1 to 1½ hours, covering with foil after 50 minutes of baking to prevent excess browning. Let cool completely in pan. Run a thin silicone or nylon offset spatula around edges of pan to loosen. Serve cake from pan using a nylon or silicone cake server, or transfer to desired serving plate. Dust with confectioners' sugar (if using). Serve with crème fraîche.

This recipe can also be made in a light-colored 9-inch springform pan. If using a springform pan, bake for 1 hour.

PRO TIP

When removing your baked goods from copper pans, use silicone spatulas or wooden spoons. Using sharp metal utensils will scratch through the tin lining and into your lovely copper.

MONT BLANC CAKE SQUARES

Makes 12 cake squares

Recipe by Frank Barron and Jennifer Drew

In this tribute to the chestnut-topped pastry that resembles France's highest peak, a surprise well of sweet chestnut spread is hidden beneath Chestnut Buttercream and a dollop of meringue.

1½   cups (340 grams) unsalted butter, softened
2   cups (400 grams) castor sugar
6   medium eggs (282 grams), lightly beaten
3½   cups (438 grams) all-purpose flour
4   teaspoons (20 grams) baking powder
½   teaspoon (1.5 grams) kosher salt
¾   cup (180 grams) whole milk
2   teaspoons (8 grams) vanilla extract
Chestnut Buttercream (recipe follows)
1   cup (324 grams) chestnut spread (see Note)
French Meringue (recipe follows)

1. Preheat oven to 325°F (170°C). Butter a 13x9-inch baking pan. Line pan with parchment paper, letting excess extend over sides of pan.
2. In the bowl of a stand mixer fitted with the paddle attachment, beat butter and castor sugar at medium speed until fluffy, 3 to 4 minutes, stopping to scrape sides of bowl. With mixer on low speed, add beaten eggs in small increments, beating well after each addition.
3. In a medium bowl, sift together flour, baking powder, and salt. Add half of flour mixture to butter mixture, and beat until combined. Add milk and vanilla, and beat until combined. Add remaining flour mixture, and beat just until combined. Pour batter into prepared pan.
4. Bake until a wooden pick inserted in center comes out clean, 45 to 50 minutes. Let cool in pan for 15 minutes. Using excess parchment as handles, remove from pan, and let cool completely on a wire rack.
5. Using a serrated knife or cake leveler, level top of cake. Using a regular straight-edge knife, cut cake into 12 (3-inch) squares. (You will have cake left over.) Using a melon baller or a teaspoon, scoop out a small hole in center of each square. Carefully spread a thin layer of Chestnut Buttercream onto each square to create a crumb coat, being careful not to spread over opening in center. Refrigerate for 20 minutes.
6. Spread remaining Chestnut Buttercream onto each square, being careful not to spread over opening in center. Fill each square with 1 tablespoon chestnut spread. Top each square with a French Meringue.

Note: *We used Clement Faugier Chestnut Spread, available at amazon.com. To make your own chestnut spread, bring 1½ cups (360 grams) water, 1¼ cups (194 grams) roasted peeled chestnuts,*

and ½ cup (100 grams) granulated sugar to a boil over medium-high heat, and cook until sugar is dissolved, about 10 minutes. Transfer mixture to the work bowl of a food processor, and purée until a spreadable consistency is reached.

CHESTNUT BUTTERCREAM
Makes about 5 cups

1¼   cups (194 grams) roasted peeled chestnuts
2   tablespoons (30 grams) water
1⅔   cups (377 grams) unsalted butter, softened
5   cups (600 grams) confectioners' sugar
½   cup plus 2 tablespoons (150 grams) heavy whipping cream
2   teaspoons (8 grams) vanilla extract

1. In the work bowl of a food processor, place chestnuts and 2 tablespoons (30 grams) water; purée until a smooth paste forms. Set aside.
2. In the bowl of a stand mixer fitted with the paddle attachment, beat butter at medium speed until creamy. Add confectioners' sugar, 1 cup (120 grams) at a time, beating until combined. Add cream and vanilla, and beat until well combined. Gradually add 5 tablespoons (74 grams) chestnut purée, beating until combined. Use immediately.

FRENCH MERINGUE
Makes about 12 meringues

1½   cups (300 grams) castor sugar
5   large egg whites (150 grams)

1. Preheat oven to 400°F (200°C). Line a baking sheet with parchment paper.
2. Spread castor sugar on prepared pan.
3. Bake for 7 minutes. Reduce oven temperature to 212°F (100°C).
4. Line another baking sheet with parchment paper.
5. In the bowl of a stand mixer fitted with the whisk attachment, beat egg whites at low speed, gradually increasing mixer speed to medium-high, and beat until stiff peaks form. With mixer on high speed, slowly spoon hot sugar into egg whites. Beat until mixture is smooth and glossy and sugar is dissolved, about 5 minutes.
6. Spoon mixture into a piping bag fitted with a round tip. Holding piping bag ¾ inch above prepared pan, pipe meringue in dollops, letting go before pulling up to get a nice peak to form.
7. Bake until glossy and just set (it shouldn't be sticky to the touch and should easily unstick from the parchment paper), 35 to 45 minutes.

Photo by Joann Pai

BERRY FINANCIERS

Makes 12 financiers

Recipe by David Lebovitz

These financiers are perfect for springtime and can be made using blackberries as well. When browning butter, which the French call beurre noisette (literally, "hazelnut butter," but colloquially, "brown butter"), you want to get the butter rather dark so it smells like noisettes. This involves cooking it until it stops sputtering and takes on the color of maple syrup. That color is key to the flavor of these financiers.

7   tablespoons (98 grams) unsalted butter
1¾   cups (200 grams) sliced blanched almonds
½   cup (100 grams) granulated sugar
½   cup (60 grams) confectioners' sugar
5   tablespoons (40 grams) all-purpose flour
¾   teaspoon (2.25 grams) kosher salt
4   large egg whites (120 grams)
½   teaspoon (2 grams) almond extract
6   ounces (175 grams) fresh raspberries*
Apricot jam, for brushing

1. Preheat the oven to 350°F (180°C). Butter a 12-cup muffin tin.
2. In a sauté pan, heat the butter until it begins to sizzle. Continue to cook over low heat until the edges darken and the butter gives off a nutty flavor. It'll sputter and splatter a bit as the water cooks off, so be careful. Remove from heat, and set aside.
3. In a food processor, grind the almonds with the granulated sugar and confectioners' sugar, the flour, and the salt. While the machine is running, add the egg whites and the almond extract. Stop the machine, and add the butter, pulsing as you add it, until the butter is just mixed.
4. Divide the batter evenly amongst the buttered muffin tins, and poke 3 to 4 berries into the top of each one.
5. Bake until each cake is browned on top, about 18 to 20 minutes. While still warm, brush tops with apricot jam.

*Frozen berries can be used to make these. No need to defrost the berries before using.

Photo by Joann Pai

CRÈME FRAÎCHE POUND CAKE

Makes 1 (9-inch) cake

With crème fraîche in the batter, this triple-berry cake is an elevated version of pound cake and one of our editor-in-chief's go-to recipes because you can make it with any fruit. We used strawberries, blueberries, and blackberries, but feel free to substitute with fruit you have on hand. Berries, apples, pears, and fruits with low moisture content work best.

¾ cup (170 grams) unsalted butter, softened
1 cup (200 grams) granulated sugar
½ cup (110 grams) firmly packed light brown sugar
3 large eggs (150 grams)
1 tablespoon (18 grams) vanilla bean paste
1 tablespoon (3 grams) lemon zest (about 1 lemon)
2 cups (250 grams) all-purpose flour
1¾ teaspoons (8.75 grams) baking powder
1 teaspoon (3 grams) kosher salt
¾ cup (180 grams) crème fraîche
⅓ cup (54 grams) plus ¼ cup (41 grams) fresh blueberries, divided
⅓ cup (54 grams) diced fresh blackberries
⅓ cup (52 grams) diced fresh strawberries

3 fresh strawberries (46 grams), quartered
4 fresh blackberries (25 grams), halved
2 tablespoons (24 grams) turbinado sugar
Crème Fraîche Chantilly (recipe follows)

1. Preheat oven to 350°F (180°C). Butter a 9-inch springform pan. Line bottom of pan with parchment paper.
2. In the bowl of a stand mixer fitted with the paddle attachment, beat butter, granulated sugar, and brown sugar at medium speed until fluffy, 3 to 4 minutes, stopping to scrape sides of bowl. Add eggs, one at a time, beating well after each addition. Beat in vanilla bean paste and lemon zest.
3. In a medium bowl, whisk together flour, baking powder, and salt. With mixer on low speed, gradually add flour mixture to butter mixture alternately with crème fraîche, beginning and ending with flour mixture, beating just until combined after each addition. Fold in ⅓ cup (54 grams) blueberries, diced blackberries, and diced strawberries. Spread batter in prepared pan. Top with quartered strawberries, halved blackberries, and remaining ¼ cup (41 grams) blueberries. Sprinkle with turbinado sugar.

4. Bake until a wooden pick inserted in center comes out clean, about 1 hour. Let cool in pan for 15 minutes. Remove from pan, and let cool completely on a wire rack. Serve with Crème Fraîche Chantilly.

PRO TIP

You can make this cake using any fruit (fresh or frozen) you like. Substitute 1 cup of any fruit for the berries in this recipe. Fruit with lots of moisture (like peaches) will add to your bake time and the final product will have a wetter crumb.

CRÈME FRAÎCHE CHANTILLY

Makes about 1 cup

1 cup (240 grams) heavy whipping cream
2 tablespoons (14 grams) confectioners' sugar
½ teaspoon (2 grams) vanilla extract
⅓ cup (80 grams) crème fraîche

1. In the bowl of a stand mixer fitted with the whisk attachment, beat cream, confectioners' sugar, and vanilla until stiff peaks form. Fold in crème fraîche. Serve immediately.

BERRY JAM CAKE

Make 1 (9-inch) cake

In this one-layer stunner, the pillowy butter cake gets subtle spice from ground ginger while a layer of blackberry-blueberry jam filling adds sweetness to every bite. Topped with sugar for extra crunch, this is the effortless, elegant dessert your summer soirées have been waiting for.

¾ cup (222 grams) Berry Jam (recipe follows)
2 tablespoons (16 grams) cornstarch
¾ cup (170 grams) unsalted butter, softened
1¼ cups (250 grams) plus 1 tablespoon (12 grams) granulated sugar, divided
2 large eggs (100 grams), room temperature
1 teaspoon (4 grams) vanilla extract*
2¾ cups (344 grams) all-purpose flour
1½ teaspoons (7.5 grams) baking powder
1 teaspoon (3 grams) kosher salt
1 teaspoon (2 grams) ground ginger
1¼ cups (300 grams) sour cream, room temperature
Garnish: fresh blackberries, fresh blueberries

1. Preheat oven to 350°F (180°C). Butter and flour a 3-inch-tall, 8-inch round cake pan. Wrap pan with foil, shiny side out. Trim edges of foil even with rim of pan. (This prevents the bottom and sides of cake from getting too dark.)
2. In a small bowl, stir together Berry Jam and cornstarch. Set aside.
3. In the bowl of a stand mixer fitted with the paddle attachment, beat butter and 1¼ cups (250 grams) sugar at medium speed until fluffy, 3 to 4 minutes, stopping to scrape sides of bowl. Add eggs, one at a time, beating well after each addition. Beat in vanilla.
4. In a medium bowl, whisk together flour, baking powder, salt, and ginger. With mixer on low speed, gradually add flour mixture to butter mixture alternately with sour cream, beginning and ending with flour mixture, beating just until combined and stopping to scrape sides of bowl after each addition. (Batter will be thick.)
5. Spoon 2¼ cups (about 531 grams) batter into prepared pan. Using a small offset spatula, spread batter in pan, and smooth top. Spoon jam mixture onto batter. Using an offset spatula,

spread jam mixture to within ½ inch of edges of pan. Spoon remaining batter onto jam mixture, smoothing top with offset spatula.
6. Bake for 30 minutes. Sprinkle with remaining 1 tablespoon (12 grams) sugar, and loosely cover with foil. Bake until golden brown and a wooden pick inserted in center comes out clean, about 1 hour more. Let cool in pan for 25 minutes. Remove from pan, and let cool completely on a wire rack. Garnish with berries, if desired.

We used Heilala.

BERRY JAM
Makes about 3 cups

18 ounces (510 grams) fresh blackberries (about 3½ cups)
14 ounces (400 grams) fresh blueberries (about 2⅔ cups)
2 cups (400 grams) granulated sugar
¼ cup (60 grams) almond liqueur
1 vanilla bean, split lengthwise, seeds scraped and reserved

1. In the container of a blender, process blackberries until puréed. Strain through a fine-mesh sieve into a medium bowl, discarding seeds. Place 1⅔ cups (400 grams) blackberry juice in a medium Dutch oven. Add blueberries, sugar, liqueur, and vanilla bean and reserved seeds, stirring to combine. Let stand for 30 minutes.
2. Bring berry mixture to a boil over medium heat. Cook, stirring frequently, until mixture is thickened and jam leaves a trace when a spoon is dragged across bottom of pot, 20 to 25 minutes. Remove from heat, and let cool for 1 hour. Transfer jam to a clean jar. Jam will keep refrigerated for up to 2 weeks.

PRO TIP
Instead of making the Berry Jam, you can use high-quality store-bought blackberry or blueberry jam. We suggest Bonne Maman Blackberry Preserves or Bonne Maman Wild Blueberry Preserves, available at specialty food stores or online.

GUAVA JAM CAKE

Makes 1 (8-inch) cake

This pillowy cake is our homage to the Bahamian guava duff. Because it's more widely available in grocery stores, we used guava paste instead of fresh guavas to make the jammy filling.

¾   cup (220 grams) guava paste*
1   tablespoon (15 grams) water
¾   cup (170 grams) unsalted butter, softened
1¼   cups (250 grams) granulated sugar
2   large eggs (100 grams), room temperature
1   teaspoon (4 grams) vanilla extract
2¼   cups (281 grams) all-purpose flour
1½   teaspoons (7.5 grams) baking powder
1   teaspoon (3 grams) kosher salt
½   teaspoon (1 gram) ground cinnamon
¼   teaspoon ground allspice
1¼   cups (300 grams) sour cream, room temperature
Confectioners' sugar, for dusting
Butter Rum Glaze (recipe follows)

1. Preheat oven to 350°F (180°C). Butter a 3-inch-tall*, 8-inch round cake pan; line bottom of pan with parchment paper, and flour sides of pan. Wrap pan with foil, shiny side out; trim edges even with rim of pan. (This prevents the bottom and sides of cake from getting too dark.)
2. In a small microwave-safe bowl, heat guava paste and 1 tablespoon (15 grams) water on high in 20-second intervals, stirring between each, until smooth and spreadable (1 to 1½ minutes total). Let cool slightly. Spoon guava mixture into a large piping bag, and cut a ½-inch opening in tip. Set aside.
3. In the bowl of a stand mixer fitted with the paddle attachment, beat butter and granulated sugar at medium speed until fluffy, 3 to 4 minutes, stopping to scrape sides of bowl. Add eggs, one at a time, beating well after each addition. Beat in vanilla; scrape sides of bowl.
4. In a medium bowl, whisk together flour, baking powder, salt, cinnamon, and allspice. With mixer on low speed, gradually add flour mixture to butter mixture alternately with sour cream, beginning and ending with flour mixture, beating just until combined and stopping to scrape sides of bowl after each addition. (Batter will be quite thick.)

5. Spoon 2¼ cups (about 531 grams) batter into prepared pan. Using a small offset spatula, spread batter into bottom edges of pan, and smooth top. Fill a large piping bag with remaining batter, and cut a ½-inch opening in tip; pipe a ring of batter along edges of pan. Pipe guava mixture inside batter ring (it's fine if mixture is still a little warm); spread evenly with a small offset spatula. Pipe remaining batter on top of guava mixture. (You can cut the piping bag opening to 1 inch to make piping easier.) Smooth top with a small offset spatula.
6. Bake until golden brown, 50 to 55 minutes. Loosely cover with foil, and bake until a wooden pick inserted in center comes out clean, 20 to 25 minutes more. Let cool in pan for 10 minutes. Remove from pan, and let cool completely on a wire rack. Place cake on desired serving plate. Dust with confectioners' sugar. (See Note.) Working quickly, drizzle cake with Butter Rum Glaze. Serve immediately.

We used Conchita Guava Paste, available at local grocery stores and online. This recipe also works in a regular 8-inch round cake pan with 2-inch-tall sides, but the top of your cake will be darker.

Note: *The glaze sets up within a few minutes. Have your cake cooled and dusted with confectioners' sugar beforehand. To revive glaze, place in a small microwave-safe bowl. Heat on high in 5-second intervals, stirring between each, until melted and smooth.*

BUTTER RUM GLAZE
Makes ⅓ cup

2   tablespoons (28 grams) unsalted butter
1   cup (120 grams) confectioners' sugar, sifted
1   tablespoon (15 grams) whole milk
1   teaspoon (5 grams) spiced rum
¼   teaspoon kosher salt

1. In small saucepan, heat butter over medium heat until just starting to brown, 5 to 7 minutes. Remove from heat. Add confectioners' sugar, milk, rum, and salt; whisk until smooth. Use immediately.

SOUR CREAM COFFEE CAKE

Makes 1 (9-inch) cake

This endlessly customizable classic comes together in a flash. The warm notes of vanilla complement the subtle tanginess from the sour cream beautifully in the irresistibly tender crumb. When topped with the nutty crunch from the almond-cinnamon streusel, it's pure magic.

1 cup (200 grams) granulated sugar
½ cup (113 grams) unsalted butter, melted and cooled
2 large eggs (100 grams)
2 teaspoons (8 grams) vanilla extract
1½ cups (188 grams) all-purpose flour
1½ teaspoons (7.5 grams) baking powder
½ teaspoon (1.5 grams) kosher salt
½ cup (120 grams) sour cream
¼ cup (60 grams) whole milk
Almond Streusel (recipe follows)
Sour Cream Glaze (recipe follows)

1. Preheat oven to 350°F (180°C). Spray a 9-inch springform pan with baking spray with flour.
2. In a medium bowl, whisk together sugar, melted butter, eggs, and vanilla.
3. In another medium bowl, whisk together flour, baking powder, and salt. Whisk flour mixture into butter mixture. Add sour cream and milk, whisking just until combined. Pour into prepared pan, smoothing top with an offset spatula. Sprinkle with Almond Streusel.
4. Bake until a wooden pick inserted in center comes out clean, 35 to 40 minutes. Let cool in pan for 15 minutes. Remove from pan, and drizzle with Sour Cream Glaze. Serve warm or at room temperature.

ALMOND STREUSEL
Makes about 1 cup

½ cup (63 grams) all-purpose flour
¼ cup (50 grams) granulated sugar
½ teaspoon (1 gram) ground cinnamon
¼ teaspoon kosher salt
½ cup (57 grams) sliced almonds
3 tablespoons (42 grams) unsalted butter, melted

1. In a medium bowl, stir together flour, sugar, cinnamon, and salt. Stir in almonds. Add melted butter, stirring until mixture is crumbly. Crumble with your fingertips until desired consistency is reached.

SOUR CREAM GLAZE
Makes about ½ cup

1 cup (120 grams) confectioners' sugar
2 tablespoons (30 grams) sour cream
1 tablespoon (15 grams) whole milk
½ teaspoon (2 grams) vanilla extract

1. In a small bowl, whisk together all ingredients until smooth.

MADELEINES

Makes about 36 madeleines

Recipe by Marjorie Taylor and Kendall Smith Franchini

These small, buttery cakes are baked in fluted tins, giving them their shell-like shape. When baked in a hot oven, they puff up to create the classic hump on their backs. Warm madeleines are served with coffee after every class at The Cook's Atelier. They are best eaten the day they are made, served slightly warm.

⅔ cup (150 grams) unsalted butter
1 tablespoon (3 grams) freshly grated lemon zest
1 tablespoon (15 grams) freshly squeezed lemon juice
¾ cup (150 grams) granulated sugar
3 large eggs (150 grams), room temperature
1 large egg yolk (19 grams), room temperature
½ teaspoon (1.5 grams) fleur de sel
1½ cups (190 grams) unbleached all-purpose flour, plus more for the pans
1 teaspoon (5 grams) baking powder
Confectioners' sugar, for dusting

1. In a small saucepan, melt the butter over low heat. Let cool slightly and then use a pastry brush to generously coat 2 to 3 madeleine tins (see Note) with butter. Dust the pans with flour, tapping out any excess, and refrigerate to set.
2. Add the lemon zest and juice to the cooled butter and set aside.
3. In the bowl of a stand mixer fitted with the whisk attachment, combine the granulated sugar, eggs, egg yolk, and fleur de sel. Beat at medium-high speed until the mixture is pale and thick and has a ribbon-like consistency when the batter is picked up with the whisk and drizzled over the remaining batter, about 5 minutes.
4. Sift the flour and baking powder into the egg mixture and use a large rubber spatula to gently fold until just combined. Slowly drizzle the melted butter into the batter, folding gently, until fully incorporated. Cover and refrigerate at least 1 hour and up to 12 hours.
5. Set a rack in the upper third of the oven and preheat the oven to 375°F (190°C).
6. Place the madeleine batter in a piping bag fitted with a large tip. Starting near the "base," pipe into the bottom of each mold, filling about two-thirds of the way and not spreading the batter.
7. Bake in the upper third of the oven until the madeleines feel set to the touch, 7 to 8 minutes. Cool slightly and then serve immediately. Garnish with confectioners' sugar, if desired.

Note: *For darker madeleines, use a darker pan. For paler madeleines, use a lighter colored pan.*

Photo by Joann Pai

CANNOLI SHEET CAKE

Makes 1 (13x9-inch) cake

Embedded with dark chocolate chunks and topped with an ethereal ricotta frosting, this sheet cake is a delicate, soft take on the crunchy Italian classic.

1¾ cups (385 grams) firmly packed light brown sugar
¾   cup (170 grams) unsalted butter, melted
3   large eggs (150 grams)
1   tablespoon (13 grams) vanilla extract
3   cups (375 grams) all-purpose flour
1   tablespoon (15 grams) baking powder
1   teaspoon (5 grams) baking soda
1   teaspoon (3 grams) kosher salt
1½   cups (360 grams) whole buttermilk
1   cup (170 grams) chopped 60% cacao bittersweet chocolate
Whipped Ricotta Icing (recipe follows)
Garnish: chopped chocolate, chopped pistachios

1. Preheat oven to 350°F (180°C). Line a 13x9-inch baking pan with parchment paper, letting excess extend over sides of pan.
2. In a large bowl, stir together brown sugar and melted butter until combined. Add eggs and vanilla, stirring until well combined.
3. In a medium bowl, whisk together flour, baking powder, baking soda, and salt. Gradually add flour mixture to sugar mixture alternately with buttermilk, beginning and ending with flour mixture, stirring just until combined after each addition. Fold in chocolate. Pour batter into prepared pan, smoothing top with an offset spatula.

4. Bake until a wooden pick inserted in center comes out clean, 40 to 45 minutes. Let cool in pan for 15 minutes. Using excess parchment as handles, remove from pan, and let cool completely on a wire rack. Top with Whipped Ricotta Icing. Garnish with chocolate and pistachios, if desired. Cover and refrigerate until ready to serve.

WHIPPED RICOTTA ICING
Makes about 6 cups

¾   cup (169 grams) whole-milk ricotta cheese*
2   ounces (55 grams) cream cheese, softened
1   tablespoon (15 grams) fresh orange juice
½   teaspoon (2 grams) vanilla extract
¼   teaspoon kosher salt
2   cups (240 grams) confectioners' sugar
2   cups (480 grams) heavy whipping cream

1. In the work bowl of a food processor, pulse together ricotta, cream cheese, orange juice, vanilla, and salt until completely smooth, about 1 minute. Transfer to a large bowl; whisk in confectioners' sugar.
2. In the bowl of a stand mixer fitted with the whisk attachment, beat cream at medium-high speed until stiff peaks form. Fold whipped cream into ricotta mixture in three additions. Use immediately, or cover and refrigerate until ready to use.

It is important to use a high-quality ricotta cheese so it won't break when creating the icing. We used Polly-O, available at local grocery stores.

CHOCOLATE OLIVE OIL CAKE

Makes 1 (9-inch) cake

A grown-up chocolate cake, this olive oil stir-together batter has sophisticated cocoa notes complemented by a dark ganache frosting.

⅔ cup (50 grams) Dutch process cocoa powder, sifted
½ cup (120 grams) boiling water
1 cup (200 grams) granulated sugar
1 cup (220 grams) firmly packed light brown sugar
¾ cup (168 grams) extra-virgin olive oil
3 large eggs (150 grams), room temperature
1 teaspoon (4 grams) vanilla extract
2 cups (250 grams) all-purpose flour
1¼ teaspoons (6.25 grams) baking powder
1 teaspoon (3 grams) kosher salt
Whipped Ganache (recipe follows)

1. Preheat oven to 350°F (180°C). Line bottom of a 9-inch springform pan with parchment paper; butter sides of pan.
2. In a small bowl, whisk together cocoa and ½ cup (120 grams) boiling water. Let cool slightly.
3. In a large bowl, whisk together sugars, oil, eggs, and vanilla until well combined.
4. In a medium bowl, whisk together flour, baking powder, and salt. Gradually add flour mixture to sugar mixture alternately with cocoa mixture, beginning and ending with flour mixture, whisking just until combined after each addition. (Batter will be thin.) Pour batter into prepared pan.
5. Bake until a wooden pick inserted in center comes out with just a few moist crumbs, 45 to 50 minutes. Let cool in pan for 10 minutes. Remove from pan, and let cool completely on a wire rack. Top with Whipped Ganache. Serve immediately. Cover and refrigerate for up to 3 days.

WHIPPED GANACHE
Makes about 2½ cups

10.5 ounces (315 grams) 60% cacao bittersweet chocolate, chopped
1¼ cups (300 grams) heavy whipping cream
2 tablespoons (28 grams) unsalted butter, softened
1 teaspoon (4 grams) vanilla extract

1. In a large heatproof bowl, place chopped chocolate.
2. In a small saucepan, heat cream over medium-low heat just until bubbles form around edges of pan. (Do not boil.) Pour half of hot cream over chocolate; let stand for 30 seconds. Starting in center of bowl, slowly stir with a rubber spatula until combined. Add remaining hot cream, and slowly stir to combine. Add butter and vanilla, stirring until well combined. Refrigerate until thickened, about 30 minutes.
3. Transfer ganache to the bowl of a stand mixer fitted with the whisk attachment. With mixer on low speed, beat ganache until it lightens in color. Increase mixer speed to medium, and beat until mixture thickens and holds stiff peaks. (If ganache texture starts to look granular, you've overwhipped.) Use immediately.

MARBLED PUMPKIN SPICE CHEESECAKE

Makes 1 (9-inch) cake

In this velvety two-tone marvel, creamy cheesecake gets swirled with sweet and spicy pumpkin batter for a dessert packed with fall flavor. Our gingersnap crust rounds out this recipe with extra crunch and caramelized notes.

30   gingersnap cookies* (210 grams)
1¾   cups (350 grams) granulated sugar, divided
3   tablespoons (42 grams) unsalted butter, melted
32   ounces (900 grams) cream cheese, softened
⅓   cup (80 grams) sour cream, room temperature
2   tablespoons (16 grams) all-purpose flour
2   teaspoons (8 grams) vanilla extract
4   large eggs (200 grams), lightly beaten
1   cup (244 grams) canned pumpkin
2   teaspoons (4 grams) pumpkin spice (see Note)
Sweetened whipped cream, to serve
Garnish: pumpkin spice

1. Preheat oven to 350°F (180°C). Line bottom of a 9-inch springform pan with parchment paper.

2. In the work bowl of a food processor, pulse gingersnap cookies until very finely crushed. Add ¼ cup (50 grams) sugar and melted butter, pulsing until well combined. Press mixture into bottom and ½ inch up sides of prepared pan. Bake for 10 minutes. Let cool slightly on a wire rack. Reduce oven temperature to 325°F (170°C).

3. In the bowl of a stand mixer fitted with the paddle attachment, beat cream cheese and remaining 1½ cups (300 grams) sugar at medium speed until smooth, 2 to 3 minutes. Add sour cream, flour, and vanilla, beating until smooth. Stir in eggs just until combined. Transfer 2 cups batter to a medium bowl; add pumpkin and pumpkin spice, stirring just until combined.

4. Pour 2 cups plain batter into prepared crust, smoothing with an offset spatula. Pour 1 cup pumpkin batter in center of plain batter. Using a spoon, dollop both remaining batters randomly onto surface of cheesecake. Using the tip of a knife, swirl batters together. (To get full marbled effect throughout cake, place knife almost to the crust when swirling.) Wrap bottom and sides of pan with a large sheet of foil (at least 18 inches wide), shiny side out. Place pan in a large roasting pan. Fill roasting pan with enough boiling water to come 1 inch up sides of springform pan.

5. Bake until center is set but still slightly jiggly, about 1 hour and 45 minutes. Carefully remove springform pan from roasting pan, and let cool completely on a wire rack. Remove foil, and refrigerate overnight. Remove from pan, and serve with sweetened whipped cream. Garnish with pumpkin spice, if desired.

*We used Nabisco Ginger Snaps.

Note: *Save a trip to the store and try our homemade Pumpkin Spice on page 19.*

MINI PINEAPPLE UPSIDE-DOWN CAKES

Makes 12 (2-inch) cakes

In this miniature take on the classic American summertime dessert, the pineapple rings caramelize while baking, the perfect topping for the tender cake. We recommend buying and coring a fresh pineapple yourself rather than buying precut and cored from the store. This way, you control the amount of pineapple you take out when coring it.

¼ cup (60 grams) unsalted butter, melted
¾ cup (168 grams) firmly packed light brown sugar
1 fresh pineapple (about 905 grams), peeled and cored
6 maraschino cherries (42 grams), drained and halved
½ cup (113 grams) unsalted butter, softened
1 cup (200 grams) granulated sugar
2 large eggs (100 grams), room temperature
1 tablespoon (18 grams) vanilla bean paste*

1½ cups (188 grams) all-purpose flour
1½ teaspoons (7.5 grams) baking powder
½ teaspoon (1.5 grams) kosher salt
½ cup (120 grams) whole milk

1. Preheat oven to 350°F (180°C). Spray a 12-cup muffin pan (see Note) with baking spray with flour.
2. In each prepared muffin cup, place 1 teaspoon (5 grams) melted butter. Add 1 tablespoon (14 grams) brown sugar to each cup, pressing lightly to form an even layer.
3. Cut pineapple crosswise into ¼-inch-thick slices. (You will need 12 slices for this recipe; reserve remaining pineapple for another use.) Using a round cutter the same diameter as the bottom of your muffin cups, cut mini pineapple rings, being careful to center cutter around cored hole. (We used a 2-inch cutter.) Place pineapple rings and cherries, cut side up, in muffin cups.
4. In the bowl of a stand mixer fitted with the paddle attachment, beat softened butter and granulated sugar at medium speed until fluffy, 3 to 4 minutes, stopping to scrape sides of bowl. Add eggs, one at a time, beating well after each addition. Beat in vanilla bean paste.
5. In a medium bowl, whisk together flour, baking powder, and salt. With mixer on low speed, gradually add flour mixture to butter mixture alternately with milk, beginning and ending with flour mixture, beating just until combined after each addition. Divide batter among prepared cups (about 3 tablespoons each).
6. Bake until a wooden pick inserted in center comes out clean, 15 to 20 minutes. Let cool in pan for 10 minutes. Carefully invert cakes onto a baking sheet. Serve warm or at room temperature.

*We used Heilala.

Note: *These look best when baked in a muffin pan with cups that have straight sides rather than sloped sides.*

TARTA DE SANTIAGO

Makes 1 (8-inch) cake

This delicately sweet, slightly eggy cake has been a Spanish favorite for centuries, and with subtle notes of lemon and almond permeating throughout, you'll understand why. Be sure to pair it with a generous scoop of dulce de leche for optimal enjoyment.

6   large eggs (300 grams)
1¼   cups (250 grams) granulated sugar
2½   cups (240 grams) blanched almond flour
3   tablespoons (9 grams) orange zest
     (about 1 orange)
½   teaspoon (1.5 grams) kosher salt
Confectioners' sugar, for dusting
Dulce de leche, to serve

1. Preheat oven to 350°F (180°C). Line bottom of an 8-inch round cake pan with parchment paper.
2. In a large bowl, whisk together eggs and granulated sugar. Add flour, orange zest, and salt, whisking until well combined. Pour batter into prepared pan.
3. Bake until a wooden pick inserted in center comes out clean, 35 to 40 minutes. Let cool in pan for 10 minutes. Remove from pan, and let cool completely on a wire rack.
4. Place a cross stencil (see Note) in center of cake, and dust cake with confectioners' sugar. Remove stencil. Serve immediately with dulce de leche.

Note: *Adorn your cake with the signature cross of St. James! We make it easy for you with a printable PDF stencil, available to download at bakefromscratch.com/crossstencil.*

MOLASSES TOFFEE APPLE UPSIDE-DOWN CAKE

Makes 1 (9-inch) cake

Fall spice takes center stage in this showstopping upside-down cake. Cooking the apples in molasses and brown sugar lends deep caramelized notes, and a blend of warm spices in the batter heightens the apple's richness. For an extra dose of decadence, serve with a dollop of mascarpone.

1⅔ cups (367 grams) firmly packed light brown sugar, divided
¼ cup (57 grams) unsalted butter, melted
½ cup (170 grams) plus 2 tablespoons (42 grams) molasses, divided
3 large Granny Smith apples (450 grams), peeled and thinly sliced
½ cup plus 1 tablespoon (127 grams) unsalted butter, softened
2 large eggs (100 grams)
1 large egg yolk (19 grams)
2 teaspoons (4 grams) vanilla extract
2⅔ cups (333 grams) all-purpose flour
2½ teaspoons (12.5 grams) baking powder
1½ teaspoons (3 grams) ground cinnamon
¾ teaspoon (2.25 grams) kosher salt
¾ teaspoon (1.5 grams) ground ginger
½ teaspoon (1 gram) ground nutmeg
⅛ teaspoon ground cloves
¾ cup (180 grams) whole milk

1. Preheat oven to 350°F (180°C). Butter sides of a 9-inch square baking pan.
2. In a small bowl, whisk together ⅔ cup (147 grams) brown sugar, melted butter, and 2 tablespoons (42 grams) molasses. Pour into prepared pan. Arrange apple slices in groups of 5 in alternating patterns on top of sugar mixture.
3. In the bowl of a stand mixer fitted with the paddle attachment, beat softened butter and remaining 1 cup (220 grams) brown sugar at medium speed until fluffy, 3 to 4 minutes, stopping to scrape sides of bowl. Beat in remaining ½ cup (170 grams) molasses until no streaks remain. Add eggs and egg yolk, one at a time, beating well after each addition. Beat in vanilla.
4. In a medium bowl, whisk together flour, baking powder, cinnamon, salt, ginger, nutmeg, and cloves. With mixer on low speed, gradually add flour mixture to butter mixture alternately with milk, beginning and ending with flour mixture, beating just until combined after each addition. Pour batter over apples, smoothing with an offset spatula.
5. Bake until a wooden pick inserted in center comes out clean, 45 to 50 minutes. Let cool in pan for 10 minutes. Run a knife around edges of pan to release sides of cake, if needed. Carefully invert cake onto a flat serving plate. Serve warm.

STRAWBERRIES AND CREAM CAKE

Makes 1 (9-inch) cake

Président® butter lends a rich, tender crumb to this elegant almond pound cake. The epitome of French elegance and simplicity, this buttery cake is topped with fresh strawberries and a generous layer of Whipped Cream Filling.

¾   cup (170 grams) unsalted butter*, softened
1½   cups (300 grams) granulated sugar
3   large eggs (150 grams), room temperature
¼   teaspoon (1 gram) almond extract
1½   cups (188 grams) cake flour
½   cup (69 grams) coarsely ground blanched almonds
2   teaspoons (10 grams) baking powder
½   teaspoon (1.5 grams) kosher salt
½   cup (120 grams) whole milk
1   pound (454 grams) large fresh strawberries, hulled
Whipped Cream Filling (recipe follows)
Garnish: quartered fresh strawberries

1. Preheat oven to 325°F (170°C). Spray a 9-inch springform pan with baking spray with flour.
2. In the bowl of a stand mixer fitted with the paddle attachment, beat butter and sugar at medium speed until fluffy, 3 to 4 minutes, stopping to scrape sides of bowl. Add eggs, one at a time, beating well after each addition. Beat in almond extract.
3. In a medium bowl, whisk together flour, ground almonds, baking powder, and salt. With mixer on low speed, gradually add flour mixture to butter mixture alternately with milk, beginning and ending with flour mixture, beating just until combined after each addition. Spoon batter into prepared pan, smoothing top with an offset spatula.
4. Bake for 30 minutes. Cover with foil, and bake until a wooden pick inserted in center comes out clean, about 15 minutes more. Let cool completely in pan, about 1½ hours.
5. Loosen edges of cake with a thin knife. Carefully remove sides of pan. Wrap a 4-inch-wide strip of parchment paper

around cake to form a collar. (You can use more than one strip of parchment, if necessary.) Replace sides of pan.
6. Cut about half of strawberries in half lengthwise. Place strawberries, cut side down, on paper towels to dry completely. Pat remaining strawberries dry with paper towels. Arrange halved strawberries, cut side out, around sides of pan. Stand remaining strawberries about 1 inch apart in center of cake, trimming bottoms as necessary to level. Spread Whipped Cream Filling over strawberries to cover completely, smoothing top with a small offset spatula. Refrigerate overnight.
7. Carefully remove sides of pan and parchment. Replace any loose strawberries, and patch any holes in Whipped Cream Filling. Garnish with quartered strawberries, if desired. Serve immediately.

We used Président® Butter.

Whipped Cream Filling
Makes 4 cups

8   ounces (225 grams) cream cheese, softened
½   cup (100 grams) granulated sugar
2   cups (480 grams) heavy whipping cream

1. In the bowl of a stand mixer fitted with the whisk attachment, beat cream cheese and sugar at medium speed until softened and well combined. With mixer on medium-low speed, gradually add one-third of cream, stopping to scrape sides of bowl. With the mixer on medium speed, gradually add remaining cream, beating until stiff peaks form. (Do not overbeat.) Use immediately.

SOUR CREAM MAPLE CAKE WITH MAPLE BUTTERCREAM FROSTING

Makes 1 (9-inch) cake

Recipe by Kevin Masse

Nothing is as comforting as maple syrup-drenched pancakes. Like a short stack with frosting, this cake has all the flavors of pancakes, baked up golden brown. The cake itself gets a hefty dose of maple syrup, giving it warm notes perfect for cozy fall afternoons. The best part about this recipe? It comes together quickly in one bowl.

2¾ cups (344 grams) all-purpose flour
1   teaspoon (5 grams) baking powder
1   teaspoon (5 grams) baking soda
½   teaspoon (2 grams) kosher salt
1   cup (295 grams) dark-grade pure maple syrup, plus more for drizzling
½   cup (112 grams) canola oil
½   cup (120 grams) whole milk, room temperature
2   large eggs (100 grams), room temperature and lightly beaten
¼   cup (50 grams) granulated sugar
¼   cup (55 grams) firmly packed light brown sugar
¼   cup (60 grams) sour cream, room temperature
1   teaspoon (4 grams) vanilla extract
Maple Buttercream Frosting (recipe follows)

1. Preheat oven to 350°F (180°C). Butter and flour a 9-inch square baking pan. Line pan with parchment paper, letting excess extend over sides of pan; butter and flour parchment.

2. In a large bowl, whisk together flour, baking powder, baking soda, and salt. Add maple syrup, oil, milk, eggs, sugars, sour cream, and vanilla, and stir with a rubber spatula just until combined and no streaks of flour remain. (There will be some lumps in batter; this is OK.) Pour batter into prepared pan. Tap pan on counter 8 times to release air bubbles.

3. Bake until deep golden and a wooden pick inserted in center comes out clean, 35 to 40 minutes, covering with foil after 20 minutes of baking to prevent excess browning. Let cool in pan for 5 minutes. Using excess parchment as handles, remove from pan, and let cool completely on a wire rack. Spread Maple Buttercream Frosting onto cooled cake. Drizzle with maple syrup.

MAPLE BUTTERCREAM FROSTING
Makes about 1½ cups

½   cup (113 grams) unsalted butter, softened
2   cups (240 grams) confectioners' sugar
3   tablespoons (45 grams) sour cream, room temperature
2   tablespoons (42 grams) dark-grade pure maple syrup
½   teaspoon (1.5 grams) kosher salt

1. In the bowl of a stand mixer fitted with the paddle attachment, beat butter at medium speed until creamy, about 3 minutes. Gradually add confectioners' sugar, beating until combined. Add sour cream, maple syrup, and salt, and beat at medium-high speed until smooth, 1 to 2 minutes. (Do not overbeat.) Use immediately.

CARROT CAKE LOAF

Makes 1 (8½x4½-inch) cake

The veggie-packed classic now comes in the compact form of a loaf cake, complete with an indulgent coat of that signature cream cheese frosting.

1   cup (200 grams) granulated sugar
½   cup (112 grams) vegetable oil
2   large eggs (100 grams)
3   tablespoons (45 grams) bourbon
1   cup (125 grams) all-purpose flour
2   teaspoons (10 grams) baking powder
1½   teaspoons (3 grams) ground cinnamon
1   teaspoon (3 grams) kosher salt
½   teaspoon (1 gram) ground ginger
¼   teaspoon (1.25 grams) baking soda
¼   teaspoon ground nutmeg
1½   cups (147 grams) shredded carrots (about 3 large carrots)
½   cup (57 grams) chopped walnuts
Cream Cheese Icing (recipe follows)

1. Preheat oven to 350°F (180°C). Line an 8½x4½-inch loaf pan with parchment paper, letting excess extend over sides of pan.
2. In a large bowl, whisk together sugar, oil, and eggs until well combined. Whisk in bourbon.
3. In a medium bowl, whisk together flour, baking powder, cinnamon, salt, ginger, baking soda, and nutmeg. Gradually add flour mixture to sugar mixture, whisking just until combined. Fold in carrots and walnuts. Pour batter into prepared pan.
4. Bake until a wooden pick inserted in center comes out clean, 45 to 50 minutes. Let cool in pan for 15 minutes. Using excess parchment as handles, remove from pan, and let cool completely on a wire rack. Top with Cream Cheese Icing. Cover and refrigerate until ready to serve.

CREAM CHEESE ICING
Makes about ¾ cup

2   ounces (55 grams) cream cheese, softened
2   tablespoons (28 grams) unsalted butter, softened
1   teaspoon (5 grams) bourbon
⅛   teaspoon kosher salt
1   cup (120 grams) confectioners' sugar

1. In the bowl of a stand mixer fitted with the paddle attachment, beat cream cheese and butter at medium speed until smooth and creamy, about 1 minute. Add bourbon and salt, beating until combined. Reduce mixer speed to low. Gradually add confectioners' sugar, beating until combined. Increase mixer speed to medium, and beat until fluffy, about 1 minute. Use immediately.

PEAR BUTTER CAKE

Makes 1 (9-inch) cake

Like most gâteaux crafted by French home bakers, this rustic pear cake is made extra tender with Président® butter. It's elegant yet simple to put together. The pillowy, buttery cake is also beautiful with a layer of fresh pear slices. Served warm with a dollop of crème fraîche, this is the epitome of comfort baking à la française.

¾   cup (170 grams) unsalted
      butter*, softened
1½   cups (300 grams) granulated sugar
2   large eggs (100 grams)
1½   teaspoons (6 grams) vanilla extract
1   teaspoon (4 grams) almond extract
¾   cup (180 grams) crème fraîche

2   cups (250 grams) all-purpose flour
1½   teaspoons (7.5 grams) baking powder
1   teaspoon (2 grams) ground cinnamon
¾   teaspoon (2.25 grams) kosher salt
½   teaspoon (1 gram) ground ginger
¼   teaspoon ground cardamom
¼   teaspoon ground cloves
1   green Anjou pear (276 grams), cored
      and sliced ⅛ inch thick (about 1½ cups)

Garnish: strained apricot preserves

1. Preheat oven to 350°F (180°C). Spray a 9-inch round cake pan with baking spray with flour; line bottom of pan with parchment paper.
2. In the bowl of a stand mixer fitted with the paddle attachment, beat butter and sugar at medium speed until fluffy, 3 to 4 minutes, stopping to scrape sides of bowl. Add eggs, one at a time, beating well after each addition. Beat in extracts. Stir in crème fraîche. (Mixture will look like it is breaking, but it is not.)
3. In a medium bowl, whisk together flour, baking powder, cinnamon, salt, ginger, cardamom, and cloves. With mixer on low speed, gradually add flour mixture to butter mixture, beating until well combined.
4. Arrange pear slices in prepared pan, fanning along outer edge and then filling center. Spread batter onto pear slices, being careful not to move pear.
5. Bake until golden brown and a wooden pick inserted in center comes out with just a few moist crumbs, 50 minutes to 1 hour. Let cool in pan for 10 minutes. Invert cake onto a wire rack; brush with apricot preserves, if desired. Let cool completely.

We used Président® Butter.

CINNAMON PERSIMMON CAKE

Makes 1 (9-inch) cake

We blended buttermilk and a persimmon together to add to this cake batter, giving the one-layer beauty the most divine texture, and crowned the luscious Honey Buttercream with slices of Sugared Persimmons.

1	Hachiya persimmon (230 grams), top removed
½	cup (120 grams) whole buttermilk
1	cup (227 grams) unsalted butter*, softened
1⅔	cups (333 grams) granulated sugar
3	large eggs (150 grams)
2	teaspoons (8 grams) vanilla extract
2½	cups (312 grams) cake flour
1	tablespoon (6 grams) ground cinnamon
1½	teaspoons (7.5 grams) baking powder
½	teaspoon (2.5 grams) baking soda
½	teaspoon (1.5 grams) kosher salt
1	cup (178 grams) chopped Fuyu persimmons

Honey Buttercream (recipe follows)
Sugared Persimmons (recipe follows)

1. Preheat oven to 350°F (180°C). Butter a 9-inch springform pan. Line bottom of pan with parchment paper.
2. In the container of a blender, place Hachiya persimmon and buttermilk; process until smooth. Set aside.
3. In the bowl of a stand mixer fitted with the paddle attachment, beat butter and sugar at medium speed until fluffy, 3 to 4 minutes, stopping to scrape sides of bowl. Add eggs, one at a time, beating well after each addition. Beat in vanilla.
4. In a medium bowl, whisk together flour, cinnamon, baking powder, baking soda, and salt. With mixer on low speed, gradually add flour mixture to butter mixture alternately with Hachiya persimmon mixture, beginning and ending with flour mixture, beating just until combined after each addition. Fold in Fuyu persimmons. Spread batter in prepared pan.
5. Bake until a wooden pick inserted in center comes out clean, about 1 hour, covering with foil halfway through baking to prevent excess browning. Let cool in pan for 15 minutes. Remove from pan, and let cool completely on a wire rack. Spread Honey Buttercream on top of cake. Top with Sugared Persimmons.

*We used Président.

HONEY BUTTERCREAM
Makes about 3 cups

1	cup (227 grams) unsalted butter, softened
8	ounces (225 grams) cream cheese, softened
1	vanilla bean, split lengthwise, seeds scraped and reserved
2	tablespoons (42 grams) honey
⅛	teaspoon kosher salt
2	cups (240 grams) confectioners' sugar

1. In the bowl of a stand mixer fitted with the paddle attachment, beat butter, cream cheese, and reserved vanilla bean seeds at medium speed until smooth and creamy. Add honey and salt, beating until combined. Gradually add confectioners' sugar, beating until smooth. Use immediately.

SUGARED PERSIMMONS
Makes about 30 sugared persimmons

¼	cup (60 grams) plus 1 tablespoon (15 grams) water, divided
½	teaspoon (3.5 grams) honey
2	Fuyu persimmons (290 grams), sliced ⅛ inch thick
¾	cup (150 grams) granulated sugar, divided

1. Preheat oven to 250°F (130°C). Line 2 baking sheets with nonstick baking mats.
2. In a small microwave-safe bowl, heat 1 tablespoon (15 grams) water and honey on high until honey is dissolved, about 15 seconds.
3. Place persimmon slices on prepared pans. Using a pastry brush, lightly brush persimmon slices with honey water.
4. Bake for 15 minutes. Turn persimmon slices, and bake until dry to the touch, 10 to 15 minutes more. Let cool completely.
5. In a small saucepan, combine ¼ cup (50 grams) sugar and remaining ¼ cup (60 grams) water. Cook over medium heat, stirring occasionally, until sugar is dissolved. Let cool completely.
6. Using a pastry brush, brush both sides of dried persimmon slices with sugar syrup; immediately toss in remaining ½ cup (100 grams) sugar. Use immediately.

PERSIMMON GINGER UPSIDE-DOWN CAKE

Makes 1 (9¾-inch) cake

Sliced persimmons give this simple cake a graphic, gorgeous look. We doubled up on holiday spice, mixing both fresh ginger and crystallized ginger into the zesty batter for a deliciously zippy kick.

¼   cup (57 grams) unsalted butter, melted
¾   cup (165 grams) firmly packed light brown sugar
3   Fuyu persimmons (435 grams), sliced ¼ inch thick and halved
½   cup (113 grams) unsalted butter, softened
1   cup plus 3 tablespoons (236 grams) granulated sugar
2   large eggs (100 grams)
1½   teaspoons (1.5 grams) lemon zest
1   teaspoon (4 grams) vanilla extract
½   teaspoon grated fresh ginger

1½   cups (188 grams) all-purpose flour
1½   teaspoons (7.5 grams) baking powder
½   teaspoon (1.5 grams) kosher salt
¼   teaspoon (1.25 grams) baking soda
⅛   teaspoon ground nutmeg
⅛   teaspoon ground cloves
⅔   cup (160 grams) whole buttermilk
½   cup (88 grams) chopped crystallized ginger

1. Preheat oven to 350°F (180°C).
2. In a 9¾-inch round tarte Tatin dish*, pour melted butter. Using a pastry brush, lightly brush butter up sides of dish. Sprinkle with brown sugar. Arrange persimmon slices in a single layer over brown sugar to completely cover bottom of dish.
3. In the bowl of a stand mixer fitted with the paddle attachment, beat softened butter and granulated sugar at medium speed until fluffy, 3 to 4 minutes, stopping to scrape sides of bowl. Add eggs, one at a time, beating well after each addition. Beat in lemon zest, vanilla, and fresh ginger.
4. In a medium bowl, whisk together flour, baking powder, salt, baking soda, nutmeg, and cloves. With mixer on low speed, gradually add flour mixture to butter mixture alternately with buttermilk, beginning and ending with flour mixture, beating just until combined after each addition. Fold in crystallized ginger. Pour batter over persimmon slices, smoothing with an offset spatula.
5. Bake until a wooden pick inserted in center comes out clean, 40 to 45 minutes. Let cool in pan for 10 minutes. Run a knife around edges of pan to release sides of cake; carefully invert cake onto a flat serving plate. Serve warm or at room temperature.

This recipe can also be made in an enamel-coated cast-iron skillet.

VANILLA APPLESAUCE CAKE

Makes 1 (9-inch) cake

Superior vanilla delivers depth and complexity to this elegant one-layer cake while applesauce gives it an extra-tender crumb. The warm notes of Heilala Vanilla's vanilla extract accentuate the natural sweetness of applesauce in the cake, and Heilala's vanilla bean paste stars in the lush Vanilla Bean Frosting. Enticing flecks of vanilla seeds enhance every billow and lend a subtle richness to round out every bite.

2   cups (250 grams) all-purpose flour
2   teaspoons (10 grams) baking powder
2   teaspoons (4 grams) ground cinnamon
1   teaspoon (3 grams) kosher salt
½   teaspoon (2.5 grams) baking soda
½   teaspoon (1 gram) ground ginger
¼   teaspoon ground cloves
1   cup (200 grams) granulated sugar
1   cup (240 grams) unsweetened applesauce
½   cup (120 grams) whole buttermilk, room temperature

½   cup (112 grams) vegetable oil
2   large eggs (100 grams)
1   teaspoon (4 grams) vanilla extract*
Vanilla Bean Frosting (recipe follows)

1. Preheat oven to 350°F (180°C). Line bottom of a 9-inch springform pan with parchment paper; lightly spray sides of pan with baking spray with flour.
2. In a large bowl, whisk together flour, baking powder, cinnamon, salt, baking soda, ginger, and cloves. In a medium bowl, whisk together sugar, applesauce, buttermilk, oil, eggs, and vanilla. Pour sugar mixture into flour mixture, and fold until well combined. Pour batter into prepared pan, smoothing top with an offset spatula.
3. Bake until a wooden pick inserted in center comes out clean, 35 to 40 minutes. Let cool in pan for 10 minutes. Remove from pan, and let cool completely on a wire rack. Spread Vanilla Bean Frosting on cooled cake.

*We used Heilala.

VANILLA BEAN FROSTING
Makes about 4 cups

8   ounces (225 grams) cream cheese, softened
½   cup (113 grams) unsalted butter, softened
4   cups (480 grams) confectioners' sugar
1   tablespoon (18 grams) vanilla bean paste*
½   teaspoon (1.5 grams) kosher salt

1. In the bowl of a stand mixer fitted with the paddle attachment, beat cream cheese at medium-low speed until smooth, about 2 minutes. Add butter, and beat until smooth, about 2 minutes. Add confectioners' sugar, 1 cup (120 grams) at a time, beating well after each addition. Increase mixer speed to medium-high. Add vanilla bean paste and salt, and beat for 2 minutes. Use immediately.

*We used Heilala.

MULLED APPLE COFFEE CAKE

Makes 1 (9-inch) cake

Brimming with mulling spices and tender chunks of apple, this aromatic cake is the epitome of comfort. We cover it in a thick Caramel Sauce that settles in sweet little pools over the Pecan Streusel.

1	cup (200 grams) granulated sugar
½	cup (113 grams) unsalted butter, melted and cooled
2	large eggs (100 grams)
2	tablespoons (6 grams) orange zest
2	teaspoons (8 grams) vanilla extract
1½	cups (188 grams) all-purpose flour
1½	teaspoons (7.5 grams) baking powder
1	teaspoon (2 grams) ground cinnamon
½	teaspoon (1.5 grams) kosher salt
½	teaspoon (1 gram) ground allspice
½	teaspoon (1 gram) ground cloves
½	teaspoon (1 gram) ground star anise
½	cup (120 grams) sour cream
¼	cup (60 grams) whole milk
1¼	cups (155 grams) chopped Pink Lady apples, divided

Pecan Streusel (recipe follows)
Caramel Sauce (recipe follows)

1. Preheat oven to 350°F (180°C). Spray a 9-inch springform pan with baking spray with flour.
2. In a medium bowl, whisk together sugar, melted butter, eggs, orange zest, and vanilla.
3. In another medium bowl, whisk together flour, baking powder, cinnamon, salt, allspice, cloves, and star anise. Whisk flour mixture into butter mixture. Add sour cream and milk, whisking just until combined. Fold in 1 cup (124 grams) apples. Pour into prepared pan, smoothing with an offset spatula. Top with remaining ¼ cup (31 grams) apples; sprinkle with Pecan Streusel.
4. Bake until a wooden pick inserted in center comes out clean, 40 to 45 minutes. Let cool in pan for 15 minutes. Remove from pan, and drizzle with Caramel Sauce. Serve warm or at room temperature.

PECAN STREUSEL
Makes about 1 cup

½	cup (63 grams) all-purpose flour
¼	cup (50 grams) granulated sugar
¼	teaspoon kosher salt
⅛	teaspoon ground cinnamon
⅛	teaspoon ground allspice
⅛	teaspoon ground cloves
⅛	teaspoon ground star anise
½	cup (57 grams) chopped pecans*
3	tablespoons (42 grams) unsalted butter, melted

1. In a medium bowl, stir together flour, sugar, salt, cinnamon, allspice, cloves, and star anise. Stir in pecans. Add melted butter, stirring until mixture is crumbly. Crumble with your fingertips until desired consistency is reached.

We used Sunnyland Farms Raw Georgia Pecan Halves.

CARAMEL SAUCE
Makes 1 cup

¼	cup (57 grams) unsalted butter
½	cup (110 grams) firmly packed dark brown sugar
1	teaspoon (1 gram) orange zest
¼	teaspoon kosher salt
½	cup (120 grams) heavy whipping cream

1. In a small saucepan, melt butter over medium heat. Whisk in brown sugar, orange zest, and salt until sugar is dissolved. Add cream, and bring to a boil. Cook for 3 minutes. Transfer to a small bowl, and let cool completely. Refrigerate in an airtight container for up to 1 month.

CRANBERRY CITRUS COFFEE CAKE

Makes 1 (9-inch) cake

This zesty cake is as merry and bright as they come. With lemon and orange zest in the batter and the Walnut Streusel and both zests and juices in the glaze, every bite of this vibrant treat offers an explosion of citrus flavor. We topped the batter with a layer of cranberries before baking for gorgeous color and extra sweetness.

1   cup (200 grams) granulated sugar
½   cup (113 grams) unsalted butter, melted and cooled
2   large eggs (100 grams)
2   tablespoons (6 grams) orange zest
1   tablespoon (3 grams) lemon zest
1   teaspoon (4 grams) vanilla extract
1½   cups (188 grams) all-purpose flour
1½   teaspoons (7.5 grams) baking powder
½   teaspoon (1.5 grams) kosher salt
½   cup (120 grams) sour cream
¼   cup (60 grams) whole milk
1¼   cups (92 grams) fresh or thawed frozen cranberries*
Walnut Streusel (recipe follows)
Citrus Glaze (recipe follows)

1. Preheat oven to 350°F (180°C). Spray a 9-inch springform pan with baking spray with flour.
2. In a medium bowl, whisk together sugar, melted butter, eggs, zests, and vanilla.
3. In another medium bowl, whisk together flour, baking powder, and salt. Whisk flour mixture into sugar mixture. Add sour cream and milk, whisking just until combined. Pour into prepared pan, smoothing top with an offset spatula. Top with cranberries; sprinkle with Walnut Streusel.
4. Bake until a wooden pick inserted in center comes out clean, 45 to 50 minutes. Let cool in pan for 15 minutes. Remove from pan, and drizzle with Citrus Glaze. Serve warm or at room temperature.

*If using thawed frozen cranberries, make sure to pat them dry before using.

WALNUT STREUSEL
Makes about 1 cup

½   cup (63 grams) all-purpose flour
¼   cup (50 grams) granulated sugar
1   teaspoon (1 gram) orange zest
1   teaspoon (1 gram) lemon zest
¼   teaspoon kosher salt
½   cup (57 grams) chopped walnuts
3   tablespoons (42 grams) unsalted butter, melted

1. In a medium bowl, stir together flour, sugar, zests, and salt. Stir in walnuts. Add melted butter, stirring until mixture is crumbly. Crumble with your fingertips until desired consistency is reached.

CITRUS GLAZE
Makes about ½ cup

1   cup (120 grams) confectioners' sugar
2   tablespoons (30 grams) sour cream
1   teaspoon (1 gram) orange zest
2   teaspoons (10 grams) orange juice
1   teaspoon (1 gram) lemon zest
1   teaspoon (5 grams) lemon juice
1   teaspoon (5 grams) whole milk

1. In a small bowl, whisk together all ingredients until smooth.

GINGERBREAD COFFEE CAKE

Makes 1 (9-inch) cake

If the holiday season could be captured in a cake, this would be it. With a divinely moist crumb, the cake's spiced ginger notes are even more delicious paired with the earthy, buttery hazelnuts in the streusel.

¾ cup (165 grams) firmly packed dark brown sugar
½ cup (113 grams) unsalted butter, melted and cooled
¼ cup (85 grams) unsulphured molasses
2 large eggs (100 grams)
2 teaspoons (8 grams) vanilla extract
1⅔ cups (208 grams) all-purpose flour
3 tablespoons (33 grams) chopped candied ginger
1½ teaspoons (7.5 grams) baking powder
1½ teaspoons (3 grams) ground ginger
1 teaspoon (2 grams) ground cinnamon
½ teaspoon (1.5 grams) kosher salt
¼ teaspoon ground nutmeg
¼ teaspoon ground cloves
½ cup (120 grams) sour cream
¼ cup (60 grams) whole milk
Hazelnut Streusel (recipe follows)
Garnish: confectioners' sugar

1. Preheat oven to 350°F (180°C). Spray a 9-inch springform pan with baking spray with flour.
2. In a medium bowl, whisk together brown sugar, melted butter, molasses, eggs, and vanilla.
3. In another medium bowl, whisk together flour, candied ginger, baking powder, ground ginger, cinnamon, salt, nutmeg, and cloves. Whisk flour mixture into sugar mixture. Add sour cream and milk, whisking just until combined. Pour into prepared pan, smoothing top with an offset spatula. Sprinkle with Hazelnut Streusel.
4. Bake until a wooden pick inserted in center comes out clean, 35 to 40 minutes. Let cool in pan for 15 minutes. Remove from pan, and garnish with confectioners' sugar, if desired. Serve warm or at room temperature.

HAZELNUT STREUSEL
Makes about 1 cup

½ cup (63 grams) all-purpose flour
¼ cup (55 grams) firmly packed dark brown sugar
¼ teaspoon kosher salt
¼ teaspoon ground cinnamon
¼ teaspoon ground ginger
½ cup (57 grams) chopped raw hazelnuts
3 tablespoons (42 grams) unsalted butter, melted

1. In a medium bowl, stir together flour, brown sugar, salt, cinnamon, and ginger. Stir in hazelnuts. Add melted butter, stirring until mixture is crumbly. Crumble with your fingertips until desired consistency is reached.

PEPPERMINT SWIRL POUND CAKE

Makes 1 (8½x4½-inch) cake

Classic pound cake goes from simple to showstopping thanks to a double dose of peppermint candies and peppermint extract swirled into marbled vanilla and cocoa batters. Topped with a Cream Cheese Glaze, this cake strikes the perfect balance between sweet and tangy.

¾ cup (170 grams) unsalted butter, softened
4 ounces (113 grams) cream cheese, softened
1 cup (200 grams) granulated sugar
½ cup (110 grams) firmly packed light brown sugar
1 teaspoon (4 grams) vanilla extract
3 large eggs (150 grams), room temperature
1½ cups (187 grams) unbleached cake flour
¾ teaspoon (2.25 grams) kosher salt
½ teaspoon (2.5 grams) baking powder
2 tablespoons (30 grams) whole milk, room temperature
3 tablespoons (25 grams) finely crushed round peppermint candies

¼ cup (21 grams) Dutch process cocoa powder, sifted
½ teaspoon (2 grams) peppermint extract
Cream Cheese Glaze (recipe follows)
Garnish: roughly crushed round peppermint candies

1. Preheat oven to 300°F (150°C). Line an 8½x4½-inch loaf pan with parchment paper, letting excess extend over sides of pan.
2. In the bowl of a stand mixer fitted with the paddle attachment, beat butter and cream cheese at medium speed until smooth, about 1 minute. Add sugars and vanilla; beat until fluffy, 3 to 4 minutes, stopping to scrape sides of bowl. Add eggs, one at a time, beating well after each addition. (Mixture may look curdled at this point, but batter will come together.)
3. In a medium bowl, whisk together flour, salt, and baking powder. With mixer on low speed, add flour mixture to butter mixture in two additions alternately with milk, beginning and ending with flour mixture, beating just until combined after each addition. Spoon 2 cups (about 406 grams) batter into a medium bowl; fold in finely

crushed peppermint candies. Add cocoa and peppermint extract to remaining batter in mixer bowl; stir until combined.
4. Using a 1-tablespoon spring-loaded scoop, alternately drop batters into prepared pan; gently swirl batters together using the tip of a knife. Tap pan on counter twice to release any air bubbles.
5. Bake until a wooden pick inserted in center comes out clean, about 1 hour and 15 minutes. Let cool in pan for 10 minutes. Run a knife around edges of pan. Using excess parchment as handles, remove cake from pan; let cool completely on a wire rack.
6. Place Cream Cheese Glaze in a small piping bag, and cut a ¼-inch opening in tip; drizzle glaze onto cooled cake. Garnish with roughly crushed peppermint candies, if desired. Store unglazed cake, wrapped tightly in plastic wrap, for up to 3 days.

CREAM CHEESE GLAZE
Makes ⅓ cup

¼ cup (30 grams) confectioners' sugar
2 ounces (55 grams) cream cheese, softened
⅛ teaspoon kosher salt
1 tablespoon (15 grams) whole milk

1. In a small bowl, stir together confectioners' sugar, cream cheese, and salt until well combined. Stir in milk until smooth. Use immediately.

BREAD

QUICK BREADS

Cozy up to warming scones, muffins, and loaves. Boasting flavors like pumpkin spice and zesty blood orange, these recipes promise comfort from scratch.

CINNAMON JAM LOAF

Makes 1 (8½x4½-inch) loaf

Filled with sweet, jammy swirls and topped with a nutty streusel, this quick bread makes for a hearty breakfast or tasty dessert. Substitute the jam for whatever fruit preserves or spreads you have at home. If you're out of cinnamon, use nutmeg, allspice, or cardamom to spice things up instead.

1   cup (220 grams) firmly packed light brown sugar
¾   cup (180 grams) sour cream*
2   large eggs (100 grams)
¼   cup plus 2 tablespoons (85 grams) unsalted butter, melted
1½   teaspoons (6 grams) vanilla extract
2   cups (250 grams) all-purpose flour
1½   teaspoons (3 grams) ground cinnamon
½   teaspoon (2.5 grams) baking powder
½   teaspoon (1.5 grams) kosher salt
¼   teaspoon (1.25 grams) baking soda
½   cup (160 grams) blueberry jam, divided
Nut Streusel (recipe follow)
Sugar Glaze (recipe follows)

1. Preheat oven to 350°F (180°C). Line an 8½x4½-inch loaf pan with parchment paper.
2. In a large bowl, whisk together brown sugar, sour cream, eggs, melted butter, and vanilla. In a medium bowl, whisk together flour, cinnamon, baking powder, salt, and baking soda. Add flour mixture to sugar mixture, whisking just until combined.
3. Spoon one-third of batter into prepared pan, spreading evenly. Top with ¼ cup (80 grams) jam, leaving a ¼-inch border. (Spread jam gently so it doesn't bleed into bottom layer too much.) Spoon another one-third of batter onto jam, spreading evenly. Top with remaining ¼ cup (80 grams) jam. Spoon remaining batter onto jam, spreading evenly. Top with Nut Streusel.
4. Bake for 30 minutes. Cover with foil, and bake until a wooden pick inserted in center comes out clean, about 45 minutes more. Let cool in pan for 10 minutes. Remove from pan, and let cool completely on a wire rack. Drizzle with Sugar Glaze.

We used sour cream, but you can also use the same amount of buttermilk, crème fraîche, or yogurt.

NUT STREUSEL
Makes about 1½ cups

½   cup (57 grams) chopped sliced almonds*
¼   cup plus 2 tablespoons (47 grams) all-purpose flour
2   tablespoons (24 grams) granulated sugar
2   tablespoons (28 grams) firmly packed light brown sugar
½   teaspoon (1 gram) ground cinnamon
¼   teaspoon kosher salt
¼   cup (57 grams) unsalted butter, cubed

1. In a small bowl, stir together almonds, flour, sugars, cinnamon, and salt. Using your fingertips, cut in butter until pea-size crumbs remain. Squeeze mixture into small and large clumps. Refrigerate until ready to use.

Use the same measurement of whichever kind of nut you prefer and have on hand.

SUGAR GLAZE
Makes ½ cup

1   cup plus 1 tablespoon (127 grams) confectioners' sugar
2   tablespoons (30 grams) whole milk

1. In a small bowl, whisk together confectioners' sugar and milk until smooth. Use immediately.

Note: *If you don't have milk on hand, you can also make this glaze with heavy whipping cream, half-and-half, or even water, although the glaze will not have as much flavor when made with water.*

BLUEBERRY LEMON LOAVES

Makes 4 large or 8 mini loaves

Bursting with fresh blueberries and bright lemon flavor, this loaf recipe is as versatile as they come. You can bake in traditional loaf sizes or in mini loaves. You can bake them in disposable pans for a bake sale, but they work well in regular pans, too. (See Note.)

2⅔ cups (533 grams) granulated sugar
1⅓ cups (320 grams) whole milk
1⅓ cups (303 grams) unsalted butter, melted and slightly cooled
5 large eggs (250 grams)
¼ cup (24 grams) packed lemon zest (from 8 to 10 lemons)
1⅓ cups (320 grams) sour cream
5¼ cups (656 grams) plus 1 tablespoon (8 grams) all-purpose flour, divided
2½ teaspoons (12.5 grams) baking powder
1½ teaspoons (4.5 grams) kosher salt
3 cups (442 grams) fresh blueberries
Garnish: sparkling sugar

1. Preheat oven to 350°F (180°C). For metal loaf pans, spray 4 large or 8 small pans with baking spray with flour. For paper loaf pans, place pans on a large baking sheet.
2. In a very large bowl, whisk together granulated sugar, milk, melted butter, eggs, and lemon zest. Whisk in sour cream.
3. In a large bowl, whisk together 5¼ cups (656 grams) flour, baking powder, and salt. Add flour mixture to sugar mixture, whisking just until dry ingredients are moistened.
4. In a medium bowl, toss together blueberries and remaining 1 tablespoon (8 grams) flour. Fold blueberries into batter.

Divide batter among prepared pans. Sprinkle with sparkling sugar, if desired.
5. Bake until a wooden pick inserted in center comes out clean. For metal loaf pans: 50 minutes to 1 hour for large loaves, or 40 to 45 minutes for small loaves. For paper loaf pans: 45 to 50 minutes. Let cool completely in pans on wire racks.

Note: *For large loaves, use 8½x4½-inch metal loaf pans. For mini loaves, use 5½x3-inch metal loaf pans. We baked our loaves in Novacart Paper Disposable Loaf Baking Molds (7x3 inches for traditional and 4x2 inches for minis), available at bakedeco.com.*

STRAWBERRIES AND CREAM SCONES

Makes about 27 scones

We jazzed up a simple scone recipe with some fresh strawberries and cream.

4 cups (500 grams) all-purpose flour
1 cup (200 grams) granulated sugar
1½ tablespoons (22.5 grams) baking powder
1½ teaspoons (4.5 grams) kosher salt
1 cup (227 grams) cold unsalted butter, cubed
1 cup (240 grams) plus 1 tablespoon (15 grams) heavy whipping cream, divided
3 large eggs (150 grams), divided
1 tablespoon (13 grams) vanilla extract
1 cup (170 grams) diced fresh strawberries
Garnish: turbinado sugar

1. Line 2 baking sheets with parchment paper.
2. In the work bowl of a food processor, pulse together flour, granulated sugar, baking powder, and salt until combined. Add cold butter, tossing to coat; pulse until mixture is crumbly. Transfer mixture to a large bowl.
3. In a small bowl, whisk together 1 cup (240 grams) cream, 2 eggs (100 grams), and vanilla. Add cream mixture to flour mixture, stirring with a fork until mixture begins to come together.
4. Turn out dough onto a heavily floured surface. Using well-floured hands, knead several times until dough comes together. Roll dough into a 14x10-inch rectangle. Spread half of strawberries onto one short side of dough; fold opposite side of dough on top of strawberries, like a book. Roll dough into a 14x10-inch rectangle again; spread remaining strawberries onto one short side of dough. Roll dough to ¾-inch thickness. Using a 2-inch round cutter dipped in flour, cut dough, rerolling scraps once. Place 2 inches apart on prepared pans. Freeze for 30 minutes.
5. Preheat oven to 400°F (200°C).
6. In a small bowl, whisk together remaining 1 egg (50 grams) and remaining 1 tablespoon (15 grams) cream. Brush egg wash onto dough. Sprinkle with turbinado sugar, if desired.
7. Bake until golden brown, 15 to 20 minutes. Let cool on pans for 10 minutes. Remove from pans, and let cool completely on wire racks.

CHAMPAGNE-POACHED PEAR MUFFINS

Makes 12 muffins

Hidden chunks of Champagne-Poached Pears bring tiny bursts of flavor to every bite of these tender muffins.

½ cup (113 grams) unsalted butter, softened
⅔ cup (133 grams) granulated sugar
⅔ cup (147 grams) firmly packed light brown sugar
2 large eggs (100 grams)
1 tablespoon (18 grams) vanilla bean paste*
2 teaspoons (8 grams) vanilla extract*
2 cups (250 grams) plus 1 tablespoon (8 grams) all-purpose flour, divided
2 teaspoons (10 grams) baking powder
½ teaspoon (1.5 grams) kosher salt
½ cup (120 grams) whole buttermilk
1¼ cups (250 grams) (¼-inch) chopped Champagne-Poached Pears (recipe follows)
⅔ cup (75 grams) sliced almonds
Garnish: confectioners' sugar

1. Preheat oven to 375°F (190°C). Butter and flour a 12-cup muffin pan.
2. In the bowl of a stand mixer fitted with the paddle attachment, beat butter, granulated sugar, and brown sugar at medium speed until fluffy, 3 to 4 minutes, stopping to scrape sides of bowl. Add eggs, one at a time, beating well after each addition. Beat in vanilla bean paste and vanilla extract.
3. In a medium bowl, whisk together 2 cups (250 grams) flour, baking powder, and salt. With mixer on low speed, gradually add flour mixture to butter mixture alternately with buttermilk, beginning and ending with flour mixture, beating just until combined after each addition.
4. Pat Champagne-Poached Pears with paper towels to absorb any excess liquid. In a small bowl, toss together pears and remaining 1 tablespoon (8 grams) flour. Fold pears into batter. Spoon batter into prepared muffin cups. Sprinkle almonds onto batter.
5. Bake until golden brown and a wooden pick inserted in center comes out clean, 25 to 30 minutes. Let cool in pan for 5 minutes. Garnish with confectioners' sugar, if desired. Serve warm or at room temperature.

We used Heilala.

CHAMPAGNE-POACHED PEARS

Makes 2 poached pears

2 large Bosc or Anjou pears (484 grams)
1 cup (240 grams) water, plus more if needed
½ cup (100 grams) granulated sugar
1 vanilla bean, split lengthwise, seeds scraped and reserved
1 cinnamon stick
1 (1-inch-wide) strip orange zest (4 grams)
2 (187-ml split) bottles Champagne

1. Peel pears, leaving stems intact. Using a melon baller, core pears from bottom.
2. In a medium saucepan, heat 1 cup (240 grams) water and sugar over medium-high heat until sugar is dissolved and mixture starts to boil. Add vanilla bean and reserved seeds, cinnamon stick, and orange zest. Add Champagne; return to a boil. Add pears; reduce heat to medium-low. (If pears are not fully submerged, add water until liquid covers pears and they start to float.) Shape a small sheet of foil into a circle. Place on top of pears to keep them fully submerged in poaching liquid. Simmer until pears are fork-tender, 30 to 35 minutes.
3. Transfer pears to a bowl. Pour poaching liquid over pears, and let cool to room temperature. Cover and refrigerate until ready to use, up to 1 week.

Note: *You will make more Champagne-Poached Pears than required for the muffins. The leftovers make a nice topper for ice cream or yogurt.*

TRIPLE-VANILLA SCONES WITH CINNAMON SUGAR FILLING

Makes 6 scones

Filling:
- ¼ cup (31 grams) all-purpose flour
- 1½ tablespoons (21 grams) firmly packed light brown sugar
- 1½ tablespoons (18 grams) vanilla sugar*
- 1 teaspoon (2 grams) ground cinnamon
- ⅛ teaspoon kosher salt
- 1½ tablespoons (21 grams) cold unsalted butter, cubed

Dough:
- 2 cups (250 grams) all-purpose flour
- ¼ cup (50 grams) plus 1½ tablespoons (18 grams) vanilla sugar, divided
- 1½ teaspoons (7.5 grams) baking powder
- 1 teaspoon (3 grams) kosher salt
- ¼ teaspoon (1.25 grams) baking soda
- ¼ cup plus 1 tablespoon (71 grams) cold unsalted butter, cubed
- 1 cup (240 grams) plus 1 teaspoon (5 grams) cold heavy whipping cream, divided
- 2 teaspoons (8 grams) vanilla extract*
- 1 large egg (50 grams)

Glaze:
- 1 cup (120 grams) confectioners' sugar
- ¼ cup (60 grams) heavy whipping cream
- ⅛ teaspoon vanilla extract
- 1 vanilla bean*, split lengthwise, seeds scraped and reserved

1. For filling: In a small bowl, combine flour, brown sugar, vanilla sugar, cinnamon, and salt. Using your fingertips, cut in cold butter until mixture is crumbly and no lumps remain. Set aside.

2. For dough: In a large bowl, whisk together flour, ¼ cup (50 grams) vanilla sugar, baking powder, salt, and baking soda. Using a pastry blender, cut in cold butter until mixture is crumbly. Add 1 cup (240 grams) cold cream and vanilla extract, stirring with a fork just until dry ingredients are moistened.

3. Turn out dough onto a sheet of parchment paper. Divide dough in half (about 311 grams each), and roll each half into a round. Cover with a second sheet of parchment paper, and press each half into a 6½-inch disk. Remove top sheet of parchment. Press filling into center of 1 disk of dough, leaving a ¼-inch border on all sides.

4. In a small bowl, whisk together egg and remaining 1 teaspoon (5 grams) cold cream. Brush egg wash onto ¼-inch border. Top with remaining disk of dough, and press around edges to seal. (Final product should be 6½ inches in diameter and 1 inch high.) Cover and freeze for 30 minutes.

5. Preheat oven to 400°F (200°C). Line a baking sheet with parchment paper.

6. Using a sharp knife, cut dough into 6 wedges. Place at least 1 inch apart on prepared pan. Brush with egg wash, and top with remaining 1½ tablespoons (18 grams) vanilla sugar.

7. Bake until golden brown, 20 to 25 minutes, covering with foil halfway through baking to prevent excess browning. Let cool on pan for 5 minutes. Remove from pan, and let cool completely on a wire rack.

8. For glaze: In a small bowl, whisk together confectioners' sugar, cream, and vanilla extract until smooth. Add reserved vanilla bean seeds, and whisk until evenly distributed. Use immediately. Drizzle glaze onto cooled scones.

We used Heilala. If you don't have a vanilla bean on hand, 1 teaspoon (4 grams) vanilla extract can be substituted.

BLOOD ORANGE GINGER SHORTCAKES WITH LABNEH WHIPPED CREAM

Makes 8 shortcakes

Recipe by Marian Cooper Cairns

This take on traditional shortcake is filled with blood oranges tossed in orange liqueur and mint. For a touch of tang, we topped them off with labneh, a Middle Eastern cream cheese. Look for rich, thick labneh near the yogurt or fresh cheese section of your grocery store.

1½   cups (188 grams) all-purpose flour
1½   cups (187 grams) cake flour
½   cup (88 grams) finely chopped candied ginger
¼   cup (50 grams) plus 3½ tablespoons (42 grams) granulated sugar, divided
1   tablespoon (15 grams) baking powder
1   teaspoon (3 grams) kosher salt
¾   teaspoon (3.75 grams) baking soda
½   cup (113 grams) unsalted butter, slightly frozen
¾   cup (180 grams) whole buttermilk

1¼   cups (300 grams) heavy whipping cream, divided
2   cups (274 grams) sectioned peeled blood oranges
2   tablespoons (2 grams) thinly sliced fresh mint
2   tablespoons (30 grams) orange liqueur
½   cup (120 grams) labneh

1. Preheat oven to 450°F (230°C). Line a baking sheet with parchment paper.
2. In a large bowl, whisk together flours, ginger, ¼ cup (50 grams) sugar, baking powder, salt, and baking soda. Grate slightly frozen butter on the large holes of a box grater. Fold into flour mixture.
3. In a small bowl, stir together buttermilk and ½ cup (120 grams) cream. Using a fork, stir buttermilk mixture into flour mixture until a soft dough forms.
4. Turn out dough onto a lightly floured surface, and knead just until dough comes together, 2 to 3 times. With floured hands,

pat dough into a 7x6-inch rectangle. Cut dough in half, and stack halves on top of each other. Repeat procedure twice. Pat dough to 1- to 1¼-inch thickness. Using a 3-inch round cutter dipped in flour, cut dough, re-patting scraps once. Place on prepared pan. Freeze for 15 minutes.
5. Bake until golden brown, 15 to 18 minutes.
6. In a medium bowl, gently toss together oranges, mint, liqueur, and 2 tablespoons (24 grams) sugar. Let stand, stirring occasionally, until sugar is dissolved, about 15 minutes. Cover and refrigerate for up to 4 hours, if desired.
7. In the bowl of a stand mixer fitted with the paddle attachment, beat labneh, remaining ¾ cup (180 grams) cream, and remaining 1½ tablespoons (18 grams) sugar at medium speed until medium peaks form. Serve oranges and whipped labneh between halved shortcakes. Serve immediately.

Photo by Matt Armendariz

JOHNNY BREAD

Makes 8 johnny breads

Every Sunday morning in households and eateries across Bermuda, johnny bread is served with boiled potatoes, bananas, and codfish. With a golden-brown exterior and tender, fluffy crumb, johnny bread is versatile enough to enjoy with dinner or as a snack smeared with jam or honey. Traditionally, Bermudians cook the dough in a hot skillet. For our recipe, we baked the bread for a few minutes after frying.

2   cups (250 grams) all-purpose flour
¼   cup (50 grams) granulated sugar
1   tablespoon (15 grams) baking powder
1   teaspoon (3 grams) kosher salt
¼   cup (57 grams) cold unsalted butter, cubed
½   cup (120 grams) whole milk
1   large egg (50 grams), room temperature
1   tablespoon (14 grams) vegetable oil
Honey, jam, and butter, to serve

1. Preheat oven to 400°F (200°C). Line a baking sheet with parchment paper.
2. In a large bowl, whisk together flour, sugar, baking powder, and salt. Using a pastry blender, cut in cold butter until mixture is crumbly. In a small bowl, whisk together milk and egg. Gradually add milk mixture to flour mixture, stirring just until dry ingredients are moistened.
3. Turn out dough onto a lightly floured surface, and gently knead 4 to 5 times. Divide into 8 equal portions (68 grams each). Shape each portion into a ball, and gently flatten to ¾-inch thickness.
4. In a 12-inch skillet, heat oil over medium heat. Place johnny bread in skillet; cook until lightly browned, about 2 minutes per side. Transfer to prepared pan.
5. Bake until centers are set, 8 to 10 minutes. Serve warm with honey, jam, and butter. Store in an airtight container for up to 1 week.

PECAN SHORTCAKES WITH FRESH PEACHES AND WHIPPED CREAM

Makes 6 shortcakes

These fluffy shortcakes are studded with pecans to add crunch and rich, nutty flavor to every buttery bite. Served with fresh peaches and homemade Whipped Cream, this classic summertime sweet is rounded out by a final sprinkling of toasted pecans.

1 cup (113 grams) chopped pecans*
2 cups (250 grams) all-purpose flour
3 tablespoons (36 grams) plus 1 teaspoon (4 grams) granulated sugar, divided
1½ teaspoons (7.5 grams) baking powder
1½ teaspoons (4.5 grams) kosher salt
¼ teaspoon (1.25 grams) baking soda
¾ cup (170 grams) cold unsalted butter, cubed
¾ cup (180 grams) plus 2 teaspoons (10 grams) cold whole buttermilk, divided
Peach Filling (recipe follows)
Whipped Cream (recipe follows)

1. Preheat oven to 350°F (180°C).
2. Spread pecans on a rimmed baking sheet.
3. Bake until pecans are just beginning to color, 6 to 7 minutes, stirring occasionally. Let cool completely.
4. In a large bowl, whisk together flour, 3 tablespoons (36 grams) sugar, baking powder, salt, and baking soda. Using a pastry blender, cut in cold butter until mixture is crumbly. Refrigerate for 30 minutes.
5. Preheat oven to 425°F (220°C). Line a baking sheet with parchment paper.
6. Add ½ cup (57 grams) cooled toasted pecans to flour mixture, stirring to combine. Add ¾ cup (180 grams) cold buttermilk, stirring until a shaggy dough forms.
7. Turn out dough and any remaining flour mixture onto a lightly floured surface, and gently knead 2 to 3 times. Pat dough into a rectangle, 1 inch thick. Cut rectangle into fourths. Stack each fourth on top of each other, and pat into a 1-inch-thick rectangle again. Repeat procedure 3 more times. Pat dough to 1-inch thickness. Using a 3-inch round cutter dipped in flour, cut 4 rounds

without twisting cutter, re-patting scraps to get 2 more rounds. Place 2 inches apart on prepared pan. Freeze for 10 minutes.
8. Brush top of dough with remaining 2 teaspoons (10 grams) cold buttermilk, and sprinkle with remaining 1 teaspoon (4 grams) sugar.
9. Bake until golden brown, 13 to 16 minutes. Remove from pan and let cool slightly on a wire rack.
10. To serve, finely chop 2 tablespoons (14 grams) of remaining toasted pecans. Cut shortcakes in half horizontally, and layer with Peach Filling and Whipped Cream. Sprinkle Whipped Cream with finely chopped pecans. Serve with remaining toasted pecans.

We used Sunnyland Farms Georgia Pecan Halves.

PEACH FILLING
Makes about 3 cups

3 cups (462 grams) sliced fresh peaches (about 3 medium peaches)
3 tablespoons (36 grams) granulated sugar

1. In a large bowl, place peaches. Sprinkle with sugar, and toss to combine. Let stand for 30 minutes.

WHIPPED CREAM
Makes 2 cups

1 cup (240 grams) heavy whipping cream
2 tablespoons (24 grams) granulated sugar

1. In the bowl of a stand mixer fitted with the whisk attachment, beat cream at medium speed until slightly thickened. Add sugar, and beat until soft peaks form. Refrigerate until ready to serve.

PUMPKIN SPICE MUFFINS WITH PECAN STREUSEL

Makes 12 muffins

These hearty muffins will be your go-to breakfast all season long. Pumpkin purée makes the crumb extra tender while a dash of pumpkin spice creates sweet heat. Don't skip our Pecan Streusel. It lends nuttiness and an addictive crunch to every bite.

2   cups (250 grams) all-purpose flour
1½   cups (330 grams) firmly packed light brown sugar
2   teaspoons (4 grams) pumpkin spice (see Note)
1   teaspoon (5 grams) baking soda
¾   teaspoon (2 grams) kosher salt
1   cup (244 grams) canned pumpkin
½   cup (113 grams) unsalted butter, melted
2   large eggs (100 grams)
⅓   cup (80 grams) whole milk, room temperature
Pecan Streusel (recipe follows)

1. Preheat oven to 350°F (180°C). Butter and flour a 12-cup muffin pan.
2. In a large bowl, whisk together flour, brown sugar, pumpkin spice, baking soda, and salt. In a medium bowl, whisk together pumpkin, melted butter, eggs, and milk. Add pumpkin mixture to flour mixture, and fold until well combined.
3. Spoon batter into prepared muffin cups, filling three-fourths full (about 74 grams each). Spoon 2 tablespoons (about 22 grams) Pecan Streusel on top of batter in each muffin cup.
4. Bake until a wooden pick inserted in center comes out clean, 18 to 22 minutes. Serve warm.

PECAN STREUSEL
Makes about 2 cups

¾   cup (94 grams) all-purpose flour
½   cup (57 grams) chopped pecans*
¼   cup (55 grams) firmly packed light brown sugar
1   teaspoon (2 grams) pumpkin spice (see Note)
¼   cup (57 grams) unsalted butter, melted

1. In a medium bowl, stir together flour, pecans, brown sugar, and pumpkin spice. Add melted butter, stirring until large clumps form. Squeeze mixture together with hands to create clumps. Freeze until ready to use.

*We used Sunnyland Farms Raw Georgia Pecan Halves.

Note: *Save a trip to the store and try our homemade Pumpkin Spice on page 17.*

CHEDDAR AND ONION BEER BREAD

Makes 1 (8½x4½-inch) loaf

This stir-together loaf can be made in a pinch with ingredients you probably have on hand, but don't let that fool you—this isn't your average quick bread. Beer's natural leavening abilities give this a little extra lift, and gluten-inhibiting alcohol lends it an especially tender crumb. Amber ale deepens the bread's flavor with complex, toasty notes of amber malt and bright citrus, which are complemented beautifully by the earthy tang of Cheddar cheese and oven-roasted sweet onion.

1   small sweet onion (about 215 grams)
1   tablespoon (14 grams) olive oil
2   teaspoons (6 grams) kosher salt, divided

3   cups (375 grams) all-purpose flour
3   tablespoons (36 grams) granulated sugar
1   tablespoon (15 grams) baking powder
½   teaspoon (1 gram) coarse ground black pepper
1   (12-ounce) bottle (340 grams) amber ale
1   cup (84 grams) freshly grated Cheddar cheese
2   tablespoons (28 grams) unsalted butter, melted

1. Preheat oven to 400°F (200°C).
2. Clean and quarter onion. Separate layers, and place in a single layer on a small rimmed baking sheet. Drizzle with oil, and sprinkle with ½ teaspoon (1.5 grams) salt.
3. Bake until tender and brown, about 20 minutes, stirring halfway through baking. Let cool completely; dice.
4. Reduce oven temperature to 350°F (180°C). Spray an 8½x4½-inch loaf pan with cooking spray.
5. In a large bowl, stir together flour, sugar, baking powder, pepper, and remaining 1½ teaspoons (4.5 grams) salt. Add beer, stirring just until combined. Fold in diced roasted onion and cheese. Spoon batter into prepared pan. Pour melted butter over batter.
6. Bake until golden brown and a wooden pick inserted in center comes out clean, about 1 hour and 10 minutes. Let cool in pan for 10 minutes. Remove from pan, and let cool slightly on a wire rack. Serve warm.

DATE AND PECAN SCONES

Makes 8 scones

These buttery scones are simple to make (they come together in a flash) and loaded with flavor. The tender, fluffy crumb is studded with pecans and dates, which offer a lovely caramellike sweetness that's amplified by the maple syrup glaze.

3 cups (375 grams) all-purpose flour
¼ cup (55 grams) firmly packed light brown sugar
1 tablespoon plus 1 teaspoon (20 grams) baking powder
1 teaspoon (3 grams) kosher salt
1 teaspoon (2 grams) ground cinnamon
½ cup (113 grams) cold unsalted butter, cubed
½ cup (87.5 grams) chopped dates
½ cup (57 grams) chopped pecans*

¾ cup (180 grams) cold heavy whipping cream
2 teaspoons (8 grams) vanilla extract
1 large egg (50 grams)
1 tablespoon (15 grams) water
Maple Glaze (recipe follows)

1. Preheat oven to 375°F (190°C). Line a baking sheet with parchment paper.
2. In a large bowl, whisk together flour, brown sugar, baking powder, salt, and cinnamon. Using a pastry blender, cut in cold butter until mixture is crumbly. Stir in dates and pecans. Add cold cream and vanilla, stirring with a fork just until dry ingredients are moistened.
3. Turn out dough onto a lightly floured surface, and gently knead until it comes together. Press dough into a 7-inch circle, 1 inch thick. Using a sharp knife or bench scraper, cut dough into

8 wedges. Place on prepared pan.
4. In a small bowl, whisk together egg and 1 tablespoon (15 grams) water. Brush dough with egg wash.
5. Bake until golden brown, 24 to 28 minutes. Let cool on pan for 5 minutes. Dip top of scones in Maple Glaze. Let set. Serve warm.

We used Sunnyland Farms Raw Georgia Pecan Halves.

MAPLE GLAZE
Makes about ¾ cup

1   cup (120 grams) confectioners' sugar
¼   cup (85 grams) maple syrup
1½   teaspoons (7.5 grams) whole milk

1. In a small bowl, whisk together all ingredients until smooth. Use immediately.

PUMPKIN SPICE BREAD WITH CREAM CHEESE SWIRL

Makes 1 (8½x4½-inch) loaf

We took the humble pumpkin quick bread to a whole new luscious level by adding a surprise cream cheese center. With Pumpkin Spice Glaze drizzled on top, this loaf strikes the perfect balance between sweet and tangy.

1⅓   cups (167 grams) all-purpose flour
1   tablespoon (6 grams) pumpkin spice (see Note)
2   teaspoons (10 grams) baking powder
¾   teaspoon (2 grams) kosher salt
½   teaspoon (3 grams) baking soda
1   cup (244 grams) canned pumpkin
¾   cup (165 grams) firmly packed dark brown sugar
½   cup (120 grams) plain Greek yogurt
2   large eggs (100 grams)
¼   cup (56 grams) vegetable oil
2   teaspoons (8 grams) vanilla extract
Cream Cheese Swirl (recipe follows)
Pumpkin Spice Glaze (recipe follows)

1. Preheat oven to 350°F (180°C). Butter and flour an 8½x4½-inch loaf pan.
2. In a large bowl, whisk together flour, pumpkin spice, baking powder, salt, and baking soda. In a medium bowl, whisk together pumpkin, brown sugar, yogurt, eggs, oil, and vanilla. Add pumpkin mixture to flour mixture, and fold until well combined.
3. Pour half of batter into prepared pan; create a well with the back of a spoon. Add Cream Cheese Swirl, leaving a ¼-inch border around edges of pan. Top with remaining batter, smoothing top.
4. Bake until a wooden pick inserted in center comes out clean, 1 hour and 5 minutes to 1 hour and 10 minutes. Let cool in pan for 10 minutes. Remove from pan, and let cool completely on a wire rack. Drizzle Pumpkin Spice Glaze onto cooled cake.

CREAM CHEESE SWIRL
Makes about 1 cup

3   ounces (86 grams) cream cheese, softened
3   tablespoons (36 grams) granulated sugar
1   large egg yolk (19 grams)
1   tablespoon (8 grams) all-purpose flour
½   teaspoon (2 grams) vanilla extract

1. In the bowl of a stand mixer fitted with the paddle attachment, beat cream cheese and sugar at medium speed until smooth, about 2 minutes. Add egg yolk and flour, and beat until smooth, about 2 minutes. Beat in vanilla. Use immediately.

PUMPKIN SPICE GLAZE
Makes about ¾ cup

1   cup (120 grams) confectioners' sugar
5   tablespoons (75 grams) heavy whipping cream
¼   teaspoon pumpkin spice (see Note)

1. In a small bowl, stir together all ingredients until smooth. Cover and store at room temperature until ready to use.

Note: *Save a trip to the store and try our homemade Pumpkin Spice on page 19.*

TRADITIONAL ENGLISH SCONES

Makes about 14 scones

Recipe by Lisa Heathcote

English scones have stood the test of time, starring on three-tiered platters during teatime for centuries. Today, they come in many different shapes (from wedges to rounds) and are dressed up with every mix-in imaginable. When it came to creating scones for the set of Downton Abbey, though, food stylist Lisa Heathcote knew only traditional scones would do. They needed to be round, fluffy on the inside, crisp on the outside, and have a beautifully golden top. This recipe checks every box.

1¾ cups plus 2 teaspoons (225 grams) self-rising flour
⅛ teaspoon kosher salt
¼ cup (57 grams) cold unsalted butter
2 tablespoons (24 grams) castor sugar
½ cup plus 2 tablespoons (150 grams) whole milk
1 large egg (50 grams), lightly beaten
Apricot jam and clotted cream, to serve

1. Preheat oven to 425°F (220°C). Lightly butter and flour 2 baking sheets.
2. In a large bowl, stir together flour and salt; gently rub in cold butter with fingertips, being careful not to overwork mixture. Stir in castor sugar. Add milk, stirring until a soft dough forms.

3. Turn out dough onto a lightly floured surface, and knead very gently. (Do not overwork.) Pat to ¾-inch thickness. Using a 2-inch round cutter, cut dough without twisting cutter, re-patting scraps as necessary. Place on prepared pans. Brush top of scones with egg wash.
4. Bake until well risen and golden, about 12 minutes. Remove from pan, and let cool on a wire rack, or serve warm. Serve with jam and clotted cream.

BUTTERMILK BISCUITS

Makes 12 biscuits

Rich, buttery, and flaky, these are an ode to the perfect Southern biscuit. White Lily flour is the not-so-secret ingredient, giving them a soft, pillowy crumb that'll keep you coming back for more.

3½   cups (438 grams) all-purpose flour*
2   tablespoons (24 grams) granulated sugar
1   tablespoon (9 grams) kosher salt
1   tablespoon (15 grams) baking powder
½   teaspoon (2.5 grams) baking soda
1¼   cups (284 grams) cold unsalted butter, cubed
1   cup (240 grams) cold whole buttermilk
1   large egg (50 grams), lightly beaten
Flaked sea salt, for sprinkling
Softened butter and honey, to serve

1. Preheat oven to 425°F (220°C). Line a baking sheet with parchment paper.
2. In a large bowl, whisk together flour, sugar, kosher salt, baking powder, and baking soda. Using a pastry blender, cut in cold butter until mixture is crumbly. Stir in cold buttermilk until a shaggy dough forms.
3. Turn out dough onto a lightly floured surface. Pat dough into a rectangle, and cut into fourths. Stack each fourth on top of each other, and pat down into a rectangle again. Repeat procedure 3 more times. Pat or roll dough to 1-inch thickness. Using a 2½-inch round cutter dipped in flour, cut dough without twisting cutter, rerolling scraps as necessary. Place 2 inches apart on prepared pan. Freeze until cold, about 10 minutes. Brush with egg wash, and sprinkle with sea salt.
4. Bake until golden brown, about 15 minutes. Serve warm with softened butter and honey.

*We used White Lily.

PERSIMMON SCONES

Makes about 7 scones

The floral sweetness and spicy undertones of persimmons really sing in these extra-tender cinnamon-scented scones brimming with fresh pieces of the fruit. A maple syrup glaze brings an extra dose of warmth.

2   cups (250 grams) all-purpose flour
5   tablespoons (70 grams) firmly packed light brown sugar, divided
1½   teaspoons (7.5 grams) baking powder
1   teaspoon (3 grams) kosher salt
1   teaspoon (2 grams) ground cinnamon
¼   teaspoon (1.25 grams) baking soda
¼   teaspoon ground ginger
⅛   teaspoon ground cardamom
¼   cup plus 1 tablespoon (71 grams) cold unsalted butter, cubed
¾   cup (134 grams) diced Fuyu persimmons
¾   cup plus 2 tablespoons (210 grams) plus 1 teaspoon (5 grams) cold heavy whipping cream, divided
2   teaspoons (8 grams) vanilla extract*
1   large egg (50 grams)
Maple Glaze (recipe follows)

1. Line a baking sheet with parchment paper.
2. In a large bowl, whisk together flour, 3 tablespoons (42 grams) brown sugar, baking powder, salt, cinnamon, baking soda, ginger, and cardamom. Using a pastry blender, cut in cold butter until mixture is crumbly. Toss persimmons in flour mixture. Add ¾ cup plus 2 tablespoons (210 grams) cold cream and vanilla, stirring with a fork just until dry ingredients are moistened.
3. Turn out dough onto a lightly floured surface, and knead gently 4 to 5 times. Roll dough to 1-inch thickness. Using a 2½-inch round cutter, cut dough, rerolling scraps as necessary. Place 2 inches apart on prepared pan. Cover and refrigerate for at least 30 minutes.
4. Preheat oven to 400°F (200°C).
5. In a small bowl, whisk together egg and remaining 1 teaspoon (5 grams) cold cream. Using a pastry brush, brush top of scones with egg wash. Sprinkle with remaining 2 tablespoons (28 grams) brown sugar.
6. Bake until golden brown, 16 to 18 minutes. Let cool on pan for 5 minutes. Remove from pan, and let cool completely on a wire rack. Drizzle with Maple Glaze. Store in an airtight container for up to 3 days.

*We used Heilala.

MAPLE GLAZE
Makes ⅔ cup

1   cup (120 grams) confectioners' sugar
2½   tablespoons (53 grams) maple syrup
¼   cup plus 1 tablespoon (75 grams) heavy whipping cream

1. In a small bowl, place confectioners' sugar. Whisk in maple syrup; slowly whisk in cream until smooth. Use immediately.

YEAST
BREADS

Featuring savory bagels, herbaceous ciabatta, and
strawberry-filled sweet rolls, our yeast breads will take you
from breakfast to dessert and every moment in between

PAIN AU RAISIN SWEET ROLLS

Makes 6 rolls

Baked to tall, golden perfection in copper soufflé molds, these rolls are a home baker-friendly version of the original, with an easy-to-use frangipane filling replacing the crème pâtissière.

3½   tablespoons (52.5 grams) warm whole milk (105°F/41°C to 110°F/43°C)
3½   tablespoons (42 grams) granulated sugar, divided
1¼   teaspoons (3.75 grams) active dry yeast
2   cups (250 grams) all-purpose flour, divided
3   large eggs (150 grams), room temperature
½   teaspoon (1.5 grams) kosher salt
9   tablespoons (126 grams) unsalted butter, softened
⅔   cup (114 grams) raisins
⅓   cup (60 grams) golden raisins
3   tablespoons (45 grams) warm brandy
1   tablespoon (14 grams) unsalted butter, melted
Frangipane (recipe follows)
1   large egg white (30 grams)
2   tablespoons (30 grams) water, divided
1½   teaspoons (6 grams) Swedish pearl sugar
⅓   cup (107 grams) apricot preserves

1. In the bowl of a stand mixer fitted with the paddle attachment, combine warm milk, 1 tablespoon (12 grams) granulated sugar, and yeast. Let stand until mixture is foamy, about 10 minutes.

2. Add 1 cup (125 grams) flour and eggs to yeast mixture; beat at medium-low speed until mostly smooth, 2 to 3 minutes, stopping to scrape sides of bowl. (Some small lumps remaining are OK.) Cover and let stand in a warm, draft-free place (75°F/24°C) until slightly puffed, with small bubbles forming over top and at edges, 30 to 45 minutes.

3. Using the dough hook attachment, add salt, remaining 1 cup (125 grams) flour, and remaining 2½ tablespoons (30 grams) granulated sugar; beat at low speed just until combined. Increase mixer speed to medium, and beat until dough is elastic and quite

smooth, 7 to 10 minutes, stopping to scrape sides of bowl. Add softened butter, 1 tablespoon (14 grams) at a time, beating until combined after each addition. (Dough should pass the windowpane test; see PRO TIP.)

4. Spray a large bowl with cooking spray. Place dough in bowl, turning to grease top. Cover and let rise in a warm, draft-free place (75°F/24°C) until doubled in size, 40 minutes to 1 hour.

5. On a lightly floured surface, turn out dough; fold dough 4 to 6 times to knock out air. Return dough to bowl; cover and refrigerate for at least 5 hours or up to 8 hours. (You can also do an overnight proof for a maximum of 12 hours. Make sure to place the dough in a large bowl, giving it room to grow.)

6. In a medium bowl, combine raisins and warm brandy; let soak for 20 minutes.

7. Line a rimmed baking sheet with parchment paper. Using a pastry brush, coat 6 (3-inch) copper soufflé molds* with melted butter, using vertical strokes up sides. Flour molds, shaking out excess. Place molds on prepared pan.

8. Turn out dough onto a heavily floured surface; lightly sprinkle top of dough with flour. Roll dough into a 16x10-inch rectangle. Using a small offset spatula, dot Frangipane onto dough; spread into an even layer, leaving a ½-inch border on one long side. Sprinkle soaked raisins onto Frangipane. Starting with opposite long side, roll dough into a 16-inch log. Gently shape log with hands to right length and more even thickness, if necessary. Using a serrated knife dipped in flour, cut log into 6 (2½-inch-thick) slices, trimming ends if necessary. Place rolls, cut side down, in prepared molds. Loosely cover and let rise in a warm, draft-free place (75°F/24°C) until dough springs back when touched, 20 to 35 minutes.

9. Preheat oven to 350°F (180°C).

10. In a small bowl, whisk together egg white and 1 tablespoon (15 grams) water. Using a pastry brush, brush top of rolls with egg wash; sprinkle with pearl sugar.

11. Bake until golden brown and an instant-read thermometer inserted in center

registers 190°F (88°C), 20 to 30 minutes. Let cool in molds for 5 minutes. Carefully remove from molds, and place on a wire rack.

12. In a small microwave-safe bowl, combine preserves and remaining 1 tablespoon (15 grams) water. Heat on high in 10-second intervals, stirring between each, until melted. Pour mixture through a fine-mesh sieve; discard solids. Using a pastry brush, glaze top of rolls with apricot mixture. Serve warm.

We used Mauviel M'Passion Mini Copper Soufflé Molds. This recipe also works in tall (2-inch-high) 8-ounce ramekins or jumbo muffin cups.

PRO TIP
Test the dough for proper gluten development. Pinch off (don't tear) a small piece of dough. Slowly pull dough out from center. If dough is ready, you will be able to stretch it until it's thin and translucent. If dough tears, it's not quite ready. Beat for 1 minute more, and test again.

FRANGIPANE

Makes 1⅓ cups

7   tablespoons (98 grams) unsalted butter, very softened
1   cup (96 grams) very finely ground almond flour
½   cup (100 grams) granulated sugar
1   large egg (50 grams)
2½   tablespoons (20 grams) all-purpose flour
¾   teaspoon (2.25 grams) kosher salt
¾   teaspoon (3 grams) almond extract

1. In a large bowl, whisk butter until creamy. Add almond flour and all remaining ingredients, whisking until well combined. Use immediately, or cover with a piece of plastic wrap, pressing wrap directly onto surface of paste to prevent a skin from forming. Refrigerate for up to 4 days. Microwave refrigerated Frangipane in 5-second intervals just until spreadable.

BRAIDED BLACK COCOA AND PEANUT BUTTER BRIOCHE

Makes 1 (10-inch) loaf

This bread ring combines creamy peanut butter and rich black cocoa into one elegant braid. Our visual tutorial below shows how to make this dramatic two-toned twisted beauty.

1 cup (240 grams) warm whole milk (105°F/41°C to 110°F/43°C)

2¼ teaspoons (7 grams) active dry yeast

2 large eggs (100 grams)

½ cup (113 grams) plus 3 tablespoons (42 grams) unsalted butter, melted and divided

4 teaspoons (16 grams) vanilla extract, divided

4¾ cups (594 grams) all-purpose flour

¼ cup (50 grams) granulated sugar

1 tablespoon (9 grams) kosher salt

¾ cup (90 grams) plus ⅔ cup (80 grams) confectioners' sugar, divided

⅔ cup (170 grams) creamy peanut butter

½ cup (113 grams) unsalted butter, softened

½ cup (85 grams) chopped bittersweet chocolate, melted

⅓ cup (25 grams) black cocoa powder

1 large egg white (30 grams)

1 tablespoon (15 grams) water

1. In the bowl of a stand mixer fitted with the paddle attachment, stir together warm milk and yeast. Let stand until mixture is foamy, about 5 minutes.

2. Add eggs, ½ cup (113 grams) melted butter, and 2 teaspoons (8 grams) vanilla to yeast mixture. Add flour, granulated sugar, and salt; beat at low speed until well combined, about 1 minute. Switch to the dough hook attachment, and beat at low speed until smooth, about 4 minutes. Turn out dough onto a lightly floured surface, and shape into a smooth round.

3. Spray a large bowl with cooking spray. Place dough in bowl, turning to grease top. Cover and let rise in a warm, draft-free place (75°F/24°C) until doubled in size, about 1 hour.

4. In the bowl of a stand mixer fitted with the paddle attachment, beat ⅔ cup (80 grams) confectioners' sugar, peanut butter, 1 teaspoon (4 grams) vanilla, and remaining 3 tablespoons (42 grams) melted butter at medium speed until smooth. Transfer peanut butter filling to a small bowl; set aside.

5. Clean bowl of stand mixer and paddle attachment. Using the paddle attachment, beat softened butter, melted chocolate, black cocoa, remaining ¾ cup (90 grams) confectioners' sugar, and remaining 1 teaspoon (4 grams) vanilla at medium speed until smooth. Set aside.

6. Punch down dough, and turn out onto a lightly floured surface. Divide dough in half (about 555 grams each). Roll half of dough into a 20x9-inch rectangle. (Keep remaining half covered to prevent it from

drying out.) Spread peanut butter filling onto dough, leaving a ½-inch border on one long side. Starting on opposite long side, roll up dough, jelly roll style; pinch seam to seal. Set aside, placing seam side down. Repeat with remaining dough and chocolate filling. Using a bench scraper, cut each roll in half lengthwise, leaving 1 inch intact at top. Place cut side up, and carefully twist dough pieces around each other.

7. Spray a 10-inch removable-bottom tube pan with cooking spray. Gently lift and place dough in prepared pan, circling tube and tucking ends under. Cover and let rise in a warm, draft-free place (75°F/24°C) until puffed, about 30 minutes.

8. Preheat oven to 350°F (180°C).

9. In a small bowl, whisk together egg white and 1 tablespoon (15 grams) water. Brush top of dough with egg wash (peanut butter pieces first and then chocolate to keep from messing up top).

10. Bake until top is golden and an instant-read thermometer inserted near center registers 190°F (88°C), 50 to 55 minutes, covering with foil halfway through baking to prevent excess browning. Let cool in pan for 15 minutes. Remove from pan, and let cool completely on a wire rack.

1. Using a bench scraper, cut your chocolate-and peanut butter-filled rolls in half lengthwise, leaving 1 inch of each roll intact at top.

2. Place rolls cut side up, and carefully twist dough pieces around each other, making sure the split pieces are firmly sandwiched together and not gapping open.

3. Gently lift and place dough in prepared pan, circling tube and tucking ends under to form a neat round.

CHEDDAR-SAUSAGE PULL-APART BREAD

Makes 1 (10-inch) loaf

Breakfast sausage and pockets of melted Cheddar make this savory round the unquestionable star of the breakfast table. With flaky pull-apart layers that are perfect for sharing, this is the recipe your weekend brunch has been waiting for.

1	cup (240 grams) warm whole milk (105°F/41°C to 110°F/43°C)
1½	tablespoons (14 grams) active dry yeast
4	large eggs (200 grams)
½	cup (113 grams) plus 6 tablespoons (84 grams) unsalted butter, melted and divided
5¾	cups (719 grams) all-purpose flour
¼	cup (50 grams) granulated sugar
1	tablespoon (9 grams) kosher salt
1	teaspoon (6 grams) garlic salt
2	cups (225 grams) coarsely grated sharp Cheddar cheese
¼	cup (8 grams) chopped fresh chives
1	(16-ounce) package (455 grams) hot breakfast sausage, cooked and drained

Garnish: flaked sea salt

1. In the bowl of a stand mixer fitted with the paddle attachment, stir together warm milk and yeast. Let stand until mixture is foamy, about 5 minutes.

2. Add eggs and ½ cup (113 grams) melted butter to yeast mixture. Add flour, sugar, kosher salt, and garlic salt; beat at low speed until well combined, about 1 minute. Switch to the dough hook attachment, and beat at low speed until smooth, about 8 minutes. Turn out dough onto a lightly floured surface, and shape into a smooth round.

3. Spray a large bowl with cooking spray. Place dough in bowl, turning to grease top. Cover and let rise in a warm, draft-free place (75°F/24°C) until doubled in size, about 45 minutes.

4. Punch down dough, and turn out onto a lightly floured surface. Divide dough in half (about 670 grams each). Roll half of dough into an 18x12-inch rectangle. (Keep remaining half of dough covered with plastic wrap to prevent it from drying out.) Brush dough with 2 tablespoons (28 grams) melted butter, and sprinkle with half of cheese, half of chives, and half of cooked sausage. Cut into 24 (3-inch) squares. Stack squares on top of each other into 6 equal stacks. Repeat with remaining dough, 2 tablespoons (28 grams) melted butter, remaining cheese, remaining chives, and remaining sausage.

5. Spray a 10-inch removable-bottom tube pan with cooking spray. Place dough stacks horizontally around tube. (Don't be afraid to pack dough tightly.) Cover and let rise in a warm, draft-free place (75°F/24°C) until puffed, about 20 minutes.

6. Preheat oven to 350°F (180°C).

7. Bake until top is golden and an instant-read thermometer inserted near center registers 190°F (88°C), 50 to 55 minutes, covering with foil halfway through baking to prevent excess browning. Brush with remaining 2 tablespoons (28 grams) melted butter. Sprinkle with sea salt, if desired. Let cool in pan for 15 minutes. Serve warm, or let cool completely on a wire rack.

PEANUT BUTTER-CHOCOLATE BABKAS

Makes 12 rolls

These dreamy baby babkas are filled with creamy peanut butter and melted pieces of chocolate, so you can twist and bake them up for breakfast or dessert. The best part? Shaping them is a breeze. You may never go back to the traditional braided loaf again.

4½   cups (563 grams) all-purpose flour, divided
½   cup (100 grams) granulated sugar
1   (0.25-ounce) package (7 grams) instant yeast*
1½   teaspoons (4.5 grams) kosher salt
1   cup (240 grams) plus 1 tablespoon (15 grams) water, divided
½   cup (113 grams) plus 1 tablespoon (14 grams) unsalted butter, melted and divided
2   large eggs (100 grams), room temperature and divided
1   large egg yolk (19 grams), room temperature
1   cup (256 grams) creamy peanut butter
¼   cup (30 grams) confectioners' sugar
1   teaspoon (4 grams) vanilla extract
⅓   cup (57 grams) chopped 60% cacao bittersweet chocolate

1. In the bowl of a stand mixer fitted with the paddle attachment, stir together 4 cups (500 grams) flour, granulated sugar, yeast, and salt by hand.
2. In a small saucepan, heat 1 cup (240 grams) water and ½ cup (113 grams) melted butter over medium heat until an instant-read thermometer registers 120°F (49°C) to 130°F (54°F). Add water mixture to flour mixture, and beat at medium speed for 2 minutes. Add 1 egg (50 grams) and egg yolk, and beat for 2 minutes. Beat in enough remaining ½ cup (63 grams) flour until a soft dough forms. (Dough will be sticky.)
3. Switch to the dough hook attachment. Beat at low speed until dough is smooth and elastic, 6 to 8 minutes. Shape dough into a smooth ball.
4. Lightly oil a large bowl. Place in bowl, turning to grease top. Cover and let rise in a warm, draft-free place (75°F/24°C) until doubled in size, about 45 minutes.
5. Butter a 12-cup muffin pan.
6. In a small bowl, stir together peanut butter, confectioners' sugar, vanilla, and remaining 1 tablespoon (14 grams) melted butter.

7. Lightly punch down dough. On a lightly floured surface, roll dough into a 20x12-inch rectangle. Spread peanut butter mixture onto dough. Sprinkle with chocolate. Fold rectangle crosswise into thirds, forming a smaller rectangle, about 12x6½ inches. Cut rectangle crosswise into 12 (about 1-inch-wide) strips. Gently stretch and twist each strip; coil 1 strip into each prepared muffin cup, tucking end inside edge of cup to create a rounded top. Cover and let rise in a warm, draft-free place (75°F/24°C) until puffed, about 30 minutes.
8. Preheat oven to 325°F (170°C).
9. In a small bowl, whisk together remaining 1 egg (50 grams) and remaining 1 tablespoon (15 grams) water. Brush top of dough with egg wash.
10. Bake until golden brown and an instant-read thermometer inserted in center registers 190°F (88°C), 15 to 20 minutes. Serve warm.

We used Red Star® Quick Rise Yeast.

COCONUT-ALMOND TWISTS

Makes 12 twists

Starring the always delicious flavor pairing of tropical coconut and nutty almonds, these beautiful breads are a new twist—literally—on an old favorite.

4¼ to 4½ cups (531 to 563 grams) all-purpose flour, divided
⅓ cup (67 grams) granulated sugar
1 (0.25-ounce) package (7 grams) active dry yeast
2 teaspoons (6 grams) kosher salt
1¼ cups (300 grams) plus 1 tablespoon (15 grams) whole milk, divided
½ cup (113 grams) unsalted butter, softened
2 large eggs (100 grams), divided
Coconut-Almond Filling (recipe follows)
Garnish: coarsely chopped sliced almonds

1. In the bowl of a stand mixer fitted with the paddle attachment, combine 1½ cups (188 grams) flour, sugar, yeast, and salt.
2. In a medium saucepan, heat 1¼ cups (300 grams) milk and butter over medium heat until an instant-read thermometer registers 120°F (49°C) to 130°F (54°C). Add warm milk mixture to flour mixture, and beat at medium speed for 2 minutes. Add 1 egg (50 grams), and beat at medium-high speed for 2 minutes. With mixer on low speed, gradually add 2¾ cups (344 grams) flour, beating just until combined and stopping to scrape sides of bowl.
3. Switch to the dough hook attachment. Beat at medium speed until a soft, somewhat sticky dough forms, 6 to 8 minutes, stopping to scrape dough hook and sides of bowl. Add up to remaining ¼ cup (31 grams) flour, 1 tablespoon (8 grams) at a time, if necessary. (Dough should pass the windowpane test [see PRO TIP on page 170] but may still stick slightly to sides of bowl.)
4. Lightly oil a large bowl. Place dough in bowl, turning to grease top. Cover and let rise in a warm, draft-free place (75°F/24°C) until doubled in size, 40 minutes to 1 hour. (See Make Ahead tip on page 170 for make-ahead method.)
5. Line 2 baking sheets with parchment paper.
6. Lightly punch down dough. Cover and let stand for 5 minutes. Turn out dough onto a lightly floured surface, and divide in half (about 536 grams each). Roll each half into a 12-inch square. Cut each square into 6 (6x4-inch) rectangles. Spread about 1 tablespoon (about 20 grams) Coconut-Almond Filling onto each rectangle. Starting from one long side, roll up rectangles, jelly roll style; pinch seam to seal. Using a serrated knife dipped in flour, cut each log in half lengthwise, leaving ½ inch at top intact. Carefully twist dough pieces around each other, pinching ends to seal. Place 6 buns on each prepared pan. Cover and let rise in a warm, draft-free place (75°F/24°C) until doubled in size, 30 to 45 minutes.
7. Preheat oven to 375°F (190°C).
8. In a small bowl, whisk together remaining 1 egg (50 grams) and remaining 1 tablespoon (15 grams) milk. Brush egg wash onto buns. Top with almonds, if desired, pressing some into filling.
9. Bake until golden brown and an instant-read thermometer inserted in center registers 190°F (88°C), about 15 minutes. Let cool completely on pan.

COCONUT-ALMOND FILLING
Makes about 1¼ cups

¾ cup (60 grams) unsweetened desiccated coconut*
½ cup (100 grams) granulated sugar
¼ cup (24 grams) superfine almond flour
¼ cup (57 grams) unsalted butter, very softened
1 large egg (50 grams)
¼ cup (31 grams) all-purpose flour
¾ teaspoon (2.25 grams) kosher salt
⅛ teaspoon almond extract

1. In a small bowl, stir together all ingredients until smooth. Use immediately, or refrigerate until ready to use.

Desiccated coconut is unsweetened, very finely ground coconut with most of the moisture removed. If your local grocery store doesn't carry it, check specialty food stores or online.

PRO TIP
There are two ways to bloom active dry yeast. The first is by dissolving it in lukewarm milk or water and sugar. In this recipe, we use the second method of blooming the yeast using a stand mixer. This is completed at the beginning of step 2.

DRIED HERB CIABATTA

Makes 2 loaves

If you know in advance that you want to make this herbaceous ciabatta, get your Poolish ready the day before. We used dried basil, oregano, parsley, and rosemary, but you can load this dough up with whichever dried herbs you prefer or have on hand. If you don't have bread flour, all-purpose flour will also work, though it will make the bread less chewy.

Poolish (recipe follows)
1   cup (240 grams) water (60°F/16°C)
2   tablespoons (28 grams) olive oil
½   teaspoon (1.5 grams) instant yeast*
¾   teaspoon dried basil
¾   teaspoon dried oregano
¾   teaspoon dried parsley
½   teaspoon dried rosemary
2½ cups (318 grams) bread flour
½   cup (62 grams) white whole wheat flour
1   tablespoon (9 grams) kosher salt

1. In the bowl of a stand mixer fitted with the paddle attachment, place Poolish. Add 1 cup (240 grams) water, oil, yeast, basil, oregano, parsley, and rosemary. Add flours and salt, and beat at low speed for 4 minutes. Increase mixer speed to medium, and beat for 5 to 6 minutes. (To test if dough is mixed enough, dust a small section of dough with flour. Pinch off a small portion, and slowly stretch to form a thin, translucent sheet. If dough tears, the dough is not ready. Beat for 1 minute more, test again.) Turn out dough onto a heavily floured surface, and shape into a round.
2. Oil a large bowl. Place dough in bowl. Cover with plastic wrap, and let rise in a warm, draft-free place (75°F/24°C) for 2½ hours, folding dough in bowl every 30 minutes. (To fold, use a floured hand to reach under one side of dough, and pull gently over center; repeat with opposite side of dough.)
3. Place 2 (16x12-inch) sheets of parchment paper on a work surface, and generously dust with flour. On a lightly floured surface, turn out dough, and shape roughly into a 14x10½-inch

rectangle; dimple surface with fingertips. Using a bench scraper, cut dough in half lengthwise; transfer halves to prepared parchment sheets.
4. Gently stretch each portion of dough into a 15½x5-inch rectangle. Dimple surface again with fingertips. Cover with plastic wrap, and let rise for 1 hour.
5. Preheat oven to 425°F (220°C). Line 2 baking sheets with parchment paper.
6. Quickly turn out each portion of dough onto a prepared pan.
7. Bake until golden and an instant-read thermometer inserted in center registers 205°F (96°C), 12 to 15 minutes. Let cool completely on wire racks.

We used Platinum® Yeast from Red Star®.

POOLISH
Makes 4 cups

1¼ cups plus 2½ tablespoons (179 grams) bread flour
2   tablespoons (14 grams) white whole wheat flour*
¹⁄₁₆ teaspoon instant yeast
¾   cup plus 1 tablespoon (195 grams) water (70°F/21°C)

1. In a medium bowl, stir together flours, yeast, and ¾ cup plus 1 tablespoon (195 grams) water until dry ingredients are completely moistened. Cover with plastic wrap, and let stand at room temperature for 14 to 16 hours.

If you do not have white whole wheat flour on hand, the same amount of bread flour or regular whole wheat flour can be used instead.

PRO TIP
Because the Poolish is a 100% hydration starter (meaning it's fed with water and flour in equal measurements), the ciabatta dough will be wet and sticky. Don't be alarmed—this is what gives the bread its signature chewy, open crumb.

RAISIN BREAD

Makes 2 (8½x4½-inch) loaves

The unexpectedly sweet bookends to the classic Bermuda fish sandwich, this enriched dough is brimming with rum-soaked raisins and flavored with a pinch of cinnamon. The best part about this bread is that you don't need fried snapper and all the fixings to enjoy it. It's just as delicious on its own. For even more visual appeal, we added a distinctive raisin-filled swirl to our version of the bread.

1⅓   cups (320 grams) warm whole milk (105°F/41°C to
      110°F/43°C)
4   teaspoons (12 grams) active dry yeast
⅔   cup (133 grams) plus 4½ teaspoons (18 grams) granulated
      sugar, divided
6   cups (762 grams) bread flour
3   large eggs (150 grams), divided
2   teaspoons (6 grams) kosher salt
½   cup (113 grams) plus 1 tablespoon (14 grams) unsalted
      butter, softened and divided
1   cup (167 grams) raisins
½   cup (120 grams) spiced rum
½   teaspoon (1 gram) ground cinnamon
1   tablespoon (15 grams) whole milk, room temperature

1. In the bowl of a stand mixer fitted with the dough hook attachment, whisk together warm milk, yeast, and 3 teaspoons (12 grams) sugar by hand. Let stand until mixture is foamy, about 10 minutes.

2. Add flour, ⅔ cup (133 grams) sugar, 2 eggs (100 grams), and salt to yeast mixture, and beat at medium speed for 5 minutes. Add ½ cup (113 grams) butter, 1 tablespoon (14 grams) at a time, beating for 8 to 10 minutes. Test dough using the windowpane test. (See PRO TIP.) If dough is not ready, beat for 1 minute more, and test again.

3. Spray a large bowl with cooking spray. Place dough in bowl, turning to grease top. Cover and let rise in a warm, draft-free place (75°F/24°C) until doubled in size, about 1 hour.

4. In a small bowl, toss together raisins and rum. Cover and let stand while dough is rising. Drain excess liquid before using.

5. Lightly spray 2 (8½x4½-inch) loaf pans with cooking spray; line pans with parchment paper, letting excess extend over sides of pan.

6. In a small bowl, stir together cinnamon and remaining 1½ teaspoons (6 grams) sugar.

7. Punch down dough, and divide in half. On a lightly floured surface, roll half of dough into a 14x6-inch rectangle. Brush with ½ tablespoon (7 grams) butter, leaving a ¼-inch border. Sprinkle with half of cinnamon-sugar mixture; top with half of plumped raisins. Starting at one short side, roll up dough, jelly roll style. Place in a prepared pan, seam side down. Repeat with remaining dough, remaining ½ tablespoon (7 grams) butter, remaining cinnamon-sugar mixture, and remaining raisins. Cover and let rise in a warm, draft-free place (75°F/24°C) until doubled in size, 30 to 40 minutes.

8. Preheat oven to 350°F (180°C).

9. In a small bowl, whisk together room temperature milk and remaining 1 egg (50 grams). Brush dough with egg wash.

10. Bake for 30 minutes. Loosely cover with foil, and bake until an instant-read thermometer inserted in center registers 190°F (88°C), 10 to 15 minutes more. Using excess parchment as handles, remove from pans, and let cool completely on wire racks. Store in an airtight container for up to 1 week.

PRO TIP

Test the dough for proper gluten development by using the windowpane test. Pinch off (don't tear) a small piece of dough. Slowly pull the dough out from the center. If the dough is ready, you will be able to stretch it until it's thin and translucent like a windowpane. If the dough tears, it's not quite ready. Beat for 1 minute more, and test again.

PAIN DE MIE

Makes 1 (9x4-inch) Pullman loaf or 1 (8½x4½-inch) loaf

This sweet bread's soft texture and lack of chewy crust make it the go-to sandwich bread in France. The addition of crème fraîche gives our Pain de Mie an extra-moist crumb, so it's the ultimate vessel for croque monsieur. We like ours baked in a Pullman pan to follow the traditional method, but use a traditional loaf pan if you want a domed top. We got great results with both.

3   cups (375 grams) all-purpose flour
2   tablespoons (24 grams) granulated sugar
2½   teaspoons (7.5 grams) kosher salt
2¼   teaspoons (7 grams) instant yeast
½   cup (120 grams) crème fraîche
½   cup (120 grams) whole milk
1   large egg (50 grams), room temperature
2   tablespoons (28 grams) unsalted butter, melted
Vegetable oil, for greasing pan

1. In the bowl of a stand mixer fitted with the paddle attachment, combine flour, sugar, salt, and yeast.
2. In a medium microwave-safe bowl, combine crème fraîche and milk. Heat on high until an instant-read thermometer registers 100°F (38°C). Whisk in egg and melted butter.

3. With mixer on low speed, add crème fraîche mixture to flour mixture, beating just until combined, about 30 seconds. Switch to the dough hook attachment. Beat at low speed until dough is smooth and elastic and pulls away from sides and bottom of bowl, about 4 minutes. Shape dough into a smooth round.
4. Spray a medium bowl with cooking spray. Place dough in bowl, turning to grease top. Cover and let rise in a warm, draft-free place (75°F/24°C) until doubled in size, about 1 hour.
5. Turn out dough onto a lightly floured surface, and shape into an 8x7-inch rectangle. Fold top third of dough over center, pressing to seal; continue to fold over remaining third, pressing to seal. Fold end in slightly; tighten loaf by folding top third over center and rolling it up, pressing to seal. (The final length should be 9 inches.)
6. Lightly brush a Pullman pan or an 8½x4½-inch loaf pan with oil. Place dough in prepared pan, and gently press top of dough flat. (If made in loaf pan, you do not need to press flat.) Cover and let rise in a warm, draft-free place (75°F/24°C) until dough has risen ½ inch from top of pan, about 1 hour. (If using loaf pan, dough should rise ¾ inch over top of pan.)
7. Preheat oven to 375°F (190°C).
8. Bake until crust is golden and an instant-read thermometer inserted in center registers 200°F (93°C), about 40 minutes. (If made in a loaf pan, cover with foil halfway through baking.)

HAWAIIAN BUNS WITH HONEY CITRUS GLAZE

Makes 15 buns

There's little to improve upon in the traditional Hawaiian bun formula, but we found that orange juice and a sticky honey glaze act as delightful complements to the classic recipe.

2   tablespoons (30 grams) warm water (105°F/41°C to 110°F/43°C)
1   tablespoon (9 grams) active dry yeast
½   cup (120 grams) canned pineapple juice
⅓   cup (73 grams) firmly packed dark brown sugar
¼   cup (60 grams) fresh orange juice
¼   cup (57 grams) unsalted butter, melted
3   large eggs (150 grams), room temperature and divided
1   large egg yolk (19 grams)
2   teaspoons (6 grams) kosher salt
1   teaspoon (4 grams) vanilla extract
4   cups (500 grams) all-purpose flour
¼   cup (42 grams) finely ground potato flour
1   tablespoon (15 grams) water or whole milk, room temperature
¼   cup (85 grams) clover honey
1   tablespoon (14 grams) unsalted butter
1   teaspoon (3 grams) tightly packed orange zest

1. In the bowl of a stand mixer fitted with the paddle attachment, stir together 2 tablespoons (30 grams) warm water and yeast by hand. Let stand until foamy, about 10 minutes.
2. Add pineapple juice, brown sugar, orange juice, melted butter, 2 eggs (100 grams), egg yolk, salt, and vanilla to yeast mixture; beat at medium-low speed until well combined, 2 to 3 minutes, stopping to scrape sides of bowl.
3. In a large bowl, whisk together flours. With mixer on low speed, gradually add flour mixture to pineapple juice mixture, beating just until combined, stopping to scrape sides of bowl. (Dough will still be quite shaggy.) Increase mixer speed to medium; beat for 2 minutes, stopping to scrape sides of bowl. Switch to the dough hook attachment. Beat at medium-low speed until dough is smooth and elastic and passes the windowpane test (see PRO TIP), 5 to 8 minutes, stopping to scrape sides of bowl and dough hook. (Dough will still stick to sides of bowl.)
4. Oil a large bowl. Place dough in bowl, turning to grease top. Cover and let rise in a warm, draft-free place (75°F/24°C) until doubled in size, about 1 hour.
5. Lightly spray a 13x9-inch baking pan with cooking spray; line with parchment paper, letting excess extend over sides of pan.
6. Punch down dough; divide into 15 equal portions (about 65 grams each). Roll into balls, and place in prepared pan. Cover and let rise in a warm, draft-free place (75°F/24°C) until almost doubled in size, 45 minutes to 1 hour.
7. Preheat oven to 350°F (180°C).
8. In a small bowl, whisk together 1 tablespoon (15 grams) water or milk and remaining 1 egg (50 grams); gently brush rolls with egg wash.
9. Bake until golden brown, 20 to 25 minutes.
10. In a small microwave-safe bowl, combine honey, butter, and orange zest. Heat on high in 10-second intervals until butter is melted. Stir and strain honey mixture. Brush rolls with glaze.

Note: *When kneading this dough, keep an eye on your mixer. Some models may "walk" off your countertop if not kept under close watch.*

PRO TIP

Test the dough for proper gluten development using the windowpane test. Pinch off (don't tear) a small piece of dough. Slowly pull the dough out from the center. If the dough is ready, you will be able to stretch it until it's thin and translucent like a windowpane. If the dough tears, it's not quite ready.

DOUBLE-VANILLA CREAM CHEESE BRAID

Makes 1 loaf

Below this bread's braid is a decadent cream cheese filling loaded with vanilla sugar and paste.

¾ cup (180 grams) warm whole milk (105°F/41°C to 110°F/43°C)
2¼ teaspoons (7 grams) active dry yeast
1 large egg (50 grams), room temperature
3 tablespoons (42 grams) unsalted butter, melted
1 tablespoon (18 grams) vanilla bean paste
2 teaspoons (8 grams) vanilla extract
3 cups (381 grams) bread flour
3 tablespoons (36 grams) granulated sugar
1 teaspoon (3 grams) kosher salt
Vanilla Cream Cheese Filling (recipe follows)
1 large egg white (30 grams)
1 tablespoon (15 grams) water
3 tablespoons (36 grams) vanilla sugar
Vanilla Glaze (recipe follows)

1. In the bowl of a stand mixer fitted with the paddle attachment, stir together warm milk and yeast by hand. Let stand until mixture is foamy, about 5 minutes.
2. Add egg, melted butter, vanilla bean paste, and vanilla extract to yeast mixture, stirring to combine.
3. In a medium bowl, stir together flour, granulated sugar, and salt. Add half of flour mixture to yeast mixture, and beat at low speed until combined, about 30 seconds. Add remaining flour mixture, and beat until combined, about 30 seconds. Switch to the dough hook attachment. Beat at low speed until dough is smooth and elastic and pulls away from sides and bottom of bowl, about 4 minutes. Turn out dough onto a lightly floured surface, and shape into a smooth round.
4. Spray a medium bowl with cooking spray. Place dough in bowl, turning to grease top. Cover and let rise in a warm, draft-free place (75°F/24°C) until doubled in size, about 1 hour.
5. Punch down dough, and turn out onto a lightly floured surface. Roll into a 15x10-inch oval, and place on a sheet of parchment paper. Spread Vanilla Cream Cheese Filling down center third of dough, leaving a 2-inch border at top and bottom of dough. Cut 1-inch-wide strips along each side of

filling. At top and bottom, trim ends to width of filling, and fold over filling. Starting on left side, fold top strip over filling, ending just below opposite top strip. Repeat with top strip on right side. Continue pattern, alternating left and right, until you reach end of strips. Tuck and pinch last strip. Transfer parchment and dough to a baking sheet. Cover and let rise in a warm, draft-free place (75°F/24°C) until puffed, about 45 minutes.
6. Preheat oven to 350°F (180°C).
7. In a small bowl, whisk together egg white and 1 tablespoon (15 grams) water. Brush top and sides of dough with egg wash. Sprinkle with vanilla sugar.
8. Bake until golden brown and an instant-read thermometer inserted in center registers 190°F (88°C), 20 to 25 minutes. Drizzle with Vanilla Glaze. Serve warm or at room temperature.

VANILLA CREAM CHEESE FILLING
Makes about 1 cup

½ cup (112 grams) cream cheese, softened
¼ cup (50 grams) vanilla sugar
¼ cup (30 grams) confectioners' sugar
1 large egg yolk (19 grams)
1 tablespoon (8 grams) all-purpose flour
½ tablespoon (9 grams) vanilla bean paste
½ teaspoon (2 grams) vanilla extract
¼ teaspoon kosher salt

1. In the bowl of a stand mixer fitted with the paddle attachment, beat cream cheese at medium speed until smooth. Add sugars and all remaining ingredients, and beat until smooth. Use immediately.

VANILLA GLAZE
Makes ½ cup

1 cup (120 grams) confectioners' sugar
2 tablespoons (30 grams) whole milk
½ teaspoon (2 grams) vanilla extract

1. In a small bowl, whisk together all ingredients until smooth. Use immediately.

CHEDDAR JALAPEÑO SOURDOUGH BOULE

Makes 1 round boule

Spicy and cheesy, this Cheddar- and jalapeño-packed boule takes the satisfying flavor of sourdough one step further.

Leaven:
⅓ cup (80 grams) lukewarm water (80°F/27°C)
1 tablespoon (16 grams) sourdough starter (see How to Start Your Sourdough Starter on page 167)
¼ cup plus 1 tablespoon (40 grams) bread flour
¼ cup plus 1 tablespoon (40 grams) whole wheat flour

Dough:
1 cup plus 3 tablespoons (285 grams) lukewarm water (80°F/27°C)
2¾ cups plus 1 tablespoon (357 grams) bread flour
1¼ cups (171 grams) (¼-inch) cubed sharp Cheddar cheese
¾ cup (94 grams) whole wheat flour
2 tablespoons (18 grams) diced seeded jalapeño
1 tablespoon (9 grams) kosher salt

1. For leaven: In a large bowl, stir together ⅓ cup (80 grams) lukewarm water and sourdough starter. Add flours, and stir thoroughly until smooth and no dry bits of flour remain. Loosely cover bowl, and let stand at room temperature overnight.
2. For dough: In the bowl of a stand mixer fitted with the dough hook attachment, place leaven and 1 cup plus 3 tablespoons (285 grams) lukewarm water. Add bread flour, cheese, whole wheat flour, jalapeño, and salt, and beat at low speed for 4 minutes. Dough will come together and should not tear when pulled.
3. Lightly oil a large bowl. Place dough in bowl. Cover and let rise in a warm, draft-free place (75°F/24°C) until dough feels smooth and soft, 2 to 2½ hours, turning every 30 minutes. (To complete a turn, grab underside of dough, stretch it up, and fold it to center of dough. Do this 4 times around the bowl.)
4. Turn out dough onto a lightly floured surface. Gently press dough flat into a 9-inch circle. Fold right third of dough over to center; fold left third over first fold. Cover with a kitchen towel, and let stand for 20 to 30 minutes.
5. For final shape, press dough flat again. Grab bottom edge, and gently stretch and fold bottom third over to center. Stretch right side out, and fold right third over to center; repeat with left side. Finish by folding top third over previous folds. Roll loaf away from you, and using both hands, cup dough and pull it toward you to seal. Turn dough 90 degrees, and pull again until a tight, smooth boule forms. Place, seam side up, in a banneton (proofing basket) or a small bowl lined with a kitchen towel heavily dusted with bread flour. Loosely cover dough with towel, and let rise for 3 hours. (Alternatively, place in refrigerator to cold-ferment overnight. Let stand at room temperature for 1 hour before baking.)
6. When dough has 30 minutes left to rise, place a Dutch oven and lid in cold oven. Preheat oven to 500°F (260°C).
7. Turn out boule onto a sheet of parchment paper dusted with flour. Dust top of boule lightly with flour. Using a lame or razor blade, score top of loaf. Carefully remove hot Dutch oven from oven; remove lid, and place boule, still on parchment paper, in Dutch oven. Cover with lid, and place back in oven.
8. Immediately reduce oven temperature to 425°F (220°C). Bake for 30 minutes. Remove lid, and bake until deep golden brown and an instant-read thermometer inserted in center registers 205°F (96°C), 10 to 15 minutes more. Immediately remove loaf from Dutch oven, and let cool completely on a wire rack.

CHOCOLATE CHERRY SOURDOUGH BOULE

Makes 1 round boule

Dark chocolate and tart dried cherries are folded into our traditional sourodugh boule to give it a bittersweet twist.

Leaven:
⅓ cup (80 grams) lukewarm water (80°F/27°C)
1 tablespoon (16 grams) sourdough starter (see How to Start Your Sourdough Stater on page 167)
¼ cup plus 1 tablespoon (40 grams) bread flour
¼ cup plus 1 tablespoon (40 grams) whole wheat flour

Dough:
1 cup plus 3 tablespoons (285 grams) lukewarm water (80°F/27°C)
2¾ cups plus 1 tablespoon (357 grams) bread flour
¾ cup (94 grams) whole wheat flour
⅔ cup (113 grams) chopped 60% cacao dark chocolate
½ cup (80 grams) dried cherries
1 tablespoon (9 grams) kosher salt

1. For leaven: In a large bowl, stir together ⅓ cup (80 grams) lukewarm water and sourdough starter. Add flours, and stir thoroughly until smooth and no dry bits of flour remain. Loosely cover bowl, and let stand at room temperature overnight.

2. For dough: In the bowl of a stand mixer fitted with the dough hook attachment, place leaven and 1 cup plus 3 tablespoons (285 grams) lukewarm water. Add flours, chocolate, cherries, and salt, and beat at low speed for 4 minutes. Dough will come together and should not tear when pulled.

3. Lightly oil a large bowl. Place dough in bowl. Cover and let rise in a warm, draft-free place (75°F/24°C) until dough feels smooth and soft, 2 to 2½ hours, turning every 30 minutes.

(To complete a turn, grab underside of dough, stretch it up, and fold it to center of dough. Do this 4 times around the bowl.)

4. Turn out dough onto a lightly floured surface. Gently press dough flat into a 9-inch circle. Fold right third of dough over to center; fold left third over first fold. Cover with a kitchen towel, and let stand for 20 to 30 minutes.

5. For final shape, press dough flat again. Grab bottom edge, and gently stretch and fold bottom third over to center. Stretch right side out, and fold right third over to center; repeat with left side. Finish by folding top third over previous folds. Roll loaf away from you, and using both hands, cup dough and pull it toward you to seal. Turn dough 90 degrees, and pull again until a tight, smooth boule forms. Place, seam side up, in a banneton (proofing basket) or a small bowl lined with a kitchen towel heavily dusted with bread flour. Loosely cover dough with towel, and let rise for 3 hours. (Alternatively, place in refrigerator to cold-ferment overnight. Let stand at room temperature for 1 hour before baking.)

6. When dough has 30 minutes left to rise, place a Dutch oven and lid in cold oven. Preheat oven to 500°F (260°C).

7. Turn out boule onto a sheet of parchment paper dusted with flour. Dust top of boule lightly with flour. Using a lame or razor blade, score top of loaf. Carefully remove hot Dutch oven from oven; remove lid, and place boule, still on parchment paper, in Dutch oven. Cover with lid, and place back in oven.

8. Immediately reduce oven temperature to 425°F (220°C). Bake for 30 minutes. Remove lid, and bake until deep golden brown and an instant-read thermometer inserted in center registers 205°F (96°C), 10 to 15 minutes more. Immediately remove loaf from Dutch oven, and let cool completely on a wire rack.

SOURDOUGH BOULE

Makes 1 round boule

Four simple ingredients combine with one highly cultured leaven to form the ideal sourdough: chewy crust, open crumb, and well-developed flavor. It's the baker's simplest triumph.

Leaven:

⅓ cup (80 grams) lukewarm water (80°F/27°C)
1   tablespoon (16 grams) sourdough starter (see How to Start Your Sourdough Starter below)
¼   cup plus 1 tablespoon (40 grams) bread flour
¼   cup plus 1 tablespoon (40 grams) whole wheat flour

Dough:

1   cup plus 3 tablespoons (285 grams) lukewarm water (80°F/27°C)
2¾ cups plus 1 tablespoon (357 grams) bread flour
¾   cup (94 grams) whole wheat flour
1   tablespoon (9 grams) kosher salt

1. For leaven: In a large bowl, stir together ⅓ cup (80 grams) lukewarm water and sourdough starter. Add flours, and stir thoroughly until smooth and no dry bits of flour remain. Loosely cover bowl, and let stand at room temperature overnight.

2. For dough: In the bowl of a stand mixer fitted with the dough hook attachment, place leaven and 1 cup plus 3 tablespoons (285 grams) lukewarm water. Add flours and salt, and beat at low speed for 4 minutes. Dough will come together and should not tear when pulled.

3. Lightly oil a large bowl. Place dough in bowl. Cover and let rise in a warm, draft-free place (75°F/24°C) until dough feels smooth and soft, 2 to 2½ hours, turning every 30 minutes. (To complete a turn, grab underside of dough, stretch it up, and fold it to center of dough. Do this 4 times around the bowl.)

4. Turn out dough onto a lightly floured surface. Gently press dough flat into a 9-inch circle. Fold right third of dough over to center; fold left third over first fold. Cover with a kitchen towel, and let stand for 20 to 30 minutes.

5. For final shape, press dough flat again. Grab bottom edge, and gently stretch and fold bottom third over to center. Stretch right side out, and fold right third over to center; repeat with left side. Finish by folding top third over previous folds. Roll loaf away from you, and using both hands, cup dough and pull it toward you to seal. Turn dough 90 degrees, and pull again until a tight, smooth boule forms. Place, seam side up, in a banneton (proofing basket) or a small bowl lined with a kitchen towel heavily dusted with bread flour. Loosely cover dough with towel, and let rise for 3 hours. (Alternatively, place in refrigerator to cold-ferment overnight. Let stand at room temperature for 1 hour before baking.)

6. When dough has 30 minutes left to rise, place a Dutch oven and lid in cold oven. Preheat oven to 500°F (260°C).

7. Turn out boule onto a sheet of parchment paper dusted with flour. Dust top of boule lightly with flour. Using a lame or razor blade, score top of loaf. Carefully remove hot Dutch oven from oven; remove lid, and place boule, still on parchment paper, in Dutch oven. Cover with lid, and place back in oven.

8. Immediately reduce oven temperature to 425°F (220°C). Bake for 25 minutes. Remove lid, and bake until deep golden brown and an instant-read thermometer inserted in center registers 205°F (96°C), 5 to 10 minutes more. Immediately remove loaf from Dutch oven, and let cool completely on a wire rack.

HOW TO START YOUR SOURDOUGH STARTER

DAY 1 | MIX: 180 grams room temperature water, 90 grams bread flour, and 90 grams whole wheat flour

REST: 48 to 72 hours at room temperature, loosely covered with lid or towel

DAY 3 | DISCARD: 180 grams (half) starter mixture

ADD: 180 grams room temperature water, 90 grams bread flour, and 90 grams whole wheat flour

REST: 24 hours at room temperature, loosely covered with lid or towel

NEXT 2 WEEKS | REPEAT: Every 24 hours, repeat process from day 3 (discarding half and replenishing with the 1:1:1 ratio) for 2 weeks, or until sourdough starter shows consistent activity and rises and falls.

PECAN STICKY BUNS

Makes 12 buns

From the cinnamon swirl in the center to the gooey pecan-studded caramel topping, these breakfast-ready sticky buns are the ultimate fall wake-up call.

6   cups (750 grams) all-purpose flour
⅓   cup (67 grams) granulated sugar
4½ teaspoons (14 grams) instant yeast
2¼ teaspoons (6 grams) kosher salt, divided
1¼ cups (300 grams) whole milk
1   cup (227 grams) unsalted butter, divided
2   teaspoons (8 grams) vanilla extract
2   large eggs (100 grams), lightly beaten
1½ cups (330 grams) firmly packed light brown sugar, divided
½   cup (170 grams) golden syrup
¼   cup (60 grams) heavy whipping cream
2   cups (284 grams) pecan halves*
1   tablespoon (6 grams) ground cinnamon
3   tablespoons (42 grams) unsalted butter, softened
¾   cup (85 grams) pecan pieces*

1. In the bowl of a stand mixer fitted with the paddle attachment, whisk together flour, granulated sugar, yeast, and 1½ teaspoons (4.5 grams) salt by hand.

2. In a small saucepan, heat milk, ½ cup (113.5 grams) butter, and vanilla over medium-low heat until an instant-read thermometer registers 120°F (49°C) to 130°F (54°C).

3. With mixer on low speed, slowly pour warm milk mixture into flour mixture, beating until combined, about 30 seconds. Add eggs, beating until combined. Switch to the dough hook attachment. Beat at low speed until dough is smooth and elastic, 5 to 6 minutes. Turn out dough onto a lightly floured surface, and shape into a smooth round.

4. Spray a large bowl with cooking spray. Place dough in bowl, turning to grease top. Loosely cover and let rise in a warm, draft-free place (75°F/24°C) until doubled in size, 30 to 45 minutes.

5. Spray a 13x9-inch baking pan with cooking spray.

6. In a medium saucepan, melt remaining ½ cup (113.5 grams) butter over medium heat. Add 1 cup (220 grams) brown sugar, golden syrup, cream, and ½ teaspoon (1.5 grams) salt; bring to a boil, stirring occasionally. Pour caramel into prepared pan; arrange pecan halves on top in a single layer. Let cool completely.

7. Lightly punch down dough. Turn out dough onto a lightly floured surface, and roll into an 18x14-inch rectangle.

8. In a small bowl, stir together cinnamon, remaining ½ cup (110 grams) brown sugar, and remaining ¼ teaspoon salt. Spread softened butter onto dough, and sprinkle with cinnamon-sugar mixture, leaving a ½-inch border on one long side. Top with pecan pieces. Starting with opposite long side, roll dough into a log; place log, seam side down, on work surface. Trim ends. Using a serrated knife, cut log into 12 (1½-inch) rolls. Place rolls on top of pecan halves in pan. Let rise in a warm, draft-free place (75°F/24°C) until puffed and rolls are touching, 30 to 45 minutes.

9. Preheat oven to 350°F (180°C).

10. Bake until golden brown and an instant-read thermometer inserted in center registers 190°F (88°C), 35 to 40 minutes. Let cool in pan for 5 minutes. Invert rolls onto a rimmed serving platter. If any pecan caramel remains in pan, spoon out, and place on top of rolls. Serve warm.

We used Sunnyland Farms Raw Georgia Pecan Halves and Pecan Pieces.

RUSSIAN RICOTTA BREAD

Makes 1 (10-inch) loaf

We reimagined the original bulochki, an Eastern European yeasted roll, as an oversize sweet roll baked in cast iron and topped with a generous drizzle of Meringue. With ricotta added to the dough, this giant roll boasts an extra-tender crumb that makes a delicious contrast to the crunchy Meringue swirl.

½	cup (120 grams) whole buttermilk
⅓	cup (76 grams) unsalted butter
4¼	cups (531 grams) all-purpose flour, divided
⅓	cup (67 grams) granulated sugar
1	tablespoon (9 grams) kosher salt
2¼	teaspoons (7 grams) instant yeast
1⅓	cups (300 grams) whole-milk ricotta cheese*, room temperature
2	large eggs (100 grams), divided
1	large egg yolk (19 grams)
1	tablespoon (15 grams) water
	Meringue (recipe follows)

1. In a small saucepan, heat buttermilk and butter over medium-low heat until butter is melted and an instant-read thermometer registers 120°F (49°C) to 130°F (54°C). Remove from heat; set aside.

2. In the bowl of a stand mixer fitted with the paddle attachment, whisk together 2 cups (250 grams) flour, sugar, salt, and yeast by hand. Add buttermilk mixture; beat at low speed until combined. Add ricotta, beating until combined. Add 1 egg (50 grams) and egg yolk, beating until combined. Add remaining 2¼ cups (281 grams) flour, and beat until a soft dough forms, about 30 seconds.

3. Switch to the dough hook attachment. Beat at low speed until dough is elastic and pulls away from sides and bottom of bowl, about 12 minutes. Turn out dough onto a lightly floured surface, and shape into a smooth round.

4. Spray a large bowl with cooking spray. Place dough in bowl, turning to grease top. Loosely cover and let rise in a warm, draft-free place (75°F/24°C) until almost doubled in size, 45 minutes to 1 hour. To test if dough is ready, make a dent in dough about 1 inch deep. If dough springs back fully, it is not ready. If dent remains and springs back only

a little bit, dough is properly proofed.

5. Oil a 10-inch enamel-coated cast-iron skillet.

6. Punch down dough well. Let stand for 5 minutes. Turn out dough onto a lightly floured surface, and shape into a 12-inch log. Roll dough to 40 inches long with slightly tapered ends. Roll dough into a spiral, tucking ends under. (It's OK if the spiral isn't super tight. The shape turns out better when it is kept flat instead of building it up.) Use hands to lift and place in prepared skillet. Cover and let rise in a warm, draft-free place (75°F/24°C) until puffed, 30 to 45 minutes.

7. Preheat oven to 350°F (180°C).

8. In a small bowl, whisk together 1 tablespoon (15 grams) water and remaining 1 egg (50 grams). Brush dough with egg wash. Pipe Meringue into grooves of spiral. (Not all Meringue will be used. It is OK to have about ¼ cup left after piping.)

9. Bake until golden brown and an instant-read thermometer inserted in center registers 190°F (88°C), 50 to 55 minutes, covering with foil after 30 minutes of baking to prevent excess browning, if necessary. Let cool for 15 minutes in pan. Serve warm or at room temperature.

*We used Polly-O Ricotta Cheese.

MERINGUE
Makes ⅔ cup

1	large egg white (30 grams), room temperature
½	cup (100 grams) granulated sugar

1. In a medium bowl, beat egg white with a mixer at medium speed; gradually add sugar, beating until glossy and thick and ribbons form. Use immediately.

GIANT BLUEBERRY BUN

Makes 10 to 12 servings

Meet your new brunch centerpiece, studded with blueberries and spiced with cinnamon and ginger.

4¼ to 4½ cups (531 to 563 grams) all-purpose flour, divided
⅓ cup (67 grams) granulated sugar
1   (0.25-ounce) package (7 grams) active dry yeast
2¼ teaspoons (6 grams) kosher salt, divided
1¼ cups (300 grams) whole milk
1   cup (227 grams) unsalted butter, softened and divided
1   large egg (50 grams)
¾   cup (165 grams) firmly packed light brown sugar
2   teaspoons (4 grams) ground cinnamon
½   teaspoon (1 gram) ground ginger
¾   cup (90 grams) fresh blueberries, divided
Berry Glaze (recipe follows)

1. In the bowl of a stand mixer fitted with the paddle attachment, combine 1½ cups (188 grams) flour, granulated sugar, yeast, and 2 teaspoons (6 grams) salt.
2. In a medium saucepan, heat milk and ½ cup (113.5 grams) butter over medium heat until an instant-read thermometer registers 120°F (49°C) to 130°F (54°C). Add warm milk mixture to flour mixture, and beat at medium speed for 2 minutes. Add egg, and beat at medium-high speed for 2 minutes. With mixer on low speed, gradually add 2¾ cups (344 grams) flour, beating just until combined and stopping to scrape sides of bowl.
3. Switch to the dough hook attachment. Beat at medium speed until a soft, somewhat sticky dough forms, 6 to 8 minutes, stopping to scrape sides of bowl and dough hook. Add up to remaining ¼ cup (31 grams) flour, 1 tablespoon (8 grams) at a time, if necessary. (Dough should pass the windowpane test [see PRO TIP] but may still stick slightly to sides of bowl.)
4. Lightly oil a large bowl. Place dough in bowl, turning to grease top. Cover and let rise in a warm, draft-free place (75°F/24°C) until doubled in size, 40 minutes to 1 hour. (See Make Ahead tip for make-ahead method.)
5. Spray a 9-inch springform pan with cooking spray; line bottom of pan with parchment paper.
6. In a medium bowl, stir together brown sugar, cinnamon, ginger, and remaining ¼ teaspoon salt.
7. Lightly punch down dough. Cover and let stand for 5 minutes. On a lightly floured surface, roll dough into a 12x10-inch rectangle. Using a small offset spatula, spread remaining ½ cup (113.5 grams) butter onto dough. Sprinkle with brown sugar mixture. (Layer will be thick.) Using a pizza cutter, cut dough into 4 (10x3-inch) strips. Scatter ½ cup (60 grams) blueberries over strips, lightly pressing into dough. Gently roll up 1 strip. Continue to roll each remaining strip around previous, creating a spiral. Secure end of outer layer with thin wooden picks, if necessary. Place bun

in prepared pan. (Bun will not completely fill pan at this point.) Gently tuck remaining ¼ cup (30 grams) blueberries into spiral as desired. Cover and let rise in a warm, draft-free place (75°F/24°C) until doubled in size, 30 to 45 minutes. Remove any wooden picks.
8. Line a rimmed baking sheet with foil, and place on bottom rack of oven to catch any drips. Preheat oven to 350°F (180°C).
9. Bake on center rack of oven for 15 minutes. Loosely cover with foil, and bake until golden brown and an instant-read thermometer inserted in center registers 190°F (88°C), about 1 hour more. Let cool in pan on a wire rack for 30 minutes. Remove from pan, and drizzle with Berry Glaze.

PRO TIP

Test the dough for proper gluten development by using the windowpane test. Pinch off (don't tear) a small piece of dough. Slowly pull the dough out from the center. If the dough is ready, you will be able to stretch it until it's thin and translucent like a windowpane. If the dough tears, it's not quite ready. Beat for 1 minute more, and test again. Test the dough for proper gluten development by using the windowpane test. Pinch off (don't tear) a small piece of dough. Slowly pull the dough out from the center. If the dough is ready, you will be able to stretch it until it's thin and translucent like a windowpane. If the dough tears, it's not quite ready. Beat for 1 minute more, and test again.

BERRY GLAZE

Makes about 1 cup

2   cups (240 grams) confectioners' sugar
3   tablespoons (45 grams) whole milk
1   tablespoon (20 grams) high-quality blueberry jam (see Note)

1. In a small bowl, stir together all ingredients until smooth. Use immediately.

Note: *We suggest Bonne Maman Wild Blueberry Preserves, available at specialty food stores or online. You can also use homemade Berry Jam (page 88).*

MAKE AHEAD

To make sweet bun dough ahead, follow recipe through step 4. Punch down dough, and place in a large resealable plastic bag; seal bag securely, and refrigerate overnight. To bake, prepare filling and shape as directed. Let rise, increasing proofing time by about 30 minutes, and then bake as directed.

STRAWBERRY-PISTACHIO SWEET BUNS

Makes 12 buns

Packing a filling with freeze-dried strawberries and chopped pistachios, these sweet buns pack a lot of fruity flavor. A tangy cream cheese drizzle offers an orthodox finish to very unorthodox buns.

4¼ to 4½ cups (531 to 563 grams) all-purpose flour, divided
¾ cup (150 grams) plus ⅓ cup (67 grams) granulated sugar, divided
1 (0.25-ounce) package (7 grams) active dry yeast
2¼ teaspoons (6 grams) kosher salt, divided
1¼ cups (300 grams) whole milk
1 cup (227 grams) unsalted butter, softened and divided
1 large egg (50 grams)
1 cup (16 grams) freeze-dried strawberries, coarsely crushed (see Note)
1⅓ cups (21 grams) freeze-dried strawberries, finely ground (see Note)
¼ teaspoon ground black pepper
¼ cup (28 grams) finely chopped roasted salted pistachios
Cream Cheese Glaze (recipe follows)
Garnish: crushed freeze-dried strawberries

1. In the bowl of a stand mixer fitted with the paddle attachment, combine 1½ cups (188 grams) flour, ⅓ cup (67 grams) sugar, yeast, and 2 teaspoons (6 grams) salt.
2. In a medium saucepan, heat milk and ½ cup (113.5 grams) butter over medium heat until an instant-read thermometer registers 120°F (49°C) to 130°F (54°C). Add warm milk mixture to flour mixture, and beat at medium speed for 2 minutes. Add egg, and beat at medium-high speed for 2 minutes. With mixer on low speed, gradually add 2¾ cups (344 grams) flour, beating just until combined and stopping to scrape sides of bowl.
3. Switch to the dough hook attachment. Beat at medium speed until a soft, somewhat sticky dough forms, about 5 minutes, stopping to scrape sides of bowl and dough hook. Add crushed strawberries, and beat until dough is smooth and elastic, 1 to 3 minutes, adding up to remaining ¼ cup (31 grams) flour, 1 tablespoon (8 grams) at

a time, if necessary. (Dough should pass the windowpane test [see PRO TIP] but may still stick slightly to sides of bowl.)
4. Lightly oil a large bowl. Place dough in bowl, turning to grease top. Cover and let rise in a warm, draft-free place (75°F/24°C) until doubled in size, 40 minutes to 1 hour. (See Make Ahead tip for make-ahead method.)
5. Spray a 13x9-inch baking pan with cooking spray. Line pan with parchment paper, letting excess extend over sides of pan.
6. In a small bowl, stir together ground strawberries, pepper, remaining ¾ cup (150 grams) sugar, remaining ½ cup (113.5 grams) butter, and remaining ¼ teaspoon salt until well combined.
7. Lightly punch down dough. Cover and let stand for 5 minutes. Turn out dough onto a lightly floured surface, and roll into an 18x12-inch rectangle. Using a small offset spatula, spread strawberry mixture onto dough, leaving a ½-inch border on one long side. Sprinkle with pistachios. Starting with opposite long side, roll up dough, jelly roll style; pinch seam to seal. Gently shape log to 18 inches long and even thickness, if necessary. Using a serrated knife dipped in flour, cut log into 12 slices (about 1½ inches thick). Place slices, cut side down, in prepared pan. Cover and let rise in a warm, draft-free place (75°F/24°C) until doubled in size, 30 to 45 minutes.
8. Preheat oven to 375°F (190°C).
9. Bake until lightly golden and an instant-read thermometer inserted in center registers 190°F (88°C), 25 to 30 minutes, loosely covering with foil to prevent excess browning, if necessary. Let cool in pan for 20 minutes. Using excess parchment as handles, remove from pan. Drizzle with Cream Cheese Glaze. Garnish with freeze-dried strawberries, if desired. Serve warm. Cover and store in refrigerator.

Note: *To crush whole freeze-dried strawberries, place in a large resealable plastic bag, and pound with a rolling pin. To grind whole freeze-dried strawberries, pulse in the work bowl of a food processor until ground to desired consistency.*

PRO TIP
Test the dough for proper gluten development by using the windowpane test. Pinch off (don't tear) a small piece of dough. Slowly pull the dough out from the center. If the dough is ready, you will be able to stretch it until it's thin and translucent like a windowpane. If the dough tears, it's not quite ready. Beat for 1 minute more, and test again.

CREAM CHEESE GLAZE
Makes ½ cup

3 ounces (86 grams) cream cheese, softened
⅔ cup (80 grams) confectioners' sugar
1 teaspoon (5 grams) whole milk
¼ teaspoon (1 gram) vanilla extract
⅛ teaspoon kosher salt

1. In a small bowl, stir together all ingredients until smooth. Spoon glaze into a small piping bag; cut a ¼-inch opening in tip. Use immediately.

MAKE AHEAD
To make sweet bun dough ahead, follow recipe through step 4. Punch down dough, and place in a large resealable plastic bag; seal bag securely, and refrigerate overnight. To bake, prepare filling and shape as directed. Let rise, increasing proofing time by about 30 minutes, and then bake as directed.

ORANGE SWEET BUNS

Makes 12 buns

A nod to the classic sweet bun recipe, these orange buns have the same sunny disposition, only with a new and improved crème fraîche glaze.

4¼ to 4½ cups (532 to 563 grams) all-purpose flour, divided
1⅓ cups (267 grams) granulated sugar, divided
1 (0.25-ounce) package (7 grams) active dry yeast
2 teaspoons (6 grams) kosher salt
1¼ cups (300 grams) whole milk
1 cup (227 grams) unsalted butter, softened and divided
1 large egg (50 grams)
2 tablespoons (24 grams) packed orange zest (about 2 large oranges)
¼ teaspoon ground cardamom
Orange-Crème Fraîche Glaze (recipe follows)
Garnish: orange zest

1. In the bowl of a stand mixer fitted with the paddle attachment, combine 1½ cups (188 grams) flour, ⅓ cup (67 grams) sugar, yeast, and salt.
2. In a medium saucepan, heat milk and ½ cup (113.5 grams) butter over medium heat until an instant-read thermometer registers 120°F (49°C) to 130°F (54°C). Add warm milk mixture to flour mixture, and beat at medium speed for 2 minutes. Add egg, and beat at medium-high speed for 2 minutes. With mixer on low speed, gradually add 2¾ cups (344 grams) flour, beating just until combined and stopping to scrape sides of bowl.
3. Switch to the dough hook attachment. Beat at medium speed until a soft, somewhat sticky dough forms, 6 to 8 minutes, stopping to scrape sides of bowl and dough hook. Add up to remaining ¼ cup (31 grams) flour, 1 tablespoon (8 grams) at a time, if necessary. (Dough should pass the windowpane test [see PRO TIP] but may still stick slightly to sides of bowl.)
4. Lightly oil a large bowl. Place dough in bowl, turning to grease top. Cover and let rise in a warm, draft-free place (75°F/24°C) until doubled in size, 40 minutes to 1 hour. (See Make Ahead tip for make-ahead method.)
5. Spray a 13x9-inch baking pan with cooking spray. Line pan with parchment paper, letting excess extend over sides of pan.
6. In a small bowl, stir together orange zest, cardamom, remaining 1 cup (200 grams) sugar, and remaining ½ cup (113.5 grams) butter until well combined.
7. Lightly punch down dough. Cover and let stand for 5 minutes. Turn out dough onto a lightly floured surface, and roll into an 18x12-inch rectangle. Using a small offset spatula, spread zest

mixture onto dough, leaving a ½-inch border on one long side. Starting with opposite long side, roll up dough, jelly roll style; pinch seam to seal. Gently shape log to 18 inches long and even thickness, if necessary. Using a serrated knife dipped in flour, cut log into 12 slices (about 1½ inches thick). Place slices, cut side down, in prepared pan. Cover and let rise in a warm, draft-free place (75°F/24°C) until doubled in size, 30 to 45 minutes.
8. Preheat oven to 375°F (190°C).
9. Bake until lightly golden and an instant-read thermometer inserted in center registers 190°F (88°C), 25 to 30 minutes, loosely covering with foil to prevent excess browning, if necessary. Let cool in pan for 20 minutes. Using excess parchment as handles, remove from pan. Using a small offset spatula, spread Orange-Crème Fraîche Glaze onto rolls. Garnish with zest, if desired. Serve warm.

PRO TIP
Test the dough for proper gluten development by using the windowpane test. Pinch off (don't tear) a small piece of dough. Slowly pull the dough out from the center. If the dough is ready, you will be able to stretch it until it's thin and translucent like a windowpane. If the dough tears, it's not quite ready. Beat for 1 minute more, and test again.

ORANGE-CRÈME FRAÎCHE GLAZE
Makes about 1 cup

1⅔ cups (200 grams) confectioners' sugar
⅔ cup (160 grams) cold crème fraîche
1 teaspoon (4 grams) packed orange zest
⅛ teaspoon kosher salt

1. In a small bowl, stir together all ingredients until smooth. Use immediately.

MAKE AHEAD
To make sweet bun dough ahead, follow recipe through step 4. Punch down dough, and place in a large resealable plastic bag; seal bag securely, and refrigerate overnight. To bake, prepare filling and shape as directed. Let rise, increasing proofing time by about 30 minutes, and then bake as directed.

SHORTCUT SOURDOUGH BOULE

Makes 1 oval boule

Sourdough without homemade sourdough starter sounds impossible, but this recipe and its revolutionary ingredient—Platinum Instant Sourdough Yeast from Red Star—guarantees it. With dried sourdough starter mixed with high-powered yeast, this sourdough boule skips the starter without missing any flavor. For a bit of variety, we swap our round Dutch oven and boule shape for a long oval.

4½ cups (572 grams) bread flour
1   (0.63-ounce) package (18 grams) instant sourdough yeast*
1   tablespoon (9 grams) kosher salt
1¾ cups (420 grams) warm water (105°F/41°C to 110°F/43°C)

1. In the bowl of a stand mixer fitted with the paddle attachment, combine flour, instant sourdough yeast, and salt. Add 1¾ cups (420 grams) warm water, and beat at medium-low speed until a sticky dough forms, about 30 seconds. Cover and let rise in a warm, draft-free place (75°F/24°C) for 2 hours. Refrigerate for at least 2 hours.

2. Line a sheet pan with parchment paper, and generously dust with bread flour.

3. Turn out dough onto a floured surface. Gently stretch and fold bottom third over to center. Stretch right side out, and fold right third over to center; repeat with left side. Finish by folding top third over previous folds. Roll loaf away from you, and using both hands, cup dough and pull it toward you to seal. Turn dough 180 degrees, and pull again until a tight,

smooth, oval boule forms. Place dough, seam side down, on prepared pan. Cover and let rise in a warm, draft-free place (75°F/24°C) for 1 hour. (Alternatively, place dough on prepared pan; cover and refrigerate overnight. The next day, remove dough from refrigerator, and let rise in a warm, draft-free place [75°F/24°C] for 1 hour.)

4. When dough has 30 minutes left to rise, place a 5- to 7-quart oval enamel-coated Dutch oven and lid in cold oven. Preheat oven to 500°F (260°C).

5. Using a lame or razor blade, score top of loaf. Carefully remove hot Dutch oven from oven; remove lid, and place dough, still on parchment, in Dutch oven. Cover with lid, and place back in oven.

6. Immediately reduce oven temperature to 425°F (220°C). Bake for 30 minutes. Remove lid, and bake until an instant-read thermometer inserted in center registers 205°F (96°C), 10 to 15 minutes more. Immediately remove loaf from Dutch oven, and let cool completely on a wire rack.

We used Platinum® Instant Sourdough Yeast from Red Star®.

SHEET PAN METHOD:

Although we prefer the Dutch oven method, this recipe can be baked on a sheet pan. To bake on a sheet pan, cover loaf with foil, and tightly seal foil around rim of pan. Bake at 425°F (220°C) for 30 minutes. Uncover and bake until an instant-read thermometer inserted in center registers 205°F (96°C), 10 to 15 minutes more.

TOMATO SOURDOUGH FOCACCIA

Make 1 (16x12-inch) loaf

With a chewy interior and an addictive caramelized crust adorned with fresh grape tomatoes, this rosemary-scented focaccia has all the tangy comfort of sourdough but without the hassle, thanks to Platinum Instant Sourdough Yeast from Red Star. A revolutionary blend of instant yeast, sourdough culture, and dough strengtheners, this new product from Red Star is changing the baking game—one dough at a time.

4   cups (500 grams) all-purpose flour
1   (0.63-ounce) package (18 grams) instant sourdough yeast*
2   teaspoons (6 grams) kosher salt
1½ cups (360 grams) warm water (120°F/49°C to 130°F/54°C)
5   tablespoons (70 grams) olive oil, divided
1½ cups (250 grams) grape tomatoes, halved
1   tablespoon (2 grams) chopped fresh rosemary
1   clove garlic (5 grams), minced
2   teaspoons (6 grams) flaked sea salt

1. In the bowl of a stand mixer fitted with the paddle attachment, stir together flour, instant sourdough yeast, and kosher salt by hand. Add 1½ cups (360 grams) warm water and 2 tablespoons (28 grams) oil, and beat at medium speed for 5 minutes.
2. Lightly oil a large bowl. Place dough in bowl, turning to grease top. Cover and let rise in a warm, draft-free place (75°F/24°C) until doubled in size, 45 minutes to 1 hour.
3. Grease a rimmed baking sheet with 2 tablespoons (28 grams) oil. Turn out dough onto prepared pan. With oiled fingers, gently press dough into a 10-inch circle. Loosely cover with plastic wrap, and let stand in a warm, draft-free place (75°F/24°C) for 30 minutes.
4. With oiled fingers, press dough into a 14x11-inch oval. Loosely cover with plastic wrap, and let rise in a warm, draft-free place (75°F/24°C) until puffed, 25 to 30 minutes.
5. Preheat oven to 425°F (220°C).
6. Gently press dimples into surface of dough. Drizzle with remaining 1 tablespoon (14 grams) oil. Top with tomatoes, rosemary, and garlic. Sprinkle with sea salt.
7. Bake until golden brown, 15 to 20 minutes. Let cool on pan for 10 minutes. Serve warm or at room temperature.

*We used Platinum® Instant Sourdough Yeast from Red Star®. Platinum Instant Sourdough Yeast can be substituted with 1 (0.25-ounce) package (7 grams) Platinum® Yeast from Red Star®. Increase bake time to 20 to 25 minutes.

BASIC BAGELS

Makes 12 bagels

Plain and perfect, these bagels are the ideal chewy canvases for your choice of toppings, a customizable bagel experience for those who want an assorted spread. But any way you top them, these ringed beauties are primed for lox, schmears, and plenty of butter.

7   cups (889 grams) bread flour
2   tablespoons (18 grams) kosher salt
1¾   teaspoons (5.25 grams) instant yeast
2⅓   cups (560 grams) warm water (120°F/49°C to 130°F/54°C)
½   cup (170 grams) plus 2 tablespoons (42 grams) barley malt syrup, divided
8   cups (1,920 grams) plus 1 tablespoon (15 grams) water, divided
1   large egg white (30 grams)
Toppings: everything bagel seasoning, sesame seeds, poppy seeds, freshly grated Asiago cheese

1. In the bowl of a stand mixer fitted with the paddle attachment, whisk together flour, salt, and yeast by hand. Add 2⅓ cups (560 grams) warm water and 2 tablespoons (42 grams) barley malt syrup, and beat at low speed until a shaggy dough forms, about 1 minute. Switch to the dough hook attachment. Beat at low speed until dough pulls away from sides and bottom of bowl, about 8 minutes. (Dough will be elastic but may not look completely smooth.) Turn out dough onto a lightly floured surface, and shape into a smooth ball.

2. Lightly oil a large bowl. Place dough in bowl, turning to grease top. Cover and let rise in a warm, draft-free place (75°F/24°C) until doubled in size, 45 minutes to 1 hour.

3. Place a large sheet of parchment paper in a warm, draft-free place (75°F/24°C); dust parchment with flour.

4. Divide dough into 12 portions (about 107 grams each). Shape each portion into a ball. Place 1 ball in your hand. Using your thumb and forefinger, pinch a hole in center of ball, and stretch hole to about 3 inches wide. Place on prepared parchment. Repeat with remaining dough. (Once dough contracts, the hole should be 1 to 1½ inches wide.) Cover and let rise until puffed, 15 to 30 minutes.

5. Preheat oven to 400°F (200°C). Line 2 sheet pans with parchment paper.

6. In a large stockpot, bring 8 cups (1,920 grams) water and remaining ½ cup (170 grams) barley malt syrup to a very low simmer over medium-low heat. (Do not boil.) Carefully drop bagels, 1 to 2 at a time, into pot. Cook for 10 seconds per side; immediately transfer to prepared pans.

7. In a small bowl, whisk together egg white and remaining 1 tablespoon (15 grams) water. Brush dough with egg wash, and sprinkle with desired toppings.

8. Bake until golden brown, 20 to 25 minutes. Let cool on pans for 10 minutes. Serve warm or at room temperature.

CHAI RAISIN BAGELS

Makes 12 bagels

Like the more familiar cinnamon raisin flavor, only with a richer, spicier chai twist. The secret to this bagel is that it lets the raisins bring the sweetness—no sugar added.

7	cups (889 grams) bread flour
⅔	cup (85 grams) raisins
2	tablespoons (18 grams) kosher salt
4	teaspoons (8 grams) chai spice
1¾	teaspoons (5.25 grams) instant yeast
2⅓	cups (560 grams) warm water (120°F/49°C to 130°F/54°C)
½	cup (170 grams) plus 2 tablespoons (42 grams) barley malt syrup, divided
8	cups (1,920 grams) plus 1 tablespoon (15 grams) water, divided
1	large egg white (30 grams)

1. In the bowl of a stand mixer fitted with the paddle attachment, whisk together flour, raisins, salt, chai spice, and yeast by hand. Add 2⅓ cups (560 grams) warm water and 2 tablespoons (42 grams) barley malt syrup, and beat at low speed until a shaggy dough forms, about 1 minute. Switch to the dough hook attachment. Beat at low speed until dough pulls away from sides and bottom of bowl, about 8 minutes. (Dough will be elastic but may not look completely smooth.) Turn out dough onto a lightly floured surface, and shape into a smooth ball.

2. Lightly oil a large bowl. Place dough in bowl, turning to grease top. Cover and let rise in a warm, draft-free place (75°F/24°C) until doubled in size, 45 minutes to 1 hour.

3. Place a large sheet of parchment paper in a warm, draft-free place (75°F/24°C); dust parchment with flour.

4. Divide dough into 12 portions (about 114 grams each). Shape each portion into a ball. Place 1 ball in your hand. Using your thumb and forefinger, pinch a hole in center of ball, and stretch hole to about 3 inches wide. Place on prepared parchment. Repeat with remaining dough. (Once dough contracts, the hole should be 1 to 1½ inches wide.) Cover and let rise until puffed, 15 to 30 minutes.

5. Preheat oven to 400°F (200°C). Line 2 sheet pans with parchment paper.

6. In a large stockpot, bring 8 cups (1,920 grams) water and remaining ½ cup (170 grams) barley malt syrup to a very low simmer over medium-low heat. (Do not boil.) Carefully drop bagels, 1 to 2 at a time, into water. Cook for 10 seconds per side; immediately transfer to prepared pans.

7. In a small bowl, whisk together egg white and remaining 1 tablespoon (15 grams) water. Brush dough with egg wash.

8. Bake until golden brown, 20 to 25 minutes. Let cool on pans for 10 minutes. Serve warm or at room temperature.

FOUR-CHEESE PULL-APART MILK BREAD

Makes 1 (9-inch) loaf

We gave Japanese milk bread a savory twist by filling this loaf with a quartet of melted mozzarella, provolone, fontina, and cream cheese. With buttery pull-apart layers, this recipe is made for sharing. Just put it on the table and watch your guests tear off their own piece of downy perfection.

1¼   cups (300 grams) warm whole milk (100°F/38°C to 110°F/43°C)
⅔   cup (133 grams) granulated sugar
4½   teaspoons (14 grams) active dry yeast
6   cups (762 grams) bread flour
Tangzhong (recipe follows)
2   large eggs (100 grams)
4   teaspoons (12 grams) kosher salt
6   tablespoons (84 grams) unsalted butter, softened
4   ounces (115 grams) cream cheese, softened
¾   cup (85 grams) freshly grated fontina cheese
¾   cup (85 grams) freshly grated mozzarella cheese
¾   cup (85 grams) freshly grated provolone cheese
2   tablespoons (28 grams) unsalted butter, melted
Flaked sea salt, for sprinkling

1. In the bowl of a stand mixer fitted with the paddle attachment, whisk together warm milk, sugar, and yeast by hand. Let stand until mixture is foamy, about 10 minutes.
2. Add flour, Tangzhong, eggs, and kosher salt to yeast mixture, and beat at very low speed until combined, about 30 seconds. Switch to the dough hook attachment. Beat at low speed until smooth and elastic, about 6 minutes. Add softened butter, 1 tablespoon (14 grams) at a time, beating until combined after each addition, about 3 minutes total. Beat until dough is smooth and elastic, about 1 minute. Turn out dough onto a lightly floured surface, and shape into a smooth round.
3. Spray a large bowl with cooking spray. Place dough in bowl, turning to grease top. Cover and let rise in a warm, draft-free place (75°F/24°C) until doubled in size, 45 minutes to 1 hour.

4. Spray a 9-inch square baking pan with cooking spray. Line pan with parchment paper, letting excess extend over sides of pan.
5. Punch down dough, and turn out onto a lightly floured surface. Roll dough into a 22x10-inch rectangle, about ½ inch thick. Spread cream cheese onto dough, and sprinkle with fontina, mozzarella, and provolone. Trim ½ inch off each side of dough, creating a 21x9-inch rectangle. Using a pastry cutter, cut dough into 3 (21x3-inch) rectangles. Cut each rectangle into 14 (3x1½-inch) pieces. Stack pieces in 3 rows in prepared pan, squishing dough as needed. Cover and let rise in a warm, draft-free place (75°F/24°C) until puffed, 20 to 30 minutes.
6. Preheat oven to 350°F (180°C).
7. Bake until golden brown and an instant-read thermometer inserted in center registers 190°F (88°C), 45 to 50 minutes, covering with foil after 30 minutes of baking to prevent excess browning. Let cool in pan for 10 minutes. Using excess parchment as handles, remove from pan. Brush with melted butter, and sprinkle with sea salt. Serve warm.

TANGZHONG
Makes about ¾ cup

¾   cup (180 grams) whole milk
¼   cup (32 grams) bread flour

1. In a small saucepan, whisk together milk and flour. Cook over medium-low heat, whisking constantly, until mixture is thickened, an instant-read thermometer registers 149°F (65°C), and whisk leaves lines on bottom of pan. Transfer to a small bowl, and let cool to room temperature before using.

PEAR CARDAMOM BUNS

Makes 16 buns

With a mesmerizing yet easy-to-execute shape, these buns are spiced with bold, complex cardamom—the ideal companion for the subtly flavored pear. Slathered in every twist and curve of the golden dough, the homemade Pear Butter is a great way to make use of overripe pears and melts in your mouth with every bite. The best news of all? You'll have leftover butter to enjoy for the rest of the season.

1   cup (240 grams) warm whole milk (105°F/41°C to 110°F/43°C), divided
2¼ teaspoons (7 grams) active dry yeast*
⅓   cup (67 grams) plus ¼ cup (50 grams) granulated sugar, divided
⅓   cup (76 grams) unsalted butter, melted and slightly cooled
¼   cup (60 grams) sour cream, room temperature
1   large egg (50 grams), room temperature
2   teaspoons (8 grams) vanilla extract
4½ to 4¾ cups (563 to 594 grams) all-purpose flour
2   teaspoons (6 grams) kosher salt
1¼ teaspoons (2.5 grams) ground cardamom, divided
½   teaspoon (1 gram) ground cinnamon
1¼ cups (360 grams) Pear Butter (recipe follows)
1   large egg white (30 grams)
1   tablespoon (15 grams) whole milk, room temperature

1. In a medium bowl, stir together ¾ cup (180 grams) warm milk and yeast. Let stand until mixture is foamy, about 10 minutes.
2. In the bowl of a stand mixer fitted with the paddle attachment, stir together ⅓ cup (67 grams) sugar, melted butter, sour cream, egg, vanilla, and remaining ¼ cup (60 grams) warm milk until combined.
3. In a large bowl, whisk together flour, salt, ¾ teaspoon (1.5 grams) cardamom, and cinnamon. Stir 4 cups (500 grams) flour mixture into sugar mixture. With mixer on low speed, add yeast mixture, beating just until combined. Beat in remaining ½ to ¾ cup (63 to 94 grams) flour mixture. (Dough should be slightly sticky.) Switch to the dough hook attachment. Beat at low speed until dough is smooth and elastic, 4 to 5 minutes. Turn out dough onto a lightly floured surface, and shape into a smooth round.
4. Spray a large bowl with cooking spray. Place dough in bowl, turning to grease top. Loosely cover and let rise in a warm, draft-free place (75°F/24°C) until doubled in size, 1 to 1½ hours.
5. Punch down dough. Refrigerate for 15 to 30 minutes.
6. Line 2 baking sheets with parchment paper.
7. Turn out dough onto a lightly floured surface, and roll into a 20x16-inch rectangle. Spread Pear Butter onto dough, leaving a ½-inch border on short sides. In a small bowl, whisk together egg white and room temperature milk. Brush one border with

egg wash. Fold dough in half crosswise, trimming if needed, to create a 16x10-inch rectangle. Gently roll over dough to ensure filling is even. Cut dough into 16 (1-inch-wide) strips. Twist each strip, spiral dough, and tuck end under. Place on prepared pans. Cover and let rise in a warm, draft-free place (75°F/24°C) until puffed, about 30 minutes.
8. Preheat oven to 350°F (180°C).
9. Brush buns with egg wash. In a small bowl, stir together remaining ¼ cup (50 grams) sugar and remaining ½ teaspoon (1 gram) cardamom. Top buns with cardamom sugar.
10. Bake, in batches, until golden brown and an instant-read thermometer inserted in center registers 190°F (88°C), 20 to 25 minutes. Let cool on pans for 10 minutes. Serve warm, or let cool completely on wire racks. Store in an airtight container at room temperature for up to 3 days.

*We used Red Star® Active Dry Yeast.

Pear Butter
Makes about 3 cups

4   pounds (1,814 grams) Bartlett pears (about 8 large pears), peeled, cored, and roughly chopped into ½-inch cubes
1   cup (240 grams) water
1   tablespoon (3 grams) lemon zest (about 1 lemon)
½   cup (120 grams) fresh lemon juice
1   teaspoon (5 grams) grated fresh ginger
1   whole star anise
1   cup (220 grams) firmly packed light brown sugar
½   cup (100 grams) granulated sugar
1   tablespoon (18 grams) vanilla bean paste
½   teaspoon (1 gram) ground cardamom
½   teaspoon (1 gram) ground cinnamon
½   teaspoon (1 gram) ground nutmeg

1. In a large stainless steel stockpot, bring pears, 1 cup (240 grams) water, lemon zest and juice, ginger, and star anise to a boil over medium-high heat. Reduce heat to medium; simmer, stirring occasionally, until tender, 20 to 25 minutes. Discard star anise.
2. Working in batches, transfer mixture to the work bowl of a food processor; purée just until a uniform texture is achieved and no large chunks remain. (Do not liquefy. It should look like applesauce.)
3. Return mixture to pot; add sugars, vanilla bean paste, cardamom, cinnamon, and nutmeg. Bring to a boil over medium-high heat, stirring frequently, until sugars are dissolved. Reduce heat to medium; simmer, stirring frequently, until mixture thickens and holds its shape with a spoon and liquid does not separate, 45 to 55 minutes. Refrigerate for up to 1 month, or freeze for up to 1 year.

HERBED FONTINA ROLLS
WITH MARINARA SAUCE

Makes 23 rolls

Perfect for sharing and packed with melted fontina cheese and a quartet of aromatic herbs, these yeasted potato rolls will chase away even the coldest of winter chills. Fluffy, buttery, and savory but with a touch of sweet from honey, they make for a fun appetizer or side for your holiday spread.

3 to 3¼	cups (381 to 413 grams) bread flour, divided
3	tablespoons (6 grams) finely chopped fresh basil, divided
1	(0.25-ounce) package (7 grams) active dry yeast*
1¾	teaspoons (5.25 grams) kosher salt
1	teaspoon (2 grams) garlic powder
2	teaspoons finely chopped fresh thyme, divided
2	teaspoons finely chopped fresh oregano, divided
2	teaspoons finely chopped fresh rosemary, divided
½	cup (120 grams) plus 1 tablespoon (15 grams) whole milk, divided
10	tablespoons (140 grams) unsalted butter, softened and divided
½	cup (122 grams) plain mashed potatoes
3	tablespoons (63 grams) honey
2	large eggs (100 grams), divided

5.75 ounces (161 grams) fontina cheese
Marinara Sauce (recipe follows), to serve
Garnish: flaked sea salt, crushed red pepper

1. In the bowl of a stand mixer fitted with the paddle attachment, combine 1 cup (127 grams) flour, 2 tablespoons (4 grams) basil, yeast, kosher salt, garlic powder, 1 teaspoon thyme, 1 teaspoon oregano, and 1 teaspoon rosemary until well combined.
2. In a medium saucepan, combine ½ cup (120 grams) milk and 6 tablespoons (84 grams) butter; cook over medium heat until butter is melted and an instant-read thermometer registers 120°F (49°C) to 130°F (54°C). Add milk mixture to flour mixture; beat at medium speed for 2 minutes. Add potatoes, honey, and 1 egg (50 grams); beat at medium-high speed for 2 minutes. With mixer on medium-low speed, gradually add 2 cups (254 grams) flour, beating just until combined.
3. Switch to the dough hook attachment; beat at medium-low speed for 4 to 6 minutes, adding up to remaining ¼ cup (32 grams) flour, 1 tablespoon (8 grams) at a time, until a smooth, elastic dough forms, stopping to scrape sides of bowl and dough hook. (Dough should pass the windowpane test; see Note.)
4. Spray a large bowl with cooking spray; place dough in bowl, turning to grease top. Cover and let rise in a warm, draft-free place (75°F/24°C) until doubled in size, 40 minutes to 1 hour.
5. Line a rimmed baking sheet with parchment paper. Cut cheese into 0.25-ounce (7-gram) cubes.

6. Punch down dough. Turn out dough, and divide into 23 portions (about 35 grams); cover with a piece of plastic wrap. (You should not need much additional flour, if any.) Flatten 1 piece of dough, and place 1 cheese cube in center; pinch dough closed, and gently shape into a ball, pressing together any seams, if needed. Repeat with remaining dough. Place balls, seam side down, on prepared pan in a Christmas tree shape, starting with 2 balls for the trunk and 6 balls for the first row; reduce each following row by 1 ball, leaving a ¼-inch gap between each. Cover and let rise in a warm, draft-free place (75°F/24°C) until doubled in size, 40 minutes to 1 hour.
7. Preheat oven to 375°F (190°C).
8. In a small bowl, whisk together remaining 1 egg (50 grams) and remaining 1 tablespoon (15 grams) milk; brush onto rolls.
9. Bake until golden brown and an instant-read thermometer inserted in the center registers 190°F (88°C), 15 to 20 minutes.
10. In a small bowl, stir together remaining 4 tablespoons (56 grams) butter, remaining 1 tablespoon (2 grams) basil, remaining 1 teaspoon thyme, remaining 1 teaspoon oregano, and remaining 1 teaspoon rosemary. Brush herb butter onto rolls. Serve warm with Marinara Sauce. Garnish with sea salt and crushed red pepper, if desired.

*We used Red Star® Active Dry Yeast.

Note: *Test the dough for proper gluten development using the windowpane test. Pinch off (don't tear) a small piece of dough. Slowly pull the dough out from the center. If the dough is ready, you will be able to stretch it until it's thin and translucent like a windowpane. If the dough tears, it's not quite ready. Beat for 1 minute more, and test again.*

MARINARA SAUCE
Makes 1½ cups

1	tablespoon (14 grams) olive oil
6	cloves garlic (30 grams), minced
1	tablespoon (15 grams) tomato paste
1	(15-ounce) can (425 grams) crushed tomatoes
2	tablespoons (4 grams) chopped fresh basil
2	teaspoons (14 grams) honey
1¼	teaspoons (3.75 grams) kosher salt
½	teaspoon (1 gram) ground black pepper

1. In a small saucepan, heat oil over medium heat. Add garlic and tomato paste; cook, stirring frequently, for 2 minutes. Add tomatoes, and bring to a boil. Reduce heat to medium-low; simmer for 10 minutes. Stir in basil, honey, salt, and pepper.

SOURDOUGH PUMPKIN ROLLS

Makes 12 rolls

Sourdough elevates these soft pull-apart rolls by imparting deeper, heightened flavor and an even fluffier, chewier crumb. And it's all thanks to the addition of Platinum Instant Sourdough Yeast from Red Star. Combining the pleasant tang of sourdough with mildly sweet pumpkin and baked in a cast-iron skillet, these bread rolls embody fall comfort baking at its finest. We finished them off with a savory topping of pepitas and flaked sea salt, delivering a welcome note of crunch to the rolls' pillowy perfection.

3½ cups (438 grams) all-purpose flour
1 (0.63-ounce) package (18 grams) instant sourdough yeast
2 teaspoons (6 grams) kosher salt
½ teaspoon (1 gram) ground cinnamon
¾ cup (183 grams) canned pumpkin
½ cup (120 grams) whole milk
¼ cup (57 grams) unsalted butter
¼ cup (85 grams) honey

1 large egg (50 grams), lightly beaten
3 tablespoons (27 grams) raw pepitas
1 tablespoon (9 grams) flaked sea salt

1. In the bowl of a stand mixer fitted with the paddle attachment, beat flour, instant sourdough yeast, kosher salt, and cinnamon at low speed until combined.
2. In a small saucepan, heat pumpkin, milk, butter, and honey over medium heat until butter is melted and an instant-read thermometer registers 120°F (49°C) to 130°F (54°C). Remove from heat; let cool slightly, if necessary.
3. With mixer on low speed, add warm pumpkin mixture to flour mixture, beating until combined, about 2 minutes. Switch to the dough hook attachment. Beat at low speed until dough is smooth and elastic, 12 to 13 minutes. Turn out dough onto a lightly floured surface, and shape into a smooth ball.

4. Lightly oil a large bowl. Place dough in bowl, turning to grease top. Cover and let rise in a warm, draft-free place (75°F/24°C) until doubled in size, 45 minutes to 1 hour.
5. Oil a 10-inch cast-iron skillet.
6. Punch down dough, and turn out onto a lightly floured surface. Divide dough into 12 equal portions (about 75 grams each). Shape each portion into a smooth round, and place in prepared skillet. Cover and let rise in a warm, draft-free place (75°F/24°C) until doubled in size, 30 to 45 minutes.
7. Preheat oven to 350°F (180°C).
8. Brush top of rolls with egg wash, and sprinkle with pepitas and flaked salt.
9. Bake until deep golden brown and an instant-read thermometer inserted in center registers 190°F (88°C), 25 to 30 minutes. Let cool slightly. Serve warm.

We used Platinum® Instant Sourdough Yeast from Red Star®.

WALNUT POTICA

Makes 1 (15-cup) loaf

Potica is a traditional celebratory yeasted bread from Slovenia. The soft, rich dough is rolled out and spread with filling and then rolled up to create a mesmerizing spiral and baked in the shape of a ring or loaf.

1   cup (240 grams) warm whole milk (105°F/41°C to 110°F/43°C)
4½ teaspoons (14 grams) active dry yeast
5¾ cups (719 grams) all-purpose flour
½   cup (100 grams) granulated sugar
2   teaspoons (6 grams) kosher salt
2   large eggs (100 grams), room temperature
1   cup (227 grams) unsalted butter, melted and slightly cooled
Walnut Filling (recipe follows)
Garnish: confectioners' sugar

1. In a small bowl, whisk together warm milk and yeast. Let stand until mixture is foamy, about 10 minutes.
2. In the bowl of a stand mixer fitted with the paddle attachment, combine flour, granulated sugar, and salt. Add eggs. With mixer on low speed, gradually add melted butter. Add yeast mixture, beating until combined,

about 30 seconds. Switch to the dough hook attachment. Beat at low speed until dough is smooth and elastic, about 5 minutes. Turn out dough onto a lightly floured surface, and shape into a smooth ball.
3. Spray a large bowl with cooking spray. Place dough in bowl, turning to grease top. Cover and let rise in a warm, draft-free place (75°F/24°C) until doubled in size, about 1 hour.
4. Lightly butter a 15-cup Bundt pan*.
5. Punch down dough. On a lightly floured surface, roll dough into a 21x18-inch rectangle. Spread Walnut Filling onto dough, leaving a 1-inch border on one short side. Lightly brush border with water. Starting with opposite short side, roll dough into a log; press seam to seal. (Be sure to press gently, because dough may tear if pinched.) Trim ends. Place log seam side up, and shape into a circle. Brush ends with water, and press together. Use hands to lift and place in prepared pan. Gently press dough flat. (Don't worry if dough doesn't look beautiful. It will fill out and bake well once it proofs.) Cover and let rise in a warm, draft-free place (75°F/24°C) until puffed and dough fills three-fourths of pan, 30 to 45 minutes.

6. Preheat oven to 350°F (180°C).
7. Bake until deep golden and an instant-read thermometer inserted near center registers 190°F (88°C), about 50 minutes. Let cool in pan for 15 minutes. Invert potica onto a wire rack, and let cool completely. Garnish with confectioners' sugar, if desired.

*We used Nordic Ware Anniversary Bundt Pan.

PRO TIP
Because of this bread's hefty size and intricate spiral shape, the soft dough may lose its shape easily. If the dough loses its circular shape when transfering to the pan, reposition it as best you can once you've placed it. It doesn't have to be perfect. The dough will rise sumptuously while baking, and you will end up with a beautiful bread.

WALNUT FILLING
Makes 2½ cups

2   cups (284 grams) walnuts
½   cup (100 grams) granulated sugar
½   cup (170 grams) honey
½   cup (120 grams) whole milk
1   teaspoon (3 grams) kosher salt
1   large egg (50 grams)
1   large egg yolk (19 grams)
1   teaspoon (4 grams) vanilla extract

1. In the work bowl of a food processor, process walnuts until finely ground and uniform in size.
2. In a medium saucepan, stir together sugar, honey, and milk. Cook over medium-low heat until sugar is dissolved and mixture starts to boil. Stir in ground walnuts and salt. Whisk in egg and egg yolk. Cook, stirring constantly, until mixture is slightly thickened, becomes glossy, and an instant-read thermometer registers 175°F (79°C) to 180°F (82°C), 6 to 7 minutes.
3. Pour mixture into a medium bowl; stir in vanilla. Cover with a piece of plastic wrap, pressing wrap directly onto surface of filling. Refrigerate until completely cooled. (For a quick cool down, place bowl in an ice water bath, and let stand, stirring every 5 minutes, until filling cools and thickens.)

WHITE CHOCOLATE-PEPPERMINT SWEET ROLLS

Makes 12 rolls

If you're on the hunt for the ultimate holiday breakfast, look no further than these pillowy sweet rolls. The white chocolate chunk, crushed peppermint, and slivered almond filling will satisfy your holiday sweet tooth while the luscious Cream Cheese Icing will keep you coming back for more.

4¼ to 4½ cups (531 to 563 grams) all-purpose flour, divided
⅓   cup (67 grams) granulated sugar
1   (0.25-ounce) package (7 grams) active dry yeast*
2   teaspoons (6 grams) kosher salt
1¼   cups (300 grams) whole milk
1   cup (227 grams) unsalted butter, softened and divided
1   large egg (50 grams)
¼   teaspoon (1 gram) peppermint extract
½   cup (86 grams) roughly crushed round peppermint candies
2   ounces (57 grams) white chocolate baking bar, roughly chopped
⅓   cup (44 grams) finely chopped slivered almonds
Cream Cheese Icing (recipe follows)
Garnish: crushed peppermint candies

1. In the bowl of a stand mixer fitted with the paddle attachment, beat 1½ cups (188 grams) flour, sugar, yeast, and salt on medium-low speed until well combined.
2. In a medium saucepan, heat milk and ½ cup (113.5 grams) butter over medium heat until an instant-read thermometer registers 120°F (49°C) to 130°F (54°C). Add milk mixture to flour mixture; beat at medium speed for 2 minutes. Add egg; beat at medium-high speed for 2 minutes. With mixer on low speed, gradually add 2¾ cups (344 grams) flour, beating just until combined and stopping to scrape sides of bowl.
3. Switch to the dough hook attachment. Beat at medium speed until a soft dough forms, 6 to 8 minutes, stopping to scrape sides of bowl and dough hook; add up to remaining ¼ cup (31 grams) flour, 1 tablespoon (8 grams) at a time, if necessary. (Dough should pass the windowpane test [see Note] but may still stick slightly to sides of bowl.)
4. Spray a large bowl with cooking spray. Place dough in bowl, turning to grease top. Cover and let rise in a warm, draft-free place (75°F/24°C) until doubled in size, 40 minutes to 1 hour. (See PRO TIP for make-ahead method.)
5. Line a 13x9-inch rimmed baking sheet with parchment paper.
6. In a small bowl, stir together peppermint extract and remaining ½ cup (113.5 grams) butter.
7. Lightly punch down dough. Cover and let stand for 5 minutes. On a lightly floured surface, roll dough into an 18x12-inch rectangle. Using a small offset spatula, spread peppermint butter onto dough, leaving a ½-inch border on one long side. Sprinkle

with peppermint candies, white chocolate, and almonds. Starting with opposite long side, roll up dough, jelly roll style; pinch seam to seal. Gently shape log to 18 inches long and even thickness, if necessary. Using a serrated knife dipped in flour, cut log into 12 slices (about 1½ inches thick), trimming edges slightly, if needed. Place slices, cut side down, in prepared pan. Cover and let rise in a warm, draft-free place (75°F/24°C) until doubled in size, 30 to 45 minutes.
8. Preheat oven to 350°F (180°C).
9. Bake until lightly golden and an instant-read thermometer inserted in center registers 190°F (88°C), 20 to 25 minutes, loosely covering with foil to prevent excess browning, if necessary. Let cool in pan for 30 minutes. Spread Cream Cheese Icing onto rolls; garnish with peppermint candies, if desired. Serve warm.

*We used Red Star® Active Dry Yeast.

Note: *Test the dough for proper gluten development using the windowpane test. Pinch off (don't tear) a small piece of dough. Slowly pull the dough out from the center. If the dough is ready, you will be able to stretch it until it's thin and translucent like a windowpane. If the dough tears, it's not quite ready. Beat for 1 minute more, and test again.*

PRO TIP
To prep ahead, follow recipe through step 3. Punch down dough; place in a large resealable plastic bag, and refrigerate. When ready to shape, prepare filling ingredients. Shape dough as directed; let rise in a warm, draft-free place (75°F/24°C) until doubled in size. Bake as directed.

CREAM CHEESE ICING
Makes 2 cups

½   cup (113 grams) unsalted butter, softened
4   ounces (113 grams) cream cheese, softened
¼   teaspoon kosher salt
2   cups (240 grams) confectioners' sugar

1. In the bowl of a stand mixer fitted with the paddle attachment, beat butter, cream cheese, and salt at medium speed until smooth, 1 to 2 minutes, stopping to scrape sides of bowl. With mixer on low speed, gradually add confectioners' sugar until combined; increase speed to medium, and beat until smooth and fluffy, 3 to 4 minutes, stopping to scrape sides of bowl. Use immediately.

ALMOND CRANBERRY WREATH

Makes 1 wreath

This celebratory bread gets its tender, pillowy texture from Platinum Yeast from Red Star, the go-to yeast for baking success every time.

4¼ to 4½ cups (531 to 563 grams) all-purpose flour, divided
¼   cup (50 grams) granulated sugar
1   (0.25-ounce) package (7 grams) instant yeast*
2   teaspoons (6 grams) kosher salt
½   cup (120 grams) plus 1 tablespoon (15 grams) water, divided
½   cup (120 grams) whole milk
½   cup (113 grams) unsalted butter
2   teaspoons (8 grams) vanilla extract
2   large eggs (100 grams), divided
1   large egg yolk (19 grams)
1   tablespoon (3 grams) orange zest
1   cup (120 grams) fresh or thawed frozen cranberries, halved (patted dry if frozen)
Almond Cream (recipe follows)
Orange Glaze (recipe follows)

1. In the bowl of a stand mixer fitted with the paddle attachment, combine 2 cups (250 grams) flour, sugar, yeast, and salt.
2. In a medium saucepan, heat ½ cup (120 grams) water, milk, butter, and vanilla over medium heat until an instant-read thermometer registers 120°F (49°C) to 130°F (54°C). Add warm milk mixture to flour mixture, and beat at medium speed until combined and cooled slightly, about 2 minutes. Add 1 egg (50 grams), egg yolk, and orange zest, and beat at medium speed until combined. With mixer on low speed, gradually add 2¼ cups (281 grams) flour, beating just until combined and stopping to scrape sides of bowl.
3. Switch to the dough hook attachment. Beat at low speed until a soft, somewhat sticky dough forms, about 12 minutes, stopping to scrape sides of bowl and dough hook. Add up to remaining ¼ cup (31 grams) flour, 1 tablespoon (8 grams) at a time, if dough is too sticky. Turn out dough onto a lightly floured surface, and shape into a smooth round.
4. Lightly oil a large bowl. Place dough in bowl, turning to grease top. Cover and let rise in a warm, draft-free place (75°F/24°C) until doubled in size, 40 minutes to 1 hour.
5. In a small bowl, whisk together remaining 1 egg (50 grams) and remaining 1 tablespoon (15 grams) water.
6. Lightly punch down dough. Cover and let stand for 5 minutes. Turn out dough onto a lightly floured surface, and roll into a 24x12-inch rectangle. Using a small offset spatula, spread Almond Cream onto dough, leaving a ½-inch border on one long side. Sprinkle with cranberries. Brush border with egg wash. Starting

with opposite long side, roll up dough, jelly roll style; pinch seam to seal. Gently shape log to even thickness, if necessary. Trim edges flat. Place log on a sheet of parchment paper. Form dough into a circle. Brush trimmed ends with egg wash, and press together, pinching dough to seal.
7. Using a serrated knife or kitchen scissors, cut three-fourths of the way into dough, being careful not to cut all the way through dough. Make a second cut 1 inch from first cut. Repeat process around the circle until you reach first cut. Gently turn each slice onto its side, slightly overlapping with the previous piece. Slide parchment onto a baking sheet. Cover and let rise in a warm, draft-free place (75°F/24°C) until puffed, 20 to 30 minutes.
8. Preheat oven to 350°F (180°C).
9. Brush dough with egg wash.
10. Bake until lightly golden and an instant-read thermometer inserted in center registers 190°F (88°C), 30 to 45 minutes, loosely covering with foil to prevent excess browning, if necessary. Let cool on pan for 10 minutes. Remove from pan, and drizzle with Orange Glaze. Serve warm or at room temperature.

We used Platinum® Yeast from Red Star®.

ALMOND CREAM
Makes about 1¾ cups

6   tablespoons (84 grams) unsalted butter, softened
½   cup (100 grams) granulated sugar
1⅓ cups (128 grams) natural almond meal
1   large egg (50 grams)
¼   teaspoon (1 gram) almond extract
½   cup (63 grams) all-purpose flour
¼   teaspoon kosher salt

1. In the bowl of a stand mixer fitted with the paddle attachment, beat butter and sugar at medium speed until creamy, about 2 minutes. Beat in almond meal until combined. Add egg and almond extract, beating at low speed until combined. Beat in flour and salt. Refrigerate until ready to use.

ORANGE GLAZE
Makes about ½ cup

1   cup (120 grams) confectioners' sugar
1   teaspoon (1 gram) orange zest
1   tablespoon plus 2 teaspoons (25 grams) fresh orange juice

1. In a small bowl, whisk together all ingredients until smooth.

APPLE OAT BREAD

Makes 1 (9x5-inch) loaf

Is there anything more comforting than the unmistakable aroma of a loaf of bread brimming with fresh apple chunks and a symphony of fall spices wafting through the kitchen? We souped up the familiar yeasted apple bread by adding a hefty dose of apple cider for a tangy kick and a thick Oat Streusel topping for epic crunch.

3⅔ cups (466 grams) bread flour
1   cup (80 grams) old-fashioned oats
3   tablespoons (36 grams) granulated sugar
1   tablespoon (9 grams) kosher salt
1   (0.25-ounce) package (7 grams) instant yeast*
1   teaspoon (2 grams) ground cinnamon
½   teaspoon (1 gram) ground nutmeg
¼   teaspoon ground allspice
⅛   teaspoon ground cloves
1¼   cups (300 grams) warm apple cider (120°F/49°C to 130°F/54°C)
2   tablespoons (28 grams) unsalted butter, melted
1   cup (121 grams) chopped Honeycrisp apple (about 1 apple)
1   large egg (50 grams)
1   tablespoon (15 grams) water
Oat Streusel (recipe follows)
Softened butter or apple butter, to serve

1. In the bowl of a stand mixer fitted with the paddle attachment, whisk together flour, oats, sugar, salt, yeast, cinnamon, nutmeg, allspice, and cloves by hand.
2. In a small bowl, whisk together warm apple cider and melted butter. Add cider mixture to flour mixture, and beat at medium speed until combined, about 30 seconds. Switch to the dough hook attachment. Beat at low speed until dough is smooth and elastic, about 5 minutes. Add apple, and beat until most of apple pieces are picked up by dough, about 1 minute. Turn out dough onto a lightly floured surface, and knead gently to completely incorporate apple, about 5 times. Shape into a smooth ball
3. Lightly oil a large bowl. Place dough in bowl, turning to grease top. Cover and let rise in a warm, draft-free place (75°F/24°C) until doubled in size, about 1 hour.
4. Spray a 9x5-inch loaf pan with cooking spray.

5. Lightly pat dough into a 9-inch circle. Fold top third of dough to center, pressing to seal. Fold bottom third over folded portion, pressing to seal. Fold dough in half lengthwise so long edges meet. Using the heel of your hand, firmly press edges to seal. Place dough, seam side down, in prepared pan. Cover and let rise in a warm, draft-free place (75°F/24°C) until doubled in size, 30 to 45 minutes.
6. Preheat oven to 350°F (180°C).
7. In a small bowl, whisk together egg and 1 tablespoon (15 grams) water. Brush top of loaf with egg wash, and sprinkle with Oat Streusel.
8. Bake until an instant-read thermometer inserted in center registers 205°F (96°C), 50 to 55 minutes. Let cool in pan for 15 minutes. Remove from pan, and let cool completely on a wire rack. Serve with softened butter or apple butter.

*We used Platinum® Yeast from Red Star®.

OAT STREUSEL
Makes ¾ cup

¼   cup (31 grams) all-purpose flour
3   tablespoons (15 grams) old-fashioned oats
2   tablespoons (24 grams) granulated sugar
¼   teaspoon ground cinnamon
⅛   teaspoon kosher salt
⅛   teaspoon ground nutmeg
2   tablespoons (28 grams) unsalted butter, melted

1. In a small bowl, stir together flour, oats, sugar, cinnamon, salt, and nutmeg. Add melted butter, and stir until mixture is crumbly.

PRO TIP
When baking, go for apple varieties with a firm, crisp texture, which guarantees the apples' flavor and structure won't be compromised by heat while baking. We like Honeycrisp apples, but Braeburn, Ambrosia, SweeTango, Pink Lady, and Jazz apples will also work well.

PIES AND TARTS

PIES

Simply made of buttery crust and a flavor-packed filling,
pies offer endless possibilities. From the rustic berry pie to
a classic Key lime stunner, these recipes pay tribute to this
versatile dessert

BLACK BOTTOM COCONUT PIE

Makes 1 (9-inch) deep-dish pie

With an indulgent chocolate bottom, this deep-dish twist on coconut cream pie is a coconut tour de force.

8   ounces (225 grams) cream cheese, softened
1   (14-ounce) can (396 grams) sweetened condensed milk
⅓   cup (80 grams) full-fat coconut milk
¾   cup (180 grams) heavy whipping cream
¼   teaspoon (1 gram) coconut extract
1   cup (60 grams) sweetened shredded coconut
Ganache (recipe follows)
Coconut Shortbread Crust (recipe follows)
Coconut Whipped Cream (recipe on page50)
Garnish: toasted sweetened shredded coconut

1. In the bowl of a stand mixer fitted with the paddle attachment, beat cream cheese at medium-high speed until creamy, about 3 minutes. Add condensed milk and coconut milk, beating until smooth. Transfer cream cheese mixture to a large bowl; set aside.
2. Using the whisk attachment, beat cream and coconut extract at medium-high speed until stiff peaks form. Add one-third of whipped cream to cream cheese mixture, and whisk until smooth. Whisk in remaining whipped cream. Fold in shredded coconut.
3. Pour Ganache into bottom of Coconut Shortbread Crust. Freeze until set, about 5 minutes. Spoon coconut cream mixture onto Ganache until coconut cream is even with top of crust. Freeze for at least 4 hours or overnight.
4. Let pie stand at room temperature for 15 minutes before serving. Top with Coconut Whipped Cream. Garnish with toasted coconut, if desired.

GANACHE

Makes about 1 cup

⅔   cup (113 grams) chopped 60% cacao dark chocolate
½   cup (120 grams) heavy whipping cream

1. In a medium heatproof bowl, place chocolate.
2. In a small saucepan, heat cream over medium-low heat just until bubbles form around edges of pan. Pour hot cream over chocolate; let stand for 30 seconds. Starting in center of bowl, slowly stir with a rubber spatula until fully combined. Use immediately.

COCONUT SHORTBREAD CRUST

Makes 1 (9-inch) deep-dish crust

2¾   cups (303 grams) vanilla shortbread cookie crumbs
½   cup (36 grams) toasted sweetened shredded coconut
5   tablespoons (70 grams) unsalted butter, melted
2   tablespoons (24 grams) granulated sugar

1. Preheat oven to 350°F (180°C).
2. In a medium bowl, stir together all ingredients. Firmly press mixture into bottom and completely up sides of a 9-inch deep-dish pie plate.
3. Bake until edges are golden, 12 to 14 minutes. Let cool completely.

ICEBOX KEY LIME PIE

Makes 1 (9-inch) deep-dish pie

Classic Key lime pie gets a spicy upgrade with our Gingersnap Crust flecked with crystallized ginger.

1½ cups (360 grams) coconut cream
½   cup (120 grams) Key lime juice
8   ounces (225 grams) cream cheese, softened
1   cup (120 grams) confectioners' sugar
½   cup (120 grams) crème fraîche
¾   cup (180 grams) heavy whipping cream
Gingersnap Crust (recipe follows)
Garnish: lime slices

1. In a small bowl, whisk together coconut cream and Key lime juice; set aside.
2. In the bowl of a stand mixer fitted with the paddle attachment, beat cream cheese at medium-high speed until creamy, about 3 minutes. Add confectioners' sugar and crème fraîche, beating until smooth. With mixer on low speed, add coconut cream mixture, beating to combine. Transfer to a large bowl; set aside.
3. Using the whisk attachment, beat heavy cream at medium-high speed until stiff peaks form. Add one-third of whipped heavy cream to cream cheese mixture, and whisk until smooth. Whisk in remaining whipped heavy cream. Spoon mixture into prepared Gingersnap Crust until mixture is even with top of crust. Freeze for at least 4 hours or overnight. Let stand at room temperature for 15 minutes before serving. Garnish with limes, if desired.

GINGERSNAP CRUST
Makes 1 (9-inch) deep-dish crust

2¾ cups (358 grams) ground gingersnap cookies
¼   cup plus 3 tablespoons (99 grams) unsalted butter, melted
3   tablespoons (42 grams) firmly packed light brown sugar
3   tablespoons (33 grams) finely chopped crystallized ginger

1. Preheat oven to 350°F (180°C).
2. In a medium bowl, stir together all ingredients. Firmly press mixture into bottom and completely up sides of a 9-inch deep-dish pie plate.
3. Bake for 10 to 12 minutes. Let cool completely.

VANILLA MILK RUFFLE PIE

Makes 1 (9-inch) pie

Filled with velvety vanilla custard, this pie triumphs in texture and taste. Shape the phyllo rosettes in the palm of your hand with one quick motion.

8   sheets frozen phyllo pastry*, thawed
¼   cup plus 3 tablespoons (99 grams) unsalted butter, melted
3   large eggs (150 grams), room temperature
½   cup (100 grams) granulated sugar
½   teaspoon (1.5 grams) kosher salt
¼   teaspoon ground cinnamon
1   cup (240 grams) whole milk
½   cup (120 grams) heavy whipping cream
1   tablespoon (18 grams) vanilla bean paste
1   tablespoon (13 grams) vanilla extract
Garnish: confectioners' sugar

1. Preheat oven to 350°F (180°C). Butter a 9-inch round cake pan. Line bottom of pan with parchment paper (see Note); butter parchment.
2. Place thawed pastry sheets on a work surface. Keep covered with wax paper while working. (You can also cover pastry sheets with plastic wrap topped with damp paper towels.) Place 1 pastry sheet on counter, and brush with melted butter. Using your fingers, ruffle dough by pinching along the long side. (It will look like a fan. Do not worry if it tears.) Starting at one end, shape into a tight spiral, and place in center of prepared pan. Repeat with remaining sheets, and place around center spiral.
3. Bake until golden brown, 20 to 25 minutes. Let cool for 10 minutes while preparing custard.
4. In a medium bowl, whisk together eggs, granulated sugar, salt, and cinnamon.
5. In a small saucepan, heat milk, cream, and vanilla bean paste over medium-high heat until steaming. Add a small amount of hot milk mixture to egg mixture, whisking constantly. Slowly add remaining hot milk mixture, whisking to combine. Whisk in vanilla extract. Pour mixture over baked phyllo dough.
6. Bake until center is set and an instant-read thermometer inserted in center registers 170°F (77°C), 15 to 20 minutes. Serve warm or at room temperature. Garnish with confectioners' sugar, if desired.

*We used The Fillo Factory 13x18-inch phyllo pastry sheets, available at Whole Foods, and thawed according to package directions.

Note: *If you want to be able to remove the pie from the pan to serve, take 2 strips of parchment paper, and cross them in the middle of the bottom of prepared pan. Let excess parchment extend up sides of pan to be used as handles; line bottom of pan.*

ROASTED MANGO AND PINEAPPLE PIE

Makes 1 (9-inch) deep-dish pie

Smoky mango and bright pineapple unite in this tangy custard pie.

3   large mangos (1,800 grams), peeled, seeded, and cut into large pieces
3   (¾-inch-thick) fresh pineapple rings (249 grams)
¼   cup (85 grams) plus 2 tablespoons (42 grams) honey, divided
2   tablespoons (30 grams) fresh orange juice
2   tablespoons (28 grams) unsalted butter, melted
1½ tablespoons (27 grams) vanilla bean paste, divided
½   cup (100 grams) granulated sugar
½   cup (110 grams) firmly packed light brown sugar
2   teaspoons (1 gram) grated fresh ginger
1½ cups (360 grams) whole buttermilk
⅓   cup (42 grams) all-purpose flour
½   teaspoon (1.5 grams) kosher salt
Vanilla Bean Piecrust (recipe follows)
6   large eggs (300 grams), room temperature
¼   cup (57 grams) unsalted butter, cubed and softened
Fresh mango, fresh pineapple, and sweetened whipped cream, to serve

1. Preheat oven to 400°F (200°C). Line a rimmed quarter sheet pan with foil.
2. Place mango and pineapple on prepared pan. In a small bowl, whisk together 2 tablespoons (42 grams) honey, orange juice, melted butter, and ½ tablespoon (9 grams) vanilla bean paste. Brush fruit with half of honey mixture.
3. Bake for 30 minutes. Brush with remaining honey mixture, and bake for 10 minutes more. Let cool slightly.
4. In the container of a blender, place roasted mango pieces; process until smooth. Measure 2 cups (480 grams) purée. In same container, place roasted pineapple and any remaining juice from pan; process until smooth. Measure ½ cup (130 grams) purée.
5. Return both purées to container, and process until combined. Add sugars, ginger, remaining ¼ cup (85 grams) honey, and remaining 1 tablespoon (18 grams) vanilla bean paste; process until smooth and uniform in color. Add buttermilk, blending to combine. Blend in flour and salt.
6. Preheat oven to 425°F (220°C).
7. Roll chilled Vanilla Bean Piecrust dough to ³⁄₁₆-inch thickness, about 15 inches in diameter. Transfer to a 9-inch deep-dish glass pie plate, pressing into bottom and completely up sides. Trim excess dough to ½ inch beyond edge of plate. Fold edges

under, and crimp as desired. Prick dough all over with a fork. Top with a piece of parchment paper, letting ends extend over edges of plate. Add pie weights.
8. Bake for 15 minutes. Carefully remove paper and weights. Bake until crust looks dry, about 5 minutes more. Remove from oven. Reduce oven temperature to 325°F (170°C).
9. In a large saucepan, heat purée mixture over medium-low heat until steaming. In a large bowl, whisk eggs. Carefully add half of hot purée mixture to eggs, whisking constantly. Return mixture to saucepan. Cook, stirring constantly, until mixture starts to thicken and an instant-read thermometer registers 160°F (71°C).
10. Press mixture through a fine-mesh sieve, discarding solids. Add softened butter, a few pieces at a time, stirring slowly with a spatula until combined after each addition. Pour filling into warm crust.
11. Bake until edges are set but center still jiggles slightly and an instant-read thermometer registers 175°F (79°C) to 180°F (82°C), about 55 minutes. Let cool to room temperature. Cover and refrigerate for at least 4 hours or overnight. Serve with mango, pineapple, and whipped cream.

Vanilla Bean Piecrust
Makes 1 (9-inch) deep-dish crust

2½ cups (313 grams) all-purpose flour
2   tablespoons (24 grams) granulated sugar
1   teaspoon (3 grams) kosher salt
¾   cup plus 2 tablespoons (198 grams) cold unsalted butter, cubed
6   tablespoons (90 grams) ice water
1   tablespoon (18 grams) vanilla bean paste*

1. In the work bowl of a food processor, place flour, sugar, and salt; pulse until combined. Add cold butter, and pulse until mixture is crumbly.
2. In a small bowl, combine 6 tablespoons (90 grams) ice water and vanilla bean paste. With processor running, pour vanilla mixture through food chute in a slow, steady stream just until dough comes together. (Mixture may appear crumbly. It should be moist and hold together when pinched.)
3. Turn out dough, and shape into a disk. Wrap tightly in plastic wrap, and refrigerate for at least 30 minutes. Dough may be refrigerated for up to 3 days or frozen for up to 2 months.

We used Heilala.

HOMESTYLE BERRY PIE

Makes 1 (9-inch) pie

Loaded with fresh berries, this pie gets a touch of warmth from cardamom in the filling. As for that buttery crust—there's no butter. We added lard to give the crust a tender, melt-in-your-mouth texture (but you can also substitute unsalted butter, if you prefer).

Pie Dough (recipe follows)
1   pound (454 grams) fresh blackberries (about 3 cups)
1   pound (454 grams) fresh blueberries (about 3 cups)
¾   cup (150 grams) plus 2 teaspoons (8 grams) granulated sugar, divided
⅓   cup (43 grams) cornstarch
1   teaspoon (2 grams) ground cardamom
⅛   teaspoon kosher salt
1   large egg (50 grams)
1   tablespoon (15 grams) water

1. On a lightly floured surface, roll half of Pie Dough into a 12-inch circle. Transfer to a 9-inch pie plate, pressing into bottom and up sides. Refrigerate until ready to use. On a lightly floured surface, roll remaining Pie Dough into a 12-inch circle. Place on a parchment paper-lined baking sheet, and refrigerate for at least 10 minutes.
2. In a large bowl, toss together blackberries, blueberries, ¾ cup (150 grams) sugar, cornstarch, cardamom, and salt. Spoon filling into prepared crust. Place remaining dough over filling. Trim excess dough; fold edges under. Working your way around edge, gently pinch crust with thumb and knuckle of forefinger to create crimps. Cut several 1-inch vents in top of dough to release steam. Freeze for 30 minutes.
3. Preheat oven to 425°F (220°C). Line a baking sheet with parchment paper.
4. In a small bowl, whisk together egg and 1 tablespoon (15 grams) water. Place pie on prepared pan, and brush top with egg wash. Sprinkle with remaining 2 teaspoons (8 grams) sugar.
5. Bake for 30 minutes. Reduce oven temperature to 350°F (180°C). Loosely cover with foil, and bake until crust is lightly browned and filling is bubbly, about 1 hour and 10 minutes more. Let cool on a wire rack.

PIE DOUGH
Makes 1 (9-inch) double crust

3   cups (375 grams) all-purpose flour
2   tablespoons (24 grams) granulated sugar
½   teaspoon (1.5 grams) kosher salt
1   cup (227 grams) cold lard, cubed
5 to 7 tablespoons (75 to 105 grams) ice water

1. In the work bowl of a food processor, pulse together flour, sugar, and salt until combined. Add cold lard, and pulse until mixture is crumbly. With processor running, add 5 tablespoons (75 grams) ice water in a slow, steady stream until combined and dough comes together. Add remaining 2 tablespoons (30 grams) ice water, if needed. Turn out dough, and divide in half. Shape each half into a disk, and wrap in plastic wrap. Refrigerate for at least 30 minutes.

TARTS

With a crumbly crust and simple yet scrumptious filling,
our decadent chocolate-, custard- and fruit-filled tarts bring
a slice of elegance to any occasion

MACCHIATO CHOCOLATE TART

Makes 1 (9-inch) tart

Three types of ganache come together to form an outrageously rich tart with an elegant latte art design. Leftover espresso grounds add a slightly gritty texture and amplified aroma to the crust.

1⅓ cups (167 grams) all-purpose flour
⅓ cup (40 grams) confectioners' sugar
¾ teaspoon (2.25 grams) kosher salt
½ cup (113 grams) cold unsalted butter, cubed
2 tablespoons (24 grams) leftover espresso grounds, cooled
2 tablespoons (30 grams) ice water
Milk Chocolate Ganache (recipe follows)
Caramelized White Chocolate Ganache (recipe follows)
Pure White Chocolate Ganache (recipe follows)

1. Preheat oven to 350°F (180°C).
2. In the work bowl of a food processor, place flour, confectioners' sugar, and salt; pulse until combined. Add cold butter, and pulse until mixture is crumbly. Add espresso grounds. With processor running, add 2 tablespoons (30 grams) ice water, pulsing just until a dough forms.
3. Press dough into bottom and up sides of a 9-inch fluted round removable-bottom tart pan. Prick bottom of dough with a fork. Freeze for 15 minutes.
4. Top dough with a piece of parchment paper, letting ends extend over edges of pan. Add pie weights.
5. Bake until edges are set, 20 to 25 minutes. Carefully remove paper and weights. Bake until golden brown, about 10 minutes more. Let cool completely on a wire rack.
6. Spoon Milk Chocolate Ganache into prepared crust, spreading with a small offset spatula. Refrigerate until set, about 45 minutes.
7. Pour enough warm Caramelized White Chocolate Ganache over tart to cover Milk Chocolate Ganache (about 1 cup). Working quickly, alternately pour 4 to 5 concentric circles each of Caramelized White Chocolate Ganache and Pure White Chocolate Ganache over tart, creating

a bull's-eye pattern. Begin each pour in bottom third of tart, and use slightly less ganache each time. (Don't worry if your circles are not perfectly spaced.) Using a wooden skewer, draw a line from one edge of crust to opposite edge. Repeat with 3 to 5 more lines, starting from different points along edge but always ending at same point. (See opposite page for a visual tutorial.) Refrigerate until set, about 1 hour.

MILK CHOCOLATE GANACHE
Makes about 1¼ cups

6 ounces (175 grams) 45% cacao milk chocolate chips
¼ cup plus 2 tablespoons (90 grams) heavy whipping cream
3 tablespoons (42 grams) unsalted butter
1 tablespoon (6 grams) instant espresso powder

1. In a small heatproof bowl, place chocolate.
2. In a small saucepan, heat cream, butter, and espresso powder over medium heat, stirring frequently, just until bubbles form around edges of pan. (Do not boil.) Pour hot cream mixture over chocolate; let stand for 1 minute. Whisk until smooth. Use immediately.

CARAMELIZED WHITE CHOCOLATE GANACHE
Makes 1⅔ cups

9 ounces (255 grams) blond chocolate* or Caramelized White Chocolate (recipe follows), chopped
½ cup plus 1 tablespoon (135 grams) heavy whipping cream
4½ tablespoons (63 grams) unsalted butter
1 tablespoon (6 grams) espresso powder

1. In a medium heatproof bowl, place blond chocolate.
2. In a small saucepan, heat cream, butter, and espresso powder over medium heat, stirring frequently, just until bubbles form around edges of pan. (Do not boil.) Pour hot cream mixture over blond chocolate; let stand for 1 minute. Whisk until smooth. Use immediately.

You can use Valrhona Blond Dulcey 32% Chocolate or make your own with the recipe below.

CARAMELIZED WHITE CHOCOLATE
Makes about 1 cup

Recipe by Jesse Szewczyk

9 ounces (255 grams) white chocolate baking chips
⅛ teaspoon kosher salt

1. Preheat oven to 250°F (130°C).
2. In a completely dry 9-inch round cake pan, combine white chocolate and salt.
3. Bake until white chocolate is smooth and deep golden and smells like toasted marshmallows, 30 minutes to 1 hour, stirring every 10 minutes. (At times, it will look very dry and chalky, but keep stirring until smooth.) Pour onto a parchment-lined rimmed baking sheet, and let set for at least 7 hours or overnight.
4. Break into pieces, and store in an airtight container for up to 4 months.

Note: *For a lighter flavor, roast just until color starts to change, about 30 minutes. For a stronger flavor, roast until chocolate resembles peanut butter and has a strong nutty fragrance, about 1 hour. This will produce something slightly less sweet with an assertive caramel flavor.*

PURE WHITE CHOCOLATE GANACHE
Makes ⅔ cup

4 ounces (115 grams) white chocolate, chopped
¼ cup (60 grams) heavy whipping cream

1. In a small heatproof bowl, place white chocolate.
2. In a small saucepan, heat cream over medium heat just until bubbles form around edges of pan. (Do not boil.) Pour hot cream over white chocolate; let stand for 1 minute. Stir with whisk until smooth. Use immediately.

PARISIAN FLAN

Makes 1 (9-inch) flan

With a velvety custard filling, a flaky Pâte Brisée base, and a splash of Grand Marnier for added zest, our flan is authentically Parisian. It's important to cover the crust during the last few minutes of baking so you get that beautifully browned top without burning the crust. Let the flan chill overnight so it achieves the subtle jiggle it's famous for.

3¾ cups (900 grams) whole milk
1¼ cups (300 grams) heavy whipping cream
1¼ cups (250 grams) granulated sugar, divided
1 vanilla bean, split lengthwise, seeds scraped and reserved
5 large eggs (250 grams)
1 large egg yolk (19 grams)
½ cup (64 grams) cornstarch
2 tablespoons (30 grams) orange liqueur*
Pâte Brisée (recipe follows)
2 tablespoons (40 grams) apricot jam, warmed and strained
1 teaspoon (5 grams) water

1. In a large saucepan, heat milk, cream, ¼ cup (50 grams) sugar, and vanilla bean and reserved seeds over medium heat until steaming and an instant-read thermometer registers 180°F (82°C).
2. In a medium bowl, whisk together eggs, egg yolk, cornstarch, and remaining 1 cup (200 grams) sugar until smooth. Slowly add hot milk mixture to egg mixture, whisking constantly. Return mixture to saucepan, and cook, stirring constantly, until mixture is thickened and an instant-read thermometer registers 185°F (85°C), 5 to 8 minutes. Remove from heat. Strain mixture through a fine-mesh sieve into a large bowl; stir in orange liqueur. Cover with a piece of plastic wrap, pressing wrap directly onto surface of custard to prevent a skin from forming. Refrigerate until chilled, 2 to 3 hours.
3. Preheat oven to 375°F (190°C). Lightly butter a 9-inch springform pan; line bottom of pan with parchment paper.
4. Let Pâte Brisée stand at room temperature for 5 minutes. On a lightly floured surface, roll Pâte Brisée into a 14-inch

circle. Transfer to prepared pan, pressing into bottom and up sides. Freeze for 15 minutes.
5. Trim dough to a height of 2 inches inside of pan. Pour filling into prepared crust, smoothing top with an offset spatula.
6. Bake until crust is golden and top of custard is mostly set but still jiggly, 40 to 45 minutes. Remove flan from oven, and increase oven temperature to broil. Cover crust with foil, pressing foil down into pan to reach crust. (The custard should remain exposed.) Return flan to oven, and broil for 2 to 3 minutes, depending on desired level of char. Let cool to room temperature. Refrigerate overnight.
7. When ready to serve, stir together warmed jam and 1 teaspoon (5 grams) water. Brush top of flan with jam mixture. Serve immediately.

We used Grand Marnier.

PÂTE BRISÉE
Makes 1 (9-inch) crust

2 cups (250 grams) all-purpose flour
1 tablespoon (12 grams) granulated sugar
1 tablespoon (11 grams) tightly packed orange zest (about 2 large oranges)
½ teaspoon (1.5 grams) kosher salt
¾ cup (170 grams) cold unsalted butter*, cubed
¼ cup (60 grams) whole milk
1 large egg yolk (19 grams)

1. In the work bowl of a food processor, place flour, sugar, orange zest, and salt; pulse until combined. Add cold butter, and pulse until mixture is crumbly, about 5 pulses. Add milk and egg yolk, pulsing until a dough forms. Turn out dough, and shape into a disk. Wrap tightly in plastic wrap, and refrigerate for 1 hour.

We used Président® Butter.

PASSION FRUIT AND LEMON CURD TART

Makes 1 (9-inch) tart

This tart strikes a satisfying balance between sweet and tart.

4   large eggs (200 grams)
4   large egg yolks (74 grams)
1   cup (200 grams) granulated sugar
¾   cup (180 grams) passion fruit purée*
2   tablespoons (6 grams) lemon zest
¼   cup (60 grams) fresh lemon juice
½   teaspoon (1.5 grams) kosher salt
½   cup (113 grams) unsalted butter, cubed and softened
Pâte Sablée (recipe follows)
Italian Meringue (recipe follows)

1. Place a fine-mesh sieve over a medium bowl; set aside. In another medium bowl, whisk together eggs and egg yolks until well combined; set aside.
2. In a medium saucepan, whisk together sugar, passion fruit purée, lemon zest and juice, and salt. Cook over medium-low heat until sugar is dissolved and mixture begins to steam. (Do not boil.) Pour hot sugar mixture into egg mixture in a slow, steady stream, whisking constantly. Return mixture to saucepan. Cook, stirring slowly and constantly in a figure eight motion with a silicone spatula, until curd is thickened and can coat the back of a spoon and an instant-read thermometer registers 180°F (82°C) and 182°F (83°C), 10 to 12 minutes.
3. Press curd through prepared sieve into bowl, discarding solids. Add butter, 1 to 2 cubes at a time, lstirring until melted after each addition. Pour curd into prepared Pâte Sablée. Cover with a piece of plastic wrap, pressing wrap directly onto surface of curd to prevent a skin from forming. Chill until set; refrigerate for at least 4 hours, and freeze for 30 minutes. Alternatively, refrigerate for 24 hours.
4. When ready to serve, top with Italian Meringue. Using a handheld kitchen torch, carefully brown meringue. Serve immediately.

We used Canoa Passion Fruit Purée, available at Latin American food stores or online.

PÂTE SABLÉE

Makes 1 (9-inch) crust

½   cup (113 grams) unsalted butter, softened
⅓   cup (40 grams) confectioners' sugar
1   tablespoon (3 grams) lemon zest
½   teaspoon (1.5 grams) kosher salt
1   large egg yolk (19 grams)
1½ cups (188 grams) pastry flour

1. In the bowl of a stand mixer fitted with the paddle attachment, beat butter at medium speed until smooth, about 1 minute. Add confectioners' sugar, lemon zest, and salt, and beat until smooth, about 1 minute. Add egg yolk, and beat until combined, about 1 minute. Add flour in two additions, beating just until combined.
2. Turn out dough onto a lightly floured surface, and gently knead 3 to 4 times. Shape dough into a disk, and wrap in plastic wrap. Refrigerate for 1 hour.
3. Preheat oven to 325°F (170°C).
4. On a lightly floured surface, roll dough into an 11-inch circle, about ¼ inch thick. Transfer to a 9-inch round tart pan, gently pressing into bottom and completely up sides. Trim excess dough. Freeze until hardened, about 10 minutes.
5. Top dough with a piece of parchment paper, letting ends extend over edges of pan. Add pie weights.
6. Bake until edges are light golden brown, about 30 minutes. Carefully remove paper and weights. Bake until crust is golden brown, about 10 minutes more. Let cool completely on a wire rack.

ITALIAN MERINGUE

Makes 4 cups

1¼ cups (250 grams) granulated sugar
⅓   cup (80 grams) water
½   cup (120 grams) pasteurized egg whites (about 3), room temperature

1. In a small saucepan, heat sugar and ⅓ cup (80 grams) water over high heat until an instant-read thermometer registers 240°F (116°C).
2. Meanwhile, in the bowl of a stand mixer fitted with the whisk attachment, beat egg whites at medium speed until soft peaks form.
3. With mixer running, slowly pour hot sugar syrup into egg whites. Increase mixer speed to high, and beat until bowl is cool to the touch, about 7 minutes. Use immediately.

STRAWBERRY TARTLETS WITH SOFT CREAM

Makes 8 (4-inch) tartlets

Recipe by Marjorie Taylor and
Kendall Smith Franchini

*This recipe is a crowd favorite at Beaune,
France's cooking school The Cooks Atelier,
run by mother-daughter duo Marjorie Taylor
and Kendall Smith Franchini. When preparing
these tartlets, use the tiniest strawberries you
can find. Be sure not to overfill the tarts with
the pastry cream—you want a nice balance
between the cream and the fruit.*

Pâte Sucrée (recipe follows)
Unbleached all-purpose flour, for work surface
1   **large egg yolk (19 grams)**
½   **cup (120 grams) plus 2 to
     3 tablespoons (30 to 45 grams)
     heavy whipping cream, divided**
Granulated sugar, for sprinkling
1   **tablespoon (7 grams) confectioners'
     sugar, plus more for dusting**
Crème Pâtissière (recipe follows), chilled
1   **pound (455 grams) tiny organic
     strawberries, hulled and sliced**

1. Preheat the oven to 350°F (180°C).
2. Remove Pâte Sucrée dough from the
refrigerator 10 to 15 minutes before rolling
to ensure it is slightly soft and ready to roll.
3. Use a bench scraper to divide each disk
into 4 triangular pieces. Using your hands,
gently shape each triangular piece into a small
ball and then flatten the balls into small disks.
4. Place the dough on a lightly floured
surface. Lightly flour a rolling pin. Begin
rolling the dough balls into ⅛-inch-thick,
5- to 6-inch-diameter rounds, turning the
dough as you roll to make an even circle. Be
sure to check you have enough flour under
the dough so it doesn't stick.
5. Once the dough is slightly larger than
your 4-inch tartlet pans, gently roll it around
the rolling pin, brushing off any excess flour
with a pastry brush as you go. Place it in the
tartlet pans, being careful not to stretch it.
Begin trimming the edges by pushing your
thumb against the side edges of the pan.
Use your other thumb to trim away the

extra dough at the edge. Be careful to make
the dough the same thickness all the way
around to create a uniform edge.
6. Freeze for 15 to 20 minutes before baking.
(If you want to freeze the tart shells for
longer, wrap in a double layer of plastic wrap
and freeze for up to 2 months. Frozen tart
shells can be baked straight from the freezer
without thawing.)
7. Line the tartlet shells with parchment
paper, leaving a 1-inch overhang, and place
them on a baking sheet. Fill with dried beans
or pie weights.
8. Bake until the edges are set and just
beginning to turn golden, 8 to 10 minutes.
Remove the parchment paper and beans.
In a small bowl, whisk together the egg yolk
and 2 to 3 tablespoons (30 to 45 grams)
of the heavy cream. Use a pastry brush to
lightly brush the egg wash on the bottom
of the tartlet shells and then sprinkle with
a little granulated sugar. Continue baking
until the tart shells are golden and cooked
through, about 10 minutes. Set on a wire
rack to cool completely before assembling.
9. In a large bowl, combine the confectioners'
sugar and the remaining ½ cup (120 grams)
heavy cream and then use a balloon whisk to
beat until soft peaks form. Add a spoonful
to the Crème Pâtissière and stir to lighten
it. Remove the cooled tartlet shells from the
pans and then spoon the lightened Crème
Pâtissière into the tartlet shells, spreading it
evenly, and top with strawberries. Dust the
tartlets with confectioners' sugar, and serve
immediately.

PÂTE SUCRÉE
Makes enough for 8 (4-inch) tartlets

1½   **cups (188 grams) unbleached
     all-purpose flour**
¼   **cup (50 grams) granulated sugar**
⅛   **teaspoon fleur de sel**
½   **cup (113 grams) cold unsalted butter,
     cut into small pieces**
2   **tablespoons (30 grams) heavy whipping
     cream**
1   **large egg yolk (19 grams)**

1. In a large bowl, whisk together the flour,
sugar, and salt. Add the butter. Using your
hands, gently toss to coat the butter in the
flour mixture. Scoop the mixture in your
hands and gently press the flour mixture
and butter between your fingertips until the
mixture looks grainy with some small pieces
of butter still visible. Work quickly to ensure
the butter stays cold.
2. In a small bowl, whisk together the
heavy cream and egg yolk. Drizzle over the
dough and use a fork to gently toss until
incorporated. Continue working the dough,
gently squeezing it between your fingertips
until it comes together and there is no dry
flour visible. Be careful not to overwork the
dough. You will know it's ready as soon as
you can squish the dough in one hand and it
stays together.
3. Divide the dough in half and shape each
half into a disk. Wrap in plastic wrap and
refrigerate for at least 1 hour, preferably
overnight. Pâte Sucrée can be wrapped in a
double layer of plastic wrap and frozen for
up to 2 weeks.

CRÈME PÂTISSIÈRE
Makes about 1¼ cups

2   **cups (480 grams) whole milk**
½   **cup (100 grams) granulated sugar,
     divided**
1   **vanilla bean, split lengthwise, seeds
     scraped and reserved**
5   **large egg yolks (93 grams)**
3   **tablespoons (24 grams) unbleached
     all-purpose flour**
1   **tablespoon (14 grams) unsalted butter**

1. In a medium saucepan, heat the milk, all
but 1 tablespoon of the sugar, and vanilla
bean and reserved seeds over medium heat
until the sugar is dissolved and the milk is
just under a boil.
2. In a medium bowl, combine the egg yolks
and the reserved 1 tablespoon sugar and
whisk until thick and pale yellow. Sift the
flour over the lightened egg yolks and whisk
to combine.

3. Very slowly add the warm milk mixture to the egg mixture, whisking constantly. Pour the mixture back into the saucepan and place over medium heat. Cook, whisking constantly, until the mixture thickens and just comes to a boil, 2 to 4 minutes. Push the pastry cream through a fine-mesh sieve into a large bowl; discard the vanilla bean.

Whisk in the butter. Press plastic wrap directly on the surface of the pastry cream to prevent a skin from forming. Let cool slightly and then refrigerate until chilled and set, about 2 hours.

Photo by Joann Pai

PRO TIP

This dough is a great base for variations. For a nut dough, replace ¼ cup (31 grams) all-purpose flour with ¼ cup (35 grams) hazelnuts or almonds, toasted, skins removed (if using hazelnuts), and finely chopped. For a citrus dough, add 1 to 2 teaspoons (1 to 2 grams) finely grated lemon or orange zest.

CLASSIC APPLE TARTE TATIN

Makes 1 (10-inch) tarte Tatin

Recipe by Susan Spungen

Susan Spungen first became a true expert at making tarte Tatin while working on the movie Julie & Julia, and is a firm believer that making a good tarte Tatin is all about technique.

½ recipe Extra Flaky Dough (recipe follows)
7 to 8 large Pink Lady or Gala apples (about 1,300 grams)
½ lemon (50 grams)
¾ cup (150 grams) granulated sugar
¼ cup (57 grams) cold unsalted butter, cubed
½ vanilla bean, split lengthwise, seeds scraped and reserved
Crème fraîche, to serve

1. Preheat oven to 400°F (200°C).
2. On a lightly floured sheet of parchment paper, roll Extra Flaky Dough into a 12-inch circle, about ⅛ inch thick. (When rolling dough out on parchment, make sure the paper is long so you can keep it in place by leaning up against the counter with the paper between you and the counter.) Place on a lightly floured plate, and refrigerate until ready to use.
3. Peel apples, cut them into thirds off core, and cut out any remaining seeds. Squeeze lemon over them.
4. In a 12-inch skillet, cook sugar over medium heat until it begins to liquefy, 2 to 4 minutes. (Do not stir.) When it starts to melt more and brown, reduce heat slightly, give it one good stir with a whisk to avoid any sugar clumps, and don't stir again. Remove from heat; add cold butter, and swirl skillet to melt.
5. Return skillet to heat; add apples and vanilla bean and reserved seeds. Cook over medium heat, gently stirring and turning, until apples soften and start to become translucent at the edges, about 10 minutes. Remove from heat; let cool slightly. Discard vanilla bean.
6. Using tongs, transfer apples, rounded side down, one at a time, to a 10-inch ovenproof skillet. (You could also use a 10-inch pie plate if you don't have a skillet.) Arrange apples in a circle around outside, overlapping and crowding them. Arrange remaining apples in center of ring. Scrape any leftover caramel over apples in skillet. Top with Extra Flaky Dough, tucking edges in all around. (The pastry should cradle the apples completely.) Cut a few vents in center, and place skillet on a baking sheet.
7. Bake until pastry is nicely browned and apples are bubbling around edges, 30 to 35 minutes. Run a knife around edges to loosen. Let cool in pan for 15 minutes. If it has cooled completely before you serve, either return to oven to warm up, or place over low heat for a few minutes to melt caramel again. Invert tart onto a serving plate. (If any apples stick to pan, just place them where they should go on the tart.) Serve warm with crème fraîche.

PRO TIP

To test the true color of the caramel, which can be hard to judge in a dark pan, drizzle a little onto a white paper towel or scrap paper as it cooks. If you are comfortable with your caramel-making abilities, you can cook until your caramel is a deep amber.

EXTRA FLAKY DOUGH

Makes dough for 2 (10-inch) tarts or 8 (4- to 5-inch) tarts

By mimicking the folding and laminating process of puff pastry, starting with larger-than-usual chunks of butter, you can quickly create Extra Flaky Dough that, with its extra bit of sturdiness, is better suited to sit upon (or below) caramelized fruit. Therefore, this dough is perfect for tarte Tatin.

1 cup plus 2 tablespoons (255 grams) cold unsalted butter, cut into tablespoon-size pieces
2½ cups (313 grams) all-purpose flour
1 teaspoon (4 grams) granulated sugar
¾ teaspoon (2.25 grams) kosher salt
6 to 8 tablespoons (90 to 120 grams) ice water
1 tablespoon (15 grams) apple cider vinegar

1. Place butter in freezer for 10 to 15 minutes.
2. In the work bowl of a food processor; place flour, sugar, and salt; pulse until combined. (See Note.) Add frozen butter, and pulse until butter is in nickel- to quarter-size pieces. (It should still be making a thumping sound when pulsed.) Transfer mixture to a large bowl.
3. In a small bowl or measuring cup, stir together 6 tablespoons (90 grams) ice water and vinegar. (See PRO TIP.) Drizzle water mixture into flour mixture, stirring with a fork until combined. Add enough remaining ice water until dough holds together when squeezed. If it still looks powdery and dry, add more water, 1 tablespoon (15 grams) at a time, until it holds together.
4. Press dough together into a rough mass in bowl, and transfer to a sheet of parchment paper. Shape dough into a rough rectangle, and very lightly dust with flour. Roll dough into a 16x8-inch rectangle. Fold dough into thirds. Give dough a quarter or 90-degree turn, lightly flour again, and roll into a 16x8-inch rectangle again. Fold dough into thirds again, and freeze for 10 to 15 minutes. Repeat procedure, giving dough 2 more turns. Wrap dough tightly in plastic wrap, and refrigerate for at least 2 hours or preferably overnight.
5. Divide dough in half, and gently press each half into a rounder shape before rolling out.

Note: *To make a savory variation, which can be used for the Tomato Tarte Tatin (page 225), add ½ cup (48 grams) freshly grated Parmesan cheese and 1 tablespoon (2 grams) fresh thyme leaves to the flour mixture.*

PRO TIP

When making ice water for dough, use a liquid-measuring cup (or any spouted container) filled with ice cubes and water, and measure what you need in a smaller liquid-measuring cup.

Photo by Jason Varney

TOMATO TARTE TATIN

Makes 1 (10-inch) tarte Tatin

Recipe by Susan Spungen

You can use any tomatoes you like for this tart, but the most consistent results will come from using brown supermarket tomatoes such as Kumato or Brunetta. These are quite flavorful when roasted, available year-round, and have a moisture content that's predictable, an important factor when making a tarte Tatin with tomatoes. This savory triumph goes well with rich, creamy Burrata.

2   pounds (910 grams) Kumato tomatoes (preferably larger ones)
1   tablespoon (14 grams) plus 2 teaspoons (10 grams) olive oil, divided
1¼   teaspoons (3.75 grams) plus ⅛ teaspoon kosher salt, divided
Ground black pepper, to taste
½   recipe Extra Flaky Dough, savory variation (recipe on page 220)
1   tablespoon (14 grams) plus 2 teaspoons (10 grams) cold unsalted butter
4   small shallots (133 grams), sliced lengthwise (1¼ cups)
1   sprig fresh thyme
2   tablespoons (30 grams) sherry vinegar, divided
1   tablespoon (15 grams) water
⅓   cup (67 grams) granulated sugar
Burrata, to serve
Garnish: Aleppo pepper, fresh thyme leaves

1. Preheat oven to 300°F (150°C). Line a large baking sheet with parchment paper.
2. Cut tomatoes in half horizontally. In a large bowl, toss together tomatoes, 1 tablespoon (14 grams) oil, ¾ teaspoon (2.25 grams) salt, and black pepper. Spread tomatoes on prepared pan, cut side up.
3. Bake until quite shriveled around edges but still soft and juicy in center, about 1½ hours. Let cool slightly. (Let cool in oven if you have time. This can be done up to 1 day ahead of time.) Increase oven temperature to 400°F (200°C).
4. On a lightly floured sheet of parchment paper, roll Extra Flaky Dough into a 12-inch circle, about ⅛ inch thick. (When rolling dough out on parchment, make sure the paper is long

so you can keep it in place by leaning up against the counter with the paper between you and the counter.) Place on a lightly floured plate, and refrigerate until ready to use.
5. In a 10-inch ovenproof skillet, heat 2 teaspoons (10 grams) cold butter and remaining 2 teaspoons (10 grams) oil over medium-high heat. Add shallots, thyme sprig, and ½ teaspoon (1.5 grams) salt; cook, stirring occasionally, until shallots are deep golden brown and very soft, 12 to 15 minutes. Stir in 1 tablespoon (15 grams) vinegar and 1 tablespoon (15 grams) water, scraping browned bits from bottom of skillet with a wooden spoon. Cook until all liquid is absorbed, about 30 seconds. Transfer shallots to a small bowl; discard thyme.
6. Wipe skillet clean; add sugar. Cook over medium heat until sugar begins to liquefy, 2 to 4 minutes. (Do not stir.) When it starts to melt more and brown, reduce heat slightly, give it one good stir with a whisk to avoid any sugar clumps, and don't stir again. Gently and carefully swirl skillet until sugar is amber, about 5 minutes. Remove from heat; add remaining 1 tablespoon (14 grams) cold butter, and swirl skillet to melt. Add remaining 1 tablespoon (15 grams) vinegar, and stand back to avoid any spattering. When it dies down, add remaining ⅛ teaspoon salt, and whisk until smooth. Let cool slightly.
7. Arrange tomatoes, cut side down, in skillet, being careful not to touch hot caramel. You can place some of them cut side up for variety. Nudge them together so they are fairly tight with no spaces. If you have a few extra pieces, simply layer them on top. Top with shallots. Place Extra Flaky Dough on top, tucking edges in all around. Cut a few vents in center, and place skillet on a baking sheet.
8. Bake until pastry is nicely browned and tomatoes are bubbling around edges, 30 to 35 minutes. Let cool in pan for at least 45 minutes to allow juices to thicken and cool. If making ahead of time, leave in pan until ready to serve, reheating if desired. Invert onto a serving plate. Serve with Burrata. Sprinkle with Aleppo pepper and thyme leaves, if desired.

Note: *The longer-than-usual time ranges for this recipe are given because times for cooking caramel can vary greatly depending on the thickness of the pan and what kind of stove you have, in addition to many other variables. Use the times given as guidelines, but pay close attention to the visual clues for the greatest success.*

Photo by Jason Varney

PINEAPPLE TARTES TATIN

Makes 4 (4- to 5-inch) tartes Tatin

Recipe by Susan Spungen

Fruit that is not overly juicy, like pineapple, works well for a tarte Tatin. Too much moisture (like you might get with peaches or berries) dilutes the caramel and makes the crust soggy after you turn it over. For another tropical twist, substitute chunks of mango for the pineapple.

1   large pineapple (1,800 grams) (about 4 pounds)
½   recipe Extra Flaky Dough (recipe on page 220)
⅔   cup (133 grams) granulated sugar
3   tablespoons (42 grams) unsalted butter, cubed
½   vanilla bean, split lengthwise, seeds scraped and reserved
Vanilla ice cream, to serve
½   cup (42 grams) unsweetened coconut flakes, toasted

1. Preheat oven to 400°F (200°C). Line a baking sheet with parchment paper.
2. Using a large sharp knife, cut top and bottom off pineapple. Standing it on one end, cut lengthwise into quarters. Cut core out of each quarter, and using a smaller knife, carefully cut flesh away from rind, wasting as little as possible. Cut each quarter lengthwise down center, and cut crosswise into ½-inch slices, which will result in flat trapezoid-shape pieces. Set aside.
3. On a lightly floured sheet of parchment paper, roll Extra Flaky Dough to about ⅛-inch thickness. (When rolling dough out on parchment, make sure the paper is long so you can keep it in place by leaning up against the counter with the paper between you and the counter.) Cut 4 (5- to 6-inch) circles (slightly larger than your baking dishes). Lightly flour pastry circles, and stack on a plate. Refrigerate until ready to use.

4. In a 12-inch skillet, cook sugar over medium heat until it begins to liquefy, 2 to 4 minutes. (Do not stir.) When it starts to melt more and brown, reduce heat slightly, give it one good stir with a whisk to avoid any sugar clumps, and don't stir again. Gently and carefully swirl skillet until sugar is amber, about 5 minutes. Remove from heat; add butter, and swirl skillet to melt.
5. Return skillet to heat; add pineapple and vanilla bean and reserved seeds. Cook over high heat, stirring frequently, until fruit has softened and caramel starts to thicken, 7 to 8 minutes. Transfer to a large bowl; let cool slightly.
6. Divide fruit and caramel among 4 (4- to 5-inch) ceramic baking dishes, arranging fruit in one flat, tight layer, fitting pieces in like a puzzle. Top each with an Extra Flaky Dough circle, and tuck dough in all around edges. Cut a vent in center of each, and place on prepared pan.
7. Bake until pastry is nicely browned and fruit is bubbling around edges, 25 to 30 minutes. Using a spatula, immediately transfer dishes to a wire rack. Let cool in dishes for at least 15 minutes and preferably 45 minutes to 1 hour. Invert each tart onto a dessert plate. Serve with vanilla ice cream, and top with coconut.

> **PRO TIP**
> To ensure that the fruit won't stick to the dish, gently spin the tart in the dish as soon as it is cool enough to handle and again just before unmolding. Press gently on the pastry and rotate.

Photo by Jason Varney

FRUIT TARTLETS

Makes 12 tartlets

Inverting the muffin pan to bake this Tart Dough on the outside of the muffin cups gives the shells defined shape and flaky texture. Top your tartlets with whichever berries or sliced fruit you like.

Tart Dough (recipe follows)
Pastry Cream (recipe follows)
4   cups (about 560 grams) assorted fresh berries (such as blackberries, blueberries, and raspberries)
½   cup (160 grams) apricot preserves
1   tablespoon (15 grams) water

1. Preheat oven to 350°F (180°C). Invert a 12-cup muffin pan.
2. On a lightly floured surface, roll Tart Dough to ⅛-inch thickness. Using a 3¾- to 4-inch fluted round cutter*, cut 12 rounds (about 16 grams each), rerolling scraps as necessary. Drape 1 round onto bottom of each muffin cup. Prick each several times with a fork.
3. Bake until crusts are golden brown, 15 to 18 minutes. Let cool on pan for 10 minutes. Remove from pan, and let cool completely on a wire rack.
4. Pipe about ¼ cup (85 grams) Pastry Cream into each prepared tart shell. Top with desired berries.
5. In a small microwave-safe bowl, heat preserves and 1 tablespoon (15 grams) water just until bubbly; stir until combined. Strain mixture through a medium-mesh sieve. Carefully brush mixture onto fruit. Serve immediately.

Fluted pastry cutters will work fine, but we chose to cut our pastry with an inverted 3⅞-inch fluted tart pan for a prettier scallop design.

Tart Dough

Makes dough for 12 tartlets

½   cup (113 grams) cold unsalted butter*
1⅓ cups all-purpose flour (167 grams)
1   tablespoon (12 grams) granulated sugar
1   teaspoon (3 grams) kosher salt
1½ tablespoons (22.5 grams) whole milk
1   large egg yolk (19 grams)

1. Cut butter into ¼-inch cubes. Freeze until firm, about 10 minutes.
2. In the bowl of a stand mixer fitted with the paddle attachment, stir together flour, sugar, and salt by hand. Add frozen butter, and beat at low speed until butter is broken into small pieces, 1 to 2 minutes. (If any large pieces of butter remain, squeeze between fingers to break up.)
3. In a 1-cup liquid-measuring cup, whisk together milk and egg yolk. With mixer on lowest speed, add milk mixture to flour mixture, beating just until moist clumps form. Transfer mixture to a large piece of plastic wrap. Using your hands, bring mixture together to form a cohesive dough. (It is fine if there are visible pieces of butter—they help create a flakier crust.) Shape dough into a disk, and wrap in plastic wrap. Refrigerate for at least 1 hour or overnight. (Dough can be made ahead and refrigerated for up to 3 days or frozen for up to 1 month.)

We used Président® Butter.

Pastry Cream

Makes about 3 cups

3   cups (720 grams) whole milk
1   cup (200 grams) granulated sugar, divided
1   teaspoon (6 grams) vanilla bean paste
8   large egg yolks (149 grams)
¼   cup plus 3 tablespoons (56 grams) cornstarch
¼   teaspoon kosher salt
¼   cup (57 grams) unsalted butter, softened

1. In a large saucepan, whisk together milk, ½ cup (100 grams) sugar, and vanilla bean paste. Heat over medium heat until steaming.
2. In a large bowl, whisk together egg yolks, cornstarch, salt, and remaining ½ cup (100 grams) sugar. Gradually add warm milk mixture to egg yolk mixture, whisking constantly. Pour mixture back into saucepan, and cook over medium heat, whisking constantly, until thickened and bubbly, 4 to 5 minutes. Cook until cornstarch flavor has cooked out, about 1 minute.
3. Strain mixture through a fine-mesh sieve into a large bowl. Stir in butter in two additions. Cover with a piece of plastic wrap, pressing wrap directly onto surface of cream to prevent a skin from forming. Refrigerate until cold. Whisk until smooth before using.

PEAR AND HONEYED GOAT CHEESE GALETTE

Makes 1 (10-inch) galette

It's time to up your galette game. This buttery beauty is great for breakfast or cocktail hour. A sugared golden crust encircles warm, tangy goat cheese topped with sweet Bosc pears, which bake into a deep rustic hue. Thanks to the layered pears, the gorgeous design is effortless and accentuates the fruit's natural shape.

2	cups (250 grams) all-purpose flour
1	teaspoon (3 grams) kosher salt
¾	cup (170 grams) cold unsalted butter*, cubed
4	ounces (115 grams) cold goat cheese
1	tablespoon (15 grams) apple cider vinegar
2	tablespoons (30 grams) ice water

Honeyed Goat Cheese Filling (recipe follows)

3	slightly firm medium Bosc pears (537 grams)
1	large egg (50 grams)
1	tablespoon (15 grams) water
1	tablespoon (12 grams) granulated sugar

Garnish: clover honey, fresh rosemary

1. In the work bowl of a food processor, place flour and salt; pulse until combined. Add cold butter and cold goat cheese, and pulse until mixture is crumbly. Add vinegar, pulsing until combined. With processor running, add 2 tablespoons (30 grams) ice water, 1 tablespoon (15 grams) at a time, just until dough comes together. Turn out dough, and shape into a disk. Wrap tightly in plastic wrap, and refrigerate for at least 30 minutes.

2. Preheat oven to 425°F (220°C). Line a baking sheet with parchment paper.

3. On a lightly floured surface, roll dough into a 14-inch circle, about ¼ inch thick. Transfer to prepared pan. Spread Honeyed Goat Cheese Filling onto dough, leaving a 2-inch border.

4. Cut pears in half vertically through stems. Scoop out core of each half. Place pears cut side down, and cut into thin slices, leaving about ½ inch intact below stem. Fan pears out, and place on top of filling, overlapping as needed. Fold edges of dough over pears.

5. In a small bowl, whisk together egg and 1 tablespoon (15 grams) water. Brush egg wash onto dough, and sprinkle with sugar.

6. Bake until crust is golden and bottom is browned, 25 to 35 minutes. Let cool on pan for 10 minutes. Garnish with honey and rosemary, if desired. Serve warm or at room temperature.

*We used Président® Butter.

HONEYED GOAT CHEESE FILLING

Makes ¾ cup

6	ounces (175 grams) goat cheese
3	tablespoons (63 grams) clover honey
1½	tablespoons (21 grams) firmly packed light brown sugar
¼	teaspoon ground nutmeg

1. In a medium bowl, whisk together goat cheese and honey until smooth. Whisk in brown sugar and nutmeg. Use immediately, or refrigerate until ready to use.

BAKEWELL TART

Makes 1 (9-inch) tart

Fans of frangipane, rejoice: this Bakewell Tart is the dessert for you. Instead of the traditional raspberry jam this legendary British recipe calls for, we used sweet plum preserves. Amp up the almond even further with our glaze flavored with almond liqueur.

Pâte Sablée (recipe follows)
¾ cup (240 grams) plum preserves*
½ cup (113 grams) unsalted butter, softened
½ cup (100 grams) granulated sugar
2 large eggs (100 grams)
1 tablespoon (15 grams) almond liqueur
1¼ cups (120 grams) almond flour
2 tablespoons (16 grams) all-purpose flour
⅓ cup (38 grams) sliced almonds
Almond Glaze (recipe follows)

1. Preheat oven to 325°F (170°C).
2. On a lightly floured surface, roll Pâte Sablée into an 11-inch circle, about ¼ inch thick. Transfer to a 9-inch round tart pan, gently pressing into bottom and up sides. Trim excess dough. Freeze until hard, about 10 minutes. Prick bottom of dough with a fork. Top with a piece of parchment paper, letting ends extend over edges of pan. Add pie weights.
3. Bake until edges look dry, about 15 minutes. Carefully remove paper and weights. Bake until crust is dry, about 10 minutes more. Let cool completely on a wire rack.
4. Preheat oven to 350°F (180°C).
5. Spread preserves into prepared Pâte Sablée. Refrigerate while preparing filling.
6. In the bowl of a stand mixer fitted with the paddle attachment, beat butter and sugar at medium speed until creamy, 3 to 4 minutes, stopping to scrape sides of bowl. Add eggs, one at a time, beating well after each addition. Beat in liqueur.

7. In a medium bowl, whisk together flours. With mixer on low speed, gradually add flour mixture to butter mixture, beating just until combined. Spread filling onto preserves, and sprinkle with almonds.
8. Bake until golden and set, 45 to 50 minutes. Let cool in pan for 15 minutes. Remove from pan, and drizzle with Almond Glaze. Serve warm or at room temperature.

We used Wilkin & Sons Tiptree Damson Preserves.

PÂTE SABLÉE
Makes dough for 1 (9-inch) crust

½ cup (113 grams) unsalted butter, softened
⅓ cup (40 grams) confectioners' sugar
1 tablespoon (3 grams) lemon zest
½ teaspoon (1.5 grams) kosher salt
1 large egg yolk (19 grams)
1½ cups (188 grams) pastry flour

1. In the bowl of a stand mixer fitted with the paddle attachment, beat butter at medium speed until smooth, about 1 minute. Add confectioners' sugar, lemon zest, and salt, and beat until smooth, about 1 minute. Add egg yolk, and beat until combined, about 1 minute. Add flour in two additions, beating just until combined after each addition. Turn out dough onto a lightly floured surface, and gently knead 3 to 4 times. Shape dough into a disk, and wrap in plastic wrap. Refrigerate for 1 hour.

ALMOND GLAZE
Makes ¼ cup

½ cup (60 grams) confectioners' sugar
4 teaspoons (20 grams) almond liqueur

1. In a medium bowl, whisk together confectioners' sugar and liqueur until smooth. Use immediately.

JAM AND CREAM BRIOCHE TART

Makes 1 (9-inch) tart

In a 1997 episode of Julia Child's Baking with Julia, Nancy Silverton baked a brioche tart that was so good it made Julia cry. In our take on this groundbreaking dessert, we filled a pillowy brioche "crust" with velvety cream cheese custard and swirled it with fruit preserves. Finished off with crunchy pearl sugar, this stunner might just make you shed a tear, too.

2¾	cups (344 grams) all-purpose flour
3	tablespoons (36 grams) granulated sugar
2¼	teaspoons (7 grams) instant yeast
1½	teaspoons (4.5 grams) kosher salt
⅓	cup plus 1 tablespoon (95 grams) warm whole milk (120°F/49°C to 130°F/54°C)
3	large eggs (150 grams), room temperature and divided
1	teaspoon (4 grams) vanilla extract
6	tablespoons (84 grams) unsalted butter, softened
	Cream Cheese Filling (recipe follows)
2	tablespoons (40 grams) fruit preserves*
1	tablespoon (15 grams) water
1½	tablespoons (18 grams) Swedish pearl sugar

1. In the bowl of a stand mixer fitted with the paddle attachment, beat flour, granulated sugar, yeast, and salt at very low speed until combined, about 30 seconds. Slowly add warm milk, and beat at medium speed until combined. Add 2 eggs (100 grams) and vanilla, and beat until combined, about 1 minute.
2. Switch to the dough hook attachment. Beat at low speed until smooth and elastic, about 8 minutes. Add butter, 1 tablespoon (14 grams) at a time, beating until combined after each addition, about 8 minutes total. Beat until a smooth and elastic dough forms, about 6 minutes. Turn out dough onto a lightly floured surface, and knead 4 to 5 times. Shape dough into a smooth round.
3. Spray a large bowl with cooking spray. Place dough in bowl, turning to grease top. Cover and let rise in a warm, draft-free place (75°F/24°C) until doubled in size, 30 to 45 minutes.
4. Spray a 9-inch square baking pan with cooking spray. Line pan with parchment paper, letting excess extend over sides of pan.

5. On a lightly floured surface, roll dough into an 11-inch square. Score a 9-inch square in center of dough. Fold outside 2 inches over score mark, creating a crust around edges. Lift dough, and place in prepared pan, making sure dough is even and fills corners of pan. Cover and let rise until puffed, 20 to 30 minutes.
6. Preheat oven to 325°F (170°C).
7. Using your fingertips, dimple center of dough back down, leaving outside crust as is. Pour Cream Cheese Filling into center of dough. Make small indentations in Cream Cheese Filling. Fill indentations with teaspoonfuls of preserves. Using a knife, swirl preserves into Cream Cheese Filling.
8. In a small bowl, whisk together 1 tablespoon (15 grams) water and remaining 1 egg (50 grams). Brush dough with egg wash, and sprinkle with pearl sugar.
9. Bake until crust is golden brown, filling is set around outside edges and slightly jiggly in center, and an instant-read thermometer inserted in center registers 175°F (79°C), 35 to 40 minutes. Let cool in pan for 10 minutes. Using excess parchment as handles, remove from pan. Serve warm, or let cool completely on a wire rack.

We used Bonne Maman Four Fruits Preserves.

CREAM CHEESE FILLING
Makes 1½ cups

2	tablespoons (28 grams) unsalted butter, softened
⅓	cup (67 grams) granulated sugar
1	teaspoon (6 grams) vanilla bean paste
¼	teaspoon kosher salt
8	ounces (225 grams) cream cheese, softened
1	large egg (50 grams), room temperature
3	tablespoons (24 grams) all-purpose flour

1. In the bowl of a stand mixer fitted with the paddle attachment, beat butter, sugar, vanilla bean paste, and salt at medium speed until well combined. Gradually add cream cheese, beating until smooth. Add egg, beating until combined. Beat in flour.

TRIPLE-CHOCOLATE PEPPERMINT TART

Makes 1 (13¾x4½-inch) tart

For the Williams Sonoma Peppermint Bark Off in 2018, Erin Clarkson of the blog Cloudy Kitchen made the most epic Peppermint Bark and Milk Chocolate Tart with Swiss Meringue Buttercream. We decided to give her recipe a triple-chocolate spin studded with sea salt and packed with crushed peppermint candies. The Simple Salted Peppermint Bark rounds out every bite of this indulgent dessert with wintry freshness.

1½ cups (170 grams) chocolate graham cracker crumbs (about 11 sheets)
2   tablespoons (24 grams) granulated sugar
6   tablespoons (84 grams) unsalted butter, melted
½   teaspoon (2 grams) vanilla extract
10 ounces (284 grams) 64% cacao semisweet chocolate, chopped
¼   teaspoon kosher salt
1¼ cups (300 grams) heavy whipping cream
¾   teaspoon (3 grams) peppermint extract
White Chocolate Frosting (recipe follows)
Garnish: Simple Salted Peppermint Bark (recipe follows), crushed peppermint candies

1. Preheat oven to 350°F (180°C). Spray a 13¾x4½-inch removable-bottom tart pan with cooking spray.
2. In the work bowl of a food processor, combine graham cracker crumbs and sugar. Pulse until well combined, about 4 pulses. Add melted butter and vanilla; pulse until combined and mixture holds together when pinched. Press mixture into bottom and up sides of prepared pan.
3. Bake until set and fragrant, about 10 minutes. Let cool completely on a wire rack.
4. In a large heatproof bowl, place chocolate and salt.
5. In a medium saucepan, heat cream over medium heat just until bubbles form around edges of pan. (Do not boil.) Pour cream over chocolate; let stand for 5 minutes. Stir until chocolate is melted and mixture is smooth. Stir in peppermint extract. Slowly pour chocolate mixture into prepared crust, carefully smoothing into an even layer with a small offset spatula. (Tart shell will be quite full.) Refrigerate until filling is set, at least 4 hours.
6. Place White Chocolate Frosting in a large piping bag fitted with a coupler; pipe frosting onto tart using a variety of piping tips*. Garnish with Simple Salted Peppermint Bark and peppermint candies, if desired.

We used Wilton No. 21 and No. 32 piping tips.

WHITE CHOCOLATE FROSTING
Makes about 1 cup

3   ounces (85 grams) cream cheese, softened
1   teaspoon (5 grams) unsalted butter, softened
2   ounces (55 grams) white chocolate, melted and cooled for 5 minutes
1   cup (120 grams) confectioners' sugar
¼   teaspoon (1 gram) vanilla extract
⅛   teaspoon kosher salt

1. In a medium bowl, beat cream cheese and butter with a mixer at medium speed until smooth, 1 to 2 minutes. Beat in melted white chocolate. Add confectioners' sugar, vanilla, and salt; beat until well combined, stopping to scrape sides of bowl. Use immediately.

SIMPLE SALTED PEPPERMINT BARK
Makes about 1 pound

6   ounces (170 grams) dark chocolate melting wafers
¾   teaspoon (3 grams) peppermint extract, divided
¼   teaspoon (1 gram) vanilla extract
8   ounces (225 grams) white chocolate melting wafers
8   round peppermint candies (36 grams), roughly crushed
¼   teaspoon (1 gram) flaked sea salt

1. Line a 9-inch square baking pan with parchment paper, letting excess extend over sides of pan.
2. In a small microwave-safe bowl, place dark chocolate; heat on high in 10-second intervals, stirring between each, until melted and smooth, 1 to 1½ minutes. Stir in ½ teaspoon (2 grams) peppermint extract and vanilla.
3. Spread melted dark chocolate on bottom of prepared pan. Firmly tap pan on counter several times to release any air bubbles; let stand for 10 minutes.
4. Meanwhile, in another small microwave-safe bowl, place white chocolate; heat on high in 10-second intervals, stirring between each, until melted and smooth, 1 to 1½ minutes. Stir in remaining ¼ teaspoon (1 gram) peppermint extract.
5. Spread melted white chocolate onto dark chocolate. Sprinkle with crushed peppermints and sea salt. Let stand until hardened, about 1 hour. Use immediately, or store in an airtight container.

MAIDS OF HONOUR TARTS

Makes 12 tartlets

Recipe by Lisa Heathcote

Made with jam and a lightly spiced cottage cheese filling, these tarts were a go-to recipe of renowned food stylist Lisa Heathcote for Downton Abbey, the hit PBS television series and feature film. Maids of Honour Tarts are said to go back to the time of King Henry VIII of England. When Henry noticed Anne Boleyn, then still a maid, savoring these tarts with other ladies in waiting, he decided to try some for himself. He found them so delicious that he named them after the maids.

Puff Pastry Dough (recipe follows)
3½   tablespoons (50 grams) unsalted butter, softened
¼   cup (50 grams) castor sugar
½   cup (50 grams) almond flour
1   medium free-range egg (47 grams), beaten
6   tablespoons (18 grams) lemon zest
1   tablespoon (8 grams) all-purpose flour
½   teaspoon grated fresh nutmeg or ground mace
14   tablespoons (100 grams) full-fat small-curd cottage cheese
6   teaspoons (42 grams) raspberry jam

1. Preheat oven to 350°F (180°C).
2. Roll Puff Pastry Dough to ¹⁄₁₆-inch thickness. Using a 3½-inch round cutter, cut 12 rounds. Transfer to a 12-cup muffin pan, pressing into bottom and up sides of each cup. Refrigerate while preparing filling.
3. In a large bowl, stir together butter and castor sugar with a wooden spoon until creamy and mixture turns pale, 2 to 3 minutes. Add almond flour, egg, lemon zest, all-purpose flour, and nutmeg or mace, stirring until combined. Stir in cottage cheese.
4. Spoon ½ teaspoon (3.5 grams) jam into each prepared crust. Divide cottage cheese mixture among prepared crusts.
5. Bake until risen and lightly browned on top, about 25 minutes. Let cool completely on a wire rack.

PUFF PASTRY DOUGH
Makes enough for 12 tartlets

½   cup (113 grams) unsalted butter, cubed
1   cup (125 grams) all-purpose flour
1   teaspoon (3 grams) kosher salt
3½   tablespoons (52 grams) ice water

1. Freeze butter for 30 minutes.
2. In the work bowl of a food processor, place flour and salt; pulse until combined. Add frozen butter, and pulse until butter is dime-size. With processor running, gradually add 3½ tablespoons (52 grams) ice water just until mixture forms a ball.
3. Turn out dough onto a lightly floured surface, and shape into a disk. Wrap in plastic wrap and refrigerate for at least 30 minutes.

PECAN CARAMEL TASSIES

Makes 24 tassies

Offering sweet and simple satisfaction, there's no denying that pecan tassies are a holiday must-bake. Pecans are the secret ingredient behind these rich bites, adding irresistible crunch to the pecan pie filling and nutty notes that harmonize with the luscious caramel topping. Sprinkled with a pinch of sea salt, these classic treats will go so fast at your next holiday party that you may want to bake a double batch.

½   cup (113 grams) unsalted butter, softened
3   ounces (86 grams) cream cheese, softened
2   teaspoons (8 grams) vanilla extract, divided
1½ cups (188 grams) all-purpose flour
¾   teaspoon (1.5 grams) kosher salt, divided
¼   cup (55 grams) firmly packed dark brown sugar
¼   cup (42 grams) light corn syrup
1   tablespoon (14 grams) unsalted butter, melted
1   large egg (50 grams)

¾   cup (90 grams) pecan pieces*
Caramel Sauce (recipe follows)
Garnish: pecan pieces, flaked sea salt

1. In the bowl of a stand mixer fitted with the paddle attachment, beat softened butter and cream cheese at medium speed until smooth. Beat in ½ teaspoon (2 grams) vanilla. With mixer on low speed, gradually add flour and ½ teaspoon (1.5 grams) kosher salt, beating until combined. Shape dough into a disk, and wrap in plastic wrap. Refrigerate for at least 30 minutes.
2. Preheat oven to 350°F (180°C). Spray a 24-cup mini muffin pan with cooking spray.
3. On a lightly floured surface, roll dough to about ⅛-inch thickness. Using a 2¾-inch round cutter, cut dough, rerolling scraps as needed. Place a round in each prepared muffin cup, pressing into bottom and up sides. Freeze while preparing filling. (Alternatively, divide dough into 24 portions [about 16 grams each]; roll into a ball, and press into bottom and up sides of each muffin cup, trimming excess dough as needed.)
4. In a medium bowl, whisk together brown sugar, corn syrup, and melted butter until

smooth. Add egg and remaining ¼ teaspoon kosher salt, whisking until combined.
5. Sprinkle pecan pieces evenly in each prepared crust. Pour sugar mixture over pecans, filling each cup three-fourths full.
6. Bake until filling is set and an instant-read thermometer inserted in center registers 200°F (93°C), about 25 minutes. Let cool in pan for 10 minutes. Remove from pan, and let cool completely on a wire rack.
7. Place Caramel Sauce in a piping bag. Cut a ¼-inch opening, and pipe sauce on top of pecan filling. Garnish with pecan pieces and sea salt, if desired.

We used Sunnyland Farms Small Pecan Pieces.

Note: *Dough can be made ahead of time. If chilled for a long period of time, let dough stand at room temperature for 15 to 20 minutes before rolling.*

CARAMEL SAUCE
Makes about 1⅓ cups

1   cup (200 grams) granulated sugar
4   tablespoons (60 grams) water, divided
½   cup (120 grams) warm heavy whipping cream
6   tablespoons (84 grams) unsalted butter, cubed and softened

1. In a medium saucepan, heat sugar and 3 tablespoons (45 grams) water over medium heat until sugar is dissolved. Increase heat to high, and use remaining 1 tablespoon (15 grams) water to brush down sides of pan. (Do not stir once it starts to boil.) Cook until desired light amber color is reached. Remove from heat; slowly add warm cream, whisking to combine. Add butter, a few pieces at a time, whisking until combined. Let cool completely.

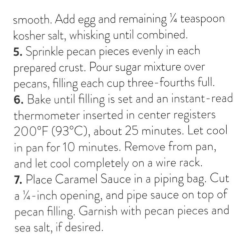

PASTRIES

CINNAMON SUGAR MORNING BUNS

Makes 14 to 18 buns

It's a callback to the cinnamon sugar-packed original but done one better. With our Danish Dough base and brown sugar and cinnamon filling, there was only one thing missing from the formula: crunchy, toasted pecans.

½   cup (113 grams) unsalted butter, melted and divided
Danish Dough (recipe below)
½   cup (110 grams) firmly packed dark brown sugar
⅓   cup (67 grams) granulated sugar, plus more for dusting
2   tablespoons (12 grams) ground cinnamon
½   teaspoon (1.5 grams) kosher salt
⅔   cup (75 grams) chopped pecans
Cinnamon sugar (see Note)

1. Brush muffin cups with 2 tablespoons (28 grams) melted butter. Dust with granulated sugar, tapping out excess.
2. Freeze Danish Dough for 15 to 30 minutes. On a lightly floured surface, roll dough into an 18x12-inch rectangle.
3. In a medium bowl, combine brown sugar, granulated sugar, cinnamon, and salt.
4. Using a pastry brush, brush remaining ¼ cup plus 2 tablespoons (85 grams) melted butter onto dough. Sprinkle brown sugar mixture onto butter, leaving a ½-inch border on one long side. Top with pecans. Starting at opposite long side, roll up dough, jelly roll style. Trim edges, if needed, and cut dough into 1-inch rolls. Place rolls, cut side up, in prepared muffin cups, gently pressing down until dough fills mold. Cover and let rise in a warm, draft-free place (75°F/24°C) until puffed, 45 minutes to 1 hour.
5. Preheat oven to 375°F (190°C).
6. Bake until golden brown and an instant-read thermometer inserted in center registers 210°F (99°C), 20 to 25 minutes, covering with foil halfway through baking to prevent excess browning, if necessary. Let cool in pans until cool enough to handle, about 10 minutes. Remove from pans, and toss in cinnamon sugar. Let cool completely on wire racks.

Note: *To make cinnamon sugar, whisk together 1 cup (200 grams) granulated sugar and 1 tablespoon (6 grams) ground cinnamon.*

DANISH DOUGH

Makes dough for 14 to 18 buns

The secret to the addictive, mind-blowing texture of the morning bun begins and ends with this Danish Dough, an enriched, laminated beauty worth every bit of effort and energy it takes to make it. Trust us.

1   cup (240 grams) whole milk, room temperature (70°F/21°C)
1   large egg (50 grams), room temperature
1   large egg yolk (19 grams), room temperature
2¼   teaspoons (7 grams) instant yeast*
4   cups plus 1½ tablespoons (520 grams) bread flour*, plus more for dusting
⅓   cup (67 grams) granulated sugar
1   cup plus 4½ tablespoons (290 grams) unsalted butter, softened and divided
1   tablespoon (9 grams) kosher salt

1. In the bowl of a stand mixer fitted with the dough hook attachment, whisk together milk, egg, egg yolk, and yeast by hand. Add flour, sugar, 3 tablespoons (42 grams) butter, and salt, and beat at low speed until dough comes together, about 1 minute. Beat until dough pulls away from sides of bowl and is smooth when a small amount is pinched off, about 5 minutes. Turn out dough onto a lightly floured surface, and shape into a smooth ball.
2. Spray a large bowl with cooking spray. Place dough in bowl, turning to grease top. Cover and let rise in a warm, draft-free place (75°F/24°C) until doubled in size, about 2 hours.
3. Using a pencil, draw a 12x8-inch rectangle on a sheet of parchment paper; turn parchment over. Place remaining 1 cup plus 1½ tablespoons (248 grams) butter on parchment. Cover with a second sheet of parchment, and shape to fit inside drawn rectangle, keeping edges straight and even. (If butter gets too soft to work with, refrigerate for 5 minutes before continuing.) Keep wrapped in parchment paper, and refrigerate overnight.
4. Line a sheet pan with parchment paper. Lightly dust with flour.
5. Turn out dough onto a lightly floured surface, and gently shape into a 10x8-inch rectangle. Place on prepared pan. Cover tightly with plastic wrap (to ensure dough does not dry out), and refrigerate overnight.
6. Place dough in freezer for 15 to 30 minutes. Let butter block stand at room temperature until pliable, 10 to 15 minutes.
7. On a lightly floured surface, roll dough into a 16x12-inch rectangle. Unwrap butter block, and place in center of dough. Fold dough over butter block, meeting in the middle, and press lightly to seal dough around butter block. Turn dough 90 degrees, and immediately roll dough into an 18x12-inch rectangle. Fold into thirds, like a letter; turn 90 degrees, and roll out again. Fold into thirds again, like a letter. Wrap dough in plastic wrap, and freeze for 15 to 30 minutes. Roll and fold, letter style, one more time. Wrap dough in plastic wrap, and refrigerate for 1½ hours. (Alternatively, wrap tightly in plastic wrap, and freeze for up to 3 months. When ready to use, let thaw in refrigerator overnight.)

We used Platinum® Yeast from Red Star® and King Arthur Bread Flour.

EVERYTHING MORNING BUNS

Makes 14 to 18 buns

The original morning bun is an epic combination of a croissant and a cinnamon roll. This goes to the savory side of things, pairing laminated texture with the umami-rich flavor blend of everything seasoning, extra-sharp Cheddar, and cream cheese associated with the bagel. It's the mash-up you never knew you needed.

½	tablespoon (7 grams) unsalted butter
¼	cup (34 grams) diced sweet onion

Danish Dough (recipe on page 240)

4	ounces (115 grams) cream cheese, softened
5	ounces (150 grams) coarsely grated extra-sharp white Cheddar cheese (about 1½ cups)
½	teaspoon garlic salt

Garnish: everything bagel seasoning*

1. Spray muffin cups with cooking spray.

2. In a medium skillet, melt butter over medium heat. Add onion; cook until translucent and slightly browned, 5 to 7 minutes. Let cool to room temperature.

3. Freeze Danish Dough for 15 to 30 minutes. On a lightly floured surface, roll dough into an 18x12-inch rectangle.

4. Spread softened cream cheese onto dough. Sprinkle onion, Cheddar, and garlic salt onto cream cheese, leaving a ½-inch border on one long side. Starting at opposite long side, roll up dough, jelly roll style. Trim edges, if needed, and cut dough into 1-inch rolls. Place rolls, cut side up, in prepared muffin cups, gently pressing down until dough fills mold. Garnish with everything bagel seasoning, if desired. Cover and let rise in a warm, draft-free place (75°F/24°C) until puffed, 45 minutes to 1 hour.

5. Preheat oven to 375°F (190°C).

6. Bake until golden brown and an instant-read thermometer inserted in center registers 210°F (99°C), 20 to 25 minutes, covering with foil halfway through baking to prevent excess browning, if necessary. Let cool in pans until cool enough to handle, about 10 minutes. Remove from pans, and let cool completely on wire racks.

*We used Trader Joe's Everything Bagel Seasoning.

MEYER LEMON MORNING BUNS

Makes 14 to 18 buns

Inspired by the orange-infused morning buns available at Tartine in San Francisco, California, we decided to imbue our sunny version with the reigning star of winter citrus: Meyer lemon. We like to finish off this tangy triumph—packing just a hint of warm cardamom within its tight spiral—with a bright Blueberry Sugar coating.

½ cup (113 grams) unsalted butter, melted and divided
Granulated sugar, for dusting
Danish Dough (recipe on page 240)
1 cup (200 grams) Meyer Lemon Sugar (recipe follows)
¼ teaspoon ground cardamom
Desired flavored sugar (recipes follow)

1. Brush muffin cups with 2 tablespoons (28 grams) melted butter. Dust with granulated sugar, tapping out excess.
2. Freeze Danish Dough for 15 to 30 minutes. On a lightly floured surface, roll dough into an 18x12-inch rectangle.

3. In a small bowl, combine Meyer Lemon Sugar and cardamom.
4. Using a pastry brush, brush remaining ¼ cup plus 2 tablespoons (85 grams) melted butter onto dough. Sprinkle sugar mixture onto butter, leaving a ½-inch border on one long side. Starting at opposite long side, roll up dough, jelly roll style. Trim edges, if needed, and cut dough into 1-inch rolls. Place rolls, cut side up, in prepared muffin cups, gently pressing down until dough fills mold. Cover and let rise in a warm, draft-free place (75°F/24°C) until puffed, 45 minutes to 1 hour.
5. Preheat oven to 375°F (190°C).
6. Bake until golden brown and an instant-read thermometer inserted in center registers 210°F (99°C), 20 to 25 minutes, covering with foil halfway through baking to prevent excess browning, if necessary. Let cool in pans until cool enough to handle, about 10 minutes. Remove from pans, and toss in desired flavored sugar. Let cool completely on wire racks.

Meyer Lemon Sugar

Make it: In the work bowl of a food processor, place 1 cup (200 grams) granulated sugar and 2 tablespoons (6 grams) Meyer lemon zest (about 2 lemons). Process until combined and uniform in color.

Blueberry Sugar

Make it: In the work bowl of a food processor, place 1 cup (200 grams) granulated sugar and ¼ cup (8 grams) freeze-dried blueberries. Process until combined and uniform in color.

MILLE-FEUILLES

Makes 9 mille-feuilles

Meaning "a thousand layers" in French, the mille-feuille is known for its seemingly countless layers of puff pastry. With a dash of crème fraîche in the airy pastry cream, our Mille-Feuilles are simple yet decadent. If you're short on time, don't worry—our quick puff makes these a cinch. We baked the dough between two baking sheets (one upside down, one right side up) so the pastry is flat enough to build those famous layers.

1⅔	cups (377 grams) unsalted butter*, cubed
3	cups (375 grams) all-purpose flour
1	tablespoon (9 grams) kosher salt
⅔	cup (160 grams) ice water

Confectioners' sugar, for dusting
Crème Fraîche Pastry Cream (recipe follows)

1. Freeze butter for 30 minutes.
2. In the work bowl of a food processor, place flour and salt; pulse until combined. Add frozen butter to flour mixture, and pulse until butter is dime-size. With processor running, gradually add ⅔ cup (160 grams) ice water, processing just until mixture forms a ball. Turn out dough onto a lightly floured surface, and shape into a disk. Wrap in plastic wrap, and refrigerate for at least 30 minutes.
3. Roll dough into a 20x10-inch rectangle. Fold dough in thirds, like a letter. Turn dough 90 degrees, and repeat procedure twice. Refrigerate for at least 20 minutes.
4. Preheat oven to 400°F (200°C). Turn 2 rimmed baking sheets over, bottom side up, and place a sheet of parchment paper on each pan. Set aside another 2 sheets of parchment paper and another 2 rimmed baking sheets.
5. On a lightly floured surface, roll dough into a 24x12-inch rectangle. Using a pastry wheel, cut dough into 36 (4x2-inch) rectangles, and place at least ½ inch apart on prepared pans. Place reserved sheets of parchment over dough; place second baking sheets, bottom side down, on top of parchment.
6. Bake for 15 minutes, rotating pans halfway through baking. Carefully remove top baking sheet and parchment, and bake until deep golden brown, 3 to 5 minutes more. Let cool completely.

7. Place 9 pieces of pastry on a sheet of parchment paper. Dust with confectioners' sugar as desired. Set aside.
8. Place chilled Crème Fraîche Pastry Cream in a piping bag fitted with an Ateco #802 round tip. Place another 9 pieces of pastry on a sheet pan. Pipe a row of large dots of Crème Fraîche Pastry Cream on top of each pastry. Top each with another piece of pastry. Pipe another layer of Crème Fraîche Pastry Cream on top of each pastry. Repeat layers one more time. Top with dusted pastries. Cover and refrigerate until ready to serve.

*We used Président® Butter.

CRÈME FRAÎCHE PASTRY CREAM
Makes about 4 cups

3	cups (720 grams) whole milk
1	cup (200 grams) granulated sugar, divided
1	vanilla bean, split lengthwise, seeds scraped and reserved
8	large egg yolks (149 grams)
¼	cup plus 3 tablespoons (56 grams) cornstarch
¼	teaspoon kosher salt
¼	cup (57 grams) unsalted butter, softened
½	cup (120 grams) crème fraîche

1. In a large saucepan, whisk together milk, ½ cup (100 grams) sugar, and vanilla bean and reserved seeds. Heat over medium heat until steaming. Discard vanilla bean.
2. In a large bowl, whisk together egg yolks, cornstarch, salt, and remaining ½ cup (100 grams) sugar. Gradually add warm milk mixture to egg yolk mixture, whisking constantly. Return mixture to saucepan, and cook over medium heat, whisking constantly, until thickened and boiling, 4 to 5 minutes. Strain mixture through a fine-mesh sieve into a large bowl. Stir in butter in two additions. Cover with a piece of plastic wrap, pressing wrap directly onto surface of cream to prevent a skin from forming. Refrigerate until completely chilled, about 4 hours or overnight.
3. Whisk pastry cream until smooth. Fold in crème fraîche. Use immediately.

CREAM PUFFS

Makes about 30 cream puffs

Also called a profiterole, the cream puff is pâtisserie's crowning achievement of simplicity. Buttery, light-as-air dough bakes into fluffy rounds with a delicate hollow center, begging to be filled with luscious crème mousseline. Dust with confectioners' sugar and pile them high; take joy in the uncomplicated perfection.

½   cup plus 1 tablespoon (127 grams) unsalted butter
½   cup (120 grams) water
½   cup (120 grams) whole milk
2   teaspoons (8 grams) granulated sugar
½   teaspoon (1.5 grams) kosher salt
1¼ cups (156 grams) all-purpose flour
5   large eggs (250 grams), room temperature
1   large egg white (30 grams), room temperature
Vanilla Crème Mousseline (recipe follows)
Garnish: confectioners' sugar

1. Preheat oven to 375°F (190°C). Using a permanent marker and a 2-inch round cutter as a guide, draw 30 circles onto 2 sheets of parchment paper. Turn parchment over, and place on 2 baking sheets.
2. In a medium saucepan, melt butter over medium heat. Add ½ cup (120 grams) water, milk, granulated sugar, and salt; bring to a boil. Using a wooden spoon, stir in flour. Cook, stirring constantly, until a skin forms on bottom of pan, 1 to 2 minutes. Transfer mixture to the bowl of a stand mixer fitted with the paddle attachment. With mixer on low speed, beat until dough is warm to the touch, about 1 minute. Add eggs and egg white, one at a time, beating until combined after each addition.
3. Transfer batter to an 18-inch piping bag fitted with a ½-inch round tip*. Place piping tip in center of one drawn circle. Hold tip perpendicular ½ inch above parchment paper. Holding tip stationary the entire time, apply even pressure until batter reaches edges of drawn circle. Stop applying pressure, and lift up. Wet your finger with water, and press down tip to create a smooth top. Repeat with remaining batter.
4. Bake for 15 minutes. Rotate pans, and bake until fully puffed and deep golden brown, about 10 minutes more. Remove from pans, and let cool completely on wire racks.
5. Using a ¼-inch round piping tip*, poke a hole in center of bottom of each puff. Insert a skewer into hole, and move it around to ensure cream will fill entire puff. Place Vanilla Crème Mousseline in a piping bag fitted with same ¼-inch piping tip. Place piping tip into hole, and apply gentle pressure to fill. Repeat with remaining puffs and Vanilla Crème Mousseline. Garnish with confectioners' sugar, if desired. Serve immediately, or refrigerate until ready to serve. Best served same day.

We used a Wilton 1A Round Tip for piping and an Ateco #802 Plain Piping Tip for filling.

VANILLA CRÈME MOUSSELINE
Makes about 5 cups

3   cups (720 grams) whole milk
1   cup (200 grams) granulated sugar, divided
1   vanilla bean, split lengthwise, seeds scraped and reserved
8   large egg yolks (149 grams)
¼   cup plus 3 tablespoons (56 grams) cornstarch
¼   teaspoon kosher salt
¼   cup (57 grams) unsalted butter, softened
1½ cups (340 grams) unsalted butter, room temperature

1. In a large saucepan, whisk together milk, ½ cup (100 grams) sugar, and vanilla bean and reserved seeds. Heat over medium heat until steaming. Discard vanilla bean.
2. In a large bowl, whisk together egg yolks, cornstarch, salt, and remaining ½ cup (100 grams) sugar. Gradually add warm milk mixture to egg yolk mixture, whisking constantly. Return mixture to saucepan, and cook over medium heat, whisking constantly, until thickened and boiling, 4 to 5 minutes. Strain mixture through a fine-mesh sieve into a large bowl. Stir in softened butter in two additions. Cover with a piece of plastic wrap, pressing wrap directly onto surface of pastry cream to prevent a skin from forming. Refrigerate until an instant-read thermometer registers 65°F (18°C) to 70°F (21°C), 2½ to 3 hours.
3. In the bowl of a stand mixer fitted with the paddle attachment, beat room temperature butter at medium speed until smooth, about 1 minute. Whisk pastry cream until smooth. (At this point, butter and pastry cream should be the same temperature.) With mixer on low speed, slowly add pastry cream to butter, beating just until combined after each addition and stopping to scrape sides of bowl. Use immediately.

ÉCLAIRS

Makes 18 to 20 éclairs

The term éclair translates literally to "flash of lightning," a reference to how quickly these oblong treats are eaten. Our version is a decadent chocolate affair, with a glossy Chocolate Glaze and silky cocoa crème mousseline filling.

½	cup plus 1 tablespoon (127 grams) unsalted butter
½	cup (120 grams) water
½	cup (120 grams) whole milk
2	teaspoons (8 grams) granulated sugar
½	teaspoon (1.5 grams) kosher salt
1¼	cups (156 grams) all-purpose flour
5	large eggs (250 grams), room temperature
1	large egg white (30 grams), room temperature

Chocolate Crème Mousseline (recipe follows)
Chocolate Glaze (recipe follows)
Garnish: flaked sea salt

1. Preheat oven to 375°F (190°C). Using a marker and a ruler, draw 20 (4¼-inch) lines onto 2 sheets of parchment paper. Turn parchment over, and place on 2 baking sheets.
2. In a medium saucepan, melt butter over medium heat. Add ½ cup (120 grams) water, milk, sugar, and kosher salt; bring to a boil. Using a wooden spoon, stir in flour. Cook, stirring constantly, until a skin forms on bottom of pan, 1 to 2 minutes. Transfer mixture to the bowl of a stand mixer fitted with the paddle attachment. With mixer on low speed, beat until dough is warm to the touch, about 1 minute. Add eggs and egg white, one at a time, beating until combined after each addition.
3. Transfer batter to an 18-inch piping bag fitted with ⁹⁄₁₆-inch French star piping tip*. Starting on lines farthest from you, hold tip about ¾ inch above parchment paper; applying even pressure, and slowly pipe out oblong shapes. Begin to lessen pressure on piping bag as you reach end of line; stop applying pressure, and lift up, leaving a small curl at end of éclair. Wet your finger with water, and press down tip. Repeat with remaining batter.

4. Bake for 15 minutes. Rotate pans, and bake until puffed and golden brown, about 10 minutes more. Remove from pans, and let cool completely on wire racks.
5. Using a ¼-inch round piping tip*, poke 2 holes about ¾ inch from each end on bottom of each éclair. Insert a skewer into holes, and move it around to ensure cream will fill entire éclair. Place Chocolate Crème Mousseline in a piping bag fitted with same ¼-inch piping tip. Place piping tip into one hole, and apply gentle pressure to begin filling éclair. Pipe cream into second hole until éclair feels heavy. Repeat with remaining éclairs.
6. Holding éclair by bottom half and parallel to surface of Chocolate Glaze, dip top of éclair in glaze. Still parallel, lift éclair out of glaze. Slowly lift one end of éclair, letting excess chocolate run off. Repeat with remaining éclairs. Garnish with flaked salt, if desired. Serve immediately, or refrigerate until ready to serve. Best served same day.

We used an Ateco #867 French Star Tip for piping and an Ateco #802 Plain Piping Tip for filling.

CHOCOLATE CRÈME MOUSSELINE
Makes about 6 cups

3	cups (720 grams) whole milk
1	cup (200 grams) granulated sugar, divided
1	vanilla bean, split lengthwise, seeds scraped and reserved
8	large egg yolks (149 grams)
¼	cup plus 3 tablespoons (56 grams) cornstarch
¼	teaspoon kosher salt
¼	cup (57 grams) unsalted butter, softened
1½	cups (255 grams) 60% cacao bittersweet chocolate, melted and slightly cooled
1½	cups (340 grams) unsalted butter, room temperature

1. In a large saucepan, whisk together milk, ½ cup (100 grams) sugar, and vanilla bean and reserved seeds. Heat over medium heat until steaming. Discard vanilla bean.

2. In a large bowl, whisk together egg yolks, cornstarch, salt, and remaining ½ cup (100 grams) sugar. Gradually add warm milk mixture to egg yolk mixture, whisking constantly. Return mixture to saucepan, and cook over medium heat, whisking constantly, until thickened and boiling, 4 to 5 minutes. Strain mixture through a fine-mesh sieve into a large bowl. Stir in softened butter in two additions. Fold in melted chocolate. Cover with a piece of plastic wrap, pressing wrap directly onto surface of pastry cream to prevent a skin from forming. Refrigerate until an instant-read thermometer registers 65°F (18°C) to 70°F (21°C), 2½ to 3 hours.
3. In the bowl of a stand mixer fitted with the paddle attachment, beat room temperature butter at medium speed until smooth, about 1 minute. Whisk pastry cream until smooth. (At this point, butter and pastry cream should be the same temperature.) With mixer on low speed, slowly add pastry cream to butter, beating just until combined after each addition and stopping to scrape sides of bowl. Use immediately.

CHOCOLATE GLAZE
Makes about 2 cups

8	ounces (225 grams) 60% cacao bittersweet chocolate, chopped
1	cup plus 2 tablespoons (270 grams) heavy whipping cream
1	tablespoon plus 1 teaspoon (28 grams) light corn syrup
¼	teaspoon kosher salt
2	tablespoons (28 grams) unsalted butter, softened

1. In a medium heatproof bowl, place chocolate.
2. In a small saucepan, bring cream, corn syrup, and salt to a boil. Pour hot cream mixture over chocolate. Let stand for 30 seconds; slowly stir until chocolate is melted. Add butter, and gently stir to combine. Use immediately.

PARIS-BREST

Makes about 14 Paris-Brest

Invented to commemorate the famous bicycle race that ran from Paris to Brest, the Paris-Brest is choux piped to resemble a bicycle tire, covered in toasted almonds, and filled with a rich hazelnut cream. Our incarnation returns to the rich hazelnut roots with velvet Praline Crème Mousseline filling and a hazelnut-studded caramel topcoat.

½   cup plus 1 tablespoon (127 grams) unsalted butter
½   cup (120 grams) water
½   cup (120 grams) whole milk
2   teaspoons (8 grams) granulated sugar
½   teaspoon (1.5 grams) kosher salt
1¼ cups (156 grams) all-purpose flour
5   large eggs (250 grams), room temperature
1   large egg white (30 grams), room temperature
Caramel (recipe follows)
Candied Hazelnuts (recipe follows)
Praline Crème Mousseline (recipe follows)

1. Preheat oven to 375°F (190°C). Using a marker and a 3-inch round cutter as a guide, draw 14 circles onto 2 sheets of parchment paper. Turn parchment over, and place on 2 baking sheets.
2. In a medium saucepan, melt butter over medium heat. Add ½ cup (120 grams) water, milk, sugar, and salt; bring to a boil. Using a wooden spoon, stir in flour. Cook, stirring constantly, until a skin forms on bottom of pan, 1 to 2 minutes. Transfer mixture to the bowl of a stand mixer fitted with the paddle attachment. With mixer on low speed, beat until dough is warm to the touch, about 1 minute. Add eggs and egg white, one at a time, beating until combined after each addition.
3. Transfer batter to an 18-inch piping bag fitted with a ⁹⁄₁₆-inch French star piping tip*. Hold tip about ¾ inch above line of a drawn circle on parchment paper; applying even pressure, slowly pipe around drawn circle. Begin to lessen pressure on piping bag as you come to end of circle; stop applying pressure, letting it overlap slightly. Wet your finger with water, and smooth down overlap. Repeat with remaining batter.

4. Bake for 15 minutes. Rotate pans, and bake until puffed and golden brown, about 10 minutes more. Remove from pans, and let cool completely on wire racks.
5. Place a sheet of parchment paper on work surface. Holding Paris-Brest by bottom half and parallel to surface of Caramel, carefully dip top of pastry in Caramel. Still parallel, lift pastry out of Caramel, letting excess drip off. Gently set on prepared parchment. Immediately sprinkle with chopped Candied Hazelnuts. Repeat with remaining Paris-Brest.
6. Using a serrated knife, cut each Paris-Brest in half horizontally. Place Praline Crème Mousseline in a piping bag fitted with a ⅜-inch open star piping tip*. Pipe tall rosettes around bottom half of each Paris-Brest. Cover with top half of each Paris-Brest, and press down gently. Serve immediately, or refrigerate until ready to serve. Best served same day.

We used an Ateco #867 French Star Tip for piping and an Ateco #824 French Star Tip for filling.

CARAMEL
Makes about 2 cups

3   cups (600 grams) granulated sugar
¾   cup (180 grams) water, plus more for brushing

1. In a medium saucepan, combine sugar and ¾ cup (180 grams) water. (Mixture should look like wet sand.) Heat over medium heat. Using a pastry brush, brush down sides of pan with water. Stir gently while sugar is dissolving. Increase heat to high. (Do not stir after sugar mixture starts to boil.) Cook until mixture is amber colored. Remove from heat, and immediately plunge pan into an ice bath for 5 seconds to stop the cooking process. Let cool for 5 minutes before using.

CANDIED HAZELNUTS
Makes about 4½ cups

2⅔ cups (379 grams) raw hazelnuts
1½ cups (300 grams) granulated sugar
4½ tablespoons (68 grams) water, plus more for brushing
1½ teaspoons (5 grams) flaked sea salt

1. Preheat oven to 300°F (150°C).
2. On a rimmed baking sheet, spread hazelnuts in an even layer.
3. Bake until fragrant and toasted, about 15 minutes. Rub hazelnuts with a kitchen linen while still warm to remove outside skin. (It does not have to be perfect.) Let cool completely. Chop hazelnuts. Line a rimmed baking sheet with a nonstick baking mat.
4. In a medium saucepan, combine sugar and 4½ tablespoons (68 grams) water. (Mixture should look like wet sand.) Heat over high heat. Using a pastry brush, brush down sides of pan with water. Stir gently while sugar is dissolving. (Do not stir after sugar mixture starts to boil.) Cook until mixture is light amber colored. Remove from heat, and quickly stir in chopped hazelnuts. Pour onto prepared pan. Using a heatproof spatula, spread hazelnuts in a single layer, and sprinkle with sea salt. Let cool completely.
5. Gently tap hazelnuts on pan to break into smaller pieces. Using a chef's knife, chop into small pieces.

PRALINE CRÈME MOUSSELINE
Makes about 6 cups

3   cups (720 grams) whole milk
1   cup (200 grams) granulated sugar, divided
1   vanilla bean, split lengthwise, seeds scraped and reserved
8   large egg yolks (149 grams)
¼   cup plus 3 tablespoons (56 grams) cornstarch
¼   teaspoon kosher salt
¼   cup (57 grams) unsalted butter, softened
1¾ cups (225 grams) chopped Candied Hazelnuts (recipe precedes)
1½ cups (340 grams) unsalted butter, room temperature

1. In a large saucepan, whisk together milk, ½ cup (100 grams) sugar, and vanilla bean and reserved seeds. Heat over medium heat until steaming. Discard vanilla bean.
2. In a large bowl, whisk together egg yolks, cornstarch, salt, and remaining ½ cup (100 grams) sugar. Gradually add warm milk mixture to egg yolk mixture, whisking constantly. Return mixture to saucepan,

and cook over medium heat, whisking constantly, until thickened and boiling, 4 to 5 minutes. Strain mixture through a fine-mesh sieve into a large bowl. Stir in softened butter in two additions. Cover with a piece of plastic wrap, pressing wrap directly onto surface of pastry cream to prevent a skin from forming. Refrigerate until an instant-read thermometer registers 65°F (18°C) to 70°F (21°C), 2½ to 3 hours.

3. In the work bowl of a food processor, process Candied Hazelnuts until a paste forms, about 2 minutes.

4. In the bowl of a stand mixer fitted with a paddle attachment, beat hazelnut paste and room temperature butter at medium speed until smooth, about 1 minute. Whisk pastry cream until smooth. (At this point, butter and pastry cream should be the same temperature.) With mixer on low speed, slowly add pastry cream to butter mixture, beating until combined after each addition and stopping to scrape sides of bowl. Refrigerate until stiffened and desired consistency is reached, up to 1 hour, stirring every 15 minutes.

CANELÉS

Makes 12 canelés

Recipe by Marjorie Taylor and Kendall Smith Franchini

Canelés are a traditional pastry from the Bordeaux region of France and are baked in little copper molds specific to this pastry.

2   cups (480 grams) whole milk
3½   tablespoons (50 grams) unsalted butter
1   vanilla bean
2   large eggs (100 grams)
2   large egg yolks (37 grams)
1¼   cups (250 grams) granulated sugar
Pinch fleur de sel
2   tablespoons (30 grams) rum
¾   cup plus 2 teaspoons (100 grams) unbleached all-purpose flour
Clarified Butter* (recipe follows)

1. In a small saucepan, combine the milk, unsalted butter, and vanilla bean. Bring to a simmer and turn off the heat and let stand so the flavors meld, 15 minutes.
2. In a large bowl, whisk the eggs and yolks. Add the sugar and fleur de sel and continue whisking until incorporated. Add the rum and sift the flour over the mixture, whisking to combine. Add the milk mixture and continue whisking until well combined. Let the batter come to room temperature before placing in the refrigerator. Chill for a minimum of 24 hours and up to 48 hours.
3. When ready to bake, remove the batter from the refrigerator and stir the batter, as it will have separated. Try not to incorporate too much air into the batter. Return to the refrigerator until ready to bake.
4. Coat the inside of 12 canelé molds with Clarified Butter. Set the molds upside down to allow any excess butter to run off. Place the molds in the freezer to let rest for at least 1 hour before baking.
5. Preheat the oven to 375°F (190°C). Line a sheet pan with foil and place in the oven to preheat.
6. Remove the chilled molds from the freezer and fill each mold three-fourths of the way full with the chilled batter and place on the preheated sheet pan. Place the sheet pan in the oven. After 20 minutes, check that the batter is not bubbling over the molds. If so, take the pan out of the oven and let the batter settle for a few moments and then return to the oven. Continue to bake and turn the sheet pan every 15 minutes to ensure even baking. The canelés will be fully baked in approximately 1 hour and 10 minutes. The canelés are done when the sides are caramelized and the interiors are still soft. Once baked, remove the canelés from the molds while they are still hot and let cool. They will firm up as they cool.

*You can also use ghee.

CLARIFIED BUTTER
Makes about 1½ cups

2   cups (454 grams) unsalted butter, cut into pieces

1. In a small saucepan, melt the butter over low heat. Remove from the heat and let it stand for 3 to 4 minutes to settle. Using a small spoon, remove the white foam from the surface. Gently pour off the clear yellow butter into a glass jar, leaving the white solids in the bottom of the saucepan. Let cool and then store in an airtight container in the refrigerator; the Clarified Butter will keep for at least 1 month.

Photo by Joann Pai

ORANGE PARIS-BREST

Makes 12 Paris-Brest

Give your holiday table a touch of elegance with this citrusy take on one of France's most iconic pastries, the Paris-Brest. Président® butter delivers exceptional light and airy texture to the signature pâte à choux base while imparting a velvety richness to the orange zest- and liqueur-spiked buttercream.

½   cup plus 1 tablespoon (127 grams) unsalted butter*
½   cup (120 grams) water
½   cup (120 grams) whole milk
2   teaspoons (8 grams) granulated sugar
½   teaspoon (1.5 grams) kosher salt
1¼ cups (156 grams) all-purpose flour
5   large eggs (250 grams), room temperature
1   large egg white (30 grams), room temperature
Orange French Buttercream (recipe follows)
Garnish: sliced almonds, sugared rosemary, and sugared cranberries

1. Preheat oven to 375°F (190°C). Using a permanent marker and a 3-inch round cutter as a guide, draw 6 circles each on 2 sheets of parchment paper (12 circles total). Turn parchment over, and place on 2 baking sheets.
2. In a medium saucepan, melt butter over medium heat. Add ½ cup (120 grams) water, milk, granulated sugar, and salt; bring to a boil. Using a wooden spoon, stir in flour. Cook, stirring constantly, until a skin forms on bottom of pan, 1 to 2 minutes. Transfer mixture to the bowl of a stand mixer fitted with the paddle attachment. With mixer on low speed, beat until dough is warm to the touch, about 1 minute. Add eggs and egg white, one at a time, beating until combined after each addition.
3. Transfer batter to an 18-inch piping bag fitted with a ⁹⁄₁₆-inch star tip. Hold tip about ¾ inch above line of a drawn circle on parchment paper; applying even pressure slowly pipe around drawn circle. Begin to lessen pressure on piping bag as you come to end of circle; stop applying pressure, letting it overlap slightly. Wet your finger with water,

and smooth down overlap. Repeat with remaining batter. Top with sliced almonds.
4. Bake for 15 minutes. Rotate pans, and bake until puffed and golden brown, about 10 minutes more. Remove from pans, and let cool completely on wire racks.
5. Using a serrated knife, cut each Paris-Brest in half horizontally. Place Orange French Buttercream in a piping bag fitted with a ⅜-inch open star tip. Pipe tall rosettes around bottom half of each Paris-Brest. Cover with top half of each Paris-Brest, and press down gently. Garnish with sliced almonds, sugared rosemary, and sugared cranberries, if desired. Serve immediately, or refrigerate until ready to serve. These are best served the same day.

*We used Président® Butter.

ORANGE FRENCH BUTTERCREAM
Makes about 4½ cups

1¾ cups (350 grams) granulated sugar
¼   cup (24 grams) packed orange zest (about 4 oranges)
4   large egg yolks (76 grams), room temperature
2   large eggs (100 grams)
2   cups (454 grams) unsalted butter, softened
1   tablespoon (15 grams) orange liqueur
¼   teaspoon kosher salt

1. In the bowl of a stand mixer, whisk together sugar and orange zest by hand until combined. Whisk in egg yolks and eggs. Place mixer bowl over a saucepan of simmering water. Cook, whisking occasionally, until an instant-read thermometer registers 155°F (68°C) to 160°F (71°C).
2. Carefully return bowl to stand mixer fitted with the whisk attachment, and beat at high speed until bowl is cool to the touch, about 8 minutes. Add butter, 2 tablespoons (28 grams) at a time, beating until combined after each addition. Beat in liqueur and salt. Use immediately, or refrigerate in an airtight container for up to 3 days. If refrigerating, let frosting come to room temperature, and rewhip before using.

BERRY PALMIERS

Makes 24 palmiers

Made of buttery rough puff pastry shaped into an iconic double swirl, palmiers take the crown as the most delicate of French pastries. We filled ours with a homemade blackberry-blueberry jam for a summertime twist on the classic.

½	recipe Rough Puff Pastry Dough (recipe follows)
3	tablespoons (36 grams) turbinado sugar
½	cup (148 grams) Berry Jam (recipe follows)
1	tablespoon (8 grams) cornstarch

1. On a lightly floured surface, roll Rough Puff Pastry Dough into a 12-inch square. Sprinkle with turbinado sugar. Using a rolling pin, gently roll over sugar to press sugar into dough. Carefully turn dough over so sugar side faces down.

2. In a small bowl, stir together Berry Jam and cornstarch. Spread jam mixture onto dough. Roll up dough from two opposite sides, jelly roll style, meeting in the middle. Place log on its side on a baking sheet (coiled portions stacked to look similar to a capital "B"). Freeze until firm enough to slice, about 15 minutes.

3. Preheat oven to 400°F (200°C). Line several baking sheets with parchment paper.

4. Place log on its side on a cutting board. Using a serrated knife, cut dough into ½-inch-thick slices. Place slices, cut side up, 2 inches apart on prepared pans. Freeze until firm, 10 to 15 minutes.

5. Bake until bottoms are golden brown, 15 to 20 minutes. Let cool on pans for 5 minutes. Remove from pans, and let cool completely on wire racks. Store in an airtight container for up to 2 days.

ROUGH PUFF PASTRY DOUGH

Makes about 2 pounds

1⅔	cups (377 grams) cold unsalted butter, cubed
3	cups (375 grams) all-purpose flour
1	tablespoon (9 grams) kosher salt
⅔	cup (160 grams) ice water

1. Freeze butter for 30 minutes.

2. In the work bowl of a food processor, pulse together flour and salt until combined. Add frozen butter, and pulse until butter is dime-size. With processor running, gradually add ⅔ cup (160 grams) ice water in a slow, steady stream just until mixture forms a ball. Turn out dough onto a lightly floured surface, and shape into a disk. Wrap in plastic wrap, and refrigerate for at least 30 minutes.

3. Roll dough into a 20x10-inch rectangle. Fold dough in thirds, like a letter. Turn dough 90 degrees, and repeat procedure twice. Divide dough in half (about 454 grams each), and wrap each half tightly in plastic wrap. Refrigerate for at least 20 minutes, or freeze for up to 3 months.

BERRY JAM

Makes about 3 cups

18	ounces (510 grams) fresh blackberries (about 3½ cups)
14	ounces (400 grams) fresh blueberries (about 2⅔ cups)
2	cups (400 grams) granulated sugar
¼	cup (60 grams) almond liqueur
1	vanilla bean, split lengthwise, seeds scraped and reserved

1. In the container of a blender, process blackberries until puréed. Strain through a fine-mesh sieve into a medium bowl, discarding seeds. Place 1⅔ cups (400 grams) blackberry juice in a medium Dutch oven. Add blueberries, sugar, almond liqueur, and vanilla bean and reserved seeds, stirring to combine. Let stand for 30 minutes.

2. Bring berry mixture to a boil over medium heat. Cook, stirring frequently, until mixture is thickened and jam leaves a trace when a spoon is dragged across bottom of pot, 20 to 25 minutes. Remove from heat, and let cool for 1 hour. Transfer jam to a clean jar. Jam will keep refrigerated for up to 2 weeks.

> **PRO TIP**
> Instead of making the Berry Jam, you can also use high-quality store-bought blackberry or blueberry jam. We suggest Bonne Maman Blackberry Preserves or Bonne Maman Wild Blueberry Preserves, available at specialty food stores or online.

PEPPERMINT CREAM PUFFS

Makes about 24 cream puffs

Filled with velvety Peppermint Pastry Cream, these airy pâte à choux puffs combine French elegance with holiday flair. We used crushed peppermint candies to lend refreshing sweetness to the pastry cream, and a dusting of peppermint sugar on top of the pastries makes for a simple, festive finish.

½   cup plus 1 tablespoon (127 grams) unsalted butter*
½   cup (120 grams) plus 1 tablespoon (15 grams) water, divided
½   cup (120 grams) whole milk
2   teaspoons (8 grams) granulated sugar
½   teaspoon (1.5 grams) kosher salt
1¼ cups (156 grams) all-purpose flour
6   large eggs (300 grams), room temperature and divided
1   large egg white (30 grams), room temperature
Peppermint Pastry Cream (recipe follows)
2   tablespoons (16 grams) finely crushed soft peppermint candies
2   tablespoons (14 grams) confectioners' sugar
Garnish: crushed soft peppermint candies

1. Preheat oven to 375°F (190°C). Using a permanent marker and a 2-inch round cutter as a guide, draw 24 circles evenly spaced onto 2 sheets of parchment paper. Turn parchment over, and place on 2 baking sheets.
2. In a medium saucepan, melt butter over medium heat. Add ½ cup (120 grams) water, milk, granulated sugar, and salt; bring to a boil. Using a wooden spoon, stir in flour. Cook, stirring constantly, until a skin forms on bottom of pan, 1 to 2 minutes. Transfer mixture to the bowl of a stand mixer fitted with the paddle attachment. With mixer on low speed, beat until dough is warm to the touch, about 1 minute. Add 5 eggs (250 grams) and egg white, one at a time, beating until combined after each addition.
3. Transfer batter to an 18-inch piping bag fitted with a ½-inch round tip (Wilton 1A). Place piping tip in center of a drawn circle. Hold tip perpendicular ½ inch above parchment paper. Holding tip stationary the entire time, apply even pressure until batter reaches edges of drawn circle. Stop applying pressure, and lift up. Wet your finger with water, and press down tip to create a smooth top. Repeat with remaining batter.
4. In a small bowl, whisk together remaining 1 egg (50 grams) and remaining 1 tablespoon (15 grams) water. Brush tops of batter rounds with egg wash.
5. Bake for 15 minutes. Rotate pans, and bake until fully puffed and deep golden brown, about 10 minutes more. Remove from pans, and let cool completely on wire racks.
6. Using a ¼-inch round piping tip, poke a hole in center of bottom of each puff. Insert a skewer into hole, and move it around to ensure cream will fill entire puff. Place Peppermint

Pastry Cream in a pipping bag fitted with same ¼-inch piping tip. Place piping tip into hole, and apply gentle pressure to fill. Repeat with remaining puffs and remaining Peppermint Pastry Cream.
7. When ready to plate, stir together finely crushed peppermint candies and confectioners' sugar in a small bowl. Using a fine-mesh sieve, dust peppermint sugar mixture onto cream puffs. Garnish with peppermint candy pieces, if desired. Serve immediately, or refrigerate until ready to serve. Best served same day.

*We used Président® Butter.

PEPPERMINT PASTRY CREAM
Makes about 3½ cups

3   cups (720 grams) whole milk
⅔   cup (133 grams) granulated sugar, divided
6   tablespoons (48 grams) cornstarch
½   teaspoon (1.5 grams) kosher salt
4   large egg yolks (74 grams)
2   tablespoons (28 grams) unsalted butter, softened
¾   teaspoon (3 grams) peppermint extract
½   teaspoon (2 grams) vanilla extract
¼   cup (32 grams) finely crushed soft peppermint candies

1. In a medium saucepan, combine milk and ⅓ cup (66.5 grams) sugar. Cook over medium heat, stirring frequently, just until bubbles form around edge of pan. (Do not boil.)
2. In a medium bowl, whisk together cornstarch, salt, and remaining ⅓ cup (66.5 grams) sugar. Whisk in egg yolks until well combined. (Mixture will be very thick.) Gradually add milk mixture to egg yolk mixture, whisking constantly. Return mixture to saucepan. Bring to a boil over medium heat, whisking constantly. Cook, whisking constantly, until thickened and an instant-read thermometer registers 190°F (88°C), 2 to 3 minutes.
3. Remove from heat. Stir in butter and extracts until butter is melted. Strain through fine-mesh sieve into a glass bowl. Cover with a piece of plastic wrap, pressing wrap directly onto surface of pastry cream to prevent a skin from forming. Refrigerate until thoroughly chilled, 2 to 3 hours or overnight.
4. When ready to use, whisk pastry cream until smooth; stir in crushed peppermint candies. Use immediately.

Notes: *To finely crush soft peppermint candies, place in a medium resealable plastic bag. Using a rolling pin, crush candies; continue to roll over candies in bag with rolling pin until finely crushed (peppermint pieces no larger than ⅛ inch thick).*

Peppermint Pastry Cream can be made through step 3 up to 4 days in advance and kept refrigerated. Stir in finely crushed peppermint candies just before ready to use.

VANILLA SLICE

Makes 16 squares

Few recipes are as central to New Zealand's baking culture as the vanilla slice. Consisting of a generous layer of pastry cream sandwiched between exquisitely thin layers of flaky pastry, this classic dessert wouldn't be complete without a dose of New Zealand's own Heilala Vanilla. Heilala's premium vanilla beans bring depth and complexity to the custardy filling. Served with a glass of bubbly, this recipe offers indulgence by the slice.

2¼   cups (281 grams) all-purpose flour
2½   teaspoons (7.5 grams) kosher salt, divided
1¼   cups (284 grams) cold unsalted butter, cubed
½   cup (120 grams) ice water
4   cups (960 grams) whole milk
1⅓   cups (266 grams) granulated sugar, divided
2   vanilla beans*, split lengthwise, seeds scraped and reserved
10   large egg yolks (186 grams)
½   cup (64 grams) cornstarch
¼   cup (57 grams) unsalted butter, softened
Garnish: confectioners' sugar

1. In the work bowl of a food processor, place flour and 2 teaspoons (6 grams) salt; pulse until combined. Add cold butter, and pulse until butter is dime-size. With processor running, add ½ cup (120 grams) ice water in a slow, steady stream just until dough comes together. Turn out dough onto a lightly floured surface, and shape into a disk. Wrap in plastic wrap, and refrigerate for at least 30 minutes.
2. Divide dough in half (about 342 grams each). Roll half of dough into a 12x8-inch rectangle. Fold dough in thirds, like a letter. Turn dough 90 degrees, and repeat procedure twice; wrap in plastic wrap. Repeat with remaining dough. Refrigerate for at least 20 minutes.
3. Preheat oven to 400°F (200°C). Line a rimmed baking sheet with parchment paper.

4. Roll half of dough into an 11x10-inch rectangle (⅛ inch thick). Place on prepared pan. Cover with another piece of parchment, and place another rimmed baking sheet on top of dough.
5. Bake for 15 minutes. Press down on middle of top pan to release some of the air from the pastry. Bake until deep golden brown, about 10 minutes more, pressing down on top pan halfway through baking. Press down on top pan again. Remove top pan and parchment; let cool completely on bottom pan. Repeat with remaining dough.
6. In a large saucepan, whisk together milk, ⅔ cup (133 grams) granulated sugar, and vanilla beans and reserved seeds. Heat over medium heat until steaming. Discard vanilla beans.
7. In a large bowl, whisk together egg yolks, cornstarch, remaining ⅔ cup (133 grams) granulated sugar, and remaining ½ teaspoon (1.5 grams) salt. Gradually add warm milk mixture to egg yolk mixture, whisking constantly. Return mixture to saucepan. Bring to a boil over medium heat, whisking constantly. Cook, stirring constantly, for 3 minutes. (Mixture will be thick with a pudding-like consistency.) Strain mixture through a fine-mesh sieve into a large bowl. Stir in softened butter in two additions. Cover with a piece of plastic wrap, pressing wrap directly onto surface of pastry cream to prevent a skin from forming. Let stand at room temperature for 10 minutes.
8. Line an 8-inch square baking pan with parchment paper, letting excess extend over sides of pan. Cut each pastry into an 8-inch square, trimming as needed to fit. Place 1 pastry square in bottom of prepared pan. Pour warm pastry cream on top, smoothing flat, and top with remaining pastry square. Cover and refrigerate until set, 3 to 4 hours.
9. Using excess parchment as handles, remove from pan. Using a serrated knife, cut into squares. Garnish with confectioners' sugar, if desired. Serve immediately.

We used Heilala.

COOKIES AND BARS

COOKIES

Dig in to these epic sablés, thumbprints, and sandwich cookies. Highlighting flavors like sweet-tart pineapple, wintry peppermint, and zesty lemon, we have a cookie for every craving.

VANILLA BEAN MACARONS

Makes about 20 macarons

We sandwiched Caramelized White Chocolate Buttercream between vanilla bean–speckled shells for our most luscious macarons yet.

1⅓ cups (128 grams) blanched almond flour
1 cup plus 1 tablespoon (127 grams) confectioners' sugar
⅛ teaspoon kosher salt
3 large egg whites (90 grams), room temperature
½ cup (100 grams) granulated sugar
1 vanilla bean*, split lengthwise, seeds scraped and reserved
¼ teaspoon (1 gram) vanilla extract*
Caramelized White Chocolate Buttercream (recipe follows)
Garnish: vanilla sugar

1. Using a permanent marker, draw 1½-inch circles 1 inch apart on 2 sheets of parchment paper. Place parchment on 2 rimmed baking sheets; top with nonstick baking mats.
2. In the work bowl of a food processor, place flour, confectioners' sugar, and salt; process until well combined. Sift flour mixture through a fine-mesh sieve.
3. In the bowl of a stand mixer fitted with the whisk attachment, beat egg whites at medium-high speed until foamy. Gradually add granulated sugar, and beat at high speed until stiff peaks form. Gently fold in flour mixture in three additions until a loose batter forms. Fold in reserved vanilla bean seeds and vanilla extract.
4. Transfer batter to a piping bag fitted with a medium round tip (Ateco #804). Pipe batter onto drawn circles underneath mats, holding piping tip perpendicular to pans. Apply pressure, leaving tip stationary, until batter reaches drawn circle. Move and lift tip in a quick circular motion as you finish piping each macaron shell to prevent a point from forming on top. Slam pans vigorously on counter 5 to 7 times to release air bubbles. Let stand at room temperature until a skin forms on top of macaron shells, about 1 hour. (The batter should feel dry to the touch and should not stick to your finger.)
5. Preheat oven to 275°F (140°C).
6. Bake in batches until firm to the touch, about 15 minutes, rotating pan every 5 minutes. Let cool completely on pans. (If you have trouble removing macaron shells from pans, place pans in freezer for about 15 minutes.)
7. Place Caramelized White Chocolate Buttercream in a piping bag fitted with a small round tip (Ateco #802). Pipe buttercream onto flat side of half of macaron shells. Place remaining macaron shells, flat side down, on top of buttercream. Roll edges in vanilla sugar, if desired.

We used Heilala.

> **MAKE AHEAD**
> Bake macaron shells the day before assembling. Once cool, wrap top of baking sheets in plastic wrap, and let stand overnight.

CARAMELIZED WHITE CHOCOLATE BUTTERCREAM

Makes about 1½ cups

6 ounces (175 grams) high-quality white chocolate baking chips*
¼ teaspoon kosher salt
½ cup (113 grams) unsalted butter, softened
1 cup (120 grams) confectioners' sugar
½ vanilla bean, split lengthwise, seeds scraped and reserved
¼ teaspoon (1 gram) vanilla extract

1. Preheat oven to 250°F (130°C).
2. In a completely dry 9-inch round baking pan, combine white chocolate chips and salt.
3. Bake until golden, about 30 minutes, stirring every 10 minutes. (At times, white chocolate will look very dry and chalky, but keep stirring until smooth.) Pour white chocolate into a medium bowl; let stand, stirring every 2 to 3 minutes, until cool.
4. In the bowl of a stand mixer fitted with the paddle attachment, beat butter at medium speed until smooth, about 3 minutes. Add cooled white chocolate, beating well. Reduce mixer to low speed. Gradually add confectioners' sugar, reserved vanilla bean seeds, and vanilla extract, beating until light and fluffy, 2 to 3 minutes. Use immediately.

White chocolate needs to be over 30% cocoa butter. We used Valrhona Ivoire 35% White Chocolate.

> **MAKE AHEAD**
> Caramelize your white chocolate (steps 2 and 3) up to 4 months before making your buttercream. After step 3, pour cooled chocolate onto a parchment paper-lined rimmed baking sheet, and let cool for at least 7 hours or overnight. Break into pieces, and store in an airtight container for up to 4 months. When ready to make the buttercream, melt caramelized white chocolate in the top of a double boiler, and let cool before continuing with step 4.

HAMANTASCHEN

Makes about 14 hamantaschen

Recipe by Jake Cohen

This dough is a little softer than a traditional one, allowing for an extra tender crust. Attention to detail is your key to success. Make sure you pinch the heck out of these bad boys. Otherwise, they'll open up as they bake, which isn't fun for anyone. Proper chilling time is essential to prevent overspreading in the oven.

¾   cup (170 grams) unsalted butter, softened
⅔   cup (133 grams) granulated sugar
1   large egg (50 grams)
1   teaspoon (4 grams) vanilla extract
2¾   cups (344 grams) all-purpose flour
½   teaspoon (1.5 grams) kosher salt
Desired filling (recipes follow)
Garnish: almonds

1. Line baking sheets with parchment paper.
2. In the bowl of a stand mixer fitted with the paddle attachment, beat butter and sugar at medium speed until creamy, 3 to 4 minutes, stopping to scrape sides of bowl. Add egg, beating until combined. Beat in vanilla.
3. In a medium bowl, whisk together flour and salt. With mixer on low speed, gradually add flour mixture to butter mixture, beating until a smooth dough forms.
4. Between 2 sheets of parchment paper, roll dough to ¼-inch thickness. Remove top sheet of parchment. Using a 3¼-inch round cutter, cut dough, rerolling scraps as necessary. Spoon 2 teaspoons desired filling into center of each dough circle. Fold dough in from three sides, and pinch edges together to seal, leaving a small opening over filling. Place 2 inches apart on prepared pans. Garnish with almonds, if desired. Refrigerate for 1 hour.
5. Preheat oven to 350°F (180°C).
6. Re-pinch corners of Hamantaschen to ensure they're well sealed.
7. Bake until bottoms and corners are golden, 20 to 25 minutes, rotating pans halfway through baking. Let cool completely.

Cardamom Frangipane Filling
Makes about 1 cup

Consider these cookies a nod to Middle Eastern almond cookies. The resulting hamantasch is the perfect blend of texture: a crispy exterior and a chewy, tender frangipane interior. While cardamom can be a polarizing flavor, cinnamon is just as lovely and aromatic in this recipe.

1¼   cups (105 grams) sifted fine blanched almond flour
½   cup (100 grams) granulated sugar
2   tablespoons (16 grams) all-purpose flour
1   large egg (50 grams)
1   tablespoon (14 grams) unsalted butter, melted
1   teaspoon (2 grams) ground cardamom
½   teaspoon (1.5 grams) kosher salt

1. In a medium bowl, stir together all ingredients until a smooth paste forms.

Strawberry Vanilla Rhubarb Filling
Makes about 1¼ cups

Keep an eye on the water content of your fruit because if they are overly juicy, you may need to cook the mixture down for a few extra minutes. Just look for a thick, syrupy texture before you remove from heat and let cool.

2   cups (340 grams) fresh strawberries, hulled and roughly chopped
¾   cup (150 grams) granulated sugar
½   cup (110 grams) (¼-inch) diced fresh or frozen rhubarb (about 1 stalk)
2   tablespoons (30 grams) rice vinegar
1   vanilla bean, split lengthwise, seeds scraped and reserved
½   teaspoon (1.5 grams) kosher salt

1. In a medium saucepan, combine strawberries, sugar, rhubarb, vinegar, vanilla bean and reserved seeds, and salt over medium heat. Cook, stirring frequently, until fruit has broken down and mixture is reduced to 1¼ cups, 20 to 25 minutes. Remove from heat, and discard vanilla bean. Let cool completely.

Raspberry Rose Filling
Makes about 1¼ cups

Raspberries sing when combined with lime juice and rose water for a fragrant filling that isn't overly floral, but you definitely can tell there is a little something special in the mix. The seeds then add a pleasant crunch when you start enjoying these vibrant beauties.

1   pound (455 grams) fresh raspberries
¾   cup (150 grams) granulated sugar
2   tablespoons (30 grams) fresh lime juice
½   teaspoon (1.5 grams) kosher salt
1½   tablespoons (19.5 grams) rose water

1. In a medium saucepan, heat raspberries, sugar, lime juice, and salt over medium heat. Cook, stirring frequently, until raspberries have broken down and mixture is reduced to 1¼ cups, 20 to 25 minutes. Remove from heat; stir in rose water. Let cool completely.

Burnt Lemon Curd Filling
Makes 2 cups

The idea for this filling came out of a desire to use up the entire lemon. After zesting and juicing, the remaining lemon halves are chopped, blanched, and caramelized in sugar. This then serves as the base of your curd, amping up the lemon flavor to extreme, tangy levels.

2   medium lemons (220 grams)
¾   cup (150 grams) granulated sugar, divided
2   large eggs (100 grams)
½   teaspoon (1.5 grams) kosher salt
¼   cup (57 grams) unsalted butter

1. Zest and juice lemons; transfer 3 tablespoons (9 grams) zest and 6 tablespoons (90 grams) juice to a medium bowl. Whisk in ½ cup (100 grams) sugar, eggs, and salt until smooth; set aside.
2. Quarter juiced lemon halves, and thinly slice. In a medium saucepan, bring sliced lemons and water to cover to a boil over high heat; cook for 3 minutes. Drain, and pat dry with paper towels.
3. Return lemon slices to pan; add remaining ¼ cup (50 grams) sugar, and cook over

medium-high heat, stirring constantly, until caramelized, 5 to 6 minutes. Remove from heat; let cool for 2 minutes. Stir caramelized lemons into lemon juice mixture. Pour mixture into pan; cook over medium-low heat until thickened, 2 to 3 minutes. Remove from heat; stir in butter. Let cool completely.

Classic Poppy Seed Filling
Makes 2⅓ cups

This is as old-school as they come. Ground poppy seeds are folded into a quick custard filling. A common ingredient found in Eastern European pastries, poppy seeds add both a nutty flavor and a lovely textural component to this tender treat.

1	cup (142 grams) poppy seeds
¾	cup (150 grams) granulated sugar, divided
½	teaspoon (1.5 grams) kosher salt
1	cup (240 grams) whole milk
¼	cup (57 grams) unsalted butter
1	large egg (50 grams)

1. In the work bowl of a food processor, place poppy seeds, ½ cup (100 grams) sugar, and salt; process until a coarse powder with a damp appearance forms, 3 to 4 minutes. Set aside.

2. In a small saucepan, cook milk and butter over medium heat just until bubbles form around edges of pan. (Do not boil.) In a medium bowl, whisk together egg and remaining ¼ cup (50 grams) sugar. Slowly add hot milk mixture to egg mixture, whisking constantly. Return mixture to saucepan, and cook over medium-low heat until thickened, 1 to 2 minutes. Strain mixture into a clean bowl. Stir in poppy seed mixture. Let cool completely. Cover with a piece of plastic wrap, pressing wrap directly onto surface to prevent a skin from forming. Refrigerate until chilled.

Photo by Mark Weinberg

CAFÉ MOCHA COOKIES

Makes 24 cookies

Our mocha brownie cookies positively crackle with ground chocolate-covered coffee beans and freshly brewed espresso in the dough, but for the ultimate decadent finish, we opted for a generous swoop of dulce de leche.

1½	cups (255 grams) 63% cacao dark chocolate chips
¼	cup (57 grams) unsalted butter, softened
1¼	cups (192 grams) dark chocolate-covered coffee beans
3	large eggs (150 grams), room temperature
1	cup (200 grams) granulated sugar
¾	cup (94 grams) all-purpose flour
¾	teaspoon (3.75 grams) baking powder
¾	teaspoon (2.25 grams) kosher salt
2	tablespoons (30 grams) brewed espresso, cooled
1½	teaspoons (6 grams) vanilla extract
1	cup (304 grams) dulce de leche*

Garnish: flaked sea salt, crushed coffee beans

1. In the top of a double boiler, heat chocolate and butter over simmering water, stirring frequently, until melted and smooth. Let cool to room temperature.

2. Preheat oven to 350°F (180°C). Line baking sheets with parchment paper.

3. In the work bowl of a food processor, pulse dark chocolate-covered coffee beans until most of beans are finely ground; set aside.

4. In the bowl of a stand mixer fitted with the whisk attachment, beat eggs and sugar at high speed until very thick and pale, 5 to 6 minutes. With mixer on low speed, add cooled chocolate mixture in three additions, beating until combined after each addition.

5. In a medium bowl, whisk together flour, baking powder, and kosher salt. With mixer on low speed, gradually add flour mixture to egg mixture, beating just until combined and stopping to scrape sides of bowl. Beat in espresso and vanilla. Fold in ground chocolate-covered coffee beans.

6. Drop batter by 2 tablespoonfuls (35 to 40 grams) about 2 inches apart onto prepared pans. (Batter will be very loose, similar to brownie batter. Use a small spatula to cleanly drop batter from tablespoon scoop.)

7. Bake until puffed and cracked, 12 to 13 minutes. Let cool completely on pans. Store in airtight containers between layers of parchment paper at room temperature until ready to serve.

8. Spread dulce de leche onto cookies. Sprinkle with sea salt and crushed coffee beans, if desired.

We used Nestlé La Lechera Dulce de Leche.

SKILLET COOKIE

Makes 1 (10-inch) skillet cookie

Get creative with this infinitely customizable skillet cookie. We used walnuts, bittersweet chocolate, and milk chocolate, but any mix-ins you have in your pantry will work. Dried fruit, oats, the last of your holiday candy, or leftover coffee grounds are fair game. You can even swirl in your favorite spreads, like peanut butter or Nutella.

¾   cup (170 grams) unsalted butter, softened
¾   cup (165 grams) firmly packed light brown sugar
¾   cup (255 grams) maple syrup
2   teaspoons (8 grams) vanilla extract
1   large egg (50 grams)
1   large egg yolk (19 grams)
2¼ cups (281 grams) all-purpose flour
½   teaspoon (2.5 grams) baking soda
½   teaspoon (1.5 grams) kosher salt
¾   cup (85 grams) chopped walnuts, divided
⅔   cup (113 grams) chopped bittersweet chocolate, divided
⅔   cup (113 grams) chopped milk chocolate, divided

1. Preheat oven to 350°F (180°C). Butter and flour a 10-inch cast-iron skillet.
2. In the bowl of a stand mixer fitted with the paddle attachment, beat butter and brown sugar at medium speed until creamy, 3 to 4 minutes, stopping to scrape sides of bowl. Add maple syrup and vanilla, and beat until well combined, about 1 minute. Add egg and egg yolk, and beat until well combined.
3. In a medium bowl, whisk together flour, baking soda, and salt. With mixer on low speed, gradually add flour mixture to butter mixture, beating until combined. Beat in ½ cup (57 grams) walnuts, ½ cup (85 grams) bittersweet chocolate, and ½ cup (85 grams) milk chocolate. Spoon batter into prepared skillet.
4. Bake until golden brown and center is just set, 40 to 50 minutes, loosely covering with foil halfway through baking. (Begin checking cookie closely for doneness starting at 40 minutes.) Sprinkle with remaining ¼ cup (28 grams) walnuts, remaining bittersweet chocolate, and remaining milk chocolate. Cover with foil, and bake 5 minutes more. Let cool on a wire rack. Serve warm or at room temperature.

Note: *If substituting mix-ins, use the same measurement of any nut or chocolate you have available.*

TOASTED ALMOND SABLÉS

Makes about 22 cookies

Président® butter makes these sparkling sablés the ultimate buttery, melt-in-your-mouth cookies. Here, it imparts a creaminess that complements the flavor of toasted almonds exquisitely. Président is France's number one butter and our go-to for all crumbly French cookies.

⅓   cup (38 grams) sliced almonds
2   cups (250 grams) all-purpose flour
¾   cup plus 2 tablespoons (198 grams) unsalted butter*, softened
⅓   cup (40 grams) confectioners' sugar
1¼   cups (250 grams) granulated sugar, divided
1   teaspoon (3 grams) kosher salt
1   vanilla bean, split lengthwise, seeds scraped and reserved
1   large egg yolk (19 grams)

1. Preheat oven to 325°F (170°C). On a rimmed baking sheet, spread almonds in an even layer.
2. Bake until fragrant and toasted, about 10 minutes. Let cool completely.
3. In the work bowl of a food processor, process toasted almonds until finely ground. (Be sure not to overprocess the almonds, or you'll end up with almond butter.) Transfer to a medium bowl; add flour, whisking to combine.
4. In the bowl of a stand mixer fitted with the paddle attachment, beat butter at medium-low speed until smooth, about 1 minute. Add confectioners' sugar, ¼ cup (50 grams) granulated sugar, and salt, and beat until smooth, about 1 minute. Add reserved vanilla bean seeds and egg yolk, and beat until combined, about 1 minute. Add flour mixture to butter mixture in two additions, beating just until combined. Turn out dough onto a work surface, and gently knead 3 to 4 times.

5. Place dough between 2 large sheets of parchment paper, and roll to ½-inch thickness. Transfer dough between parchment to refrigerator. Refrigerate until set, at least 2 hours.
6. Preheat oven to 325°F (170°C). Line 2 baking sheets with parchment paper.
7. Using a 2-inch round cutter dipped in flour, cut dough, and place at least 1 inch apart on prepared pans. Reroll scraps between parchment, if necessary. Freeze until set before cutting dough, about 5 minutes.
8. Bake in batches until bottom edges turn golden, 15 to 16 minutes. Let cool on pans for 1 minute. Place remaining 1 cup (200 grams) granulated sugar on a plate. Using a spatula, place cookies, a few at a time, in sugar. Cover tops and sides with sugar. Using spatula, lift cookies, and place on wire racks to let cool completely.

We used Président® Butter.

CREAM-FILLED BASQUE COOKIES

Makes about 18 cookies

These indulgent cream-filled cookies embody the flavors of the gâteau Basque. A timeless cake from the Basque region in southwestern France, the gâteau Basque features a pâte brisée crust filled with pastry cream. We added crème fraîche to this sugar cookie base for a tanginess that complements the cookie's sweetness perfectly.

½   cup (113 grams) unsalted butter, softened
1   cup (200 grams) granulated sugar
2   large eggs (100 grams)
1   vanilla bean*, split lengthwise, seeds scraped and reserved
2½ cups (313 grams) all-purpose flour
½   teaspoon (2.5 grams) baking powder
½   teaspoon (2.5 grams) baking soda
½   teaspoon (1.5 grams) kosher salt
⅓   cup plus 2 tablespoons (110 grams) crème fraîche
Vanilla Pastry Cream (recipe follows), chilled

1. In the bowl of a stand mixer fitted with the paddle attachment, beat butter and sugar at medium speed until fluffy, 3 to 4 minutes, stopping to scrape sides of bowl. Add eggs, one at a time, beating well after each addition. Add reserved vanilla bean seeds.
2. In a medium bowl, whisk together flour, baking powder, baking soda, and salt. With mixer on low speed, gradually add flour mixture to butter mixture alternately with crème fraîche, beginning and ending with flour mixture, beating just until combined after each addition.
3. Divide dough in half. Roll each half between 2 sheets of parchment paper to ⅛-inch thickness. Transfer dough between parchment to refrigerator. Refrigerate overnight.
4. Preheat oven to 400°F (200°C). Line 3 rimmed baking sheets with parchment paper.
5. Using a 2-inch round cutter, cut half of dough. Using a 3-inch round cutter, cut remaining dough. With floured hands, place a 3-inch round in your palm. Place 1 tablespoon chilled Vanilla Pastry Cream in center. Top with a 2-inch round, and pinch edges of circles

together to seal. If dough is too soft to handle, place in freezer until set up, 10 to 15 minutes. (Using your finger, brush edges with water if there is too much flour.) Place cookies, seam side down, at least 2 inches apart on prepared pans. Repeat with remaining dough and remaining Vanilla Pastry Cream.
6. Bake until bottom edges are golden and tops look dry, about 10 minutes. Let cool on pans for 2 minutes. Remove from pans, and let cool completely on wire racks.

We used Heilala.

Vanilla Pastry Cream
Makes about 1¾ cups

1½ cups (360 grams) whole milk
½   cup (100 grams) granulated sugar, divided
1   vanilla bean, split lengthwise, seeds scraped and reserved
4   large egg yolks (74 grams)
3½ tablespoons (28 grams) cornstarch
¼   teaspoon kosher salt
2   tablespoons (28 grams) unsalted butter, softened

1. In a large saucepan, whisk together milk, ¼ cup (50 grams) sugar, and vanilla bean and reserved seeds. Heat over medium heat until steaming. Discard vanilla bean.
2. In a large bowl, whisk together egg yolks, cornstarch, salt, and remaining ¼ cup (50 grams) sugar. Gradually add warm milk mixture to egg mixture, whisking constantly. Return mixture to saucepan, and cook over medium heat, whisking constantly, until thickened and boiling, 4 to 5 minutes. Strain mixture through a fine-mesh sieve into a large bowl. Stir in butter in two additions. Cover with a piece of plastic wrap, pressing wrap directly onto surface of pastry cream to prevent a skin from forming. Refrigerate until completely chilled, about 4 hours or overnight.

BANANA SNICKERDOODLES

Makes 24 cookies

Recipe by Julie Grayston-Smith

Try adding in some dark chocolate chips or nuts to this cookie dough for extra flavor and texture.

- 1 cup (227 grams) unsalted butter, softened
- 2 cups (400 grams) granulated sugar, divided
- 1 teaspoon (4 grams) pure vanilla extract
- 2 large eggs (100 grams)
- ¾ cup (196 grams) banana purée (about 3 small bananas)
- 4½ cups (563 grams) all-purpose flour
- 2½ teaspoons (6 grams) cream of tartar
- 1½ teaspoons (7.5 grams) baking soda
- ¼ teaspoon sea salt
- 1 heaping tablespoon (11 grams) plus ¼ teaspoon ground cinnamon, divided

1. Preheat oven to 350°F (180°C). Line baking sheets with parchment paper.
2. In the bowl of a stand mixer fitted with the paddle attachment, beat butter and 1½ cups (300 grams) sugar at medium speed until fluffy, 3 to 4 minutes, stopping to scrape sides of bowl. Beat in vanilla. Add eggs, one at a time, beating well after each addition. Beat in banana purée.
3. In a large bowl, sift together flour, cream of tartar, baking soda, and sea salt. Stir in ¼ teaspoon cinnamon. With mixer on low speed, gradually add flour mixture to butter mixture, beating until combined. (Dough will be slightly sticky.)
4. In a small bowl, stir together remaining ½ cup (100 grams) sugar and remaining 1 heaping tablespoon (11 grams) cinnamon.
5. Roll dough into 2-inch balls (57 grams each), and roll in cinnamon sugar. (Dip fingers in flour when forming dough balls so dough does not stick to fingers.) Place 1½ to 2 inches apart on prepared pans.
6. Bake until puffed and lightly browned, 10 to 12 minutes. Let cool on pans for 5 minutes. Remove from pans, and let cool completely on wire racks. Store in an airtight container for up to 2 days.

CEYLON SNICKERDOODLES

Makes 24 cookies

Recipe by Elaine Townsend

This inspired snickerdoodle offers an herbaceous Ceylon tea sugar coating and salty custard center.

1½ cups plus 1 tablespoon (364 grams) unsalted butter
3⅓ cups (665 grams) granulated sugar
3   tablespoons plus 1 teaspoon (20 grams) Ceylon black tea leaves, ground in a spice grinder
3½ large eggs (171 grams), room temperature
⅓   cup plus 1 tablespoon plus 1 teaspoon (103 grams) whole milk, room temperature
1   tablespoon plus 2 teaspoons (20 grams) vanilla extract
6½ cups (818 grams) all-purpose flour
2   tablespoons (27 grams) fine sea salt
2   tablespoons (29 grams) baking soda
2   tablespoons (18 grams) cream of tartar
Salted Yolk Custard (recipe follows)
Ceylon Sugar (recipe follows)

1. In the bowl of a stand mixer fitted with the paddle attachment, beat butter, granulated sugar, and ground tea leaves at medium speed until fluffy, 3 to 4 minutes, stopping to scrape sides of bowl. Add eggs. Stream in milk and vanilla, beating until combined. Add flour, sea salt, baking soda, and cream of tartar, beating to combine.
2. Using a 3.2-ounce scoop, scoop dough into balls (90 grams each); press 1 frozen Salted Yolk Custard into center of each dough ball. Freeze for 4 hours or overnight.
3. Preheat oven to 350°F (180°C). Line baking sheets with parchment paper.
4. Toss each frozen dough ball in Ceylon Sugar, and place on prepared pans.
5. Bake until golden, about 15 minutes. Let cool completely on pans.

SALTED YOLK CUSTARD

Makes 24 custard balls

Cured Egg Yolks (recipe follows)
¼   cup plus 1 tablespoon (70 grams) unsalted butter
⅓   cup plus 1 tablespoon (50 grams) confectioners' sugar
5   tablespoons (30 grams) milk powder
2   teaspoons (10 grams) fine sea salt
2   teaspoons (5 grams) cornstarch
1   tablespoon plus 2 teaspoons (25 grams) coconut milk

1. Preheat oven to 350°F (180°C). Grease a sheet pan with cooking oil.
2. Rinse salt mixture off prepared Cured Egg Yolks. Place cleaned yolks on prepared pan.
3. Bake until firm, about 5 minutes. Let cool; finely grate with a grater. Set aside.
4. In the bowl of a stand mixer fitted with the paddle attachment, beat butter and confectioners' sugar at medium speed until creamy. Beat in grated yolks. Add milk powder, sea salt, and cornstarch, and beat until combined. Stream in coconut milk. Scoop mixture into 24 (0.75-ounce) balls (10 grams each); freeze until firm.

CURED EGG YOLKS

Makes 3 yolks

1½ cups plus 2 tablespoons (238 grams) kosher salt
¾   cup (141 grams) granulated sugar
3   duck egg yolks* (80 grams)

1. In a large bowl, combine salt and sugar. Spread half of salt mixture on a small pan or plate. Using the bottom of a spoon, make 3 round impressions in salt mixture. Place 1 egg yolk in each impression. Cover yolks with remaining salt mixture. Cover with plastic wrap, and refrigerate for 48 hours.

Duck egg yolks are preferred for their richness, but you can use 5 large chicken egg yolks (93 grams) instead.

CEYLON SUGAR

Makes 1⅔ cups

3   tablespoons (18 grams) Ceylon black tea leaves
1½ cups (300 grams) granulated sugar

1. In a spice grinder, grind tea leaves. In a small bowl, toss together ground tea leaves and sugar.

Photo courtesy of The Bakery at Fat Rice

DULCE DE LECHE BACI DI DAMA

Makes about 42 sandwich cookies

Recipe by Rebecca Firth

Baci di dama *are petite Italian sandwich cookies made with ground hazelnuts, and the cookie base has cocoa powder added for that perfect hazelnut-chocolate combination that we love so much. These cookies are chocolaty without being too sweet, and they melt and crumble once bitten. The Dulce de Leche Buttercream filling is so decadent, you'll want to eat by the spoonful.*

1   cup (126 grams) raw hazelnuts, skinned and coarsely chopped
1   cup plus 1½ tablespoons (137 grams) all-purpose flour
⅓   cup (25 grams) Dutch process cocoa powder, sifted
⅓   cup (73 grams) firmly packed light brown sugar
¼   cup (30 grams) confectioners' sugar, sifted
½   teaspoon (1.5 grams) sea salt
¾   cup (170 grams) unsalted butter, cubed and softened
2   tablespoons (30 grams) whole milk
1   teaspoon (4 grams) vanilla extract
Dulce de Leche Buttercream (recipe follows)

1. Preheat oven to 325°F (170°C). Line several baking sheets with parchment paper.
2. In the work bowl of a food processor, pulse hazelnuts until finely chopped and they have the appearance of fine bread crumbs. Add flour, cocoa, sugars, and sea salt, and pulse until completely combined. Scatter butter on top of hazelnut mixture; add milk and vanilla, and pulse for about 30 seconds to combine. Using a spatula, scrape sides and bottom of bowl to make sure everything is combined. Shape dough into 1-teaspoon (6-gram) balls, and place 1 inch apart on prepared pans.
3. Bake for 10 minutes. Let cool on pans for 10 minutes. Remove from pans, and let cool completely on wire racks. Spread Dulce de Leche Buttercream onto flat side of half of cookies. Place remaining cookies, flat side down, on top of buttercream.

DULCE DE LECHE BUTTERCREAM

Makes about 2 cups

1¾ cups (420 grams) whole milk
⅔   cup (133 grams) plus ¾ cup (150 grams) granulated sugar, divided
¼   cup (60 grams) heavy whipping cream
½   vanilla bean, split lengthwise, seeds scraped and reserved
½   teaspoon sea salt, divided

¼   teaspoon (1.25 grams) baking soda
2   large egg whites (60 grams), room temperature
3   tablespoons (63 grams) corn syrup
¾   cup (170 grams) unsalted butter

1. In a large saucepan, whisk together milk, ⅔ cup (133 grams) sugar, cream, vanilla bean and reserved seeds, and ¼ teaspoon sea salt; bring to a boil over medium-high heat. Reduce to a simmer; whisk in baking soda. Cook, stirring occasionally and adjusting temperature to keep it from boiling (see PRO TIP), for 1 hour and 15 minutes to 1 hour and 30 minutes. Strain through a fine-mesh sieve into a heatproof bowl. (You will have about ⅔ cup.) Refrigerate in an airtight container until ready to use. (It will thicken more as it cools.)
2. In the bowl of a stand mixer, combine egg whites, remaining ¾ cup (150 grams) sugar, and remaining ¼ teaspoon sea salt; place bowl over a saucepan of simmering water. Cook, whisking occasionally, until mixture no longer feels gritty when rubbed between two fingers and an instant-read thermometer registers 155°F (68°C) to 160°F (71°C). Return bowl to stand mixer fitted with the whisk attachment, and beat at high speed until bowl feels cool to the touch, 5 to 6 minutes. Add butter, a piece at a time, beating until well combined after each addition. Beat until mixture is smooth, glossy, and voluminous. Beat in ⅓ cup (104 grams) dulce de leche; reserve remaining dulce de leche for another use.

Note: *The cookies come together quickly, but take note of the cook time for the dulce de leche in the buttercream so you can plan accordingly. You can also use store-bought dulce de leche in place of this homemade version.*

PRO TIP

When preparing the dulce de leche, you just want some bubbles around the edges of the pan. After 30 to 45 minutes, the color will start to deepen and the mixture will begin to thicken a bit. When this happens, it'll be more prone to a heavy boil, which is bad, so continue adjusting the temperature as needed and stirring more frequently. This dulce de leche deepens and thickens faster than usual because of the addition of cream, so keep an eye on it. You want it to have a nice, thick consistency and a bronzed and deep caramel appearance.

Photo by Rebecca Firth

BLACK-AND-WHITE THUMBPRINT COOKIES

Makes about 55 cookies

It doesn't get much simpler or more satisfying than these black-and-white cookies. With a bittersweet black cocoa base and a silky vanilla bean buttercream, this recipe is a nostalgic crowd-pleaser.

1   cup (227 grams) unsalted butter, softened
¾   cup (165 grams) firmly packed dark brown sugar
2   large egg yolks (37 grams)
1½   teaspoons (6 grams) vanilla extract
2   cups (250 grams) all-purpose flour
⅓   cup (28 grams) black cocoa powder
½   teaspoon (1.5 grams) kosher salt
¼   teaspoon (1.25 grams) baking powder
Vanilla Buttercream (recipe follows)
Garnish: crushed cookies

1. Preheat oven to 350°F (180°C). Line baking sheets with parchment paper.
2. In the bowl of a stand mixer fitted with the paddle attachment, beat butter and brown sugar at medium speed until creamy, about 3 minutes, stopping to scrape sides of bowl. Beat in egg yolks and vanilla.
3. In a medium bowl, whisk together flour, black cocoa, salt, and baking powder. With mixer on low speed, gradually add flour mixture to butter mixture, beating until combined. Shape dough into 1-inch balls (about 13 grams), and place 2 inches apart on prepared pans. Using your thumb or a ¼ teaspoon, gently make an indentation in center of each ball.
4. Bake until set, 9 to 10 minutes. Press down centers again. Let cool on pans for 10 minutes. Remove from pans, and let cool completely on wire racks.
5. Place Vanilla Buttercream in a piping bag fitted with a large round tip (Wilton No. 12).

Pipe Vanilla Buttercream into center of each cookie. Crush a few cookies, and sprinkle on top of buttercream, if desired.

VANILLA BUTTERCREAM
Makes about 1¼ cups

6   tablespoons (84 grams) unsalted butter, softened
1¾   cups (210 grams) confectioners' sugar
½   teaspoon (3 grams) vanilla bean paste
¼   teaspoon kosher salt
¼   cup (60 grams) heavy whipping cream

1. In the bowl of a stand mixer fitted with the paddle attachment, beat butter at medium speed until creamy, about 2 minutes. Gradually add confectioners' sugar, beating until combined. Beat in vanilla bean paste and salt. Add cream, beating until smooth. Use immediately.

PINEAPPLE-GINGER THUMBPRINT COOKIES

Makes about 50 cookies

We reimagined the classic Southeast Asian pineapple tart as a zingy ginger cookie topped with a ball of spiced, caramelized pineapple jam. As a nod to the original's elegant stamped shape, we piped these cookies into a mesmerizing swirl.

1   cup (227 grams) unsalted butter, softened
⅔   cup (133 grams) granulated sugar
1   large egg (50 grams)
1   teaspoon (3 grams) finely grated fresh ginger
1   teaspoon (4 grams) vanilla extract
2⅔ cups (333 grams) all-purpose flour
1   teaspoon (2 grams) ground ginger
¾   teaspoon (2.25 grams) kosher salt
¼   teaspoon (1.25 grams) baking powder
Pineapple Jam Filling (recipe follows)

1. Preheat oven to 350°F (180°C). Line baking sheets with parchment paper.
2. In the bowl of a stand mixer fitted with the paddle attachment, beat butter and sugar at medium speed until creamy, 2 to 3 minutes, stopping to scrape sides of bowl. Add egg, beating well. Beat in fresh ginger and vanilla.
3. In a medium bowl, whisk together flour, ground ginger, salt, and baking powder. With mixer on low speed, gradually add flour mixture to butter mixture, beating until combined.
4. Transfer about ½ cup dough to a piping bag fitted with an open star tip (Wilton 1M). Pipe 1½-inch rosettes 3 inches apart on prepared pans, pinching dough with fingers to release. (Spacing these cookies farther apart ensures even heating during baking for better shape.) Repeat with remaining dough, ½ cup at a time.
5. Bake for 5 minutes. Remove from oven; using the handle of a wooden spoon, gently make an indentation in center of each cookie. Top with Pineapple Jam Filling balls. Bake until cookies are light golden, 6 to 8 minutes more. Let cool on pans for 10 minutes. Remove from pans, and let cool completely on wire racks.

PINEAPPLE JAM FILLING
Makes about 1½ cups

2   medium pineapples, peeled, cored, and cubed (about 2¼ pounds)
1   cinnamon stick
½   teaspoon (1 gram) whole cloves
½   cup (100 grams) granulated sugar
1   tablespoon (15 grams) fresh lemon juice

1. In the work bowl of a food processor, place pineapple; pulse until puréed. Transfer pineapple purée to a large skillet. Add cinnamon stick and cloves; cook over medium heat, stirring frequently, until most of liquid is evaporated, about 15 minutes. Stir in sugar and lemon juice; increase heat to medium-high. Bring to a boil; cook for 5 minutes, stirring frequently to reduce spattering. Reduce heat; simmer, stirring frequently to prevent scorching, until thick and golden in color, about 40 minutes.
2. Transfer pineapple mixture to a bowl. Let cool for 30 minutes. Discard cinnamon stick and cloves. Cover and refrigerate for at least 1 hour.
3. Line a baking sheet with parchment paper. Scoop pineapple mixture by teaspoonfuls (about 7 grams each), and shape into balls. Place on prepared pan until ready to use.

PECAN THUMBPRINT COOKIES WITH CHERRY BUTTERCREAM

Makes about 55 cookies

We gave pecan sandies a summertime makeover by filling these buttery pecan-studded cookies with a tart Cherry Buttercream. The buttercream gets its bright flavor—and brilliant color—from cherry concentrate, available in the fruit juice aisle at most grocery stores.

1   cup (227 grams) unsalted butter, softened
⅔   cup (133 grams) granulated sugar
2   large egg yolks (37 grams)
1   teaspoon (4 grams) vanilla extract
¾   cup (85 grams) chopped pecans*, toasted and cooled
2¼ cups (281 grams) all-purpose flour, divided
¾   teaspoon (2.25 grams) kosher salt
Cherry Buttercream (recipe follows)

1. Preheat oven to 350°F (180°C). Line baking sheets with parchment paper.
2. In the bowl of a stand mixer fitted with the paddle attachment, beat butter and sugar at medium speed until creamy, 2 to 3 minutes, stopping to scrape sides of bowl.

Add egg yolks, one at a time, beating well after each addition. Beat in vanilla.
3. In the work bowl of a food processor, place pecans and ¼ cup (31 grams) flour; pulse until ground. Add salt and remaining 2 cups (250 grams) flour; pulse to combine.
4. With mixer on low speed, gradually add pecan mixture to butter mixture, beating until combined. Shape dough into 1-inch balls (about 13 grams each), and place 2 inches apart on prepared pans. Using your thumb or a ¼ teaspoon, gently make an indentation in center of each ball.
5. Bake until bottoms are golden brown, 15 to 17 minutes. Remove from oven, and press down centers again. Let cool on pans for 10 minutes. Remove from pans, and let cool completely on wire racks.
6. Place Cherry Buttercream in a piping bag fitted with a medium open star tip (Wilton No. 32). Pipe Cherry Buttercream into center of each cookie.

We used Sunnyland Farms Raw Georgia Pecan Halves.

CHERRY BUTTERCREAM
Makes about 2 cups

¾   cup (170 grams) unsalted butter, softened
¼   teaspoon (1 gram) almond extract
⅛   teaspoon kosher salt
3   cups (360 grams) confectioners' sugar
2   tablespoons (40 grams) pure cherry concentrate*

1. In the bowl of a stand mixer fitted with the paddle attachment, beat butter, almond extract, and salt at medium speed until creamy, 3 to 5 minutes. Gradually add confectioners' sugar and cherry concentrate, beating until smooth. Use immediately.

We used Tart Is Smart Tart Cherry Concentrate, found in the fruit juice aisle of the grocery store or online.

RAINBOW SPRINKLE SUGAR COOKIES

Makes about 30 cookies

Rainbow sprinkles bring crunch and color to these tender drop cookies.

⅓   cup (76 grams) unsalted butter, softened
¾   cup (150 grams) granulated sugar
1   large egg (50 grams)
2   large egg yolks (37 grams)
1   tablespoon (13 grams) vanilla extract
1   teaspoon (4 grams) almond extract
½   cup (120 grams) sour cream, room temperature
2½ cups (313 grams) all-purpose flour
1   teaspoon (5 grams) baking powder
¼   teaspoon (1.25 grams) baking soda
¼   teaspoon kosher salt
¾   cup (135 grams) rainbow sprinkles*, divided

1. Preheat oven to 350°F (180°C). Line baking sheets with parchment paper.
2. In the bowl of a stand mixer fitted with the paddle attachment, beat butter and sugar at medium speed just until combined, 1 to 2 minutes. Beat in egg and egg yolks. Beat in extracts. Add sour cream, beating until combined.
3. In a medium bowl, whisk together flour, baking powder, baking soda, and salt. With mixer on low speed, gradually add flour mixture to butter mixture, beating until combined. Gently fold in ¼ cup (45 grams) sprinkles. Using a 1½-teaspoon spring-loaded scoop, scoop dough (about 23 grams each), and drop onto prepared pans. Freeze for 15 minutes.
4. Place remaining ½ cup (90 grams) sprinkles in a small bowl. Roll each portion of dough into a ball, and toss in sprinkles. Place 2 inches apart on prepared pans. Flatten slightly using the bottom of a glass.
5. Bake until bottoms are golden brown, 10 to 12 minutes. Let cool on pans for 5 minutes. Remove from pans, and let cool completely on wire racks.

We used Betty Crocker Rainbow Sprinkles because the colors don't bleed.

BLUEBERRY MUFFIN COOKIES

Makes about 15 cookies

With a crunchy sugar-crusted surface and a cakey interior, this treat offers the best part of the muffin in cookie form. Président® butter gives the breakfast-ready cookies an irresistibly tender, pillowy crumb, just like the top of a muffin. Brimming with fresh blueberries and drizzled with a tart Lemon Glaze, these are summertime perfection.

½   cup (113 grams) unsalted butter*, softened
¾   cup (150 grams) granulated sugar
½   cup (110 grams) firmly packed light brown sugar
1   large egg (50 grams)
1   tablespoon (3 grams) lemon zest
1   teaspoon (4 grams) vanilla extract
2   cups (250 grams) all-purpose flour
2   teaspoons (10 grams) baking powder
½   teaspoon (1.5 grams) kosher salt
½   cup (120 grams) sour cream
2   cups (300 grams) fresh blueberries
2   tablespoons (24 grams) sparkling sugar
Lemon Glaze (recipe follows)

1. Preheat oven to 375°F (190°C). Line 3 baking sheets with parchment paper.
2. In the bowl of a stand mixer fitted with the paddle attachment, beat butter, granulated sugar, and brown sugar at medium speed until fluffy, 3 to 4 minutes, stopping to scrape sides of bowl. Add egg, beating well. Beat in lemon zest and vanilla.
3. In a medium bowl, whisk together flour, baking powder, and salt. With mixer on low speed, add flour mixture to butter mixture in two additions alternately with all of sour cream, beating just until combined after each addition. Gently fold in blueberries. Using a ¼-cup spring-loaded scoop, scoop batter, and drop 2½ to 3 inches apart onto prepared pans. (Cookies will spread during baking.) Sprinkle with sparkling sugar.
4. Bake until a wooden pick inserted in center comes out clean, about 16 minutes. Let cool on pans for 5 minutes. Remove from pans, and place on a wire rack. Drizzle with Lemon Glaze. Serve warm.

We used Président® Butter.

LEMON GLAZE
Makes about ½ cup

1⅓ cups (160 grams) confectioners' sugar, divided
1   teaspoon (1 gram) lemon zest
2   tablespoons (30 grams) fresh lemon juice

1. In a small bowl, whisk together 1 cup (120 grams) confectioners' sugar and lemon zest and juice until smooth. Add remaining ⅓ cup (40 grams) confectioners' sugar, and whisk until thick and smooth. Use immediately.

LEMON MERINGUE THUMBPRINT COOKIES

Makes about 50 cookies

Filled with a velvety Lemon Curd and topped with torched Meringue Kisses, these cookies are bite-size versions of a lemon meringue pie.

1 cup (227 grams) unsalted butter*, softened
1 cup plus 2 tablespoons (134 grams) confectioners' sugar
¾ teaspoon (2.25 grams) kosher salt
½ teaspoon (2 grams) almond extract
2 cups (250 grams) all-purpose flour
Lemon Curd (recipe follows)
Meringue Kisses (recipe follows)

1. Preheat oven to 350°F (180°C). Line baking sheets with parchment paper.
2. In the bowl of a stand mixer fitted with the paddle attachment, beat butter, confectioners' sugar, and salt at medium speed until fluffy, 2 to 3 minutes, stopping to scrape sides of bowl. Beat in almond extract. Add flour, beating until combined.
3. Shape dough into 1-inch balls (about 12 grams each), and place 2 inches apart on prepared pans. Using your thumb or a

¼ teaspoon, gently make an indentation in center of each ball.
4. Bake until bottoms are golden brown, 11 to 13 minutes. Press down centers again. Let cool on pans for 10 minutes. Remove from pans, and let cool completely on wire racks. Just before serving, spoon about ¾ teaspoon (about 6 grams) Lemon Curd into center of each cookie. Top with Meringue Kisses. Serve immediately.

We used Président® Butter.

LEMON CURD
Makes about ⅔ cup

3 large egg yolks (56 grams)
⅓ cup (67 grams) granulated sugar
2 teaspoons (4 grams) lemon zest
¼ cup (60 grams) fresh lemon juice
¼ cup (57 grams) unsalted butter, cubed

1. In a small heavy-bottomed saucepan, whisk together egg yolks, sugar, and lemon zest and juice until combined. Add butter; cook over medium heat, whisking constantly, until thickened and an instant-

read thermometer registers 170°F (77°C), about 12 minutes. (Do not boil.) Strain through a fine-mesh sieve into a small bowl. Cover with a piece of plastic wrap, pressing wrap directly onto surface of curd. Let cool slightly. Refrigerate for at least 30 minutes.

MERINGUE KISSES
Makes about 200 miniature meringues*

This recipe yields more than double what you'll need for the Lemon Meringue Thumbprint Cookies, so you'll have plenty for snacking, too.

3 large egg whites (90 grams), room temperature
¼ teaspoon (1.25 grams) cream of tartar
¼ teaspoon (1 gram) vanilla extract
¾ cup (150 grams) granulated sugar

1. Preheat oven to 225°F (107°C). Line baking sheets with parchment paper.
2. In the bowl of a stand mixer fitted with the whisk attachment, beat egg whites, cream of tartar, and vanilla at high speed until foamy, about 1 minute. Add sugar in a slow, steady stream, beating until glossy, soft peaks form, about 3 minutes.
3. Spoon meringue into a large piping bag fitted with an open star tip (Wilton No. 21 or No. 32). Pipe small stars (about ¾ inch) onto prepared pans. If torching kisses to brown, lightly press down any pointed tips to prevent burning. (See Note.)
4. Bake until firm and lightly browned, about 2 hours. Let cool completely. Store in airtight containers at room temperature.

We piped very small stars to top our thumbprints. You'll have more meringues than you'll need for the Lemon Meringue Thumbprints. If desired, pipe or spoon larger (about 1½-inch) mounds to make meringue cookies. The bake time will remain the same.

Note: *If desired, the tops of the baked and cooled kisses can be browned with a kitchen torch. Just be sure to transfer them to an unlined baking sheet before torching.*

CHOCOLATE HALVAH SANDWICH COOKIES WITH CARDAMOM BUTTERCREAM

Makes about 16 sandwich cookies

Recipe by Amisha Gurbani

Halvah has a nutty flavor and combines really well with chocolate—a match made in heaven. Add cardamom to the mix and you get luxurious cookies, especially with the chocolate coating and gold specks. These make for beautiful, festive cookies that are perfect for entertaining!

½ cup (113 grams) unsalted butter, softened
½ cup (100 grams) granulated sugar
1 teaspoon (4 grams) vanilla extract
1¼ cups (156 grams) all-purpose flour
⅓ cup (32 grams) almond flour
¼ cup (21 grams) dark cocoa powder, plus more for rolling
1 teaspoon (6 grams) table salt
½ cup (65 grams) shredded halvah
1½ cups (255 grams) chocolate chips
1½ tablespoons (21 grams) coconut oil
Small food-safe paintbrush
Edible gold paint*
Cardamom Buttercream (recipe follows)

1. In the bowl of a stand mixer fitted with the paddle attachment, beat butter and sugar at high speed until combined, about 1 minute, stopping to scrape sides of bowl with a rubber spatula. Add vanilla, and beat at low speed until combined, about 15 seconds.
2. In a medium bowl, sift together flours, cocoa, and salt. With mixer on low speed, add flour mixture to butter mixture, gradually increasing mixer speed to medium until the mixture starts coming together, about 2 minutes. Add halvah, and beat until well combined. (Dough should be dark brown without any specks of halvah showing. It will look a bit crumbly, but don't worry—it will come together in the refrigerator when it sets.) Shape dough into a disk, and wrap tightly in plastic wrap. Refrigerate for 1 hour.
3. Preheat oven to 350°F (180°C). Line 2 baking sheets with parchment paper.
4. Dust a sheet of parchment paper with cocoa. Turn out dough onto parchment, and dust with cocoa. Top with another sheet of parchment paper, and roll dough to ¼-inch thickness. Remove top layer of parchment; using a 2-inch square cutter, cut dough, rerolling scraps. Using a small offset spatula, gently remove cookies, and place on prepared pans. Freeze for 10 minutes.

5. Bake for 12 to 13 minutes. Let cool on pans for 5 minutes. Remove from pans, and let cool completely on a wire rack, about 1 hour.
6. In a small microwave-safe bowl, combine chocolate and oil; heat on high in 30-second intervals, stirring between each, until chocolate is melted and mixture is smooth (about 1½ minutes total).
7. Line 2 baking sheets with parchment paper. Dip cookies halfway into chocolate mixture, shaking off excess. Place on prepared pans, and freeze until chocolate is set, about 10 minutes.
8. Cover the undipped half of 1 cookie with a piece of parchment paper. Dip brush in edible gold paint, and flick paint onto chocolate-covered portion of cookie. Freeze for 2 minutes. Repeat process with all remaining cookies.
9. Place Cardamom Buttercream in a piping bag fitted with a ⅓-inch round tip (Ateco #804), and pipe buttercream onto flat side of half of cookies. Place remaining cookies, flat side down, on top of buttercream. Refrigerate in an airtight container for up to 1 week.

*We used AmeriColor Amerimist Airbrush Color in Gold Sheen, available at amazon.com. You can also combine dry edible gold dust with a couple drops of any alcohol, like rum or vodka, mix, and use that mixture as paint. We like Super Gold Luster Dust, available at amazon.com.

CARDAMOM BUTTERCREAM
Makes about 1⅓ cups

½ cup (113 grams) unsalted butter, softened
1 teaspoon (4 grams) vanilla extract
½ teaspoon (3 grams) table salt
½ teaspoon (1 gram) ground cardamom
2 cups (240 grams) confectioners' sugar

1. In the bowl of a stand mixer fitted with the paddle attachment, beat butter, vanilla, salt, and cardamom until combined, about 30 seconds. Scrape sides of bowl. Add confectioners' sugar, and beat at low speed for about 30 seconds. Gradually increase mixer speed to high, and beat until well combined, about 1 minute. Use immediately.

Photo by Amisha Gurbani

PUMPKIN SPICE WHOOPIE PIES

Makes 12 whoopie pies

The pumpkin spice latte, the most viral fall beverage, inspired these epic sandwiches. We packed the cakey cookies with pumpkin spice, and our airy Mascarpone Filling is a parallel to the latte's milky texture.

1   cup (227 grams) unsalted butter, softened
2   cups (440 grams) firmly packed dark brown sugar
1½   cups (366 grams) canned pumpkin
2   teaspoons (8 grams) vanilla extract
2   large eggs (100 grams)
3   cups (375 grams) all-purpose flour
2   teaspoons (4 grams) pumpkin spice (see Note)
1   teaspoon (5 grams) baking soda
½   teaspoon (2.5 grams) baking powder
½   teaspoon (1.5 grams) kosher salt
Mascarpone Filling (recipe follows)

1. Preheat oven to 350°F (180°C). Line baking sheets with parchment paper.

2. In the bowl of a stand mixer fitted with the paddle attachment, beat butter and brown sugar at medium speed until fluffy, 2 to 3 minutes, stopping to scrape sides of bowl. Beat in pumpkin and vanilla. Add eggs, one at a time, beating well after each addition.

3. In a medium bowl, whisk together flour, pumpkin spice, baking soda, baking powder, and salt. With mixer on low speed, gradually add flour mixture to butter mixture, beating until combined. Using a scant ¼-cup spring-loaded scoop, scoop batter, and drop 2 inches apart on prepared pans. Using damp fingers, pat batter to flatten tops, creating 2½-inch rounds.

4. Bake until a wooden pick inserted in center comes out clean, 13 to 15 minutes. Let cool on pans for 5 minutes. Remove from pans, and let cool completely on wire racks.

5. Place Mascarpone Filling in a piping bag fitted with a large round tip (Wilton No. 12). Pipe Mascarpone Filling onto flat side of half of cookies. Place remaining cookies, flat side down, on top of filling. Refrigerate in an airtight container for up to 3 days.

MASCARPONE FILLING
Makes 3½ cups

1   cup (227 grams) unsalted butter, softened
4   cups (480 grams) confectioners' sugar
2   tablespoons (30 grams) heavy whipping cream
1   teaspoon (2 grams) pumpkin spice (see Note)
¼   teaspoon kosher salt
8   ounces (225 grams) mascarpone cheese, room temperature

1. In the bowl of a stand mixer fitted with the paddle attachment, beat butter at medium speed until smooth, about 2 minutes. Add confectioners' sugar, 1 cup (120 grams) at a time, beating well after each addition. Beat in cream, pumpkin spice, and salt. Using a spatula, carefully fold in mascarpone. (Do not overmix, or mixture will break.) Use immediately.

Note: *Save a trip to the store and try our homemade Pumpkin Spice on page 19.*

DOUBLE-CHOCOLATE TOFFEE BISCOTTI

Makes 24 biscotti

Recipe by Michele Song

These twice-baked chocolate-toffee-almond biscotti are the perfect treat to dunk into your morning cup of coffee. The addition of espresso powder in the dough enhances the chocolate flavor, and the butter gives the biscotti a tender texture.

6   tablespoons (84 grams) unsalted butter, softened
1   cup (220 grams) firmly packed dark brown sugar
1   teaspoon (4 grams) vanilla extract
2   large eggs (100 grams), room temperature
2   cups (250 grams) unbleached all-purpose flour
¾   cup (64 grams) Dutch process cocoa powder
2   teaspoons (10 grams) baking powder
1   teaspoon (2 grams) espresso powder
½   teaspoon (1.5 grams) kosher salt
1   cup (170 grams) chopped 60% cacao bittersweet chocolate
Toffee Bits (recipe follows), divided

¾   cup (85 grams) chopped toasted almonds
1   large egg white (30 grams), lightly beaten
8   ounces (225 grams) 60% cacao bittersweet chocolate, melted

1. Line a baking sheet with parchment paper.
2. In the bowl of a stand mixer fitted with the paddle attachment, beat butter, brown sugar, and vanilla at medium speed until fluffy, 4 to 5 minutes. With mixer on low speed, add eggs, one at a time, beating well after each addition. Increase mixer speed to medium, and beat for 2 minutes, stopping to scrape sides of bowl.
3. In a medium bowl, stir together flour, cocoa, baking powder, espresso powder, and salt. Add flour mixture to butter mixture all at once, and beat at low speed just until combined. In another medium bowl, combine chopped chocolate, ¾ cup (106 grams) Toffee Bits, and almonds. Add chocolate mixture to dough, beating until combined.
4. Turn out dough onto a lightly floured surface, and divide in half. Using well-floured hands, roll each half into a log. Place logs on prepared pan, and gently pat each into a 10x2½-inch log. Dough will be

sticky, so you may need to add extra flour to surface and hands. (Make sure logs are spaced about 3 inches apart to allow for spreading.) Cover with plastic wrap, and refrigerate for at least 1 hour or overnight.
5. Preheat oven to 350°F (180°C).
6. Brush top of logs with egg white.
7. Bake until tops are cracked and firm, 30 to 35 minutes, rotating pan halfway through baking. Let cool on pan for 15 minutes. Reduce oven temperature to 300°F (150°C).
8. Transfer logs to a cutting board. Using a serrated knife, gently cut warm logs crosswise on a diagonal into ¾-inch-thick slices. Place slices, side by side and cut side down, on baking sheet.
9. Bake for 10 minutes. Turn, and bake until edges are dry but center is still slightly soft, about 10 minutes more. Let cool completely on pan.
10. Dip bottom of biscotti in melted chocolate, and immediately sprinkle with remaining Toffee Bits. Place dipped biscotti back on pans. Let stand until chocolate is set, 30 to 45 minutes.

TOFFEE BITS
Makes about 1½ cups

½   cup (113 grams) unsalted butter
½   cup (100 grams) granulated sugar
2   tablespoons (30 grams) water
2   teaspoons (14 grams) light corn syrup
½   teaspoon (1.5 grams) kosher salt
½   teaspoon (2 grams) vanilla extract

1. Line a baking sheet with a nonstick baking mat.
2. In a large saucepan, melt butter over medium heat. Add sugar, 2 tablespoons (30 grams) water, corn syrup, salt, and vanilla, stirring to combine. Bring to a boil, stirring constantly; cook until sugar begins to caramelize, about 5 minutes.
3. As soon as caramel turns a dark amber color, remove from heat, stir a few times, and pour onto prepared pan. Let toffee harden and set, about 20 minutes. Coarsely chop into bits.

Photo by Michele Song

TRIPLE-CHOCOLATE HOT COCOA COOKIES

Makes about 24 cookies

With milk chocolate and drinking chocolate in the batter and a luscious White Chocolate Ganache center, these tender cookies offer all the comfort and coziness of a cup of hot cocoa. A blend of cocoa and ground red pepper sprinkled on top adds warmth and subtle spice to each bite.

¾ cup (170 grams) unsalted butter, softened

½ cup (110 grams) firmly packed dark brown sugar

2 large egg yolks (37 grams)

1½ teaspoons (6 grams) vanilla extract

½ cup (85 grams) chopped milk chocolate, melted and slightly cooled

2 cups (250 grams) all-purpose flour

⅓ cup (40 grams) unsweetened drinking chocolate powder

½ teaspoon (1.5 grams) kosher salt

¼ teaspoon (1.25 grams) baking powder

White Chocolate Ganache (recipe follows)

1 tablespoon (5 grams) unsweetened cocoa powder

½ teaspoon (1 gram) ground red pepper

1. Preheat oven to 350°F (180°C). Line baking sheets with parchment paper.

2. In the bowl of a stand mixer fitted with the paddle attachment, beat butter and brown sugar at medium speed until creamy, about 2 minutes, stopping to scrape sides of bowl. Beat in egg yolks and vanilla. Beat in melted chocolate.

3. In a medium bowl, whisk together flour, drinking chocolate powder, salt, and baking powder. With mixer on low speed, gradually add flour mixture to butter mixture, beating until combined. Using a 1½-tablespoon spring-loaded scoop, scoop dough, and roll into smooth balls (29 grams each). Place 2 inches apart on prepared pans. Using the back of the scoop, gently make an indentation in center of each ball.

4. Bake for 9 to 11 minutes. Press down centers again. Let cool on pans for 10 minutes. Remove from pans, and let cool completely on wire racks. Pipe White Chocolate Ganache into center of each cookie. In a small bowl, stir together cocoa and red pepper. Dust cocoa mixture onto cookies.

WHITE CHOCOLATE GANACHE
Makes about 1 cup

1 cup (170 grams) chopped white chocolate

¼ cup (60 grams) heavy whipping cream

1. In a large heatproof bowl, place white chocolate.

2. In a small saucepan, bring cream just to a boil over medium heat. Pour hot cream over white chocolate. Let stand for 1 minute; whisk until smooth. Refrigerate, stirring occasionally, until slightly thickened, about 30 minutes.

GERMAN CHOCOLATE SANDWICH COOKIES

Makes 20 sandwich cookies

Recipe by Elisabeth Farris

No mixer necessary for these chewy double-chocolate cookies filled with the most delicious Coconut Pecan Filling that melts in your mouth. Coconut lovers will fall in love all over again!

2½ cups (425 grams) 60% cacao dark chocolate chips, divided
½ cup (113 grams) unsalted butter, softened
1¾ cups (219 grams) all-purpose flour
¼ cup (21 grams) unsweetened cocoa powder
1 teaspoon (5 grams) baking powder
1 teaspoon (5 grams) baking soda
½ teaspoon (1.5 grams) kosher salt
3 large eggs (150 grams)
¾ cup (150 grams) granulated sugar
¾ cup (165 grams) firmly packed light brown sugar
2 teaspoons (8 grams) vanilla extract
Coconut Pecan Filling (recipe follows)

1. In the top of a double boiler, combine 1½ cups (255 grams) chocolate chips and butter. Cook over simmering water, stirring frequently, until chocolate is melted and mixture is smooth. (Alternatively, combine chocolate chips and butter in a large microwave-safe bowl. Heat on high in 30-second intervals, stirring between each, until chocolate is melted and mixture is smooth.) Remove from heat; set aside.
2. In a medium bowl, whisk together flour, cocoa, baking powder, baking soda, and salt. Set aside.
3. Add eggs, sugars, and vanilla to chocolate mixture, and whisk to combine. Add flour mixture to chocolate mixture, stirring just until combined. Fold in remaining 1 cup (170 grams) chocolate chips. Cover and refrigerate for at least 1 hour or for up to 3 days.
4. Preheat oven to 350°F (180°C). Line 2 large baking sheets with parchment paper.
5. Using a 2-tablespoon spring-loaded scoop, scoop dough, and shape into smooth,

round balls (30 grams each). Place 2 inches apart on prepared pans.
6. Bake until slightly cracked, 8 to 10 minutes. Let cool on pans for 5 minutes. Remove from pans, and let cool completely on wire racks. Spoon 1 to 2 tablespoons Coconut Pecan Filling onto flat side of half of cookies. Place remaining cookies, flat side down, on top of filling. Store in an airtight container for up to 3 days.

Note: *If you do not want to bake all of these cookies at once, the dough can be stored in a resealable plastic bag in the freezer. Freeze the scooped dough until solid on a baking sheet before transferring to a bag.*

COCONUT PECAN FILLING
Makes about 2 cups

1 cup (220 grams) firmly packed light brown sugar
1 cup (240 grams) evaporated milk
½ cup (113 grams) unsalted butter, softened
3 large egg yolks (56 grams)
1 teaspoon (4 grams) vanilla extract
1 cup (113 grams) chopped toasted pecans
1 cup (60 grams) sweetened flaked coconut
⅛ teaspoon kosher salt

1. In a medium saucepan, bring brown sugar, evaporated milk, butter, and egg yolks to a low boil over medium heat, whisking occasionally; cook, stirring constantly, until thickened, about 5 minutes. Remove from heat; stir in vanilla, pecans, coconut, and salt. Let cool completely.

Note: *This filling can be made a day ahead and refrigerated until ready to use. Let come to room temperature before assembling cookies.*

Photo by Elisabeth Farris

CHOCOLATE PEPPERMINT MACARONS

Makes about 24 macarons

Recipe by Mike Johnson

These chocolate macarons are sprinkled with crushed candy canes and sandwiched together with a White Chocolate Peppermint Ganache. They're perfect for cookie exchanges, holiday gatherings, or alongside a cup of hot cocoa on a cold winter's night.

4	large egg whites (120 grams), room temperature
½	cup plus 2 tablespoons (124 grams) granulated sugar
1⅔	cups (200 grams) confectioners' sugar
1⅓	cups (128 grams) almond flour
2	tablespoons (10 grams) unsweetened Dutch process cocoa powder
1	tablespoon (5 grams) black cocoa powder

Finely crushed peppermint candies* (optional)
White Chocolate Peppermint Ganache (recipe follows)

1. Line baking sheets with silicone baking mats or parchment paper. If using parchment paper, use a pencil to draw 1½-inch circles 2 inches apart on parchment; turn parchment over.
2. In the bowl of a stand mixer fitted with the whisk attachment, beat egg whites at medium speed until foamy and whisk begins leaving visible trails. Gradually add granulated sugar; increase mixer speed to high, and beat until stiff peaks form. (Do not overwhip, or you risk drying out your egg whites.)
3. In a medium bowl, sift together confectioners' sugar, almond flour, and cocoas. Using a rubber spatula, fold sugar mixture into egg white mixture from bottom of bowl upward; press flat side of spatula through middle against side of bowl. (The batter will look very thick at first, but it will get thinner as you fold.) Continue folding until batter reaches a lavalike consistency. (See PRO TIP.)
4. Transfer batter to a large piping bag fitted with a medium round tip (Wilton No. 2A). Holding piping bag at a 90-degree angle to surface, pipe 1½-inch circles 2 inches apart onto baking mats, or pipe batter onto drawn circles if using parchment. Use a wet finger to gently smooth out any peaks. Lift pans to a height of 6 inches above counter, and drop to release any air bubbles. Repeat 3 or 4 times. (If you don't release the air bubbles, they will expand during baking and crack your beautiful macaron shells.) Let stand at room temperature until a skin has formed, about 30 minutes. (On a humid day, it might take 1 hour or more.) To see if your shells are ready to be baked, lightly touch batter. If it doesn't stick to your finger, they're ready.
5. Preheat oven to 300°F (150°C).
6. Bake in batches for 18 to 20 minutes, rotating pan halfway through baking. Sprinkle with crushed peppermints (if using) during final minute of baking. Let cool on pan for 10 minutes.

Remove from pan, and let cool completely on a wire rack. (If the bottoms are a bit sticky, keep them on the pan to cool for 10 to 15 minutes more. If, however, the bottoms are already browned, they peel off cleanly, or they appear overbaked, carefully take them off the pan immediately to cool down.) (See Note.)
7. Place White Chocolate Peppermint Ganache in a piping bag. Pipe ganache onto flat side of half of macaron shells (about 14 grams each). Place remaining macaron shells, flat side down, on top of ganache. Refrigerate in an airtight container for up to 5 days. Serve at room temperature.

*Be sure to crush the peppermints very finely, almost to dust, to help prevent the peppermint from baking into the macaron shells.

PRO TIP
The figure eight test is a great way to check your batter's consistency. Pick up the batter with your spatula, and let it flow into the bowl while drawing the figure "8." If it can do that without the batter breaking, immediately stop folding.

Note: *Macarons are best enjoyed the next day, after they have matured in the refrigerator (since the flavors will be absorbed into the shell). If your shells are hard, crunchy, or overbaked, letting them mature will also cause them to absorb the moisture from the filling, softening them up and giving them their signature chewy texture. It's always better to overbake rather than underbake your macarons; the maturation process can typically salvage ones that are overbaked.*

WHITE CHOCOLATE PEPPERMINT GANACHE
Makes about 1½ cups

9	ounces (250 grams) 28% cacao white chocolate, chopped
⅓	cup (80 grams) heavy whipping cream
½	teaspoon (2 grams) peppermint extract

1. In a medium heatproof bowl, place white chocolate.
2. In a small saucepan, heat cream over medium heat, stirring frequently, just until bubbles form around edges of pan. (Do not boil.) Pour hot cream over chocolate; let stand for 3 minutes. Add peppermint extract; whisk until smooth. Cover with a piece of plastic wrap, pressing wrap directly onto surface of ganache to prevent a skin from forming. Refrigerate until firm, about 1 hour.
3. Transfer ganache to the bowl of a stand mixer fitted with the whisk attachment; beat at medium speed until light and fluffy. Use immediately.

Photo by Mike Johnson

CRÈME FRAÎCHE SANDWICH COOKIES

Makes about 18 sandwich cookies

Recipe by Laura Kasavan

Sandwiched with sweet Vanilla Frosting and rolled in holiday sprinkles, these melt-in-your-mouth crème fraîche cookies will be the star of your holiday cookie platter! You'll love each buttery bite.

1½ cups (340 grams) unsalted butter, softened
¾ cup (180 grams) crème fraîche
1½ teaspoons (6 grams) vanilla extract
¼ teaspoon kosher salt
1 cup (120 grams) confectioners' sugar
3 cups (375 grams) all-purpose flour
1 tablespoon (8 grams) cornstarch
Vanilla Frosting (recipe follows)
¼ cup (45 grams) holiday sprinkles*

1. Line baking sheets with parchment paper.
2. In the bowl of a stand mixer fitted with the paddle attachment, beat butter and crème fraîche at medium speed until combined, 1 to 2 minutes. Beat in vanilla and salt. With mixer on low speed, gradually add confectioners' sugar, beating until combined.
3. In a medium bowl, whisk together flour and cornstarch. Gradually add flour mixture to butter mixture, beating until a soft dough forms. Divide dough in half. Transfer half of dough to a large piping bag fitted with a large closed star tip (Wilton No. 2D). Pipe 2½-inch spirals 2 inches apart on prepared pans. Repeat with remaining dough. Refrigerate for 30 minutes.
4. Preheat oven to 350°F (180°C).
5. Bake until lightly golden, 14 to 16 minutes, rotating pans once. Let cool on pans for 10 minutes. Remove from pans, and let cool completely on wire racks.
6. Pipe or spoon 1 to 2 tablespoons Vanilla Frosting onto flat side of half of cookies. Place remaining cookies, flat side down, on top of frosting, gently pressing together until frosting reaches edges of cookies. Roll cookies in sprinkles. Place cookies in a single layer on a baking sheet, and refrigerate for 20 minutes before serving.

*We used Wilton Holiday Nonpareils.

VANILLA FROSTING
Makes about 3 cups

1 cup (227 grams) unsalted butter, softened
¼ teaspoon kosher salt
2 teaspoons (8 grams) vanilla extract
½ teaspoon (2 grams) almond extract
3 cups (360 grams) confectioners' sugar
1 tablespoon (15 grams) milk

1. In the bowl of a stand mixer fitted with the paddle attachment, beat butter and salt at medium speed until smooth, 2 to 3 minutes. Beat in extracts. With mixer on low speed, gradually add confectioners' sugar, beating until combined. Add milk, and beat at medium speed until smooth, 1 to 2 minutes. Use immediately.

Photo by Laura Kasavan

BUTTER PECAN SNOWBALL COOKIES

Makes 24 cookies

Recipe by Marcella DiLonardo

These cookies are so simple to make, use staple pantry ingredients, and resemble little bite-size snowballs, which makes them super festive. The pecans add a little crunch to the cookies, but if you don't have pecans, try any nut you have on hand.

1   cup (227 grams) unsalted butter, softened
½   cup (60 grams) confectioners' sugar, plus more for rolling
2   teaspoons (8 grams) vanilla extract
2½   cups (313 grams) all-purpose flour
½   teaspoon (1.5 grams) fine sea salt
½   cup (57 grams) finely chopped pecans

1. Preheat oven to 350°F (180°C). Line 2 baking sheets with parchment paper.
2. In the bowl of a stand mixer fitted with the paddle attachment, beat butter and confectioners' sugar at low speed until combined, about 2 minutes. Beat in vanilla.
3. In a medium bowl, sift together flour and sea salt. Gradually add flour mixture to butter mixture, beating until dough comes together. Fold in pecans. Using a 1½-tablespoon spring-loaded scoop, scoop dough, and use hands to shape into 1½-inch dough balls (25 grams each). Place dough balls on prepared pans. Refrigerate for 15 minutes.
4. Bake until bottoms are lightly golden, 12 to 15 minutes. Let cool for 10 minutes. Roll in confectioners' sugar. Let cool completely, and roll in confectioners' sugar again. Cover and store at room temperature for up to 2 days, or freeze for up to 2 weeks.

Photo by Marcella DiLonardo

ESPRESSO CHOCOLATE SANDWICH SABLÉS

Makes 25 sandwich cookies

Recipe by Edd Kimber

The dough for these cookies is a classic vanilla sablé, but to give them another pop of flavor and a more grown-up, sophisticated hue, we added freshly ground coffee to the dough. And what cookie, especially one made with coffee, is truly finished without some element of chocolate? For these sablés, the chocolate comes in the form of a simple ganache filling.

⅔ cup (150 grams) unsalted butter, softened
1 cup (120 grams) confectioners' sugar
2 large egg yolks (37 grams)
1 teaspoon (6 grams) vanilla bean paste
2 cups (250 grams) all-purpose flour
2 tablespoons (12 grams) freshly ground coffee
½ teaspoon (1.5 grams) kosher salt
3.5 ounces (101 grams) 60% to 70% cacao dark chocolate, finely chopped
⅓ cup plus 1 tablespoon (95 grams) heavy whipping cream
1 tablespoon (14 grams) unsalted butter

1. In the bowl of a stand mixer fitted with the paddle attachment, beat softened butter at medium speed until creamy. Add confectioners' sugar, and beat until well combined and smooth, about 1 minute. Add egg yolks and vanilla bean paste, and beat just until fully combined. Add flour, coffee, and salt, and beat at low speed just until combined but before dough forms a ball.

2. Turn out dough onto a floured surface, and use your hands to bring dough together. Divide dough in half, and roll into 1½-inch-wide logs. Wrap logs in plastic wrap, and refrigerate until firm, 1 to 2 hours.

3. Preheat oven to 350°F (180°C). Line baking sheets with parchment paper.

4. Unwrap logs, and cut into ¼-inch-thick rounds. Place 1 inch apart on prepared pans.

5. Bake until just lightly browned around the edges, 10 to 12 minutes. Let cool on pans for 5 minutes. Remove from pans, and let cool completely on wire racks.

6. In a large heatproof bowl, place chocolate. In a small saucepan, heat cream and butter over medium heat just until bubbles form around edges of pan. (Do not boil.) Pour hot cream mixture over chocolate. Let stand for 1 minute; stir until a smooth, silky ganache forms. Let stand until thickened, 30 minutes to 1 hour.

7. Scoop ganache into a piping bag fitted with a small round piping tip. Pipe a round of ganache onto flat side of half of cookies. Place remaining cookies, flat side down, on top of ganache. Let stand until ganache is set, 1 to 2 hours. Unfilled cookies will keep for 2 to 3 days. Once they are filled with ganache, the cookies are best served within a day.

Photo by Edd Kimber

ORANGE ZEST SHORTBREAD WITH CRANBERRY-CHAMPAGNE BUTTERCREAM

Makes about 20 sandwich cookies

Recipe by Amisha Gurbani

A riff on the cranberry mimosa, these sparkly, elegant cookies will go very quickly at your next brunch party.

1   cup (227 grams) unsalted butter, softened
⅔   cup (133 grams) granulated sugar
1   tablespoon (3 grams) orange zest
1   tablespoon (13 grams) vanilla extract
2   cups (250 grams) all-purpose flour
⅔   cup (64 grams) almond flour
1   teaspoon (6 grams) table salt
1   teaspoon (2 grams) ground star anise
¾   cup (90 grams) confectioners' sugar
6   teaspoons (30 grams) cranberry juice
Edible silver sprinkles
Cranberry-Champagne Buttercream
     (recipe follows)

1. In the bowl of a stand mixer fitted with the paddle attachment, beat butter, granulated sugar, and orange zest at medium speed until creamy, about 2 minutes, stopping to scrape sides of bowl. Add vanilla, beating until combined.
2. In a medium bowl, combine flours, salt, and star anise. With mixer on medium-low speed, add flour mixture to butter mixture, beating just until combined. Divide dough in half, and shape each half into a disk, about 1 inch thick. Wrap tightly in plastic wrap, and refrigerate for at least 1 hour.
3. Preheat oven to 350°F (180°C). Line several baking sheets with parchment paper.
4. On a lightly floured surface, roll dough to ¼-inch thickness. Using a 2-inch fluted round cutter, cut dough, and place on prepared pans.
5. Bake until light golden brown, 12 to 15 minutes. Remove from pans, and let cool on wire racks for 30 minutes.
6. In a small bowl, stir together confectioners' sugar and cranberry juice with a small rubber spatula until well combined. Drizzle on top of half of cookies. Top with sprinkles.
7. Place Cranberry-Champagne Buttercream in a piping bag fitted with a ⅓-inch round tip (Ateco #804). Pipe buttercream onto flat side of undecorated cookies. Place decorated cookies, flat side down, on top of buttercream. Refrigerate in an airtight container for up to 1 week.

CRANBERRY-CHAMPAGNE BUTTERCREAM
Makes about 1½ cups

½   cup (113 grams) unsalted butter, softened
½   teaspoon (3 grams) table salt
1   teaspoon (4 grams) vanilla extract
2½   cups (300 grams) confectioners' sugar
2   tablespoons (30 grams) Champagne
1   tablespoon (20 grams) Cranberry Jam*
     (recipe follows)

1. In the bowl of a stand mixer fitted with the paddle attachment, beat butter, salt, and vanilla at medium speed until combined, about 30 seconds, stopping to scrape sides of bowl. Add confectioners' sugar, Champagne, and Cranberry Jam, and beat at low speed, about 30 seconds. Gradually increase mixer speed to high, beating until fully combined, about 1 minute.

You can also use any tart red store-bought jam.

CRANBERRY JAM
Makes about ⅓ cup

1   cup (170 grams) fresh or frozen cranberries
½   cup (100 grams) granulated sugar
¼   cup (60 grams) water
¼   cup (60 grams) orange juice

1. In a medium saucepan, bring cranberries, sugar, ¼ cup (60 grams) water, and orange juice to a boil over medium-high heat. Cook for about 5 minutes. Using a masher, crush cranberries to release pulp. Cook until thickened, about 5 minutes. Using a fine-mesh sieve, strain mixture, discarding solids. Pour jam into a small bottle; let cool completely in refrigerator before use.

Photo by Amisha Gurbani

SPICED SHORTBREAD COOKIES WITH CARAMELIZED WHITE CHOCOLATE

Makes 32 cookies

Recipe by Erin Clarkson

We added some of our favorite warming spices to classic shortbread dough and finished off the cookie by dipping half of it into caramelized white chocolate, also known as blond chocolate. The toasty flavor of the chocolate pairs so perfectly with the spiced shortbread.

1	cup plus 2 tablespoons (255 grams) unsalted butter, softened
⅔	cup (80 grams) confectioners' sugar
1	teaspoon (4 grams) vanilla extract
¼	teaspoon kosher salt
2¼	cups (281 grams) all-purpose flour
1	teaspoon (2 grams) ground cardamom
1	teaspoon (2 grams) ground cinnamon
¼	teaspoon ground allspice
¼	teaspoon ground cloves
¼	teaspoon ground ginger
¼	teaspoon ground nutmeg
6.5	ounces (187.5 grams) blond chocolate*, chopped
1 to 2	tablespoons (14 to 28 grams) coconut oil (optional)

1. Preheat oven to 325°F (170°C). Line several baking sheets with parchment paper.

2. In the bowl of a stand mixer fitted with the paddle attachment, beat butter, confectioners' sugar, vanilla, and salt at medium speed until light and creamy, 2 to 3 minutes.

3. In a medium bowl, sift together flour, cardamom, cinnamon, allspice, cloves, ginger, and nutmeg. Add flour mixture to butter mixture all at once, and beat at low speed just until combined.

4. Cut 2 (18x13-inch) sheets of parchment paper. Transfer dough to 1 sheet of parchment, and press into a rough rectangle using your hands. (Dough will be sticky.) Cover with second sheet of parchment. Roll dough to ¼-inch thickness. (If you get wrinkles in paper, carefully peel it off and place it back onto dough, smoothing down.) Transfer dough, between parchment, to a prepared pan. Freeze until firm, 15 to 20 minutes.

5. Remove top sheet of parchment. Using a 2½-inch fluted round cutter, cut dough, rerolling scraps as necessary. Place on prepared pans. (If dough starts to warm up too much at any point, place it in freezer to firm up.) Freeze for at least 10 minutes.

6. Bake in batches until shortbread is set and only very slightly golden around the edges, 13 to 14 minutes. Let cool on pans for 15 minutes. Remove from pans, and let cool completely on wire racks.

7. In the top of a double boiler, place blond chocolate. Heat over simmering water, stirring frequently, until melted and smooth. (Alternatively, microwave blond chocolate on high in 30-second intervals, stirring between each, until melted and smooth.) If chocolate is too thick, stir in coconut oil, 1 tablespoon (14 grams) at a time, if needed, until mixture is melted and smooth.

8. Line 2 baking sheets with parchment paper. Working with 1 cookie at a time, dip half of cookie into melted blond chocolate, letting excess drip off. Place cookies on prepared pans. Refrigerate until set. Refrigerate in an airtight container for up to 3 days.

We used Valrhona Blond Dulcey 32% Chocolate. If you'd like to make your own caramelized white chocolate, turn to page 212.

Notes: *The undipped cookies can be stored in an airtight container at room temperature, but once you have dipped them in the blond chocolate, they need to be stored in the refrigerator.*
This dough can be prepared ahead of time. Store it tightly wrapped in plastic wrap in the refrigerator. However, because the dough is frozen before being cut out, you can also skip the chilling step and roll out the dough straight from the mixer.

PRO TIP
Pre-cut parchment sheets are great for rolling out the dough. They are the same size as a half sheet pan, meaning that transferring the dough to a baking sheet to chill up is super easy. We also like to use them as a guide to roll out the dough because the dough is sticky.

Photo by Erin Clarkson

EMPIRE COOKIES

Makes 24 sandwich cookies

Recipe by Laura Kasavan

Empire biscuits are a traditional Scottish bakery treat, and it's easy to see why. Rich and buttery shortbread filled with raspberry preserves and topped with Almond Glaze makes for an irresistible sandwich cookie.

1½ cups (340 grams) unsalted butter, softened
1 cup (200 grams) granulated sugar
2 teaspoons (8 grams) vanilla extract
½ teaspoon (2 grams) almond extract
¼ teaspoon kosher salt
3½ cups (438 grams) all-purpose flour
Almond Glaze (recipe follows)
¾ cup (240 grams) raspberry preserves
12 maraschino cherries* (44 grams), halved
Garnish: sparkling sugar

1. In the bowl of a stand mixer fitted with the paddle attachment, beat butter and granulated sugar at medium speed until creamy, 1 to 2 minutes. Beat in extracts and salt. With mixer on low speed, gradually add flour, beating until combined and dough comes together in large pieces. Divide dough in half, and turn out each half onto a piece of plastic wrap. (Dough may be a little crumbly, but it will come together as you shape.) Shape each half into a disk, and wrap tightly in plastic wrap. Refrigerate until firm, about 30 minutes.
2. Preheat oven to 350°F (180°C). Line baking sheets with parchment paper.
3. On a lightly floured surface, roll half of dough to ¼-inch thickness. Using a 2-inch fluted round cutter dipped in flour, cut dough, rerolling scraps as necessary. Place 2 inches apart on prepared pans. Refrigerate for 15 minutes. Repeat with remaining dough.
4. Bake until lightly golden and set, 14 to 16 minutes, rotating pans halfway through baking. Let cool on pans for 5 minutes. Remove from pans, and let cool completely on wire racks.
5. Line baking sheets with parchment paper. Lightly dip top of half of cookies in Almond Glaze. Place glazed cookies on prepared pans. Let stand until set, about 1 hour.
6. Pipe or spoon raspberry preserves in center of unglazed cookies. Place glazed cookies, flat side down, on top of prserves, and gently sandwich together. Let stand for 1 hour. Top cookies with a cherry half, cut side down. Garnish with sparkling sugar, if desired.

Drain maraschino cherries well, and pat dry with paper towels before using.

ALMOND GLAZE
Makes about 1 cup

1½ cups (180 grams) confectioners' sugar
3 tablespoons (45 grams) hot water
¾ teaspoon (3 grams) almond extract
⅛ teaspoon kosher salt

1. In a medium bowl, whisk together confectioners' sugar, 3 tablespoons (45 grams) hot water, almond extract, and salt until smooth. Use immediately.

Photo by Laura Kasavan

HOLIDAY SPRINKLE SABLÉS

Makes about 24 cookies

Recipe by Laura Kasavan

Buttery sablés get a holiday makeover! Festive holiday sprinkles add color and crunch to these easy slice-and-bake cookies.

1   cup (227 grams) unsalted butter, softened
⅔   cup (133 grams) granulated sugar
⅓   cup (40 grams) confectioners' sugar
½   teaspoon (1.5 grams) kosher salt
1   large egg yolk (19 grams)
2   teaspoons (8 grams) vanilla extract
½   teaspoon (2 grams) almond extract
2⅓   cups (292 grams) all-purpose flour
10   tablespoons (112.5 grams) holiday sprinkles*, divided

1. In the bowl of a stand mixer fitted with the paddle attachment, beat butter at medium speed until creamy, about 1 minute. Add sugars and salt, and beat until smooth, stopping to scrape sides of bowl. Add egg yolk and extracts, and beat until combined. With mixer on low speed, gradually add flour, beating just until combined. Gently beat in 6 tablespoons (67.5 grams) sprinkles.
2. Divide dough in half, and turn out each half onto a piece of plastic wrap. Roll each half into a 7-inch log, using plastic wrap to help shape soft dough. Wrap logs tightly in plastic wrap, and refrigerate for at least 4 hours or for up to 2 days.
3. Line baking sheets with parchment paper.
4. Using a sharp knife, cut logs into ½-inch-thick rounds, and place 2 inches apart on prepared pans. Freeze for 1 hour.
5. Preheat oven to 350°F (180°C).

6. Top cookies with remaining 4 tablespoons (45 grams) sprinkles.
7. Bake until golden, 16 to 18 minutes, rotating pans halfway through baking. Let cool on pans for 5 minutes. Remove from pans, and let cool completely on wire racks.

*We used Wilton Holiday Jimmies Sprinkles because the colors don't bleed.

PRO TIP
For uniformly round slice-and-bake cookies, cut two empty paper towel rolls in half lengthwise. Refrigerate logs of dough inside center of each cardboard roll until firm.

Photo by Laura Kasavan

HOT BUTTERED RUM RUGELACH

Makes 36 cookies

Recipe by Michele Song

These rum-spiked rugelach are inspired by the classic holiday drink and are sure to be a hit at the adult table. The cream cheese rugelach dough is super buttery and flaky, and the brown sugar filling has chopped spiced pecans with hints of ground cinnamon, nutmeg, and cloves. The glaze is also spiked with rum, so don't be shy with those drizzles!

- 2 cups (250 grams) all-purpose flour
- 2 tablespoons (24 grams) granulated sugar
- ½ teaspoon (1.5 grams) kosher salt
- 1 cup (227 grams) cold unsalted butter, cubed
- 8 ounces (225 grams) cold cream cheese, cubed
- 1 teaspoon (4 grams) vanilla extract
- ¾ cup (165 grams) firmly packed dark brown sugar
- 1 tablespoon (21 grams) honey
- 1 tablespoon (15 grams) dark or spiced rum
- 2 teaspoons (4 grams) ground cinnamon
- ¼ teaspoon ground nutmeg
- ¼ teaspoon ground cloves
- Hot Buttered Rum Spiced Pecans (recipe follows), chopped
- 1 large egg (50 grams)
- 1 tablespoon (15 grams) water
- Turbinado sugar, for sprinkling
- Rum Glaze (recipe follows)

1. In the work bowl of a food processor, pulse together flour, granulated sugar, and salt until combined. Add cold butter, cold cream cheese, and vanilla, and pulse 3 to 4 times; process just until dough comes together, about 30 seconds. (Do not overwork dough.) Turn out dough onto a lightly floured surface, and divide into 3 portions. Shape each portion into a disk, and wrap in plastic wrap. Refrigerate for at least 2 hours or overnight.

2. In a medium bowl, stir together brown sugar, honey, rum, cinnamon, nutmeg, and cloves. Cover and set aside.

3. Line 2 baking sheets with parchment paper.

4. On a lightly floured surface, roll one-third of dough into a 10-inch circle. Spoon one-third of brown sugar mixture onto dough, and spread using an offset spatula. Sprinkle with one-third of Hot Buttered Rum Spiced Pecans. Gently press pecans into dough to ensure they stick. Using a pizza wheel, cut dough into 12 wedges. Starting at base of each triangle, carefully roll up dough and filling into a log. Place on prepared pans, tucking ends under. Repeat with remaining dough, remaining brown sugar mixture, and remaining Hot Buttered Rum Spiced Pecans. Refrigerate for 30 minutes.

5. Preheat oven to 350°F (180°C).

6. In a small bowl, whisk together egg and 1 tablespoon (15 grams) water. Brush egg wash onto dough, and sprinkle with turbinado sugar.

7. Bake until golden brown, 20 to 25 minutes, rotating pans halfway through baking. (See Note.) Let cool completely on pans. Drizzle with Rum Glaze. Store in an airtight container for up to 3 days.

Note: *Some of the spiced sugar filling will ooze out during baking. This is normal. Once you've let your rugelach cool completely on the pan, the puddles of spiced sugar filling will detach easily from the cookies and leave them clean and crisp.*

HOT BUTTERED RUM SPICED PECANS
Makes 1 cup

- 1 cup (100 grams) pecan halves
- 1 tablespoon (12 grams) granulated sugar
- ½ teaspoon (1.5 grams) kosher salt
- ¼ teaspoon ground cinnamon
- ⅛ teaspoon ground nutmeg
- ⅛ teaspoon ground cloves
- 2 tablespoons (30 grams) dark rum
- 1 tablespoon (14 grams) firmly packed dark brown sugar
- 1 tablespoon (14 grams) unsalted butter
- ½ teaspoon (2 grams) vanilla extract

1. Preheat oven to 350°F (180°C). Line a baking sheet with parchment paper.

2. Spread pecans in an even layer on prepared pan.

3. Bake until fragrant, 5 to 7 minutes, rotating pan halfway through baking.

4. In a medium bowl, stir together granulated sugar, salt, cinnamon, nutmeg, and cloves.

5. In a medium saucepan, bring rum, brown sugar, butter, and vanilla to a boil over medium heat, stirring constantly. Add toasted pecans, stirring to coat; cook until glaze is absorbed and pecans are shiny, 1 to 2 minutes. Transfer pecans to sugar mixture, and toss to coat. Return to parchment-lined baking sheet, and let cool. Store in an airtight container.

RUM GLAZE
Makes ½ cup

- 2 tablespoons (28 grams) unsalted butter
- 1 tablespoon (15 grams) dark or spiced rum
- ¾ cup (90 grams) confectioners' sugar
- 1 tablespoon (15 grams) milk
- ¼ teaspoon ground cinnamon

1. In a small saucepan, heat butter and rum over medium heat until butter is melted and bubbly. Remove from heat; transfer to a small bowl. Add confectioners' sugar, milk, and cinnamon, whisking until smooth. Use immediately.

Photo by Michele Song

EGGNOG THUMBPRINT COOKIES

Makes 18 cookies

Recipe by Marcella DiLonardo

There is nothing we crave more around the holiday season than a glass (or two) of eggnog. These cookies are like biting into a cup of holiday cheer featuring the three important flavors of eggnog: cinnamon, nutmeg, and rum. A unique treat perfect for endless cookie exchanges!

½   cup (113 grams) unsalted butter, room temperature
⅓   cup (73 grams) firmly packed light brown sugar
1   large egg (50 grams), room temperature
1   tablespoon (15 grams) spiced rum
1   teaspoon (4 grams) vanilla extract
1½   cups (188 grams) all-purpose flour
½   teaspoon (1 gram) ground cinnamon
½   teaspoon (1 gram) ground nutmeg
¼   teaspoon (1.25 grams) baking powder
½   teaspoon fine sea salt
Eggnog Frosting (recipe follows)
Turbinado sugar, for sprinkling

1. Preheat oven to 350°F (180°C). Line 2 baking sheets with parchment paper.
2. In the bowl of a stand mixer fitted with the paddle attachment, beat butter and brown sugar at medium speed until creamy, about 2 minutes. Beat in egg; beat in rum and vanilla.
3. In a medium bowl, sift together flour, cinnamon, nutmeg, baking powder, and sea salt. Gradually add flour mixture to butter mixture, beating until dough comes together. Shape dough into 1½-inch balls (about 23 grams each), and place 2 inches apart on prepared pans. Using your thumb or the back of a spoon, gently make an indentation in center of each ball. Refrigerate for 15 minutes.
4. Bake until edges are slightly golden, 11 to 13 minutes. Let cool completely.
5. Place Eggnog Frosting in a piping bag fitted with a star tip. Pipe a dollop of frosting into center of each cookie. Sprinkle with turbinado sugar. Cover and refrigerate for up to 2 days, or freeze for up to 2 weeks.

Eggnog Frosting
Makes about 1 cup

½   cup (113 grams) unsalted butter, softened
1   teaspoon (4 grams) vanilla extract
¼   teaspoon ground cinnamon
¼   teaspoon ground nutmeg
⅛   teaspoon fine sea salt
1½   cups (180 grams) confectioners' sugar
1   tablespoon (15 grams) eggnog

1. In the bowl of a stand mixer fitted with the paddle attachment, beat butter at medium speed until creamy, about 2 minutes. Reduce mixer speed to medium-low. Beat in vanilla, cinnamon, nutmeg, and sea salt. Gradually beat in confectioners' sugar, ¼ cup (30 grams) at a time, until creamy and smooth. Beat in eggnog until combined. Use immediately.

Photo by Marcella DiLonardo

BOURBON-SPIKED APPLE CIDER COOKIES

Makes 24 cookies

Recipe by Elisabeth Farris

Filled with real apple cider and chopped apples, these Bourbon-Spiked Apple Cider Cookies are moist and delicious. The Bourbon Glaze takes them to another level and makes them perfect for the holidays.

½   cup (113 grams) unsalted butter, softened
½   cup (100 grams) granulated sugar
¼   cup (55 grams) firmly packed light brown sugar
1   large egg (50 grams)
1   teaspoon (4 grams) vanilla extract
1¼   cups (300 grams) apple cider
1½   cups (188 grams) all-purpose flour
1   teaspoon (2 grams) ground cinnamon
½   teaspoon (1.5 grams) kosher salt
½   teaspoon (2.5 grams) baking soda
1   cup (110 grams) finely chopped Granny Smith apple
2   teaspoons (10 grams) fresh lemon juice
Bourbon Glaze (recipe follows)

1. Preheat oven to 400°F (200°C). Line 2 baking sheets with parchment paper.
2. In the bowl of a stand mixer fitted with the paddle attachment, beat butter and sugars at medium-high speed until light and fluffy, 2 to 3 minutes, stopping to scrape sides of bowl. Add egg and vanilla, beating well.
3. In a medium saucepan, heat cider over medium-high heat until thickened and reduced to 2 tablespoons, 10 to 15 minutes. (An instant-read thermometer should register at least 150°F [65°C].) You can pour the reduced cider into a glass measuring cup to check the volume. (This transfer will also help the foam to subside.) Let cool for 1 to 2 minutes. (It will harden if cooled any longer.) Beat reduced cider into butter mixture.
4. In a medium bowl, whisk together flour, cinnamon, salt, and baking soda. In a small bowl, toss together apple and lemon juice. With mixer on low speed, gradually add flour mixture to butter mixture, beating just until combined. Stir in apple mixture. Using a 1½-tablespoon spring-loaded scoop, scoop dough into balls (about 25 grams each), and place 2 inches apart on prepared pans.

5. Bake until golden brown but still soft, 8 to 10 minutes. Let cool on pans for 5 minutes. Remove from pans, and let cool completely on wire racks. Using a piping bag or spoon, drizzle Bourbon Glaze onto cooled cookies. Store in an airtight container for up to 3 days.

Note: *The apple cider reduction will harden if not used within a few minutes, so make sure to beat it into the batter while it's still warm.*

BOURBON GLAZE
Makes about ½ cup

1   cup (120 grams) confectioners' sugar
1   tablespoon (15 grams) bourbon
1   tablespoon (15 grams) apple cider

1. In a small bowl, whisk together all ingredients until smooth. Use immediately.

Photo by Elisabeth Farris

MITTEN COOKIES

Makes 10 to 12 (3½-inch) cookies

Recipe by Tessa Huff

Swapping honey in for molasses and changing up the spice blend from a typical gingerbread cookie creates a brighter flavor palette in these cookies, and the lemony icing pairs well with the punchy cardamom and other spices.

1½   cups (188 grams) all-purpose flour
1½   tablespoons (12 grams) cornstarch
¾   teaspoon (1.5 grams) ground cardamom
½   teaspoon (1.5 grams) kosher salt
½   teaspoon (1 gram) ground cinnamon
¼   teaspoon (1.25 grams) baking powder
⅛   teaspoon grated fresh nutmeg
½   cup (113 grams) unsalted butter, softened
¼   cup (50 grams) granulated sugar
3   tablespoons (63 grams) honey
1   large egg yolk (19 grams)
      Lemon Royal Icing (recipe follows)
      Gel food coloring (optional)

1. In a medium bowl, stir together flour, cornstarch, cardamom, salt, cinnamon, baking powder, and nutmeg.
2. In the bowl of a stand mixer fitted with the paddle attachment, beat butter at medium speed until creamy, about 1 minute. Add sugar, and beat for 2 minutes, stopping to scrape sides of bowl. Reduce mixer speed to low. Add honey and egg yolk, and beat until combined.
3. With mixer on low speed, gradually add flour mixture to butter mixture, beating until dough comes together. Turn out dough onto a piece of plastic wrap, and shape into a disk. Wrap in plastic wrap, and refrigerate for at least 1 hour.
4. Preheat oven to 350°F (180°C). Line a baking sheet with parchment paper.
5. On a lightly floured surface, roll dough to ¼-inch thickness. Using a 3½-inch mitten cutter, cut dough, rerolling scraps as needed, and place 1 to 2 inches apart on prepared pan. Refrigerate for 15 minutes.
6. Bake until edges begin to brown, 12 to 14 minutes. Let cool completely on pan.
7. Tint Lemon Royal Icing with food coloring

(if using). For woven design, thin a portion of Lemon Royal Icing with water until it is the consistency of runny honey to create a glaze. Using an offset spatula, spread a thin coat of glaze around top of cookie, leaving about ⅛-inch border un-iced. This prevents any cookie from showing through the piped icing. Place stiff Lemon Royal Icing in a piping bag fitted with a small petal tip (Wilton No. 101). Pipe interlocking "V" shapes in rows on cookies. Point narrow end of petal tip away from your body and toward top of cookie as you pipe down length of cookie. Turn cookie opposite way to create rows of alternating woven pattern. Alternatively, use the same technique using a small round tip (Wilton No. 5).
8. For spiraled knit design, place Lemon Royal Icing in a piping bag fitted with a small star piping tip. Starting at top of cookie, pipe tight spirals down length of cookie. Repeat at top to create rows of icing until cookie is completely decorated.
9. For mitten cuff design, thin a portion of Lemon Royal Icing with water until it is the consistency of runny honey to create a glaze. Place glaze in a shallow bowl, and dip top surface of cookie into glaze. Shake off excess, and let dry. Pipe remaining stiff

icing onto cuff of mitten using one of the techniques above. Let icing completely dry and harden before carefully storing cookies in an airtight container. Cookies are best served within 2 to 3 days.

LEMON ROYAL ICING
Makes about 1¾ cups

2⅔   cups (320 grams) confectioners' sugar
2   tablespoons (20 grams) meringue powder
3 to 4 tablespoons (45 to 60 grams) water
1   teaspoon (5 grams) fresh lemon juice

1. In the bowl of a stand mixer fitted with the whisk attachment, stir together confectioners' sugar and meringue powder. Add 3 tablespoons (45 grams) water and lemon juice, and beat at medium speed until stiff peaks form, 6 to 7 minutes. Add up to remaining 1 tablespoon (15 grams) water, beating until consistency is slightly thicker than toothpaste and easy to pipe. Use immediately. Cover any icing not being used with a damp cloth.

Photo by Tessa Huff

RED VELVET PEPPERMINT COOKIES

Makes about 22 cookies

Dipped in smooth white chocolate and finished off with soft peppermint candies, these chewy red velvet cookies are sure to satisfy your holiday sweet tooth.

½ cup (113 grams) unsalted butter, softened
⅔ cup (133 grams) granulated sugar
⅓ cup (73 grams) firmly packed light brown sugar
1 large egg (50 grams)
1 tablespoon (15 grams) liquid red food coloring
1 teaspoon (5 grams) distilled white vinegar
1 teaspoon (4 grams) vanilla extract
½ teaspoon (2 grams) peppermint extract
1½ cups (188 grams) all-purpose flour
¼ cup (21 grams) Dutch process cocoa powder
1½ teaspoons (7.5 grams) baking powder
½ teaspoon (1.5 grams) kosher salt
¼ teaspoon (1.25 grams) baking soda
1 (10-ounce) bag (283.5 grams) white chocolate melting wafers
Garnish: crushed soft peppermint candies

1. Line a baking sheet with parchment paper.
2. In the bowl of a stand mixer fitted with the paddle attachment, beat butter and sugars at medium speed until fluffy, 3 to 4 minutes, stopping to scrape sides of bowl. Add egg, beating well. Beat in food coloring, vinegar, and extracts.
3. In a medium bowl, whisk together flour, cocoa, baking powder, salt, and baking soda. With mixer on low speed, gradually add flour mixture to butter mixture, beating until combined. Using a 1½-tablespoon spring-loaded scoop, scoop dough, and place on prepared pan. Cover and refrigerate for at least 1 hour.
4. Preheat oven to 350°F (180°C). Line 2 baking sheets with parchment paper. Place chilled dough at least 2 inches apart on prepared pans.
5. Bake until cookies look dry and edges are set, 12 to 14 minutes. Let cool on pans for 5 minutes. Remove from pans, and let cool completely on a wire rack.
6. In a small microwave-safe bowl, heat white chocolate on high in 30-second intervals, stirring between each, until melted and smooth. Dip cookies halfway in melted white chocolate, and transfer to a sheet of parchment paper. Sprinkle with crushed peppermints, if desired. Let set before serving.

CHOCOLATE CHIP SANDWICH COOKIES WITH IRISH CREAM GERMAN BUTTERCREAM

Makes 20 sandwich cookies

Recipe by Erin Clarkson

Loaded with chopped chocolate, this thin cookie is sandwiched with German buttercream. Because this versatile frosting is pastry cream-based, you can infuse the milk or, in this case, sub it out for Irish cream liqueur, which makes the most luxurious and creamy buttercream, bursting with Irish cream flavor. This really is the perfect pairing.

1¼ cups (284 grams) unsalted butter, softened
1 cup plus 2 tablespoons (224 grams) granulated sugar
⅓ cup plus 2 tablespoons (101 grams) muscovado sugar
1 large egg (50 grams), room temperature
1 large egg yolk (19 grams), room temperature
1 teaspoon (4 grams) vanilla extract
2 cups (250 grams) all-purpose flour
1 teaspoon (3 grams) kosher salt
½ teaspoon (2.5 grams) baking powder
¼ teaspoon (1.25 grams) baking soda
13 ounces (375 grams) 70% cacao bittersweet chocolate, chopped
Irish Cream German Buttercream (recipe follows)

1. Preheat oven to 350°F (180°C). Line 2 to 3 baking sheets with parchment paper.
2. In the bowl of a stand mixer fitted with the paddle attachment, beat butter and sugars at medium speed until fluffy, 2 to 3 minutes, stopping to scrape sides of bowl. Add egg, egg yolk, and vanilla, beating until combined.
3. In a medium bowl, sift together flour, salt, baking powder, and baking soda. Add flour mixture to butter mixture all at once, and beat at low speed just until combined. Using a rubber spatula, fold in chocolate. (Do not overwork dough.) Use a 2-tablespoon spring-loaded scoop, scoop dough, and place 6 balls of dough on 1 prepared pan. (Leave remaining dough in bowl until ready to bake.)
4. Bake until set around edges, 11 to 12 minutes. (Cookies will puff up in the oven and then flatten out as they cool.) If the cookies come out of the oven not perfectly round, you can use a cookie cutter slightly larger than the cookie to help nudge it back into place and make it round. Let cool on pan for 10 minutes. Remove from pan, and let cool completely on a wire rack. Repeat with remaining dough.
5. Place Irish Cream German Buttercream in a large piping bag fitted with a French star tip (Ateco #865). Pipe buttercream onto flat side of half of cookies. Place remaining cookies, flat side down, on top of buttercream. Refrigerate in an airtight container for up to 3 days.

PRO TIP
The cookie dough can be made ahead and frozen. If you want to freeze the dough, scoop it all out into balls onto a parchment paper-lined baking sheet (it is OK if the balls are close together), and freeze until solid. Once frozen, transfer them to an airtight freezer-safe container. You will need to add 1 to 2 minutes to the baking time to account for the frozen dough.

IRISH CREAM GERMAN BUTTERCREAM
Makes about 3 cups

½ cup plus 1 tablespoon (112 grams) granulated sugar
1½ tablespoons (12 grams) cornstarch
1 large egg (50 grams), room temperature
1 large egg yolk (19 grams), room temperature
½ teaspoon (1.5 grams) kosher salt
¾ cup plus 1½ teaspoons (187.5 grams) Irish cream liqueur*
½ teaspoon (2 grams) vanilla extract
1½ cups (340 grams) unsalted butter, cubed and softened

1. In a medium bowl, whisk together sugar and cornstarch. Add egg, egg yolk, and salt, whisking until well combined.
2. In a medium saucepan, heat liqueur and vanilla over low heat just until bubbles form around edges of pan. (Do not boil.) Remove from heat.
3. Whisking constantly, pour half of hot liqueur mixture into egg mixture. Add egg mixture to remaining hot liqueur mixture in pan, whisking to combine. Cook over medium heat, whisking constantly, until bubbly and thickened. Cook for 1 minute more; remove from heat. Pour into a shallow container, and cover with a piece of plastic wrap, pressing wrap directly onto surface of pastry cream to prevent a skin from forming. Refrigerate for at least 4 hours or overnight. (Alternatively, place pastry cream in a bowl, and place bowl in an ice bath. Let stand, stirring frequently, until cold.)
4. In the bowl of a stand mixer fitted with the whisk attachment, beat pastry cream at medium speed until creamy and smooth. Add butter, a few cubes at a time, until fully combined. (It may look curdled at some point, but just keep whipping, and it will come together.) Switch to the paddle attachment. Beat at low speed for 2 to 3 minutes to help remove any air bubbles. Store in an airtight container until ready to use. If you need to chill it, you can let it rewarm slightly and then beat it in mixer to help smooth it out.

We used Baileys Original Irish Cream.

Photo by Erin Clarkson

GINGERBREAD CRINKLE SANDWICH COOKIES

Makes 15 sandwich cookies

Recipe by Mike Johnson

Perfectly soft, tender, and chewy, these sugar-coated gingerbread crinkle cookies are sandwiched with a creamy Vanilla Bean Cream Cheese Frosting that's so good you'll want to eat it straight from the bowl. These are likely to become your new holiday cookie-baking tradition.

2¼ cups (281 grams) all-purpose flour
⅔ cup (147 grams) firmly packed dark brown sugar
2 teaspoons (4 grams) ground cinnamon
2 teaspoons (4 grams) ground ginger
½ teaspoon (1.5 grams) kosher salt
½ teaspoon (2.5 grams) baking soda
½ teaspoon (1 gram) ground cloves
½ cup plus 1 tablespoon (127 grams) cold unsalted butter, cubed
½ cup (170 grams) unsulphured molasses
2 tablespoons (30 grams) milk
Granulated sugar, for rolling
Confectioners' sugar, for rolling
Vanilla Bean Cream Cheese Frosting (recipe follows)

1. In the bowl of a stand mixer fitted with the paddle attachment, stir together flour, brown sugar, cinnamon, ginger, salt, baking soda, and cloves until combined. Using a fork or your fingers, cut in cold butter until small pea-size crumbs remain and mixture resembles the texture of sand.
2. With mixer on low speed, gradually add molasses and milk, beating until dough is evenly moistened. Increase mixer speed to medium, and beat until thoroughly combined. (The dough will appear slightly crumbly.) Turn out dough onto a work surface, and shape into a disk. Wrap in plastic wrap, and refrigerate until firm, 1 to 2 hours or overnight.
3. Preheat oven to 350°F (180°C). Line 2 baking sheets with parchment paper.
4. Using a 1-tablespoon spring-loaded scoop, scoop dough, and roll into balls. (Do not overwork dough; it will get too warm.) Roll each ball in granulated sugar until coated. Roll each ball in confectioners' sugar until coated. Place 1½ inches apart on prepared pans.
5. Bake until centers are set, 10 to 12 minutes. Let cool on pans for 2 minutes. Remove from pans, and let cool completely on wire racks.
6. Pipe or spread Vanilla Bean Cream Cheese Frosting onto flat side of half of cookies. Place remaining cookies, flat side down, on top of frosting. Store in an airtight container for up to 1 week.

VANILLA BEAN CREAM CHEESE FROSTING
Makes about 2 cups

4 ounces (115 grams) cream cheese, room temperature
¼ cup (57 grams) unsalted butter, softened
2 cups (240 grams) confectioners' sugar
1 teaspoon (6 grams) vanilla bean paste

1. In the bowl of a stand mixer fitted with the paddle attachment, beat cream cheese and butter at high speed until smooth and creamy. Add confectioners' sugar and vanilla bean paste, and beat at low speed for 30 seconds. Increase mixer speed to high, and beat for 2 minutes. Cover and refrigerate for up to 5 days, or freeze for up to 3 months. After freezing, thaw in refrigerator, and beat for a few seconds so it's creamy again.

Photo by Mike Johnson

GINGERBREAD CHOCOLATE CHIP COOKIES

Makes 22 cookies

Recipe by Edd Kimber

Nothing says the holidays more than spiced bakes, and very few recipes will please the crowd more than a soft gingerbread cookie. Because the cookies have both muscovado sugar and molasses, there is already a hint of bitterness in them, so when choosing your chocolate, you can go a little lower in cacao percentage than you might usually; even a milk chocolate would work wonderfully here.

1   cup (220 grams) firmly packed light muscovado sugar
1   cup (227 grams) unsalted butter, softened
½   cup (170 grams) unsulphured molasses
2   large eggs (100 grams)
4   cups plus 3 tablespoons (524 grams) all-purpose flour
2   tablespoons (12 grams) grated fresh ginger
2   teaspoons (10 grams) baking soda
2   teaspoons (4 grams) ground cinnamon
1   teaspoon (2 grams) ground ginger
½   teaspoon (1.5 grams) kosher salt
¼   teaspoon grated fresh nutmeg
10.5 ounces (315 grams) 60% cacao dark chocolate, roughly chopped
½   cup (100 grams) demerara sugar

1. In a large saucepan, heat muscovado sugar, butter, and molasses over medium-high heat until butter is melted and sugar is dissolved. Remove from heat; let cool for 30 minutes. Once cool, add eggs, whisking until well combined.
2. In a large bowl, whisk together flour, grated ginger, baking soda, cinnamon, ground ginger, salt, and nutmeg. Add sugar mixture, and stir with a wooden spoon until almost fully combined. Add chocolate, and stir until a uniform dough forms. Wrap in plastic wrap, and refrigerate for 2 hours.

3. Preheat oven to 375°F (190°C). Line 2 baking sheets with parchment paper.
4. Using a ¼-cup spring-loaded scoop, scoop dough, and roll into balls. Coat dough balls in demerara sugar. Place 2 inches apart on prepared pans.
5. Bake until set and lightly browned around edges but still soft in center, 10 to 12 minutes. Let cool on pans for 10 minutes. Remove from pans, and let cool completely on wire racks. Store in an airtight container for up to 3 days.

PRO TIP
For more melty chocolate on top of your cookies, press a few pieces of chopped chocolate onto the exterior of each dough ball right before popping them in the oven.

Photo by Edd Kimber

CHAI CRESCENT COOKIES

Makes about 23 cookies

Spice up your holidays with these chai-packed crescent cookies. This buttery, crumbly dough is flecked with a homemade chai blend and rolled in chai sugar after baking for an extra dose of warmth.

1   cup (227 grams) unsalted butter, softened
¾   cup (90 grams) confectioners' sugar
1   teaspoon (4 grams) vanilla extract
2½ cups (313 grams) all-purpose flour
2   teaspoons (4 grams) ground cinnamon, divided
1   teaspoon (2 grams) ground ginger, divided
½   teaspoon ground cloves, divided
¼   teaspoon kosher salt
¼   teaspoon ground cardamom, divided
¼   teaspoon ground black pepper, divided
1   cup (200 grams) granulated sugar

1. Preheat oven to 350°F (180°C). Line 2 baking sheets with parchment paper.
2. In the bowl of a stand mixer fitted with the paddle attachment, beat butter and confectioners' sugar at medium speed until creamy, 3 to 4 minutes. Beat in vanilla.
3. In a medium bowl, stir together flour, 1 teaspoon (2 grams) cinnamon, ½ teaspoon (1 gram) ginger, ¼ teaspoon cloves, salt, ⅛ teaspoon cardamom, and ⅛ teaspoon pepper. With mixer on low speed, gradually add flour mixture to butter mixture, beating until a dough forms.
4. Using a 1½-tablespoon spring-loaded scoop, scoop dough into balls (about 25 grams each). Roll each dough ball into a 4¾-inch log with tapered ends, and bend into a crescent shape, flouring work surface as needed. Place about 1 inch apart on prepared pans.
5. In a medium bowl, stir together granulated sugar, remaining 1 teaspoon (2 grams) cinnamon, remaining ½ teaspoon (1 gram) ginger, remaining ¼ teaspoon cloves, remaining ⅛ teaspoon cardamom, and remaining ⅛ teaspoon pepper.
6. Bake in batches until edges are just beginning to turn golden (not browned), 12 to 15 minutes. Sprinkle spiced sugar onto hot cookies. Let cool completely; dust with spiced sugar again. Store in an airtight container for up to 3 weeks.

PEPPERMINT BARK COOKIES

Makes 24 cookies

Recipe by Marcella DiLonardo

A holiday twist on a classic chocolate chunk cookie inspired by peppermint bark. No rolling or cookie-cutting required—just a simple drop and bake featuring dark chocolate, white chocolate, and peppermint candy canes. This dough freezes well, so you can have cookie dough on hand at all times in case an unexpected guest arrives. Be sure to use quality chopped chocolate! The chunks make for the best gooey chocolate cookie.

1½ cups (330 grams) firmly packed light brown sugar
1   cup (227 grams) unsalted butter, melted
½   cup (100 grams) granulated sugar

2   large eggs (100 grams), room temperature
1   teaspoon (4 grams) vanilla extract
1   teaspoon (4 grams) peppermint extract
3½ cups (438 grams) all-purpose flour
1   teaspoon (5 grams) baking soda
1   teaspoon (3 grams) fine sea salt
4   ounces (115 grams) white chocolate, roughly chopped
4   ounces (115 grams) 70% cacao dark chocolate, roughly chopped
4   medium peppermint candy canes (48 grams), crushed

1. Preheat oven to 350°F (180°C). Line 2 baking sheets with parchment paper.
2. In the bowl of a stand mixer fitted with the paddle attachment, beat brown sugar, melted butter, and granulated sugar at low speed until combined, about 1 minute. Add eggs, one at a time, beating well after each addition. Beat in extracts.
3. In a medium bowl, sift together flour, baking soda, and sea salt. Gradually add flour mixture to butter mixture, beating until dough comes together. Fold in white chocolate, dark chocolate, and candy canes. Wrap dough in plastic wrap, and refrigerate for 15 minutes.
4. Using a 3-tablespoon spring-loaded scoop, scoop 24 dough balls, and place on prepared pans.
5. Bake until edges are golden brown, 10 to 12 minutes. Let cool completely on wire racks. Cover and refrigerate for up to 2 days, or freeze for up to 2 weeks.

Photo by Marcella DiLonardo

CHOCOLATE CHUNK ORANGE SHORTBREAD WITH SICHUAN PEPPERCORNS

Makes 48 cookies

Recipe by Rebecca Firth

Booze and chocolate with a touch of heat from the peppercorns— what more could you ask for in a cookie? This shortbread has chocolate chunks, orange zest, and a nice earthiness from the buckwheat flour, making it the perfect cookie to pair with a drink at the end of a holiday meal. Because you don't want any larger peppercorn bits in your cookie, make sure you grind up the peppercorns well and even sift before adding them to the dough.

1   cup (227 grams) unsalted butter, cubed and softened
¾   cup (90 grams) confectioners' sugar
1   large egg yolk (19 grams), room temperature
2   tablespoons (6 grams) orange zest
1   tablespoon (15 grams) plus 1 teaspoon (5 grams) orange liqueur*, divided
1¾   cups (219 grams) all-purpose flour
½   cup (75 grams) buckwheat flour
1   teaspoon (3 grams) kosher salt
½   teaspoon (1 gram) finely ground Sichuan peppercorns (see Note)
10.5 ounces (300 grams) 60% cacao dark chocolate, finely chopped and divided
½   cup (100 grams) sparkling sugar
3   tablespoons (45 grams) heavy whipping cream

1. In the bowl of a stand mixer fitted with the paddle attachment, beat butter and confectioners' sugar at medium speed until smooth and creamy, 2 to 3 minutes. Add egg yolk, beating until combined. Add orange zest and 1 tablespoon (15 grams) orange liqueur, beating until combined.

2. In a medium bowl, whisk together flours, salt, and peppercorns. Add flour mixture to butter mixture, and beat just until combined. Add 7 ounces (200 grams) chocolate, beating until combined.

3. Divide dough in half (about 420 grams each), and roll each half into a log (1½ inches wide and 12 inches long). Wrap tightly in plastic wrap, and freeze for 45 minutes. Transfer dough to refrigerator.

4. Preheat oven to 350°F (180°C). Line 2 baking sheets with parchment paper.

5. Place sparkling sugar on a piece of parchment paper. Roll each log in sugar to coat completely. Working with 1 log at a time (keep remaining log in refrigerator), cut log into ½-inch-thick slices, and place on prepared pans.

6. Bake in batches for 12 to 14 minutes. Let cool on pans for 10 minutes. Remove from pans, and let cool completely on wire racks.

7. In a small heatproof bowl, place remaining 3.5 ounces (100 grams) chocolate. In a small saucepan, heat cream just until bubbles form around edges of pan. (Do not boil.) Pour over chocolate, and let stand for 1 minute. Slowly stir together until smooth. Stir in remaining 1 teaspoon (5 grams) orange liqueur. Let cool slightly. Using a spoon, drizzle chocolate onto cookies.

We used Cointreau.

Note: *Sichuan peppercorns are available at most specialty food stores or online. You can also use 1 teaspoon (2 grams) finely ground black pepper.*

Photo by Rebecca Firth

HAZELNUT, FIG, AND WHITE CHOCOLATE OATMEAL COOKIES

Makes 16 cookies

Recipe by Jenn Davis

These classic oatmeal cookies have a seasonal twist with hazelnuts, sweet black Mission figs, and white chocolate chips. Dark brown sugar and cinnamon add a hint of cozy caramel spice. The easy stir-and-drop cookie dough is perfect for those cold winter evenings when all you want to do is snuggle under a blanket.

1	cup (227 grams) unsalted butter, softened
1	cup (220 grams) firmly packed dark brown sugar
½	cup (100 grams) granulated sugar
1	tablespoon (13 grams) vanilla extract
2	large eggs (100 grams)
2	cups (250 grams) all-purpose flour
1	teaspoon (5 grams) baking soda
1	teaspoon (3 grams) cornstarch
1	teaspoon (2 grams) ground cinnamon
½	teaspoon (1.5 grams) kosher salt
3	cups (240 grams) old-fashioned oats
⅔	cup (75 grams) chopped hazelnuts
½	cup (64 grams) chopped dried black Mission figs
1½	cups (255 grams) white chocolate chips, divided

1. In the bowl of a stand mixer fitted with the paddle attachment, beat butter and sugars at medium speed until fluffy, 3 to 4 minutes. Beat in vanilla. Add eggs, one at a time, beating well after each addition. Scrape bottom and sides of bowl as needed with a rubber spatula.

2. In a large bowl, whisk together flour, baking soda, cornstarch, cinnamon, and salt. Stir in oats. With mixer on medium-low speed, gradually add flour mixture to butter mixture, beating until a dough is formed. Using a small spatula, scrape dough from paddle. Using a spoon, stir in hazelnuts, figs, and ½ cup (85 grams) white chocolate chips. Cover with plastic wrap, and refrigerate for 15 minutes.

3. Preheat oven to 375°F (190°C). Line 2 baking sheets with parchment paper.

4. Using 2-tablespoon spring-loaded scoop, scoop dough, and place 2 inches apart on prepared pans. If dough is very cold and firm, flatten dough balls slightly.

5. Bake for 10 to 12 minutes. Let cool on pans for 3 to 4 minutes. Remove from pans, and let cool completely on wire racks.

6. In the top of a double boiler, heat remaining 1 cup (170 grams) white chocolate chips over simmering water until melted and smooth. (Alternatively, in a large microwave-safe bowl, heat white chocolate chips on high in 30-second intervals, stirring between each, until melted and smooth.) Transfer melted white chocolate to a bowl for dipping. Dip each cookie halfway into melted white chocolate, and place on a sheet of parchment paper. Let stand until cool and firm, about 6 minutes. Store in an airtight container for up to 2 weeks, or freeze cookies, individually wrapped in plastic wrap, in an airtight freezer-safe container for 2 to 3 months. (If refrigerating, place a small sheet of parchment or wax paper between each cookie to prevent sticking.)

> **PRO TIP**
> Cookie dough can be made the day before and stored in an airtight container in the refrigerator. Let dough warm to room temperature before baking to make sure cookies spread while baking. Super cold and firm dough won't spread as much.

Photo by Jenn Davis

CARDAMOM ESPRESSO COOKIES WITH VANILLA GLAZE

Makes about 22 cookies

Recipe by Jenn Davis

These richly spiced cookies have a hint of coffee and espresso. They are for the holiday cookie lover who doesn't like or have time to decorate with frosting. Use any holiday cookie stamp to add a little festive flare.

1	cup (227 grams) unsalted butter, softened
⅓	cup (40 grams) confectioners' sugar
¼	cup (55 grams) firmly packed light brown sugar
1	teaspoon (4 grams) vanilla extract
3	cups (391 grams) all-purpose flour
1	tablespoon plus 2 teaspoons (10 grams) instant espresso powder
2	teaspoons (4 grams) ground cinnamon
1	teaspoon (2 grams) ground cardamom
½	teaspoon (1.5 grams) sea salt

Vanilla Glaze (recipe follows)

1. In the bowl of a stand mixer fitted with the paddle attachment, beat butter and sugars at medium speed until smooth. Beat in vanilla. Scrape bottom and sides of bowl as needed with a rubber spatula.

2. In a medium bowl, whisk together flour, espresso powder, cinnamon, cardamom, and sea salt. With mixer on medium-low speed, gradually add flour mixture to butter mixture, beating until a dough is formed. Shape dough into a ball, and wrap in plastic wrap. Refrigerate for 1 hour.

3. Preheat oven to 375°F (190°C). Line 2 baking sheets with parchment paper.

4. Divide dough in half. Wrap one half in plastic wrap, and return to refrigerator. Roll dough into 1½-inch balls (about 40 grams each); place 4 inches apart on prepared pan. Dip a reindeer cookie stamp* in flour to coat design; tap out any excess flour. Pressing slowly but firmly, stamp cookie dough ball down with cookie stamp, slightly rotating wrist to make sure entire design is pressed. Gently peel cookie dough away from stamp. Coat stamp in flour between each cookie

to prevent sticking. Using a 2⅝-inch round cutter or a sharp knife, remove excess trimmings. Place on prepared pans.

5. Bake until edges start to look golden, 11 to 13 minutes. Let cool on pans for 3 to 4 minutes. Remove from pans, and let cool completely on wire racks. Repeat with remaining dough.

6. Using a small pastry brush, gently paint Vanilla Glaze onto cooled cookies. Let stand until firm, 10 to 15 minutes. Store in an airtight container for 3 to 4 weeks. (Place a small sheet of parchment or wax paper between each glazed cookie to prevent sticking.) Or freeze cookies, individually wrapped in plastic wrap, in an airtight freezer-safe container for 3 to 4 months.

We used Nordic Ware Yuletide Cookie Stamp's reindeer stamp, available at nordicware.com.

PRO TIP
This dough can be made the day before, wrapped in plastic wrap, and stored in the refrigerator. Let dough warm very slightly at room temperature, enough to scoop dough before stamping and cutting. If dough becomes too soft, place back in refrigerator for 10 to 15 minutes to firm. Refrigerate baking sheet with stamped cookies for 10 minutes before baking. This helps them keep their shape.

VANILLA GLAZE
Makes about ½ cup

1	cup (170 grams) confectioners' sugar
1	tablespoon (21 grams) light corn syrup
2	teaspoons (10 grams) water
1	teaspoon (4 grams) vanilla extract

1. In a small bowl, whisk together confectioners' sugar, corn syrup, 2 teaspoons (10 grams) water, and vanilla until smooth. Use immediately.

Photo by Jenn Davis

ORANGE CURRANT OATMEAL COOKIES

Makes 30 to 36 cookies

Recipe by Becky Sue Wilberding

Inspired by the nostalgic iced oatmeal cookies, these cardamom- and cinnamon-spiced cookies are loaded with texture and flavor. Extra-thick old-fashioned oats are whizzed in the food processor for an ultra-chewy bite. Studded with tart currants and bright orange zest, the oatmeal cookies are finished with an orange glaze to balance out the spicy flavors.

2   cups (200 grams) extra-thick old-fashioned oats*
2   cups (250 grams) all-purpose flour
1½   tablespoons (9 grams) orange zest
1   teaspoon (3 grams) fine sea salt
1   teaspoon (5 grams) baking soda
1   teaspoon (2 grams) ground cardamom
¾   teaspoon (3.75 grams) baking powder
½   teaspoon (1 gram) ground cinnamon
1   cup (227 grams) unsalted butter, softened
1   cup (220 grams) firmly packed light brown sugar
½   cup (100 grams) granulated sugar
2   large eggs (100 grams), room temperature
2   teaspoons (8 grams) vanilla extract
1½   cups (192 grams) dried currants
Orange Icing (recipe follows)

1. Preheat oven to 350°F (180°C). Line baking sheets with parchment paper or nonstick baking mats.
2. In the work bowl of a food processor, pulse oats until coarsely chopped, 10 to 20 seconds. Transfer to a large bowl; add flour, orange zest, sea salt, baking soda, cardamom, baking powder, and cinnamon, whisking to combine. Set aside.
3. In the bowl of a stand mixer fitted with the paddle attachment, beat butter and sugars at medium speed until light and fluffy, 3 to 4 minutes, stopping to scrape sides of bowl. In a liquid-measuring cup, whisk together eggs and vanilla until combined. With mixer on low speed, gradually add egg mixture.

4. Gradually add flour mixture to butter mixture in two to three additions, beating until well combined. Stir in currants just until combined. Using a 1½-tablespoon spring-loaded scoop, scoop dough, and shape into balls (31 grams each). Place 2 inches apart on prepared pans. Refrigerate overnight. (See Note.)
5. Bake until edges begin to brown and centers appear slightly underdone, 10 to 12 minutes, rotating pans halfway through baking. Let cool completely on pans. (They will continue to cook and should be crunchy around edges with a warm and chewy center.) Drizzle Orange Icing onto cooled cookies, and gently spread just to edges. Alternatively, dip top of cookies in Orange Icing. Let icing set before serving.

We used Bob's Red Mill Extra Thick Rolled Oats.

Note: *You can also bake these cookies immediately (without chilling dough), but your cookies will not be as thick.*

PRO TIP
Once scooped, this dough can be refrigerated overnight or sealed in a resealable plastic bag and frozen for up to 2 months. Bake them straight from the freezer. Baking time may require an extra minute or so.

ORANGE ICING
Makes about ¾ cup

2¼   cups (270 grams) confectioners' sugar
3   tablespoons (45 grams) fresh orange juice

1. In a small bowl, whisk together confectioners' sugar and orange juice until smooth and creamy. The glaze should run off whisk in a smooth ribbon. If it's too thick, add a bit more orange juice, ½ teaspoon (2.5 grams) at a time. If it's too thin, add confectioners' sugar, 1 tablespoon (7 grams) at a time, until desired consistency is reached.

Photo by Becky Sue Wilberding

STAMPED LEBKUCHEN

Makes 18 to 20 cookies

Recipe by Edd Kimber

Lebkuchen is a European Christmas staple. The cookies hail from Germany but can now be found all across Europe at Christmas markets all winter long. They are deeply spiced and chewy cookies, a relative of gingerbread, but they differ partly in their use of honey. This version isn't strictly authentic but is more of an homage to the classic. For a little extra Christmas cheer, use cookie stamps to emboss the cookies with a variety of patterns.

½   cup (110 grams) firmly packed
     dark brown sugar
3½ tablespoons (75 grams) honey
3½ tablespoons (75 grams) molasses
1   large egg (50 grams)
2½ cups (313 grams) all-purpose flour
2   tablespoons (10 grams) unsweetened
     cocoa powder
2   teaspoons (4 grams) ground cinnamon
2   teaspoons (4 grams) ground ginger
1   teaspoon (5 grams) baking powder

½   teaspoon (2.5 grams) baking soda
¼   teaspoon grated fresh nutmeg
⅛   teaspoon ground cloves
⅛   teaspoon ground black pepper
Granulated sugar, for sprinkling
1   cup (120 grams) confectioners' sugar
3   tablespoons (45 grams) fresh lemon
     juice

1. In a large saucepan, heat brown sugar, honey, and molasses over medium heat, stirring occasionally, until sugar is dissolved and mixture is smooth. Remove from heat; let cool for 20 minutes. Add egg, whisking until well combined.
2. In a large bowl, whisk together flour, cocoa, cinnamon, ginger, baking powder, baking soda, nutmeg, cloves, and pepper. Make a well in center of flour mixture; add sugar mixture, and stir with a wooden spoon until combined. Turn out onto a lightly floured surface, and knead until a stiff dough forms. Divide dough in half, and wrap each half in plastic wrap. Refrigerate until firm, about 2 hours.
3. Preheat oven to 350°F (180°C). Line 2 baking sheets with parchment paper.

4. On a lightly floured surface, roll half of dough to ¼-inch thickness. Using a 2¾-inch round cutter, cut dough, rerolling scraps as needed. Place 1 to 2 inches apart on prepared pans. Sprinkle with granulated sugar. Using a cookie stamp*, emboss a pattern onto each cookie. Repeat with remaining dough.
5. Bake until lightly browned around edges, 10 to 12 minutes.
6. In a small bowl, stir together confectioners' sugar and lemon juice until a thick but pourable glaze is formed. Using a pastry brush, coat top of warm cookies with glaze. (Doing this when the cookies are still warm will give them their characteristic translucent glaze.) Store in an airtight container for up to 1 week. As with most gingerbread recipes, the flavor and texture will improve after a day's rest.

We used Nordic Ware Starry Night Cookie Stamp Set and Nordic Ware Greetings Heirloom Cookie Stamps, available at nordicware.com.

Photo by Edd Kimber

VANILLA SUGAR COOKIE TREES WITH CREAM CHEESE FROSTING

Makes about 24 cookies

Recipe by Becky Sue Wilberding

These easy vanilla shortbread cookies get dressed in their holiday best with a festive flourish of Cream Cheese Frosting mini stars in wintergreen hues. They may take a while to decorate, but the gorgeous result is worth the investment. Just turn on a holiday movie or two while you decorate, and enjoy the cozy craft.

1	cup (227 grams) unsalted butter, softened
⅔	cup (133 grams) granulated sugar
1	vanilla bean, split lengthwise, seeds scraped and reserved
1	teaspoon (4 grams) vanilla extract
2⅓	cups (292 grams) all-purpose flour
1	teaspoon (3 grams) fine sea salt

Cream Cheese Frosting (recipe follows)
Green and blue natural food coloring

1. In the bowl of a stand mixer fitted with the paddle attachment, beat butter, sugar, and and reserved vanilla bean seeds at medium-high speed until light and fluffy, 5 to 7 minutes, stopping to scrape sides of bowl. With mixer on medium-low speed, add vanilla extract, beating to combine.
2. In a medium bowl, whisk together flour and sea salt. With mixer on low speed, gradually add flour mixture to butter mixture, beating until combined. Turn out dough onto a floured surface, and divide in half. Shape each half into a disk, and wrap in plastic wrap. Refrigerate for at least 1 hour.
3. Let dough stand at room temperature until slightly softened, about 5 minutes. Roll to about ¼-inch thickness. Using a 3- to 4-inch tree-shaped cutter, cut dough, rerolling scraps as necessary. Line baking sheets with parchment paper, and place cookies 1 to 2 inches apart on prepared pans. Freeze or refrigerate for at least 1 to 2 hours.
4. Preheat oven to 350°F (180°C).
5. Bake until cookies just start to turn golden brown around the edges, 10 to 12 minutes. Let cool on pans or wire racks.
6. Divide Cream Cheese Frosting among 3 small bowls. For light green color, add 1 drop of green food coloring to first bowl, and stir until combined. For medium green color, add 3 drops green food coloring to second bowl, and stir until combined.

For minty blue color, add 3 drops green food coloring and 1 drop blue coloring the third bowl, and stir until combined.
7. Place one-third of each frosting in a piping bag fitted with a small open star tip (Wilton No. 16 or No. 18). Refrigerate in piping bags for at least 20 minutes. (Cover remaining frosting in bowls with plastic wrap, and refrigerate until ready to use.)
8. To decorate cookies, hold piping bag straight up, with tip just slightly above surface. Squeeze bag, and use light pressure to form a small star; add more pressure to make a bigger star. Stop squeezing before pulling tip away. Using one color at a time, cover cookie with stars; fill in with other colors. Repeat with remaining cookies and remaining frosting. (If frosting gets too warm, the stars will not hold their shape. You may need to place the piping bags in the refrigerator for a few minutes to chill the frosting a few times throughout the decorating process.) (Alternatively, smear thick swirls of frosting on each cookie with an offset spatula.) Store decorated cookies in refrigerator. Remove from refrigerator 1 to 2 hours before serving.

PRO TIP
Be sure to fully beat the sugar and butter. You want it superlight and fluffy. This will help the cookies keep sharp edges when baking. Freeze the cut cookies, and bake from frozen for best results.

CREAM CHEESE FROSTING
Makes about 2⅔ cups

1	cup (225 grams) cream cheese, softened
6	tablespoons (84 grams) unsalted butter, softened
1	teaspoon (4 grams) vanilla extract
3½	cups (420 grams) confectioners' sugar, sifted

1. In the bowl of a stand mixer fitted with the paddle attachment, beat cream cheese, butter, and vanilla at medium speed, 1 to 2 minutes, until smooth. Gradually add confectioners' sugar, beating until thick and creamy. Use immediately.

Photo by Becky Sue Wilberding

PEANUT BUTTER EGGNOG SNOWFLAKE COOKIES

Makes 24 cookies

Recipe by Jenn Davis

These soft peanut butter cookies decorated with piped Eggnog Buttercream deliver melt-in-your-mouth goodness that screams winter is here. Use a little buttercream, or frost the whole cookie. Either way, the combo is just what a snow-loving sweet tooth craving needs.

1   cup (227 grams) unsalted butter, softened
1   cup (200 grams) granulated sugar
1   cup (220 grams) firmly packed light brown sugar
1   cup (256 grams) creamy peanut butter
1   teaspoon (4 grams) vanilla extract
3   large eggs (150 grams)
3   cups (375 grams) all-purpose flour
1   teaspoon (5 grams) baking powder
1   teaspoon (4 grams) ground cinnamon
1   teaspoon (4 grams) ground nutmeg
½   teaspoon (2.5 grams) baking soda
½   teaspoon (1.5 grams) kosher salt
Eggnog Buttercream (recipe follows)
Garnish: sparkling sugar

1. In the bowl of a stand mixer fitted with the paddle attachment, beat butter, granulated sugar, and brown sugar at medium speed until fluffy, 3 to 4 minutes, stopping to scrape sides of bowl. Add peanut butter, beating until smooth. Beat in vanilla. Add eggs, one at a time, beating well after each addition.
2. In a medium bowl, whisk together flour, baking powder, cinnamon, nutmeg, baking soda, and salt. With mixer on low speed, gradually add flour mixture to butter mixture, beating until a dough forms. Divide dough in half, and shape into disks; wrap each in plastic wrap. Refrigerate for 2 hours.
3. Preheat oven to 350°F (180°C). Line 2 baking sheets with parchment paper.

4. Place half of dough on a large sheet of parchment paper. Cover with another large sheet of parchment paper, and roll to ¼-inch thickness. Remove top sheet of parchment. Using a 3- to 5-inch snowflake cutter dipped in flour, cut dough, re-flouring cutter every 3 to 4 cookies to prevent sticking. Using a small offset spatula lightly coated in flour, transfer cookies to prepared pans. Refrigerate until firm, about 15 minutes.
5. Bake until edges start to lightly brown, 10 to 12 minutes. Let cool on pans for 3 to 4 minutes. Remove from pans, and let cool completely on wire racks. Repeat with remaining dough.
6. Place Eggnog Buttercream in a piping bag fitted with a closed star piping tip (Wilton No. 18 or No. 31). Pipe stars onto cooled cookies by gently squeezing from top of bag and then lifting while releasing pressure. Sprinkle with sparkling sugar, if desired. Store in an airtight container, separated by parchment or wax paper, for up to 3 weeks, or freeze cookies, individually wrapped in plastic wrap, in an airtight freezer-safe container for up to 4 months.

> **PRO TIP**
> Cookie dough can be made the day before and stored wrapped in plastic wrap in the refrigerator. Let dough warm slightly at room temperature to roll out but maintain a cold cookie dough.

EGGNOG BUTTERCREAM
Makes about 3 cups

1   cup (227 grams) unsalted butter, softened
¼   cup (60 grams) prepared eggnog
1   tablespoon (13 grams) vanilla extract
½   teaspoon (1.5 grams) kosher salt
4 to 5 cups (480 to 600 grams) confectioners' sugar

1. In the bowl of stand mixer fitted with the whisk attachment, beat butter, eggnog, vanilla, and salt at medium-low speed until combined. Gradually add confectioners' sugar, beating until desired thickness is reached. Use immediately.

Photo by Jenn Davis

CINNAMON SWIRL COOKIES WITH MAPLE BUTTER FROSTING

Makes 40 to 45 cookies

Recipe by Tessa Huff

These cinnamon roll-inspired cookies are packed with spice and draped with Maple Butter Frosting. The maple pays tribute to the season and pairs perfectly with the cinnamon.

1   cup (227 grams) unsalted butter, softened
1   cup (200 grams) granulated sugar
1   large egg (50 grams)
1   teaspoon (4 grams) vanilla extract
2⅔   cups (333 grams) plus ¼ cup (31 grams) all-purpose flour, divided
½   teaspoon (1.5 grams) kosher salt
¼   teaspoon (1.25 grams) baking soda
2   tablespoons (12 grams) ground cinnamon
¼   cup (85 grams) maple syrup
Maple Butter Frosting (recipe follows)

1. In the bowl of a stand mixer fitted with the paddle attachment, beat butter at medium speed until creamy, about 1 minute. Add sugar, and beat for 2 to 3 minutes. With mixer on low speed, add egg and vanilla. Increase mixer speed to medium, and beat until combined, about 2 minutes, stopping to scrape sides and bottom of bowl.
2. In a medium bowl, sift together 2⅔ cups (333 grams) flour, salt, and baking soda. With mixer on low speed, add flour mixture to butter mixture in two additions, beating until dough comes together in a loose, shaggy ball.
3. Turn out dough onto 2 sheets of parchment paper or nonstick baking mats. Divide in half, and roll each half into an 11-inch square, about ¼ inch thick. (Lightly dust with flour if dough becomes sticky while rolling.) Place dough on baking sheets, and refrigerate for 8 to 10 minutes (Do not chill the dough for too long, or it may crack when rolled.)
4. In a small bowl, stir together cinnamon and remaining ¼ cup (31 grams) flour. Stir in maple syrup to create a thin paste. Spread maple-cinnamon filling on each half of dough, leaving a ¼-inch border. Tightly roll up each portion of dough into a log. Wrap in parchment paper, and refrigerate until firm enough to slice, at least 2 hours.
5. Preheat oven to 350°F (180°C). Line 2 baking sheets with parchment paper.
6. Using a sharp knife, cut logs into ¼- to ½-inch-thick slices, and place 1 to 2 inches apart on prepared pans.
7. Bake until very lightly browned around edges, 12 to 14 minutes. Let cool completely on pans. Spread Maple Butter Frosting onto cooled cookies. Serve immediately, or store in an airtight container for up to 2 days.

MAPLE BUTTER FROSTING
Makes about ¾ cup

½   cup (113 grams) unsalted butter, softened
1¼ to 1½ cups (150 to 180 grams) confectioners' sugar
⅓   cup (105 grams) maple butter*
2   tablespoons (30 grams) heavy whipping cream
⅛   teaspoon kosher salt

1. In a medium bowl, stir unsalted butter with a small rubber spatula or spoon until smooth. Add 1¼ cups (150 grams) confectioners' sugar, maple butter, cream, and salt, and stir until smooth and creamy. Add remaining ¼ cup (30 grams) confectioners' sugar, if needed, stirring until frosting reaches a spreadable consistency. Use immediately.

Available in specialty food stores or online.

> **PRO TIP**
> If making in advance, store unfrosted cookies in an airtight container for up to 4 days.

Photo by Tessa Huff

SPICED SUGAR SANDWICH COOKIES WITH FIVE-SPICE CRANBERRY SWISS BUTTERCREAM

Makes 38 sandwich cookies

Recipe by Rebecca Firth

Picture your favorite sugar cookie recipe and then add your favorite holiday spices. That's what this cookie tastes like. It's great on its own but even better with a thick layer of Five-Spice Cranberry Swiss Buttercream. The buttercream is lightly scented with cranberries and Chinese five-spice powder.

1½	cups (340 grams) unsalted butter, cubed and softened
¾	cup (150 grams) granulated sugar
¾	cup (165 grams) firmly packed light brown sugar
2	large eggs (100 grams), room temperature
¾	teaspoon (3 grams) vanilla extract
2	teaspoons (4 grams) ground cinnamon
1	teaspoon (2 grams) ground allspice
1	teaspoon (2 grams) ground ginger
½	teaspoon (1 gram) ground cardamom
½	teaspoon (1 gram) ground cloves
2¼	cups (281 grams) all-purpose flour
2	cups (254 grams) bread flour
1	teaspoon (3 grams) sea salt
½	teaspoon (2.5 grams) baking powder
½	teaspoon (2.5 grams) baking soda

Five-Spice Cranberry Swiss Buttercream (recipe follows)
1   cup (16 grams) freeze-dried cranberries, finely ground (optional)

1. In the bowl of a stand mixer fitted with the paddle attachment, beat butter and sugars at medium speed until creamy, about 5 minutes. Add eggs, one at a time, beating well after each addition. Add vanilla, cinnamon, allspice, ginger, cardamom, and cloves, and beat until well combined, about 1 minute.
2. In a large bowl, whisk together flours, sea salt, baking powder, and baking soda. Add flour mixture to butter mixture, and beat at low speed just until combined. Divide dough in half, and shape each half into a disk. Wrap tightly in plastic wrap, and refrigerate for 1 hour. (Don't chill longer than 1 hour, or it will be too difficult to roll out. If this happens, let the dough come close to room temperature before attempting to roll out. You want it soft enough that it rolls out without cracking but cool enough that it's not too sticky.)
3. Preheat oven to 350°F (180°C). Line several baking sheets with parchment paper.
4. Let dough stand until slightly softened, about 10 minutes. Between 2 lightly floured sheets of parchment paper, roll half of dough to ¼-inch thickness. (Don't go too thin. Periodically check to make sure the dough isn't sticking; sprinkle lightly with flour when it does.) Using a 1½-inch fluted round cutter, cut dough, rerolling scraps as necessary. Place 1 inch apart on prepared pans. Repeat with remaining dough. Freeze for 15 minutes, or refrigerate for 30 minutes.
5. Bake for 10 minutes. Let cool on pans for 5 minutes. Remove from pans, and let cool completely on wire racks. Spread Five-Spice Cranberry Swiss Buttercream onto flat side of half of cookies; sprinkle with freeze-dried cranberries (if using). Place remaining cookies, flat side down, on top of buttercream.

FIVE-SPICE CRANBERRY SWISS BUTTERCREAM
Makes about 2 cups

1	cup (170 grams) fresh or frozen cranberries
⅔	cup (133 grams) plus ½ cup (100 grams) granulated sugar, divided
½	cup (120 grams) water
1½	teaspoons (3 grams) Chinese five-spice powder, divided
3	large egg whites (90 grams)
¼	teaspoon sea salt
1	cup (227 grams) unsalted butter, slightly chilled and cubed

1. In a heavy-bottomed saucepan, bring cranberries, ½ cup (100 grams) sugar, ½ cup (120 grams) water, and 1 teaspoon (2 grams) five-spice powder to a boil over medium-high heat. Reduce heat, and simmer, stirring frequently, until mixture is reduced and thickened, about 20 minutes. Strain mixture through a fine-mesh sieve, reserving 3 to 4 tablespoons (57 to 72 grams) cranberry liquid and discarding solids. Let cool completely.
2. In the bowl of a stand mixer, combine egg whites, sea salt, and remaining ⅔ cup (133 grams) sugar; place bowl over a saucepan of simmering water. Cook, whisking constantly, until thickened and opaque and no longer feels gritty when rubbed between two fingers, 3 to 4 minutes. Return bowl to stand mixer fitted with the whisk attachment, and beat at high speed until stiff peaks form.
3. Switch to the paddle attachment. With mixer on medium speed, add butter, a few cubes at a time, beating until well combined after each addition. (If mixture curdles, your butter may be too cold. If mixture is soupy, you may need to refrigerate it.) Beat until mixture is smooth, glossy, and voluminous. Add reserved 3 to 4 tablespoons (57 to 72 grams) cranberry liquid and remaining ½ teaspoon (1 gram) five-spice powder. Use immediately.

Photo by Rebecca Firth

SNOWFLAKE LINZER COOKIES

Makes 20 sandwich cookies

Recipe by Amisha Gurbani

Linzers are popular Austrian cookies made by many during the holiday season. Almond flour, citrus zest, and a touch of cinnamon and star anise make these wintry, warm, and delicious. Make them even more special by using homemade jam.

1   cup (227 grams) unsalted butter, softened
¾   cup (150 grams) granulated sugar
1   tablespoon (3 grams) orange zest
1   large egg (50 grams)
1   tablespoon (13 grams) vanilla extract
2½   cups (313 grams) all-purpose flour
⅔   cup (64 grams) almond flour
1   teaspoon (2 grams) ground cinnamon
1   teaspoon (2 grams) ground star anise
½   teaspoon (2.5 grams) baking powder
½   teaspoon (1.5 grams) kosher salt
1   cup (320 grams) raspberry jam
Garnish: confectioners' sugar

1. In the bowl of a stand mixer fitted with the paddle attachment, beat butter, granulated sugar, and orange zest at medium-high speed until pale and fluffy, about 3 minutes, stopping to scrape sides of bowl. Beat in egg and vanilla.
2. In a medium bowl, whisk together flours, cinnamon, star anise, baking powder, and salt. With mixer on low speed, gradually add flour mixture to butter mixture, beating just until combined. Using floured hands, divide dough in half. Shape each half into a 5-inch disk, and wrap in plastic wrap. Refrigerate until firm, at least 2 hours.
3. Position oven racks in upper and lower thirds of oven, and preheat oven to 350°F (180°C).

4. On a lightly floured surface, place half of dough; sprinkle top with more flour. Roll dough into an 11-inch circle, ⅛ inch thick. (If dough becomes too soft to roll, rewrap in plastic wrap, and refrigerate until firm.) Using a 3-inch snowflake cutter, cut dough, and place about 1 inch apart on 2 large baking sheets. Using a 1-inch mini snowflake cutter, cut centers from half of cookies. Reserve centers, and reroll with scraps once.
5. Bake until edges are golden, 10 to 15 minutes, rotating pans halfway through baking. Using a metal spatula, remove from pans, and let cool completely on wire racks. Repeat with remaining dough.
6. Spread about 1 teaspoon (7 grams) jam onto flat side of all solid cookies. Dust cookies with cutouts with confectioners' sugar, if desired. Place cookies with cutouts, flat side down, on top of jam.

Photo by Amisha Gurbani

SUGAR COOKIE WREATHS

Makes about 36 cookies

Is it really the holidays if you don't have festive sugar cookies? These classic cookies are topped with an elegant Royal Icing wreath that's easier to create than you might think.

1   cup (227 grams) unsalted butter, softened
2   cups (240 grams) confectioners' sugar
1   large egg (50 grams), room temperature
1½   teaspoons (6 grams) vanilla extract
½   teaspoon (2 grams) almond extract
3¼   cups (406 grams) all-purpose flour
2   teaspoons (10 grams) baking powder
1   teaspoon (3 grams) kosher salt
Royal Icing (recipe follows)

1. Preheat oven to 400°F (200°C). Line 3 baking sheets with parchment paper.
2. In the bowl of a stand mixer fitted with the paddle attachment, beat butter and confectioners' sugar at medium speed until fluffy, 3 to 4 minutes, stopping to scrape sides of bowl. Add egg and extracts, beating until combined.
3. In a medium bowl, whisk together flour, baking powder, and salt. With mixer on low speed, gradually add flour mixture to butter mixture, beating until a dough forms.
4. Divide dough in half; cover one half with plastic wrap. On a heavily floured surface, roll remaining dough to ¼-inch thickness. (Lightly flour top of dough if it sticks to rolling pin.) Using a 3¼-inch fluted round cutter, cut dough, rerolling scraps as necessary. Using a 1¾-inch fluted round cutter, cut centers from cookies. Repeat with remaining dough. Using a small offset spatula, place cookies at least 1 inch apart on prepared pans.
5. Bake in batches until lightly browned, 7 to 8 minutes. Let cool on pans for 5 minutes. Using a large offset or flat metal spatula, remove from pan, and let cool completely on wire racks.
6. Using piping bag with plain white Royal Icing, pipe an outline along both edges of each cookie. Let dry for 5 minutes. Fill in center using white Royal Icing in squeeze bottle. Immediately pipe small green dots to left and right of center of ring using small piping bottle. Using a wooden pick, continuously drag through center of cookie to create leaves. Let dry for 2 to 3 hours.

7. Pipe red Royal Icing berries in groupings around cookie. Let dry until hardened, about 30 minutes. Store in airtight containers for up to 1 week.

ROYAL ICING
Makes about 6 cups

1   (2-pound) package (907 grams) confectioners' sugar
5   tablespoons (50 grams) meringue powder
¾   cup (180 grams) warm water (105°F/41°C to 110°F/43°C)
1   tablespoon (13 grams) vanilla extract
Gel food coloring (juniper green, kelly green, Christmas red, black, yellow)
Water, as needed

1. In the bowl of a stand mixer fitted with the paddle attachment, beat confectioners' sugar and meringue powder at low speed until combined. Slowly add ¾ cup (180 grams) warm water and vanilla, beating until fluid. Increase mixer speed to medium, and beat until stiff, about 5 minutes.
2. Place 1 cup (180 grams) white icing in a piping bag fitted with a small round piping tip (Wilton No. 3).
3. In a medium bowl, place another 1 cup (180 grams) white icing. Slowly add green food colorings until desired color is reached. Add water, 1 teaspoon (5 grams) at a time, until flood-consistency is reached (about 3 teaspoons [15 grams] total). Place green icing in a small piping bottle fitted with a small round tip (Wilton No. 4).
4. In another medium bowl, place another 1 cup (180 grams) white icing. Slowly add red food coloring until desired color is reached. (Adding a touch of black and yellow will keep it from going pink.) Place in a piping bag fitted with a small round tip (Wilton No. 2), or trim end of bag to create a small opening.
5. Place remaining white icing in a large bowl. Add water, 1 tablespoon (15 grams) at a time, until fluid (5 to 7 tablespoons [75 to 105 grams] total.) (It should ribbon when a whisk is pulled up out of icing.) Place in squeeze bottle with a small opening.

BURNT SUGAR BOURBON GINGERBREAD COOKIES

Makes 50 cookies

Recipe by Rebecca Firth

Newsflash! Burnt sugar isn't really burnt, just caramelized, giving it a toasted marshmallow vibe that we jazzed up with some bourbon because why not? These cookies have heaps of holiday flavor and are just as gorgeous without the boozy buttercream as they are with it. But when all is said and done, make the buttercream—you won't regret it.

1¾ cups (350 grams) granulated sugar, divided
3 tablespoons (45 grams) bourbon, divided
1 cup (227 grams) unsalted butter, softened
2 cups (440 grams) firmly packed dark brown sugar
⅔ cup (226 grams) unsulphured molasses
2 large eggs (100 grams), room temperature
3 cups (375 grams) all-purpose flour
1½ cups (191 grams) bread flour
1 tablespoon (6 grams) ground ginger
1 tablespoon (6 grams) ground cinnamon
2 teaspoons (10 grams) baking powder
1 teaspoon (5 grams) baking soda
1 teaspoon (3 grams) sea salt
1 teaspoon (2 grams) ground allspice
½ teaspoon (1 gram) ground cloves
½ teaspoon (1 gram) ground cardamom
½ teaspoon grated fresh nutmeg
Bourbon Buttercream (recipe follows)
Garnish: demerara sugar

1. Line a rimmed baking sheet with a silicone baking mat.
2. In a medium heavy-bottomed saucepan, heat 1 cup (200 grams) granulated sugar over medium heat, stirring constantly, until sugar liquefies. Cook, stirring constantly, until sugar turns golden brown and no sugar crystals remain. Add 1 tablespoon (15 grams) bourbon. (Mixture may seize, but keep stirring until it relaxes and smooths out.) Pour onto prepared pan; using a spatula, spread to ⅛-inch thickness. Let cool and harden. Chop into chocolate chip-size pieces. Set aside.
3. Preheat oven to 350°F (180°C). Line several baking sheets with parchment paper.

4. In the bowl of a stand mixer fitted with the paddle attachment, beat butter and brown sugar at medium speed until well combined, about 4 minutes. Add molasses, beating until no streaks remain. Add eggs, one at a time, beating well after each addition. Beat in remaining 2 tablespoons (30 grams) bourbon.
5. In a medium bowl, whisk together flours, ginger, cinnamon, baking powder, baking soda, sea salt, allspice, cloves, cardamom, and nutmeg. With mixer on low speed, gradually add flour mixture to butter mixture, beating until mostly combined but with streaks of flour remaining. Add burnt sugar, and beat until evenly distributed throughout dough, about 1 minute.
6. In a shallow bowl, place remaining ¾ cup (150 grams) granulated sugar. Using a 2-tablespoon spring-loaded scoop, scoop dough, and roll into balls (about 36 grams each). Roll balls thickly in sugar, and place 3 inches apart on prepared pans.
7. Bake for 12 to 13 minutes. Using the edge of a spatula, nudge any misshapen cookies back into shape. Let cool on pans for 5 minutes. Remove from pans, and let cool completely on wire racks. Spread Bourbon Buttercream onto cooled cookies. Sprinkle with demerara sugar, if desired.

BOURBON BUTTERCREAM
Makes about 1½ cups

½ cup (113 grams) unsalted butter, softened
2½ cups (300 grams) confectioners' sugar, sifted and divided
1 tablespoon (15 grams) milk
1 tablespoon (15 grams) bourbon
1 teaspoon (4 grams) vanilla extract

1. In the bowl of a stand mixer fitted with the paddle attachment, beat butter at medium speed until creamy, about 2 minutes. Add 1 cup (120 grams) confectioners' sugar, and beat at low speed until combined. Add milk, beating until combined. Add another 1 cup (120 grams) confectioners' sugar, beating until combined; beat in bourbon. Add vanilla and remaining 1½ cups (180 grams) confectioners' sugar, beating until combined. Increase mixer speed to medium, and beat until smooth, light, and fluffy, 2 to 3 minutes. Use immediately.

Photo by Rebecca Firth

CHOCOLATE CARDAMOM SUGAR COOKIES

Makes 24 cookies

Recipe by Erin Clarkson

We kept these particular cookies soft by adding cream cheese to the dough—it also gives them a slight tang that works so well with the cardamom and chocolate. We finished them off with a generous dusting of confectioners' sugar using a snowflake stencil.

1	cup (227 grams) unsalted butter, softened
½	cup plus 2 tablespoons (140 grams) full-fat cream cheese, softened
¾	cup (150 grams) granulated sugar
¼	cup (55 grams) firmly packed dark brown sugar
1	large egg (50 grams), room temperature
1	large egg yolk (19 grams), room temperature
1	teaspoon (4 grams) vanilla extract
3	cups plus 1 tablespoon (383 grams) all-purpose flour, sifted
1	cup (85 grams) Dutch process cocoa powder
1¼	teaspoons (2.5 grams) ground cardamom
¾	teaspoon (2.25 grams) kosher salt

Garnish: confectioners' sugar

1. In the bowl of a stand mixer fitted with the paddle attachment, beat butter and cream cheese at medium speed until combined, 1 to 2 minutes. Add granulated sugar and brown sugar; increase mixer speed to high, and beat until light and creamy, 2 to 3 minutes. Reduce mixer speed to low. Add egg, egg yolk, and vanilla, beating until combined.

2. In a medium bowl, sift together flour, cocoa, cardamom, and salt. Add flour mixture to butter mixture all at once, and beat at low speed just until combined. Using a rubber spatula, briefly stir to ensure everything is combined. (Dough will be sticky.) Transfer dough to a large piece of plastic wrap, and press into a rough rectangle. Wrap tightly in plastic wrap, and refrigerate until firm, 3 to 4 hours or overnight.

3. Preheat oven to 350°F (180°C). Line 2 baking sheets with parchment paper.

4. Divide dough in half; return half of dough to refrigerator. On a lightly floured sheet of parchment paper, roll remaining dough to ⅓-inch thickness. (You may need to give dough a few bangs with the rolling pin to help flatten it a little before you start rolling. This dough is on the stickier side, so rolling it out on a sheet of parchment paper means you can easily transfer it back to the refrigerator to chill a little if needed.) Using a 3-inch round cutter, cut dough, rerolling scraps as necessary. Place on prepared pans. (If at any time dough becomes too warm and hard to work with, return to refrigerator to chill briefly.) Refrigerate for 10 to 15 minutes.

5. Bake in batches for 9 to 10 minutes. (Cookies will still look very soft when they come out of the oven but will firm up as they cool.) Let cool completely on pans. Place a stencil* on top of cooled cookies, and garnish with confectioners' sugar, if desired. Store in an airtight container for up to 3 days.

*Make your own stencil with a snowflake paper punch, available online or in local craft stores. A piece of lace draped on top of the cookies also works well.

PRO TIP

To help keep them moist, these cookies don't have any leaven in them, so the thickness that you roll the dough out to will be the thickness of your finished cookie.

Photo by Erin Clarkson

BROWNED BUTTER SNICKERDOODLE COOKIES

Makes 20 to 24 cookies

Recipe by Elisabeth Farris

The classic flavor of snickerdoodles with a unique twist! Browned butter is the perfect addition to these festive cookies, giving them the most delicious nutty flavor. Use your favorite holiday cookie cutters to make different shapes and designs, and they will be the hit of any party!

1 cup (227 grams) unsalted butter, softened
1 cup (200 grams) plus 2 tablespoons (24 grams) granulated sugar, divided
2 large eggs (100 grams)
1 teaspoon (4 grams) vanilla extract
3 cups (375 grams) all-purpose flour
2 teaspoons (4 grams) ground cinnamon, divided
½ teaspoon (2.5 grams) baking powder
½ teaspoon (1.5 grams) kosher salt
Glaze (recipe follows)
Gel food coloring, for decorating
Small food-safe paintbrush
Clear vodka, for decorating

1. In a medium heavy-bottomed saucepan, melt butter over medium heat. Cook until butter turns a medium amber color and has a nutty aroma, about 10 minutes. Remove from heat, and let cool to room temperature. Pour browned butter into a glass measuring cup, and freeze just until solidified, about 1 hour.
2. In the bowl of stand mixer fitted with the paddle attachment, beat browned butter and 1 cup (200 grams) sugar at medium speed until light and creamy, 2 to 3 minutes, stopping to scrape sides of bowl. Add eggs and vanilla, and beat until combined.
3. In a medium bowl, whisk together flour, 1 teaspoon (2 grams) cinnamon, baking powder, and salt. With mixer on low speed, gradually add flour mixture to butter mixture, beating until dough comes together. Turn out dough onto a lightly floured surface, and shape into a disk. Wrap disk in plastic wrap, and refrigerate for at least 1 hour or for up to 3 days.
4. Preheat oven to 350°F (180°C). Line 2 baking sheets with parchment paper.
5. In a small bowl, stir together remaining 2 tablespoons (24 grams) sugar and remaining 1 teaspoon (2 grams) cinnamon. Set aside.

6. On a lightly floured surface, roll dough to ¼-inch thickness. Using a 3½-inch holiday cookie cutter (use any shape you like or multiple shapes), cut dough, rerolling scraps as necessary. Place 2 inches apart on prepared pans. Sprinkle with cinnamon sugar.
7. Bake until lightly golden around edges, 8 to 10 minutes. Remove from pans, and let cool completely on wire racks.
8. Place Glaze in a piping bag, and cut off tip; outline each cookie with Glaze. After outline has set, fill it completely with Glaze, and use a wooden pick or knife to spread it out and fill in holes. Let glazed cookies stand at room temperature for at least 5 hours or overnight before decorating or painting.
9. Use a toothpick to place a few drops of gel food coloring on a sheet of wax paper or parchment paper. With a fine-tipped paintbrush, use vodka or clear extract to dilute the food coloring, and paint* your design on the cookies. After dipping your brush in the paint, lightly dab it on a paper towel so the colors don't become too wet and bleed. When changing colors, remember to rinse and dry your brush between each use. Store decorated cookies in an airtight container for up to 5 days.

We used Wilton Cake Decorating Tools, 5-Piece Brush Set.

Note: *This dough can be wrapped in plastic wrap and frozen for up to 3 months. Let thaw in the refrigerator overnight.*

GLAZE
Makes about 1½ cups

3 cups (360 grams) confectioners' sugar
4 to 6 tablespoons (60 to 90 grams) whole milk, room temperature

1. In a medium bowl, whisk together confectioners' sugar and milk until smooth. When you run your whisk through glaze, it should settle back down after 10 seconds. If glaze is too thick, add more milk, and if it's too thin, add more confectioners' sugar. Color glaze with food coloring as desired. If you're not going to use your glaze immediately, cover with a wet paper towel so it doesn't dry out.

Photo by Elisabeth Farris

VIENNESE SANDWICH COOKIES

Makes about 18 sandwich cookies

We are obsessed with Gemma Stafford's take on the traditional Viennese whirl. The recipe, Simplest Buttery Viennese Fingers, is featured in her cookbook, Bigger Bolder Baking: A Fearless Approach to Baking Anytime, Anywhere. Here, we reimagined the British teatime favorite as holiday-ready sandwich cookies packed with mulling spices for a touch of warmth and filled with sweet, sophisticated Cherry-Port Buttercream.

2   cups (454 grams) unsalted butter, softened
⅔   cup (80 grams) confectioners' sugar
2   tablespoons (16 grams) tightly packed orange zest
1½   teaspoons (3 grams) ground cinnamon
1½   teaspoons (3 grams) ground ginger
1½   teaspoons (3 grams) ground cloves
1   teaspoon (3 grams) kosher salt
1   teaspoon (2 grams) ground nutmeg
1   teaspoon (2 grams) ground allspice
½   teaspoon (1 gram) ground black pepper
3⅓   cups (417 grams) all-purpose flour
6   tablespoons (48 grams) cornstarch
Cherry-Port Buttercream (recipe follows)

1. Preheat oven to 350°F (180°C). Using a permanent marker, draw 12 (4x1-inch) rectangles on each of 3 sheets of parchment paper (36 rectangles total). Turn parchment over, and place on 3 baking sheets.
2. In the bowl of a stand mixer fitted with the paddle attachment, beat butter, confectioners' sugar, orange zest, cinnamon, ginger, cloves, salt, nutmeg, allspice, and pepper at medium speed until well combined and creamy, 2 to 3 minutes, stopping to scrape sides of bowl.
3. In a medium bowl, sift together flour and cornstarch. With mixer on low speed, gradually add flour mixture to butter mixture, beating until combined.
4. Place about 1 cup (247 grams) dough into a piping bag fitted with a medium open star tip (Wilton 4B); pipe small dots

of batter under parchment to adhere to pans. Using drawn rectangles as guides, pipe dough in a zigzag pattern. (Dough will take some effort to pipe.) Repeat with remaining dough. Refrigerate for 15 minutes.
5. Bake until lightly golden and firm to the touch, about 14 minutes, rotating pans halfway through baking. Let cool on pans for 5 minutes. Carefully remove from pans, and let cool completely on wire racks.
6. Spoon Cherry-Port Buttercream into a large piping bag fitted with a medium open star tip (Wilton 4B); pipe about 2 tablespoons (30 grams) buttercream onto flat side of half of cookies. Place remaining cookies, flat side down, on top of buttercream. Serve immediately.

CHERRY-PORT BUTTERCREAM
Makes about 2⅔ cups

¾   cup (170 grams) ruby port
¼   cup (80 grams) cherry preserves
1   cup (227 grams) unsalted butter, softened
½   teaspoon (2 grams) vanilla extract
¼   teaspoon kosher salt
4   cups (480 grams) confectioners' sugar

1. In a small saucepan, bring port and preserves to a boil over medium-high heat. Reduce heat to medium; cook, stirring occasionally, until mixture is reduced to ¼ cup, 15 to 20 minutes. Strain mixture through a fine-mesh sieve, pressing out as much liquid as possible; discard solids. Let cool completely.
2. In the bowl of a stand mixer fitted with the paddle attachment, beat butter at medium speed until smooth and creamy, 1 to 2 minutes. Beat in vanilla and salt. With mixer on low speed, gradually add confectioners' sugar until combined. Add 2 tablespoons (about 34 grams) cooled port mixture; beat at medium speed until fluffy and well combined, 1 to 2 minutes, stopping to scrape sides of bowl. Use immediately.

CASADINHOS

Makes 35 to 40 sandwich cookies

Derived from the Portuguese word for "married," these sandwich cookies are a staple at Brazilian weddings. Speckled with warm spice and spiked with rum, the tender butter cookies are joined by a sweet-tart guava jam, symbolizing the union of two people through marriage. Commonly filled with guava paste, casadinhos are so beloved in Brazil that they're also baked for any special occasion.

1	cup (227 grams) unsalted butter, softened
⅔	cup (133 grams) granulated sugar
1	large egg (50 grams), room temperature
2	large egg yolks (37 grams), room temperature
2	tablespoons (30 grams) spiced rum
1	tablespoon (13 grams) vanilla extract
2	cups (250 grams) all-purpose flour
1	cup (128 grams) cornstarch (see Note)
1	teaspoon (5 grams) baking powder
¾	teaspoon (2.25 grams) kosher salt
½	teaspoon (1 gram) ground cinnamon
¼	teaspoon ground allspice
1½	(14.1-ounce) packages (600 grams) guava paste, cubed
⅓	cup (80 grams) water
2	tablespoons plus 1 teaspoon (35 grams) fresh lemon juice

Confectioners' sugar, for dusting

1. In the bowl of a stand mixer fitted with the paddle attachment, beat butter and granulated sugar at medium speed until creamy, about 2 minutes, stopping to scrape sides of bowl. Add egg and egg yolks, one at a time, beating until well combined after each addition. Beat in rum and vanilla.

2. In a medium bowl, whisk together flour, cornstarch, baking powder, salt, cinnamon, and allspice. With mixer on low speed, gradually add flour mixture to butter mixture, beating just until combined. Divide dough in half; shape each half into a disk, and wrap in plastic wrap. Freeze until firm, about 2 hours.

3. Preheat oven to 350°F (180°C). Line baking sheets with parchment paper.

4. Unwrap one half of dough, and let stand at room temperature until slightly softened, 10 to 15 minutes. On a heavily floured surface, roll dough to ⅛-inch thickness; lightly flour dough and work surface as needed. Using a 2-inch fluted round cutter dipped in flour, cut dough, rerolling scraps as necessary, and place 1 inch apart on prepared pans. Repeat with remaining half of dough.

5. Bake, in batches if needed, until edges are lightly golden, 10 to 13 minutes, rotating pans halfway through baking. Let cool on pans for 2 minutes. Remove from pans, and let cool completely on wire racks.

6. In a small saucepan, combine guava paste, ⅓ cup (80 grams) water, and lemon juice; cook over medium heat, stirring occasionally, until melted and smooth. Remove from heat; let stand at room temperature or refrigerate until an instant-read thermometer registers 85°F (29°C).

7. Dust half of cookies with confectioners' sugar. Transfer guava mixture to a piping bag fitted with a ¼-inch round piping tip (Wilton No. 10). Pipe about 1½ to 2 teaspoons (about 12 grams) filling onto flat side of remaining cookies. Place sugar-dusted cookies, flat side down, on top of filling.

Note: *Don't be alarmed by using a whole cup of cornstarch in your cookie dough. This ingredient helps create that signature melt-in-your-mouth casadinhos texture.*

JAM-FILLED KOLACZKI COOKIES

Makes about 22 cookies

Popular throughout central and Eastern Europe around the holidays, these jewel-toned cookies consist of a tender cream cheese dough folded over your favorite thick preserves or jam and dusted with confectioners' sugar. Our recipe is true to the original, save for one decadent detail: rather than dusting with confectioners' sugar, we drizzled our cookies with a creamy glaze for a festive touch.

½ cup (113 grams) unsalted butter, softened
4 ounces (115 grams) cream cheese, softened
1 cup (120 grams) confectioners' sugar, divided
2 teaspoons (2 grams) lemon zest (about 2 medium lemons)
¾ teaspoon (3 grams) vanilla extract, divided
1¼ cups (156 grams) all-purpose flour
½ teaspoon (1 gram) ground cardamom
½ teaspoon kosher salt, divided
⅓ cup (100 grams) thick jam or preserves
2 tablespoons (30 grams) heavy whipping cream

1. In the bowl of a stand mixer fitted with the paddle attachment, beat butter and cream cheese at medium speed until smooth and well combined, about 1 minute, stopping to scrape sides of bowl. Add ⅓ cup (40 grams) confectioners' sugar, lemon zest, and ½ teaspoon (2 grams) vanilla; beat at medium speed until well combined, about 1 minute.
2. In a medium bowl, whisk together flour, cardamom, and ¼ teaspoon salt. With mixer on low speed, gradually add flour mixture to butter mixture, beating just until combined. (Dough will be sticky.) Shape dough into a 5½-inch square, about ¾ inch thick, and wrap in plastic wrap. Refrigerate until firm, at least 2 hours or overnight.
3. Preheat oven to 350°F (180°C). Line baking sheets with parchment paper.
4. On a heavily floured surface, roll dough to ⅛-inch thickness, lightly flouring dough and work surface as needed. (If dough is refrigerated overnight, let stand at room temperature until softened, 10 to 15 minutes, if needed). Using a 2½-inch square cutter, cut dough, rerolling scraps as necessary. Using a large offset or flat metal spatula, place on prepared pans.
5. Spread about ¾ teaspoon (4.5 grams) jam on each square, leaving about a ¼-inch border. Fold 2 opposite corners of dough over jam, and press together lightly to seal, using a small amount of water to adhere. Repeat with remaining cookies.
6. Bake until lightly golden, about 12 minutes. Let cool on pans for 2 minutes; remove from pans, and let cool completely on wire racks.
7. In a small bowl, stir together cream, remaining ⅔ cup (80 grams) confectioners' sugar, remaining ¼ teaspoon salt, and remaining ¼ teaspoon (1 gram) vanilla until smooth; spoon into a small piping bag, and cut a ¼-inch opening in tip. Drizzle glaze onto cookies.

ROASTED BLOOD ORANGE HAZELNUT BISCOTTI

Makes about 48 biscotti

Recipe by Marian Cooper Cairns

These biscotti take the classic pairing of chocolate and citrus to the next level. Sliced-up fresh blood oranges are tossed in honey and roasted to golden perfection. Roasting the oranges gives the biscotti an even deeper citrus flavor.

2   blood oranges (262 grams), peeled
3   tablespoons (63 grams) honey
6   tablespoons (84 grams) unsalted butter, softened
¾   cup (150 grams) granulated sugar
2   large eggs (100 grams)
1   tablespoon (3 grams) blood orange zest
2   teaspoons (8 grams) vanilla extract
2¼ cups (281 grams) all-purpose flour
1½ teaspoons (7.5 grams) baking powder
1   teaspoon (3 grams) kosher salt
½   teaspoon (1 gram) ground cinnamon
¾   cup (106 grams) toasted hazelnuts, chopped
8   ounces (225 grams) dark chocolate, chopped
Garnish: roasted sliced blood oranges

1. Preheat oven to 400°F (200°C). Line a baking sheet with parchment paper.
2. Cut blood oranges into ⅛-inch-thick slices, discarding seeds. In a medium bowl, toss together oranges and honey. Arrange in a single layer on prepared pan.
3. Bake until edges are just beginning to brown, 20 to 25 minutes, rotating pan halfway through baking. Let cool completely on wire racks. (Set aside a few slices for garnish, if desired.) Chop into ½-inch pieces.
4. Reduce oven temperature to 325°F (170°C). Line a large baking sheet with parchment paper.
5. In the bowl of a stand mixer fitted with the paddle attachment, beat butter and sugar at medium speed until fluffy, about 2 minutes, stopping to scrape sides of bowl. Add eggs, one at a time, beating well after each addition. Beat in orange zest and vanilla.
6. In a medium bowl, whisk together flour, baking powder, salt, and cinnamon. With mixer on low speed, gradually add flour mixture to butter mixture, beating until combined. Stir in roasted oranges and hazelnuts. Using lightly floured hands, divide dough in half. Shape each half into a 12x4-inch log. Place logs on prepared pan.
7. Bake until firm to the touch, about 28 minutes. Let cool on pan for 15 minutes. Using a serrated knife, gently cut logs crosswise on a diagonal into ½-inch-thick slices. Place slices, cut side down, on baking sheet.
8. Bake for 9 minutes. Turn biscotti over, and bake until dry, about 12 minutes more. Let cool completely on wire racks.
9. Spray a wire rack with cooking spray. In a small microwave-safe bowl, heat three-fourths of chocolate on medium in 30-second intervals, stirring between each, until melted and smooth. Stir in remaining one-fourth of chocolate until melted. Dip one end of each biscotti in melted chocolate. Place on prepared rack, and let stand until set, about 1 hour. Garnish with oranges, if desired.

Photo by Matt Armendariz

ITALIAN RAINBOW COOKIES

Makes 32 (3x1-inch) bars

These tender cookies are made of brightly colored almond cakes layered with apricot preserves and topped off with a thin chocolate coating. Resembling the Italian flag, they were actually created in the United States by homesick Italian American bakers to commemorate their native land around the holidays.

5 large eggs (250 grams), separated and room temperature
1 cup (200 grams) granulated sugar, divided
8 ounces (225 grams) almond paste, chopped into ¼-inch pieces
1 cup (227 grams) cold unsalted butter, cubed
1 teaspoon (4 grams) vanilla extract
1 teaspoon (4 grams) almond extract
2 cups (250 grams) all-purpose flour
¾ teaspoon (2.25 grams) kosher salt
30 drops (3 grams) red food coloring
20 drops (2 grams) green food coloring
⅔ cup (228 grams) strained apricot preserves

6 ounces (175 grams) 70% cacao bittersweet chocolate baking bars, chopped
1 teaspoon (5 grams) coconut oil
Flaked sea salt, for sprinkling

1. Preheat oven to 350°F (180°C). Line 3 (13x9-inch) baking pans with parchment paper, letting excess extend over sides of pan.
2. In the bowl of a stand mixer fitted with the whisk attachment, beat egg whites at medium-high speed until foamy, about 1 minute. Gradually add ¼ cup (50 grams) sugar, beating until stiff peaks form. Gently transfer to a medium bowl.
3. Clean bowl of stand mixer, and switch to the paddle attachment. Add almond paste to bowl. With mixer on medium-low speed, gradually add remaining ¾ cup (150 grams) sugar, beating until combined. Add cold butter, 1 tablespoon (14 grams) at a time, beating until well combined after each addition. Increase mixer speed to medium, and beat until fluffy, 2 to 3 minutes, stopping to scrape sides of bowl. Add egg yolks, one at a time, beating well after each addition. Beat in extracts.

4. In a medium bowl, whisk together flour and kosher salt. With mixer on low speed, add flour mixture to butter mixture, beating just until combined. (Batter will be thick.) Stir one-fourth of egg white mixture into batter. Gently fold in remaining egg white mixture in three additions until well combined.
5. Divide batter among 3 bowls (about 1½ cups [356 grams] each). Add red food coloring to first bowl; using a silicone spatula, fold until well combined. Add green food coloring to second bowl; using a clean silicone spatula, fold until well combined. Leave third bowl uncolored. Spread each batter separately in prepared pans.
6. Bake until layers begin to pull away from sides of pans, 10 to 12 minutes. Let cool completely in pans on wire racks.
7. To assemble, transfer green layer to a cutting board; spread half of preserves on top in an even layer. Top with uncolored layer; spread remaining preserves on uncolored layer. Top with red layer, and cover red layer with plastic wrap. Place an empty 13x9-inch baking pan on top; weigh down with cans. Refrigerate for 4 hours or up to overnight.
8. In a small microwave-safe bowl, heat chocolate on high in 10-second intervals, stirring between each, until melted and smooth (1 to 1½ minutes total). Stir in coconut oil until well combined.
9. Using a small offset spatula, spread chocolate mixture onto red layer. (It's OK if some chocolate runs down sides.) Gently tap cutting board on counter to smooth chocolate into an even layer. Refrigerate for 15 minutes. Using a warm serrated knife, trim edges. Cut into bars, dipping knife in warm water and wiping clean between each cut. Sprinkle with sea salt.

GLAZED FRUITCAKE COOKIES

Makes about 36 cookies

Studded with candied fruit and spiked with rum, these tender cookies are the from-scratch version of editor-in-chief Brian Hart Hoffman's grandfather's cookies. We finished them off with a Rum Drizzle to make them extra merry. From our family to yours, these cakey cookies are sure to become a part of your own holiday traditions.

1¼   cups (300 grams) spiced rum
½   cup (100 grams) finely chopped candied red cherries
½   cup (100 grams) finely chopped candied green cherries
½   cup (87 grams) finely chopped dried pineapple
½   cup (83 grams) finely chopped crystallized ginger
½   cup (85 grams) finely chopped candied orange
1   cup (227 grams) unsalted butter, softened
1¾   cups (350 grams) granulated sugar, divided
¼   cup (55 grams) firmly packed light brown sugar
2   large eggs (100 grams), room temperature
1   teaspoon (4 grams) rum extract
3½   cups (438 grams) all-purpose flour
1   teaspoon (5 grams) baking soda
1   teaspoon (3 grams) kosher salt
1   teaspoon (2 grams) ground nutmeg
1   teaspoon (2 grams) ground cinnamon
1   teaspoon (2 grams) ground ginger
½   teaspoon (1 gram) ground cloves
1   cup (113 grams) chopped toasted pecans
Rum Drizzle (recipe follows)

1. In a medium microwave-safe bowl, combine rum, cherries, pineapple, crystallized ginger, and orange, and heat on high until hot, 2 to 3 minutes; let stand at room temperature for at least 1 hour, stirring occasionally. Drain fruit mixture. Set aside.
2. Preheat oven to 350°F (180°C). Line 4 baking sheets with parchment paper.
3. In the bowl of a stand mixer fitted with the paddle attachment, beat butter, 1¼ cups (250 grams) granulated sugar, and brown sugar at medium speed until fluffy, 2 to 3 minutes, stopping to scrape sides of bowl. Add eggs, one at a time, beating well after each addition. Beat in rum extract.
4. In a medium bowl, whisk together flour, baking soda, salt, nutmeg, cinnamon, ground ginger, and cloves. Add flour mixture to butter mixture all at once; beat at low speed just until combined, stopping to scrape sides of bowl. Fold in fruit mixture and pecans. (Dough will be sticky.)
5. On a rimmed plate, place remaining ½ cup (100 grams) granulated sugar. Using a 2-tablespoon spring-loaded scoop, scoop dough, and shape into balls (42 grams each).

Roll in sugar, and place 1½ to 2 inches apart on prepared pans. Using the palm of your hand, gently flatten balls to 1-inch thickness.
6. Bake until light golden brown and set around edges, about 12 minutes. Let cool on pans for 3 minutes. Remove from pans, and let cool completely on wire racks. Place Rum Drizzle in a piping bag, and cut a ¼-inch opening in tip. Drizzle onto cooled cookies.

RUM DRIZZLE
Makes about ½ cup

1   cup (120 grams) confectioners' sugar
1½   tablespoons (22.5 grams) heavy whipping cream
1   tablespoon (15 grams) spiced rum
2   teaspoons (10 grams) unsalted butter, melted
¼   teaspoon kosher salt

1. In a medium bowl, stir together all ingredients until smooth. Use immediately.

LEBKUCHEN

Makes about 32 cookies

Inspired by the centuries-old lebkuchen recipe of Nuremberg, Germany, these large, cakey cookies are packed with a blend of warm spices and spiked with rum.

½ cup (113 grams) unsalted butter, softened
1½ cups (330 grams) firmly packed dark brown sugar
½ cup (170 grams) honey
2 large eggs (100 grams)
1 tablespoon (3 grams) lemon zest
1 tablespoon (15 grams) spiced rum
4 cups (500 grams) all-purpose flour
½ cup (48 grams) almond flour
3 tablespoons (15 grams) cocoa powder
1 tablespoon (6 grams) ground cinnamon
2 teaspoons (4 grams) ground ginger
1 teaspoon (3 grams) kosher salt
1 teaspoon (5 grams) baking powder
½ teaspoon (1 gram) ground cloves
½ teaspoon (1 gram) ground allspice
¼ teaspoon (1.25 grams) baking soda
¼ teaspoon ground mace
⅛ teaspoon ground cardamom

1 cup (240 grams) whole milk
128 whole blanched almonds
Rum Sugar Glaze (recipe follows)

1. Preheat oven to 325°F (170°C). Line 4 baking sheets with parchment paper.
2. In the bowl of a stand mixer fitted with the paddle attachment, beat butter and brown sugar at medium speed until fluffy, 3 to 4 minutes, stopping to scrape sides of bowl. Add honey, beating until combined. Add eggs, one at a time, beating well after each addition. Beat in lemon zest and rum.
3. In a medium bowl, whisk together flours, cocoa, cinnamon, ginger, salt, baking powder, cloves, allspice, baking soda, mace, and cardamom. With mixer on low speed, gradually add flour mixture to butter mixture alternately with milk, beginning and ending with flour mixture, beating just until combined after each addition. Using a 3-tablespoon spring-loaded scoop, scoop dough, and place 2 inches apart on prepared pans. Press 4 almonds, touching, into center of each dough ball. (Almonds will move apart as cookies bake.)
4. Bake until a wooden pick inserted in

center comes out clean, 16 to 18 minutes. Let cool on pans for 5 minutes. Remove from pans, and place on wire racks. Using a pastry brush, brush tops of cookies with Rum Sugar Glaze. (If glaze gets too thick, heat in the microwave on high for 10 seconds, stir, and continue brushing cookies.) Let dry and cool completely on wire racks before serving.

RUM SUGAR GLAZE
Makes about ¾ cup

½ cup (100 grams) granulated sugar
¼ cup (60 grams) water
2 tablespoons (30 grams) spiced rum
1 cup (120 grams) confectioners' sugar

1. In a small saucepan, whisk together granulated sugar and ¼ cup (60 grams) water. Heat over medium heat, stirring occasionally, until bubbles form around edges of pan. (Do not boil.) Simmer for 3 minutes. Remove from heat, and whisk in rum. Sift confectioners' sugar over mixture, and whisk until smooth. (Clumps will form in your glaze if you do not sift.) Transfer to a microwave-safe bowl.

ICED EGGNOG SHORTBREAD COOKIE TREES

Makes 2 cookie trees (30 cookies)

Stars aren't just for topping the tree. Turns out, the shape is perfect for stacking to create your most eye-catching centerpiece yet. We let our favorite holiday drink inspire the flavor for the tender, delicately spiced shortbread. You'll love the little kick from the spiced rum.

1   cup (227 grams) unsalted butter, softened
2   cups (240 grams) confectioners' sugar
1   large egg (50 grams), room temperature
1½ teaspoons (7.5 grams) spiced rum
½   teaspoon (2 grams) vanilla extract
3¼ cups (406 grams) all-purpose flour
2   teaspoons (10 grams) baking powder
1   teaspoon (3 grams) kosher salt
1   teaspoon (2 grams) ground cinnamon
1   teaspoon (2 grams) ground nutmeg
Spiked Royal Icing (recipe follows)
2   tablespoons (30 grams) water
Garnish: assorted sprinkles

1. Preheat oven to 375°F (190°C). Line baking sheets with parchment paper.
2. In a large bowl, beat butter and confectioners' sugar with a mixer at medium speed until fluffy, 2 to 3 minutes, stopping to scrape sides of bowl. Add egg, rum, and vanilla, beating until combined.
3. In a medium bowl, whisk together flour, baking powder, salt, cinnamon, and nutmeg. With mixer on low speed, gradually add flour mixture to butter mixture, beating until a dough forms.
4. Divide dough in half; cover one half with plastic wrap. On a lightly floured surface, roll uncovered dough to ¼-inch thickness. Using 5 graduated-size, star-shaped cookie cutters*, cut out 3 cookies for each size, rerolling scraps as necessary. Repeat with remaining dough. (Each tree will have 15 cookies.) Working in batches and using a small offset spatula, place cookies, sorted by size, at least ½ inch apart on prepared pans.

5. Bake until edges are just beginning to brown, 7 to 10 minutes. Let cool on pans for 1 minute. Remove from pans, and let cool completely on wire racks.
6. Transfer about 1 cup (206 grams) Spiked Royal Icing to a small bowl; add 2 tablespoons (30 grams) water, stirring until icing is flood-consistency. (If icing is too thick, add more water, and if it's too thin, add more confectioners' sugar. For reference, flood-consistency icing has the appearance of runny honey.) Dip tops of cooled cookies into flood-consistency Spiked Royal Icing, letting excess drip off. Let stand until dry, at least 4 hours. (Don't rush this process—if you start to move your cookies or ice with new details, you'll risk smudging.)
7. Spoon 1 cup (206 grams) Spiked Royal Icing into a small piping bag fitted with a small round piping tip (Wilton No. 2) or cut a ⅛-inch opening. Pipe desired decorations onto dipped cookies. Refill piping bag as needed. Garnish with sprinkles, if desired. Let stand until dry, at least 1 hour.
8. For first set of 15 cookies, start with largest star and stack cookies in order of size, spiraling them so points do not line up; use Spiked Royal Icing as an adhesive, piping a little icing onto the center of each cookie before layering with the next. Stand final cookie upright as a tree topper, securing with Spiked Royal Icing. (To help top cookie stand up, gently grate bottom points until flat and dot with icing before securing to the top of the tree.) Repeat procedure with second set of 15 cookies.

*Our largest cookie was 5 inches, and our smallest cookie was 1 inch. We like Williams Sonoma Stainless-Steel Star Biscuit 5-Piece Cookie Cutter Set.

Note: *Any leftover flood-consistency icing can be stored in an airtight container in the freezer for up to 3 months.*

SPIKED ROYAL ICING
Makes 2½ cups

3¾ cups (450 grams) confectioners' sugar
2½ tablespoons (22.5 grams) meringue powder*
6   tablespoons (90 grams) warm water (80°F/26°C to 105°F/41°C)
¾   teaspoon (3.75 grams) spiced rum
¾   teaspoon (3 grams) vanilla extract

1. In the bowl of a stand mixer fitted with the paddle attachment, beat confectioners' sugar, meringue powder, 6 tablespoons (90 grams) warm water, rum, and vanilla at low speed until well combined. Increase mixer speed to medium; beat until mixture is the consistency of toothpaste, 3 to 5 minutes. (See Note). Use immediately. (See PRO TIP.)

*Find meringue powder at Michaels or your local craft store.

Note: *Use gel food coloring to tint your Spiked Royal Icing. Gel food coloring won't affect the icing's consistency like liquid food coloring does. For green icing, tint Spiked Royal Icing with 1 to 2 teaspoons Wilton Gel Icing Color in Kelly Green.*

PRO TIP
It's the nature of royal icing to harden and dry out. If you're not using it immediately, cover the top of your icing with a damp paper towel to keep it fluid and fresh, but for no more than 1 hour. You can also put the icing in an airtight container.

BARS

Studded with nuts, swirled with peanut butter, or topped
with meringue, these brownies, blondies, and bars offer
satisfaction by the slice

CEREAL DESSERT BARS

Makes 9 bars

We channeled Christina Tosi, the queen of baking with cereal milk, for these bars that feature a crushed cereal crust and silky pastry cream made from cereal milk. Toasting the cereal enhances its flavor and allows it to hold up longer when soaking in milk for the base of the pastry cream. This recipe features Cinnamon Toast Crunch, but we also got delicious results with Apple Jacks and Frosted Flakes. Use any cereal you like!

6½ cups (298 grams) cinnamon toasted cereal squares*
4 cups (960 grams) whole milk
¼ cup plus 3 tablespoons (99 grams) unsalted butter, melted
1¼ cups (250 grams) granulated sugar, divided
1 teaspoon (4 grams) vanilla extract
10 large egg yolks (186 grams)
½ cup plus 1 tablespoon (72 grams) cornstarch
½ teaspoon (1.5 grams) kosher salt
¼ cup (57 grams) unsalted butter, softened
Whipped cream, to serve

1. Preheat oven to 300°F (150°C). Line a rimmed baking sheet with parchment paper.
2. Spread cereal on prepared pan; bake until toasted, about 15 minutes, stirring halfway through baking. Let cool completely on pan.
3. Place 3 cups (123 grams) toasted cereal in a large bowl. Pour milk over cereal; let stand at room temperature for 30 minutes.
4. Line an 8-inch square baking pan with plastic wrap. Place 3 cups (123 grams) toasted cereal in a large resealable plastic bag, and crush until no large pieces remain. Place crushed cereal in a medium bowl. Add melted butter and ¼ cup (50 grams) sugar, and stir until combined. Press mixture into bottom of prepared pan. Refrigerate for at least 30 minutes.
5. Strain cereal milk through a fine-mesh sieve into a large saucepan, gently pressing on cereal to release any remaining milk. Discard soaked cereal. Whisk in ½ cup (100 grams) sugar and vanilla. Heat over medium-low heat until steaming.
6. In a large bowl, whisk together egg yolks, cornstarch, salt, and remaining ½ cup (100 grams) sugar. Gradually add warm cereal milk mixture to egg yolk mixture, whisking constantly. Return mixture to saucepan, and cook over medium-low heat for 5 minutes, whisking constantly; increase heat to medium, and cook until thickened to a pudding-like consistency and just beginning to boil, 3 to 5 minutes. Strain through a fine-mesh sieve into a large bowl. Stir in softened butter. Pour mixture onto prepared crust. Cover with a piece of plastic wrap, pressing wrap directly onto surface of pastry cream to prevent a skin from forming. Refrigerate overnight.
7. Using a warm, dry chef's knife, cut into squares. Top with whipped cream. Crush remaining ½ cup (21 grams) cereal, and sprinkle onto bars.

We used General Mills Cinnamon Toast Crunch.

KAHLÚA COFFEE BROWNIES

Makes 9 brownies

With dark-roast granules in every layer, these brownies are a coffeeholic's ultimate indulgence. A splash of Kahlúa in the fudgy brownie base highlights the rich caramel notes of our Biscoff-studded buttercream. A final coat of boozy ganache takes these brownies to the next level of caffeine-laced decadence.

¾   cup (150 grams) granulated sugar
¾   cup (72 grams) Dutch process cocoa powder
½   cup (110 grams) firmly packed light brown sugar
2½ tablespoons (15 grams) dark-roast instant coffee granules
1   teaspoon (3 grams) kosher salt
½   cup (113 grams) unsalted butter, melted and slightly cooled
1   teaspoon (5 grams) Kahlúa
½   teaspoon (2 grams) vanilla extract
2   large eggs (100 grams), room temperature
⅓   cup (42 grams) all-purpose flour
Coffee Biscoff Buttercream (recipe follows)
Kahlúa Coffee Ganache (recipe follows)
Garnish: crushed Biscoff cookies, flaked sea salt

1. Preheat oven to 325°F (170°C). Butter an 8-inch square baking pan; line pan with parchment paper, letting excess extend over sides of pan.
2. In a large bowl, whisk together granulated sugar, cocoa, brown sugar, coffee, and kosher salt. Gradually add melted butter, whisking just until combined. (Mixture will be thick.) Whisk in Kahlúa and vanilla. Add eggs, one at a time, whisking well after each addition. Fold in flour just until combined. Spread batter in prepared pan.
3. Bake until a wooden pick inserted in center comes out with just a few moist crumbs, 25 to 30 minutes. Let cool completely in pan.
4. Spread Coffee Biscoff Buttercream on cooled brownie. Freeze until set, about 15 minutes. Remove from freezer, and let stand at room temperature for 15 minutes.
5. Pour Kahlúa Coffee Ganache over Coffee Biscoff Buttercream; smooth and swirl into an even layer. Garnish with crushed cookies and sea salt, if desired. Freeze until layers are firm, 45 minutes to 1 hour.
6. Using excess parchment as handles, remove from pan. Trim about ⅛ inch off edges with a hot, dry knife for a cleaner look, if desired. Cut into squares.

COFFEE BISCOFF BUTTERCREAM
Makes 1¼ cups

1   tablespoon (6 grams) dark-roast instant coffee granules
1   teaspoon (5 grams) water
½   cup (113 grams) unsalted butter, softened
1⅓ cups (160 grams) confectioners' sugar
1¼ teaspoons (5 grams) vanilla extract
½   teaspoon (1.5 grams) kosher salt
¼   cup (25 grams) finely crushed Biscoff cookies (about 4 cookies)

1. In a small bowl, stir together coffee and 1 teaspoon (5 grams) water until granules are dissolved.
2. In the bowl of a stand mixer fitted with the paddle attachment, beat butter at medium speed until creamy, 30 seconds to 1 minute. Scrape sides of bowl. Add coffee mixture, confectioners' sugar, vanilla, and salt; beat until smooth. Fold in crushed cookies. Use immediately.

KAHLÚA COFFEE GANACHE
Makes about ½ cup

2   tablespoons (30 grams) heavy whipping cream
1   tablespoon (6 grams) dark-roast instant coffee granules
⅔   cup (113 grams) chopped 64% cacao semisweet chocolate baking bars*
1   tablespoon (14 grams) unsalted butter
1   tablespoon (15 grams) Kahlúa

1. In the top of a double boiler, stir together cream and coffee until granules are mostly dissolved. Add chocolate and butter. Cook over simmering water, stirring frequently, until mixture is melted and well combined, 3 to 5 minutes. Remove from heat; whisk in Kahlúa. Use immediately.

We used Guittard 64% Cacao Semisweet Chocolate Baking Bars.

SPICED CRANBERRY-WHITE CHOCOLATE BLONDIES

Makes 10 blondies

Don't be a square this holiday season. We spruced up the traditional blondie formula with some spices, white chocolate, and cranberries. Topped with a velvety White Chocolate Frosting, these bars will be on your to-bake list all year long.

1½   cups (330 grams) firmly packed light brown sugar
¾   cup (170 grams) unsalted butter, melted and cooled
2   large eggs (100 grams), room temperature
1   teaspoon (4 grams) vanilla extract
1½   cups (188 grams) all-purpose flour
1   teaspoon (5 grams) baking powder
1   teaspoon (3 grams) kosher salt
½   teaspoon (1 gram) ground nutmeg
½   teaspoon (1 gram) ground cinnamon
½   teaspoon (1 gram) ground ginger
¼   teaspoon ground cloves
5   ounces (150 grams) white chocolate baking bars, roughly chopped
½   cup (78 grams) roughly chopped dried sweetened cranberries
White Chocolate Frosting (recipe follows)
Garnish: assorted holiday sprinkles

1. Preheat oven to 350°F (180°C). Butter a 9-inch square baking pan; line pan with parchment paper, letting excess extend over sides of pan.
2. In a large bowl, whisk together brown sugar and melted butter until well combined; whisk in eggs and vanilla.
3. In a medium bowl, combine flour, baking powder, salt, nutmeg, cinnamon, ginger, and cloves. Fold flour mixture into sugar mixture just until combined. Fold in white chocolate and cranberries. Spoon batter into prepared pan; spread into an even layer using a small offset spatula.
4. Bake until golden brown and a wooden pick inserted in center comes out with just a few moist crumbs, 25 to 30 minutes. Let cool completely in pan on a wire rack.
5. Using excess parchment as handles, remove from pan. Cut in half, creating 2 rectangles. Cut each half into 5 triangles with 3-inch bases.
6. Place White Chocolate Frosting in a large piping bag fitted with an open star piping tip (Wilton 1M); pipe frosting onto cooled blondies, working from tip to base of each triangle. Garnish with sprinkles, if desired.

WHITE CHOCOLATE FROSTING
Makes 2½ cups

⅔   cup (150 grams) unsalted butter, softened
7.5 ounces (215 grams) white chocolate baking bars, melted and cooled for 5 minutes
1¼   cups (150 grams) confectioners' sugar
¼   teaspoon vanilla extract
⅛   teaspoon kosher salt
Green gel food coloring*

1. In the bowl of a stand mixer fitted with the paddle attachment, beat butter at medium speed until smooth, 30 seconds to 1 minute. Beat in melted white chocolate. With mixer on low speed, gradually add confectioners' sugar, beating until combined. Add vanilla and salt; increase mixer speed to medium, and beat until light and fluffy, about 2 minutes, stopping to scrape sides of bowl. Stir in enough food coloring until desired color is reached. Use immediately.

We used Wilton Gel Icing Color in Kelly Green and Juniper Green.

STRAWBERRY LILLET BROWNIES

Makes 12 brownies

These ultra-fudgy brownies channel the magic of a chocolate-dipped strawberry and a sparkling French aperitif. Packed with homemade Strawberry Jam and dressed up with fresh strawberry slices, the batter has a dash of Lillet Blanc, a sweet blend of Sauvignon Blanc and Sémillon grapes from Bordeaux. A final drizzle of Crème Fraîche Glaze brings a burst of tang and one final kiss of Lillet.

2	cups (340 grams) 63% cacao dark chocolate chips*
1½	cups (340 grams) unsalted butter, cubed
2¼	cups (450 grams) granulated sugar
1½	cups (330 grams) firmly packed light brown sugar
2¼	cups (281 grams) all-purpose flour
1⅛	cups (95 grams) unsweetened cocoa powder
1	tablespoon (9 grams) kosher salt
7	large eggs (350 grams)
4	tablespoons (60 grams) Lillet Blanc, divided
	Strawberry Jam (recipe follows)
1¼	cups (227 grams) sliced fresh strawberries
	Crème Fraîche Glaze (recipe follows)

1. Preheat oven to 350°F (180°C). Lightly spray a 13x9-inch baking pan with cooking spray. Line pan with parchment paper, letting excess extend over sides of pan.
2. In the top of a double boiler, combine chocolate chips and butter. Cook over simmering water, stirring occasionally, until chocolate is melted and mixture is smooth. Turn off heat, and whisk in sugars. Remove from heat, and let cool slightly.
3. In a medium bowl, whisk together flour, cocoa, and salt. Set aside.
4. In another medium bowl, lightly whisk eggs. Add half of beaten eggs to chocolate mixture, whisking until combined. Add remaining beaten eggs, and whisk until combined. Whisk in 1 tablespoon (15 grams) Lillet Blanc. Fold in flour mixture until combined.
5. Spread half of batter (about 3½ cups) in prepared pan.

Gently spread Strawberry Jam on top of batter, leaving a ½-inch border around edges. Spread remaining batter on top of jam, being careful not to mix with jam.
6. Bake until a wooden pick inserted in center comes out with a few moist crumbs, about 55 minutes. Let cool completely in pan. Brush remaining 3 tablespoons (45 grams) Lillet on top of brownie. Using excess parchment as handles, remove from pan. Arrange sliced strawberries on top of brownie. Top with Crème Fraîche Glaze. Cut into bars.

*We used Guittard Extra Dark Chocolate Baking Chips.

STRAWBERRY JAM
Makes about ¾ cup

8	ounces (225 grams) fresh strawberries, diced
¼	cup (50 grams) granulated sugar
1	tablespoon (8 grams) cornstarch
1	tablespoon (15 grams) Lillet Blanc
⅛	teaspoon rose water

1. In a medium saucepan, bring strawberries, sugar, and cornstarch to a boil over medium heat; cook for 15 minutes. Remove from heat.
2. Line a baking sheet with a nonstick baking mat. Transfer strawberry mixture to prepared pan. Freeze for 15 minutes. Remove from freezer; stir in Lillet and rose water.

CRÈME FRAÎCHE GLAZE
Makes ½ cup

1	cup (120 grams) confectioners' sugar
2	tablespoons (30 grams) Lillet Blanc
1	tablespoon (15 grams) crème fraîche

1. In a small bowl, whisk together all ingredients until smooth. Use immediately.

PARADISE BLONDIE BROWNIES

Makes 12 brownies

Why choose between brownies and blondies when you can have both? These blondie-topped brownies are packed with island flavor.

Brownie layer:
2½ cups (500 grams) granulated sugar
1½ cups (340 grams) unsalted butter, melted
½ cup (110 grams) firmly packed light brown sugar
5 large eggs (250 grams), room temperature
1½ teaspoons (6 grams) vanilla extract
1¼ cups (156 grams) all-purpose flour
1¼ cups (106 grams) Dutch process cocoa powder, sifted
2 teaspoons (4 grams) espresso powder
1 teaspoon (3 grams) kosher salt

Blondie layer:
2 cups (440 grams) firmly packed light brown sugar
⅔ cup (150 grams) unsalted butter, melted
2 large eggs (100 grams), room temperature
1¼ teaspoons (5 grams) coconut extract
1 teaspoon (4 grams) vanilla extract
2 cups (250 grams) all-purpose flour
1 teaspoon (5 grams) baking powder
¾ teaspoon (2.25 grams) kosher salt
½ cup (67 grams) salted macadamia nuts, coarsely chopped and divided
½ cup (28 grams) unsweetened coconut flakes*, lightly toasted and divided
4 ounces (113 grams) 64% cacao semisweet chocolate baking bars*, coarsely chopped and divided

1. Preheat oven to 350°F (180°C). Line a 13x9-inch baking pan with parchment paper, letting excess extend over sides of pan.
2. For brownie layer: In the bowl of a stand mixer fitted with the whisk attachment, beat granulated sugar, melted butter, and brown sugar at medium speed until well combined, 1 to 2 minutes, stopping to scrape sides of bowl. Add eggs, one at a time, beating well after each addition. Beat in vanilla.

3. In a medium bowl, whisk together flour, cocoa, espresso powder, and salt. With mixer on low speed, gradually add flour mixture to sugar mixture, beating just until combined. Spoon batter into prepared pan; using a small offset spatula, smooth into an even layer.
4. Bake for 25 minutes.
5. Meanwhile, for blondie layer: Clean bowl of stand mixer and whisk attachment; add brown sugar and melted butter, and beat at medium speed until well combined, 1 to 2 minutes, stopping to scrape sides of bowl. Add eggs, one at a time, beating well after each addition. Beat in extracts.
6. In a medium bowl, whisk together flour, baking powder, and salt. With mixer on low speed, gradually add flour mixture to sugar mixture, beating just until combined. Stir in ¼ cup (33.5 grams) macadamia nuts, ¼ cup (14 grams) coconut flakes, and 1 ounce (28 grams) chopped chocolate.
7. Remove brownie layer from oven. Drop heaping tablespoonfuls of blondie batter on top, spreading carefully with a small offset spatula. (Don't worry if some brownie layer gets swirled in or peeks through.)
8. Bake for 25 minutes. Sprinkle with remaining 3 ounces (85 grams) chopped chocolate and remaining ¼ cup (33.5 grams) macadamia nuts, gently pressing to adhere. Tent with foil, and bake until top is golden brown and a wooden pick inserted in center comes out with a few moist crumbs, 25 to 30 minutes more. Top with remaining ¼ cup (14 grams) coconut flakes. Let cool completely in pan on a wire rack. Using excess parchment as handles, remove from pan, and cut into bars. Store in an airtight container for up to 3 days.

We used Let's Do Organic Unsweetened Untoasted Coconut Flakes and Guittard 64% Cacao Semisweet Chocolate Baking Bars.

PRO TIP
Be sure to measure out all your ingredients beforehand to make these blondie brownies with ease.

BROWNED BUTTER BLONDIES

Makes 12 blondies

Flavored with brown sugar and vanilla, our traditional blondies get a nutty spin with browned butter in the batter. With luscious butterscotch notes, this essential recipe is both a stunner in its own right and the perfect canvas for sweet new creations.

1½ cups (340 grams) unsalted butter
3   cups (660 grams) firmly packed light brown sugar
2   teaspoons (10 grams) baking powder
1   teaspoon (3 grams) kosher salt
4   large eggs (200 grams), room temperature
1   tablespoon (18 grams) vanilla bean paste
1   tablespoon (13 grams) vanilla extract
3   cups (375 grams) all-purpose flour

1. Preheat oven to 350°F (180°C). Line a 13x9-inch baking pan with parchment paper, letting excess extend over sides of pan.
2. In a medium heavy-bottomed saucepan, melt butter over medium heat. Cook, stirring occasionally, until butter turns a golden-brown color and has a nutty aroma, 5 to 10 minutes. Pour into a small bowl, and let stand at room temperature for 5 minutes.
3. In a large bowl, whisk together brown sugar, baking powder, and salt. Gradually add browned butter, whisking just until combined. Add eggs, one at a time, whisking well after each addition. Stir in vanilla bean paste and vanilla extract. Fold in flour just until combined. Spread batter in prepared pan.
4. Bake until a wooden pick inserted in center comes out with just a few moist crumbs, 35 to 40 minutes. Let cool completely in pan on a wire rack. Using excess parchment as handles, remove from pan, and cut into bars. Store in an airtight container for up to 3 days.

PRO TIP
Simplify the baking process by making the browned butter ahead and refrigerating it in an airtight container for up to 5 days. When you're ready to bake, microwave in 10-second intervals to reheat until melted.

BOURBON PECAN BLONDIES

Makes 12 blondies

The classic Southern pairing of bourbon and pecans stars in this blondie batch. The batter is as versatile as they come, so you can sub out the bourbon and pecan for any other type of liquor or nuts.

2   cups (440 grams) firmly packed light brown sugar
1   teaspoon (5 grams) baking powder
½   teaspoon (1.5 grams) kosher salt
1   cup (227 grams) unsalted butter*, melted and cooled slightly
¼   cup (60 grams) bourbon
1   teaspoon (4 grams) vanilla extract
2   large eggs (100 grams), room temperature
2   cups (250 grams) all-purpose flour
1½   cups (170 grams) chopped pecans, divided

1. Preheat oven to 350°F (180°C). Line a 13x9-inch baking pan with parchment paper, letting excess extend over sides of pan.

2. In a large bowl, whisk together brown sugar, baking powder, and salt. Gradually add melted butter, stirring just until combined. Stir in bourbon and vanilla. Add eggs, one at a time, whisking well after each addition. Stir in flour and 1 cup (113 grams) pecans just until combined. Spread batter in prepared pan. Sprinkle with remaining ½ cup (57 grams) pecans.

3. Bake until a wooden pick inserted in center comes out with just a few moist crumbs, 25 to 30 minutes. Let cool completely in pan on wire rack. Using excess parchment as handles, remove from pan, and cut into bars. Store in an airtight container for up to 3 days.

We used Président® Butter.

SPRINKLE BLONDIES

Makes 12 blondies

With a generous dose of rainbow sprinkles added to the batter, this twist on our Browned Butter Blondies is the ultimate party-ready treat.

1½   cups (340 grams) unsalted butter
3   cups (660 grams) firmly packed light brown sugar
2   teaspoons (10 grams) baking powder
1   teaspoon (3 grams) kosher salt
4   large eggs (200 grams), room temperature
1   tablespoon (18 grams) vanilla bean paste
1   tablespoon (13 grams) vanilla extract
3   cups (375 grams) all-purpose flour
¼   cup (43 grams) plus 2 tablespoons (21 grams) rainbow sprinkles, divided

1. Preheat oven to 350°F (180°C). Line a 13x9-inch baking pan with parchment paper, letting excess extend over sides of pan.
2. In a medium heavy-bottomed saucepan, melt butter over medium heat. Cook, stirring occasionally, until butter turns a golden-brown color and has a nutty aroma, 5 to 10 minutes. Pour into a small bowl, and let stand at room temperature for 5 minutes.
3. In a large bowl, whisk together brown sugar, baking powder, and salt. Gradually add browned butter, whisking just until combined. Add eggs, one at a time, whisking well after each addition. Stir in vanilla bean paste and vanilla extract. Fold in flour just until combined. Gently fold in ¼ cup (43 grams) sprinkles until combined. Spread batter in prepared pan. Sprinkle with remaining 2 tablespoons (21 grams) sprinkles.
4. Bake for 30 minutes. Cover with foil, and bake until a wooden pick inserted in center comes out with just a few moist crumbs, 10 to 15 minutes more. Let cool completely in pan on wire rack. Using excess parchment as handles, remove from pan, and cut into bars. Store in an airtight container for up to 3 days.

*We used Betty Crocker Rainbow Sprinkles (10.5-ounce container) because the colors don't bleed during baking.

LAMINGTON BLONDIES

Makes 12 blondies

Inspired by one of our favorite Australian desserts, we piled shredded coconut and melted chocolate chunks on top of our Browned Butter Blondies. A sticky sweetened condensed milk topper pushes these blondies right over the edge into indulgent gooey bliss.

1½	cups (340 grams) unsalted butter
3	cups (660 grams) firmly packed light brown sugar
2	teaspoons (10 grams) baking powder
1	teaspoon (3 grams) kosher salt
4	large eggs (200 grams), room temperature
1	tablespoon (18 grams) vanilla bean paste
1	tablespoon (13 grams) vanilla extract
3	cups (375 grams) all-purpose flour
1	cup (60 grams) sweetened flaked coconut
1	cup (170 grams) roughly chopped 60% cacao bittersweet chocolate
1	(14-ounce) can (397 grams) sweetened condensed milk

1. Preheat oven to 350°F (180°C). Line a 13x9-inch baking pan with parchment paper, letting excess extend over sides of pan.
2. In a medium heavy-bottomed saucepan, melt butter over medium heat. Cook, stirring occasionally, until butter turns a golden-brown color and has a nutty aroma, 5 to 10 minutes.

Pour into a small bowl, and let stand at room temperature for 5 minutes.
3. In a large bowl, whisk together brown sugar, baking powder, and salt. Gradually add browned butter, whisking just until combined. Add eggs, one at a time, whisking well after each addition. Stir in vanilla bean paste and vanilla extract. Fold in flour just until combined. Spread batter in prepared pan.
4. Bake for 30 minutes. (Make sure the base is fully baked and set before adding toppings. Otherwise, toppings will all sink.) Remove from oven, and sprinkle with coconut and chocolate. Pour sweetened condensed milk over coconut-chocolate topping. Bake until topping is set and a wooden pick inserted in center comes out clean, 15 to 20 minutes more. Let set and cool completely in pan on a wire rack. Using excess parchment as handles, remove from pan, and cut into bars. Store in an airtight container for up to 3 days.

PRO TIP
Simplify the baking process by making the browned butter ahead and refrigerating it in an airtight container for up to 5 days. When you're ready to bake, microwave in 10-second intervals to reheat until melted.

BANOFFEE BLONDIES

Makes 12 blondies

Blondies, meet British banoffee pie, complete with caramelized bananas, caramel drizzle, and a splash of rum in the batter.

5	bananas (750 grams), halved lengthwise
10	teaspoons (40 grams) granulated sugar
2	cups (440 grams) firmly packed light brown sugar
1	teaspoon (5 grams) baking powder
½	teaspoon (1.5 grams) kosher salt
1	cup (227 grams) unsalted butter*, melted and cooled slightly
¼	cup (60 grams) black spiced rum*
1	teaspoon (4 grams) vanilla extract
2	large eggs (100 grams), room temperature
2	cups (250 grams) all-purpose flour

Caramel (recipe follows)

1. Sprinkle cut side of each banana half with 1 teaspoon (4 grams) granulated sugar.
2. In a medium skillet, cook 2 banana slices, cut side down, over medium heat until caramelized, about 1 minute. Repeat with remaining banana slices. Set aside.
3. Preheat oven to 350°F (180°C). Line a 13x9-inch baking pan with parchment paper, letting excess extend over sides of pan.
4. In a large bowl, whisk together brown sugar, baking powder, and salt. Gradually add melted butter, stirring just until combined. Stir in rum and vanilla. Add eggs, one at a time, whisking well after each addition. Stir in flour just until

combined. Spread batter in prepared pan; place caramelized bananas, cut side up, on top of batter.
5. Bake until a wooden pick inserted in center comes out with just a few moist crumbs, about 40 minutes. Let cool completely in pan on a wire rack. Using excess parchment as handles, remove from pan, and cut into bars. Drizzle with Caramel. Store in an airtight container for up to 3 days.

We used Président® Butter and Kraken Black Spiced Rum. (Golden rum will work, too.)

CARAMEL
Makes ¾ cup

¾	cup (150 grams) granulated sugar
2	tablespoons (30 grams) water
½	tablespoon (10 grams) light corn syrup
¼	cup (60 grams) warm heavy whipping cream
2	tablespoons (28 grams) unsalted butter, softened

1. In a large saucepan, stir together sugar, 2 tablespoons (30 grams) water, and corn syrup. Cook over medium heat until mixture is amber colored, about 10 minutes. (Do not stir.) Remove from heat; slowly stir in warm cream. (Mixture will bubble and steam.) Stir in butter until melted. Transfer to a medium heatproof bowl, and let cool, stirring frequently, until slightly warm. If mixture becomes too cool, microwave in 10-second intervals to reach desired consistency.

CHOCOLATE PEANUT BUTTER BLONDIES

Makes 12 blondies

With peanut butter folded right into the batter and tempting pools of melted dark chocolate throughout, these blondies are a crowd-pleasing classic you'll turn to again and again.

2   cups (440 grams) firmly packed light brown sugar
1   cup (227 grams) unsalted butter, melted and cooled
½   cup (128 grams) creamy peanut butter*, melted
1   teaspoon (5 grams) baking powder
½   teaspoon (1.5 grams) kosher salt
2   large eggs (100 grams), room temperature
2   teaspoons (8 grams) vanilla extract
2½ cups (313 grams) all-purpose flour
1   cup (170 grams) 63% cacao dark chocolate chips*
½   cup (85 grams) lightly chopped 70% cacao dark chocolate*, divided
Garnish: sea salt

1. Preheat oven to 350°F (180°C). Line a 13x9-inch baking pan with parchment paper, letting excess extend over sides of pan.
2. In a large bowl, whisk together brown sugar, melted butter, melted peanut butter, baking powder, and kosher salt until combined. Add eggs, one at a time, whisking well after each addition. Whisk in vanilla. Stir in flour and chocolate chips just until combined. Spread batter into prepared pan. Sprinkle with ¼ cup (42.5 grams) chopped chocolate.
3. Bake for 25 to 30 minutes. Sprinkle with remaining ¼ cup (42.5 grams) chopped chocolate, and bake for 2 minutes more. Let cool completely in pan on a wire rack. Sprinkle with sea salt, if desired. Using excess parchment as handles, remove from pan, and cut into bars. Store in an airtight container for up to 3 days.

*We used Jif Creamy Peanut Butter, but you can also use crunchy peanut butter for additional texture. We used Guittard Extra Dark Chocolate Baking Chips for folding into the batter and Valrhona Guanaja 70% Dark Chocolate for the chopped pieces to place on top of the blondies.

PRO TIP
The secret behind those glossy pools of chocolate on top? High-quality chocolate. When pulling the pan from the oven after the final 2 minutes of baking, slightly tilt pan so chocolate spreads.

MAPLE PEACH BLONDIES

Makes 12 blondies

Make the most of stone fruit with our blondie ode to one of our favorite summer cocktails, the Bourbon Peach Smash. We packed these with peach preserves and diced peach and drizzled them with a bourbon glaze.

2   cups (440 grams) firmly packed light brown sugar
1   teaspoon (5 grams) baking powder
½   teaspoon (1.5 grams) kosher salt
1   cup (227 grams) unsalted butter*, melted and cooled slightly
¼   cup (60 grams) plus 1 tablespoon (15 grams) bourbon, divided
1   teaspoon (4 grams) vanilla extract
2   large eggs (100 grams), room temperature

2   cups (250 grams) all-purpose flour
½   cup (160 grams) peach preserves
1   cup (153 grams) diced fresh peach, divided (about 1 medium peach)
1½   cups (180 grams) confectioners' sugar
¼   cup (85 grams) maple syrup

1. Preheat oven to 350°F (180°C). Line a 13x9-inch baking pan with parchment paper, letting excess extend over sides of pan.
2. In a large bowl, whisk together brown sugar, baking powder, and salt. Gradually add melted butter, stirring just until combined. Stir in ¼ cup (60 grams) bourbon and vanilla. Add eggs, one at a time, whisking well after each addition. Stir in flour just until combined. Fold in preserves. Fold in ¾ cup (115 grams) diced peach. Spread

batter in prepared pan. Sprinkle with remaining ¼ cup (38 grams) diced peach.
3. Bake until a wooden pick inserted in center comes out with just a few moist crumbs, 35 to 40 minutes, covering with foil after 30 minutes of baking to prevent excess browning. Let cool completely in pan on a wire rack.
4. In a medium bowl, stir together confectioners' sugar, maple syrup, and remaining 1 tablespoon (15 grams) bourbon until smooth.
5. Using excess parchment as handles, remove blondie from pan, and drizzle with glaze. Cut into bars. Store in an airtight container for up to 3 days.

We used Président® Butter.

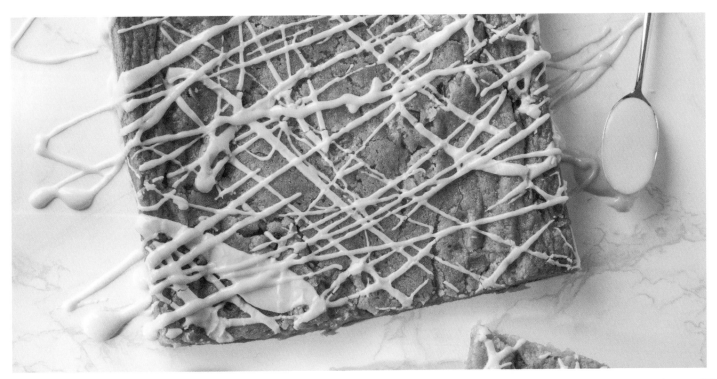

MACADAMIA-COOKIE BUTTER BLONDIES

Makes 12 blondies

Biscoff Cookie Butter and broken Biscoff Cookies bring warm spice while chopped macadamia nuts boost the crunch factor.

2 cups (440 grams) firmly packed light brown sugar
1 cup (227 grams) unsalted butter, melted and cooled
½ cup (128 grams) creamy cookie butter*, melted
1 teaspoon (5 grams) baking powder
½ teaspoon (1.5 grams) kosher salt
2 large eggs (100 grams), room temperature
2 teaspoons (8 grams) vanilla extract
2½ cups (313 grams) all-purpose flour
¾ cup (85 grams) roughly chopped macadamia nuts, divided
¾ cup (57 grams) speculoos cookie pieces*

1. Preheat oven to 350°F (180°C). Line a 13x9-inch baking pan with parchment paper, letting excess extend over sides of pan.
2. In a large bowl, whisk together brown sugar, melted butter, melted cookie butter, baking powder, and salt until combined. Add eggs, one at a time, whisking well after each addition. Whisk in vanilla. Stir in flour just until combined. Fold in ½ cup (57 grams) macadamia nuts. Spread batter in prepared pan. Sprinkle with cookie pieces and remaining ¼ cup (28 grams) macadamia nuts.
3. Bake for 30 minutes. Let cool completely in pan on a wire rack. Using excess parchment as handles, remove from pan, and cut into bars. Store in an airtight container for up to 3 days.

We used Biscoff Creamy Cookie Butter and Biscoff Cookies, but you can use any kind of cookie butter and cookies.

CLASSIC FUDGE BROWNIES

Makes 9 brownies

Recipe by Paul A. Young

Using chocolate rather than cocoa powder in these brownies gives them a seriously intense hit of indulgence. This is the base recipe for all of Paul A. Young's brownies, so go wild and add anything to the batter you fancy and then top with more of your favorite ingredients to customize further.

1½   cups plus 2 teaspoons (350 grams) unrefined light muscovado sugar
14   tablespoons (200 grams) unsalted butter
4   tablespoons plus 2 teaspoons (100 grams) golden syrup*
1¼   cups (330 grams) 70% cacao dark chocolate, chopped
6   medium free-range eggs (282 grams)
⅔   cup plus 2 tablespoons (100 grams) all-purpose flour

1. Preheat oven to 325°F (170°C). Line an 8-inch square baking pan with parchment paper, letting excess extend over sides of pan.
2. In a medium saucepan, heat muscovado sugar, butter, and golden syrup over medium heat until smooth and bubbly, 5 to 6 minutes. Remove from heat; add chocolate, stirring until melted.
3. Whisk eggs, and strain through a fine-mesh sieve over batter. Stir until fully well combined. Add flour, stirring until well combined. Pour batter into prepared pan. Tap pan on counter to level batter.
4. Bake until set but still moist in center, about 45 minutes. (It will look slightly underdone, but the residual heat will set the chocolate and make the brownie very moist.) Let cool to room temperature. Refrigerate for at least 6 hours or overnight.
5. Using a large, sharp knife dipped in hot water, cut into bars, cleaning knife between each cut. Serve warm or at room temperature. Store in an airtight container in refrigerator for up to 2 weeks or at room temperature for up to 1 week, or freeze for up to 3 months.

Corn syrup may be substituted.

> **BOURBON AND ORANGE BROWNIE VARIATION:**
> For a super fast and easy way to jazz up your brownie, zest **half an orange**, and stir in **¼ cup minus 1 teaspoon (50 grams) light muscovado sugar** and **1 tablespoon (15 grams) bourbon**. Drizzle and drop mixture onto batter, and swirl in before baking.

SOURDOUGH DISCARD BROWNIES

Makes about 12 brownies

This recipe will make you think twice about tossing the discard from your sourdough starter. Sourdough discard gives these brownies a tang and a luscious, velvety texture without being too dense. The melty pools of dark chocolate and the nutty crunch from the pecans don't hurt either. You may never go back to discard-less brownies again.

1 cup (170 grams) 63% cacao extra-dark chocolate chips
1 cup (227 grams) unsalted butter
1½ cups (300 grams) granulated sugar
1 cup (220 grams) firmly packed light brown sugar
1 cup (125 grams) all-purpose flour
¾ cup (64 grams) unsweetened cocoa powder
2 teaspoons (6 grams) kosher salt
5 large eggs (250 grams)
1 tablespoon (13 grams) vanilla extract
1 cup (251 grams) sourdough starter discard, room temperature
1¼ cups (213 grams) chopped 66% cacao dark chocolate, divided
1¼ cups (141 grams) chopped toasted pecans*, divided

1. Preheat oven to 350°F (180°C). Line a 13x9-inch baking pan with parchment paper, letting excess extend over sides of pan.
2. In the top of a double boiler, combine chocolate chips and butter. Cook over simmering water, stirring occasionally, until chocolate is melted and mixture is smooth. Turn off heat, and whisk in sugars. Remove from heat, and let cool for 15 minutes.
3. In a medium bowl, whisk together flour, cocoa, and salt. Set aside.
4. Add eggs to chocolate chip mixture, whisking until combined. Whisk in vanilla. Fold flour mixture into chocolate chip mixture until only a few bits of flour remain. Fold in sourdough discard until well combined. Fold in 1 cup (170 grams) chopped chocolate and 1 cup (113 grams) pecans. Spread batter into prepared pan.
5. Bake until a wooden pick inserted in center comes out with a few crumbs, about 38 minutes. Remove from oven, and sprinkle with remaining ¼ cup (43 grams) chopped chocolate and remaining ¼ cup (28 grams) pecans. Bake until chocolate is melted, about 2 minutes more. Let cool completely in pan. Using excess parchment as handles, remove from pan, and cut into bars.

We used Sunnyland Farms Georgia Pecan Halves.

PB&J BLONDIES

Makes 12 blondies

In a throwback to your favorite childhood lunch box item, we added luscious swirls of grape jelly and extra peanut butter to the top of our peanut butter-rich batter. Swap out the grape jelly for your favorite flavor.

2   cups (440 grams) firmly packed light brown sugar
1   cup (227 grams) unsalted butter, melted and cooled
½   cup (128 grams) creamy peanut butter*, melted
1   teaspoon (5 grams) baking powder
½   teaspoon (1.5 grams) kosher salt
2   large eggs (100 grams), room temperature
2   teaspoons (8 grams) vanilla extract
2½   cups (313 grams) all-purpose flour
½   cup (128 grams) creamy peanut butter
½   cup (160 grams) grape jelly

1. Preheat oven to 350°F (180°C). Line a 13x9-inch baking pan with parchment paper, letting excess extend over sides of pan.
2. In a large bowl, whisk together brown sugar, melted butter, melted peanut butter, baking powder, and salt until combined. Add eggs, one at a time, whisking well after each addition. Whisk in vanilla. Stir in flour just until combined. Spread batter in prepared pan.
3. In a small microwave-safe bowl, heat peanut butter in 5-second intervals, stirring between each, until warm. In another small microwave-safe bowl, heat jelly in 5-second intervals, stirring between each, until warm. (Do not heat peanut butter and jelly for more than 15 seconds. You do not want them to be liquid.) Drop warm peanut butter and jelly in alternating tablespoonfuls across top of batter, making sure to reach edges. Using the tip of a butter knife or a small offset spatula, swirl peanut butter and jelly together to create a marbled effect. (It is fine to pull through top of batter.)
4. Bake for 35 to 40 minutes. Let cool completely in pan on a wire rack. Using excess parchment as handles, remove from pan, and cut into bars. Store in an airtight container for up to 3 days.

*We used Jif Creamy Peanut Butter, but you can also use crunchy peanut butter for additional texture.

NO-BAKE PEPPERMINT SLICE

Makes about 16 bars

Recipe by Erin Clarkson

This recipe is a nod to Erin Clarkson's favorite cookie from New Zealand, the mint slice. This no-bake version has a cocoa-graham cracker crust, a minty filling, and a smooth chocolate top. A little goes a long way with this, so it is perfect for making ahead to have on hand in the refrigerator for whenever you need a little treat!

1 (14.4-ounce) box (408 grams) graham crackers
½ cup (43 grams) Dutch process cocoa powder
¼ cup (50 grams) granulated sugar
½ teaspoon (1.5 grams) kosher salt
1 cup plus 3 tablespoons (99 grams) unsweetened desiccated coconut*
1 cup plus 2 tablespoons (255 grams) unsalted butter, melted and slightly cooled
Peppermint Filling (recipe follows)
Chocolate Topping (recipe follows)

1. Butter and flour a 9-inch square baking pan. Line pan with parchment paper, letting excess extend over sides of pan.
2. In the work bowl of a food processor, pulse together graham crackers, cocoa, sugar, and salt until mixture resembles fine crumbs. Transfer mixture to a medium bowl; add coconut, stirring until combined. Add melted butter, and stir with a rubber spatula until combined. (Mixture should resemble wet sand.) Using a flat-bottomed glass or measuring cup, press mixture into bottom of prepared pan. Freeze for 20 minutes.
3. Top crust with Peppermint Filling. Use a damp offset spatula to help smooth Peppermint Filling into an even layer. Slam pan on counter to level. Refrigerate until set, about 30 minutes.
4. Top with Chocolate Topping. Slam pan on counter several times to smooth and release any air bubbles. Refrigerate until topping is set. Using a clean, sharp knife, cut into bars, wiping blade between each cut. Refrigerate in an airtight container for up to 3 days.

*Desiccated coconut is unsweetened, very finely ground coconut with most of the moisture removed. If your local grocery store doesn't carry it, check specialty food stores or online.

PEPPERMINT FILLING
Makes about 2 cups

4¾ cups (570 grams) confectioners' sugar, sifted
2 tablespoons (28 grams) unsalted butter, softened
1¼ teaspoons plus ⅛ teaspoon (5 grams) peppermint extract
½ teaspoon (3 grams) vanilla bean paste
3 to 4 tablespoons (45 to 60 grams) boiling water, divided

1. In a medium bowl, place confectioners' sugar, butter, peppermint extract, and vanilla bean paste. Add 3 tablespoons (45 grams) boiling water, and stir until combined. (It should resemble a thick paste that smooths out within about 20 seconds when bowl is left to stand.) Add remaining 1 tablespoon (15 grams) boiling water, 1 teaspoon (5 grams) at a time, if needed, to reach desired consistency. Use immediately.

CHOCOLATE TOPPING
Makes about 1 cup

9 ounces (250 grams) 70% cacao dark chocolate, chopped
3 tablespoons (42 grams) vegetable or canola oil

1. In the top of a double boiler, combine chocolate and oil. Cook over simmering water, stirring frequently, until chocolate is melted and mixture is smooth. (Alternatively, combine chocolate and butter in a medium microwave-safe bowl. Heat on high in 30-second intervals, stirring between each, until chocolate is melted and mixture is smooth.) Use immediately.

Photo by Erin Clarkson

SWEET POTATO BARS

Makes about 10 bars

With a vanilla bean Pâte Sablée crust and a custardy sweet potato filling, these bars take sweet potato pie to a whole new level. A dash of Chinese five-spice powder in the filling lends a punch of fall flavor to every bite.

Pâte Sablée (recipe follows)
2   cups (488 grams) warm mashed baked sweet potato (see Note)
1   cup (240 grams) evaporated milk
¾   cup (165 grams) firmly packed light brown sugar
3   large eggs (150 grams)
3   tablespoons (42 grams) unsalted butter, melted
2   tablespoons (16 grams) all-purpose flour
1   teaspoon (3 grams) kosher salt
1   teaspoon (2 grams) Chinese five-spice powder
1   teaspoon (4 grams) vanilla extract*
½   teaspoon (1 gram) ground cinnamon
¼   teaspoon ground nutmeg

1. Preheat oven to 350°F (180°C). Line a 9-inch square baking pan with parchment paper, letting excess extend over sides of pan; lightly spray parchment with cooking spray.
2. Press Pâte Sablée into bottom of prepared pan. Freeze until firm, about 30 minutes. Using a fork, dock dough about every 1 inch.
3. Bake until light golden brown and a wooden pick inserted in center comes out clean, 20 to 25 minutes. Let cool on a wire rack for 10 minutes.
4. In a large bowl, whisk together warm mashed sweet potato and all remaining ingredients until well combined. Pour filling onto warm crust.

5. Bake until filling is set and an instant-read thermometer inserted in center registers 175°F (79°C), 45 to 50 minutes. Let cool completely in pan. Using excess parchment as handles, remove from pan. Trim edges, and cut into bars as desired using a hot, dry knife.

*We used Heilala.

Note: *Make sure mashed baked sweet potato is completely smooth without any chunks.*

PÂTE SABLÉE
Makes 1 (9-inch) crust

½   cup (113 grams) unsalted butter, softened
¾   cup (150 grams) granulated sugar
1   large egg (50 grams)
2   large egg yolks (37 grams)
2   teaspoons (12 grams) vanilla bean paste
2   cups (250 grams) all-purpose flour
1½ teaspoons (7.5 grams) baking powder
½   teaspoon (1.5 grams) kosher salt

1. In the bowl of a stand mixer fitted with the paddle attachment, beat butter and sugar at medium speed until fluffy, 2 to 3 minutes, stopping to scrape sides of bowl. Add egg and egg yolks, beating until combined. Beat in vanilla bean paste.
2. In a medium bowl, whisk together flour, baking powder, and salt. With mixer on low speed, gradually add flour mixture to butter mixture, beating until combined. Use immediately.

SALTED HAZELNUT CHOCOLATE MAPLE RUM BARS

Makes 16 bars

Recipe by Becky Sue Wilberding

Think pecan pie filling but with chocolate, hazelnuts, and significantly less work. These nutty bars are layered with a brown sugar shortbread cookie base and topped with smooth dark chocolate and a decadent maple, rum, and hazelnut filling. To finish, the bars are liberally sprinkled with crunchy sea salt flakes to perfectly balance out the indulgent flavors.

2	cups (266 grams) raw hazelnuts
¾	cup (170 grams) unsalted butter, softened
¾	cup (165 grams) firmly packed light brown sugar
1	teaspoon (4 grams) vanilla extract
1¾	cups (219 grams) all-purpose flour
1	teaspoon (3 grams) fine sea salt
1¼	cups (213 grams) dark chocolate chips
	Maple Rum Filling (recipe follows)
2	teaspoons (6 grams) flaked sea salt

1. Preheat oven to 350°F (180°C).
2. Spread hazelnuts in an even layer on a baking sheet.
3. Bake until hazelnuts give off a nutty aroma and have browned slightly, 10 to 15 minutes. (The skins should start to blister.) Let cool slightly. Wrap nuts in a clean kitchen towel, and rub to remove loose skins. (Don't worry about skins that don't come off.) Let cool completely. Coarsely chop half of hazelnuts; leave remaining hazelnuts whole. Leave oven on.
4. Line a 9-inch square baking pan with parchment paper.
5. In the bowl of a stand mixer fitted with the paddle attachment, beat butter and brown sugar at medium-high speed until light and creamy, 5 to 7 minutes, stopping to scrape sides of bowl. Beat in vanilla.
6. In a medium bowl, whisk together flour and fine salt. With mixer on low speed, gradually add flour mixture to butter mixture, beating just until combined. Lightly press dough into prepared pan.
7. Bake until edges are golden brown and top is firm to the touch, 22 to 24 minutes. Let cool completely. Leave oven on.
8. Layer chocolate chips on top of prepared crust. Top with chopped and whole hazelnuts. Carefully pour Maple Rum Filling over top.
9. Bake until filling is set, 18 to 20 minutes. Let set for at least 1 to 2 hours before cutting. Sprinkle with flaked salt.

MAPLE RUM FILLING
Makes about 1½ cups

½	cup (110 grams) firmly packed light brown sugar
½	cup (170 grams) maple syrup
2	tablespoons (30 grams) spiced rum
1	tablespoon (14 grams) unsalted butter
1	teaspoon (4 grams) vanilla extract
2	large eggs (100 grams), room temperature

1. In a medium heavy-bottomed saucepan, cook brown sugar and maple syrup over medium heat, whisking occasionally, until sugar is dissolved. Remove from heat; add rum, butter, and vanilla. Let cool; add eggs, whisking until smooth. (Do not add the eggs while the syrup is hot, or they will begin to cook.) Use immediately.

> **PRO TIP**
> The spiced rum and sea salt really cut down the sweetness of these bars. Feel free to sub in bourbon or a coffee liqueur instead if rum isn't your jam.

Photo by Becky Sue Wilberding

PEPPERMINT CHEESECAKE SWIRL BROWNIES

Makes 16 brownies

Recipe by Mike Johnson

These rich, fudgy brownies with two layers of peppermint cheesecake filling swirled throughout are the perfect treat for the holidays!

8   ounces (225 grams) cream cheese, softened
1¼   cups (250 grams) granulated sugar, divided
4   large eggs (200 grams), room temperature and divided
½   teaspoon (2 grams) peppermint extract
20   drops red gel food coloring (optional)
4   ounces (115 grams) 70% cacao dark chocolate, chopped
¾   cup (170 grams) unsalted butter
½   cup (110 grams) firmly packed dark brown sugar
2   teaspoons (8 grams) vanilla extract
1   teaspoon (3 grams) kosher salt
½   cup (63 grams) all-purpose flour
¼   cup (21 grams) unsweetened cocoa powder

1. In the bowl of a stand mixer fitted with the paddle attachment, beat cream cheese at medium speed until smooth and creamy, about 2 minutes. Add ¼ cup (50 grams) granulated sugar, and beat at medium speed for 2 to 3 minutes. Add 1 egg (50 grams) and peppermint extract, and beat until smooth and well combined. Add food coloring (if using). Transfer cheesecake batter to a large bowl; set aside.

2. In a medium heatproof bowl, place chocolate.
3. In a small saucepan, bring butter to a low boil over medium-high heat, stirring frequently. Immediately pour hot butter over chocolate. Let stand for 2 minutes; whisk until smooth.
4. Preheat oven to 350°F (180°C).
5. Clean bowl of stand mixer. Using the whisk attachment, beat brown sugar, vanilla, salt, remaining 1 cup (200 grams) granulated sugar, and remaining 3 eggs (150 grams) at high speed for exactly 10 minutes. (It will look like a very thick batter.) With mixer on medium speed, pour in slightly cooled chocolate mixture, beating until smooth.
6. Butter an 8-inch square baking pan. Line pan with parchment paper, letting excess extend over sides of pan; butter parchment.
7. In a small bowl, sift together flour and cocoa. Using a spatula, gently fold flour mixture into chocolate mixture just until combined. Pour half of brownie batter in prepared pan, smoothing top with a spatula. Top with half of cheesecake batter. Repeat layers. Using a small spatula or butter knife, gently swirl batters together to create a marbled effect.
8. Bake until a wooden pick inserted in center comes out clean, 45 to 50 minutes. Let cool completely in pan. (Center will seem slightly underbaked, but brownies will continue to cook and set as they cool.) Using excess parchment as handles, remove from pan, and cut into bars.

Photo by Mike Johnson

COFFEE TOFFEE CHOCOLATE CHUNK COOKIE BARS

Makes 10 bars

Recipe by Tessa Huff

Simply cut into triangles like a tree instead of squares, these festive cookies are dressed up with coffee-infused ganache and sugar pearls. The caramelized toffee is perfectly balanced by the dark chocolate and coffee flavors while offering crunch to each bite. Complete the design by piping swags of ganache using a petal tip or swirl it on for a more rustic finish.

¾   cup (170 grams) unsalted butter, softened
1   cup (220 grams) firmly packed light brown sugar
½   cup (100 grams) granulated sugar
1   large egg (50 grams)
1   large egg yolk (19 grams)
2   teaspoons (8 grams) pure vanilla extract
2½   cups (313 grams) all-purpose flour
2   teaspoons (4 grams) instant espresso powder (optional)
¾   teaspoon (3.75 grams) baking soda
½   teaspoon (3 grams) kosher salt
6   ounces (175 grams) 60% to 70% cacao dark chocolate, chopped
¾   cup (120 grams) toffee bits
Coffee Ganache Frosting (recipe follows)
Garnish: sugar pearls, dragées

1. Preheat oven to 350°F (180°C). Butter a 9-inch square baking pan. Line pan with parchment paper, letting excess extend over sides of pan.
2. In the bowl of a stand mixer fitted with the paddle attachment, beat butter at medium speed until smooth, 1 to 2 minutes. Add sugars, and beat until light and fluffy, 2 to 3 minutes, stopping to scrape sides of bowl. Add egg, egg yolk, and vanilla, beating until combined, about 1 minute.
3. In a medium bowl, whisk together flour, espresso powder (if using), baking soda, and salt. With mixer on low speed, add flour mixture to butter mixture in two additions, beating just until combined and a few steaks of flour remain. Fold in chocolate and toffee bits. Press dough into prepared pan, smoothing into an even layer with an offset spatula. (You can slightly wet your hands to press dough into place before smoothing. Dough will be quite thick and stiff.)
4. Bake until center is nearly set, 31 to 35 minutes. Remove from oven, and immediately press down edges using a heatproof spatula. Let cool completely in pan on a wire rack.
5. Using excess parchment as handles, remove from pan, and cut in half, creating 2 rectangles. Cut each half into 5 triangles with 3-inch bases.

6. Place Coffee Ganache Frosting in a piping bag fitted with a petal tip (Wilton No. 104). Pointing narrow end of tip away from your body and toward top of cookie bar "tree," pipe rounded zigzags, creating swags down tree. Garnish with sugar pearls and dragées, if desired. Cookie bars are best served within 2 days of baking. Store in an airtight container for up to 3 days.

> **PRO TIP**
> Baking the bars until nearly set in the center and pressing down the edges once cooked will help keep the centers from sinking for a more even "tree." Decrease the cook time by a few minutes for a gooey, chewy center.

COFFEE GANACHE FROSTING
Makes about ¾ cup

¾   cup (180 grams) heavy whipping cream
2   tablespoons (10 grams) coffee beans, crushed
4   ounces (115 grams) 60% cacao dark chocolate, chopped

1. In a small saucepan, heat cream over medium-high heat just until bubbles form around edges of pan. (Do not boil.) Stir in crushed coffee beans. Remove from heat; let cool completely. Refrigerate in an airtight container for at least 8 hours or overnight.
2. Strain cream through a fine-mesh sieve, discarding coffee beans. Reserve ½ cup (120 grams) cream.
3. In a heatproof bowl, place chocolate.
4. In a small saucepan, heat reserved cream over medium-high heat just until bubbles form around edges of pan. (Do not boil.) Pour hot cream over chocolate. Let stand for 30 seconds to 1 minute; whisk until smooth. Let cool to room temperature, at least 1 hour. (Alternatively, refrigerate for about 30 minutes, stirring every 5 to 10 minutes.)
5. Whisk ganache by hand until it thickens and slightly lightens in color, 2 to 3 minutes. (Alternatively, transfer ganache to the bowl of a stand mixer fitted with the whisk attachment, and beat for 30 seconds to 1 minute.) (Do not overmix.) Use immediately.

> **PRO TIP**
> If the ganache sets before decorating, gently reheat in the top of a double boiler, and whisk until thick and spreadable.

Photo by Tessa Huff

CRANBERRY MERINGUE BARS

Makes 12 bars

Recipe by Michele Song

Are you looking for a new showstopper to add to your holiday tradition? These festive and vibrant cranberry-orange meringue bars are guaranteed to impress your family and friends. The tart, luscious cranberry curd filling pairs perfectly with the sweet, toasty notes of the Brown Sugar Meringue and the spiced cookie crust.

1¼ cups (145 grams) speculoos cookies
3   tablespoons (42 grams) unsalted butter, melted
1   cup (200 grams) plus 2 tablespoons (24 grams) granulated sugar, divided
½   teaspoon kosher salt, divided
12 ounces (340 grams) fresh or thawed frozen cranberries
¼   cup (60 grams) water
1   large orange (131 grams)
3   tablespoons (24 grams) cornstarch
4   large eggs (200 grams)
2   large egg yolks (37 grams)
¾   cup (180 grams) fresh orange juice
½   cup (113 grams) unsalted butter
Brown Sugar Meringue (recipe follows)

1. Preheat oven to 350°F (180°C). Line an 8-inch square baking pan with parchment paper, letting excess extend over sides of pan.
2. In the work bowl of a food processor, pulse cookies until finely ground. Add melted butter, 2 tablespoons (24 grams) sugar, and ¼ teaspoon salt; pulse until combined and mixture sticks together when rubbed between fingertips. Press into bottom of prepared pan.
3. Bake for 10 minutes. Let cool completely. Reduce oven temperature to 325°F (170°C).
4. In a medium saucepan, combine cranberries and ¼ cup (60 grams) water. Cook over medium-high heat, whisking occasionally, until cranberries start to burst, 7 to 10 minutes. Remove from heat; let cool slightly. Transfer cranberries to the container of a blender, and purée until smooth. Strain mixture, discarding skins. Set aside.
5. In a small bowl, place remaining 1 cup (200 grams) sugar. Zest orange over sugar, and rub together with fingertips to help release oils in zest. Add cornstarch, and stir until well combined.
6. In a metal or glass bowl, whisk together eggs and egg yolks. Gradually add sugar mixture, whisking constantly, until combined.

7. In a large saucepan, cook puréed cranberries, orange juice, butter, and remaining ¼ teaspoon salt over medium-high heat, whisking occasionally. Remove from heat; gradually pour half of hot cranberry mixture into egg mixture, whisking constantly. Return mixture to saucepan. Bring to a boil over medium heat, stirring constantly. Reduce heat to medium-low, and simmer for 2 minutes to ensure cornstarch is cooked through. Strain through a fine-mesh sieve. Pour mixture onto prepared crust.
8. Bake until set but slightly jiggly, 20 to 25 minutes. Let cool to room temperature, about 1 hour. Refrigerate until set, at least 4 hours or overnight.
9. Top with Brown Sugar Meringue, and create peaks using a rubber spatula. Using a kitchen torch, toast meringue until top is golden brown. Best served same day or when cold; refrigerate any leftovers in an airtight container. (To make ahead, make the cranberry bars, and refrigerate overnight; make the Brown Sugar Meringue when ready to serve.)

BROWN SUGAR MERINGUE
Makes about 4 cups

¾   cup (165 grams) firmly packed light brown sugar
¼   cup (50 grams) granulated sugar
¼   cup (60 grams) water
4   large egg whites (120 grams), room temperature
½   teaspoon (2 grams) cream of tartar
1   teaspoon (4 grams) vanilla extract

1. In a medium saucepan, combine sugars and ¼ cup (60 grams) water. Using your index finger, gently stir sugars and water together until sugar is wet and mixture resembles wet sand. Wipe any excess sugar from sides of pan using wet hands. (This will prevent sugar from crystallizing.) Cook over medium-high heat until an instant-read thermometer registers 240°F (116°C), 5 to 7 minutes.
2. Meanwhile, in the bowl of a stand mixer fitted with the whisk attachment, beat egg whites and cream of tartar at medium speed until soft peaks form, 1 to 2 minutes.
3. With mixer on medium speed, slowly pour hot sugar syrup into egg white mixture. Increase mixer speed to high, and beat until shiny, smooth, stiff peaks form. Add vanilla, and beat to combine. Use immediately.

Photo by Michele Song

CITRUS SUGAR COOKIE BARS

Makes 24 bars

Recipe by Laura Kasavan

Soft and buttery Citrus Sugar Cookie Bars are a dream for citrus lovers. You'll love the versatility of these bright, zesty bars (use any mix of citrus you love). Generous swirls of Citrus Vanilla Frosting make the perfect finish.

1¼ cups (250 grams) granulated sugar
3 tablespoons (9 grams) citrus zest*
1 cup (227 grams) unsalted butter, softened
1 large egg (50 grams)
2 teaspoons (8 grams) vanilla extract
3 cups (375 grams) all-purpose flour
1 tablespoon (8 grams) cornstarch
1 teaspoon (5 grams) baking powder
½ teaspoon (1.5 grams) kosher salt
¼ teaspoon (1.25 grams) baking soda
Citrus Vanilla Frosting (recipe follows)
Garnish: holiday sprinkles

1. Preheat oven to 350°F (180°C). Line a 13x9-inch baking pan with parchment paper, letting excess extend over sides of pan.

2. In the work bowl of a food processor, pulse together sugar and citrus zest until zest is finely ground, about 1 minute.
3. In the bowl of a stand mixer fitted with the paddle attachment, beat citrus sugar and butter at medium speed until fluffy, 1 to 2 minutes. Beat in egg and vanilla.
4. In a medium bowl, whisk together flour, cornstarch, baking powder, salt, and baking soda. With mixer on low speed, gradually add flour mixture to butter mixture, beating until a soft dough forms. Transfer dough to prepared pan. Using a sheet of parchment paper coated with cooking spray, press dough into pan.
5. Bake until lightly golden and a wooden pick inserted in center comes out clean, 20 to 24 minutes. Let cool completely in pan.
6. Using excess parchment as handles, remove from pan. Using an offset spatula, swirl Citrus Vanilla Frosting on top. Garnish with sprinkles, if desired. Refrigerate until set, about 20 minutes. Cut into bars. Refrigerate in an airtight container for up to 3 days.

We used the zests of 1 orange, 2 Meyer lemons, and 2 limes, but any combination or singular type of citrus will work.

CITRUS VANILLA FROSTING
Makes about 2 cups

½ cup (113 grams) unsalted butter, softened
¼ cup (60 grams) crème fraîche
¼ teaspoon kosher salt
1 tablespoon (3 grams) citrus zest*
1 teaspoon (4 grams) vanilla extract
3 cups (360 grams) confectioners' sugar
½ tablespoon (7.5 grams) citrus juice*

1. In the bowl of a stand mixer fitted with the paddle attachment, beat butter, crème fraîche, and salt at medium speed until smooth, 2 to 3 minutes. Beat in zest and vanilla. With mixer on low speed, gradually add confectioners' sugar, beating until combined. Add citrus juice, and beat at medium-high speed until light and fluffy, 1 to 2 minutes. Use immediately.

We used a blend of orange, Meyer lemon, and lime for the citrus zest and juice.

Photo by Laura Kasavan

"FOOD FOR THE GODS" BARS

Makes 24 bars

During the holiday season in the Philippines, these walnut- and date-studded bars are baked and given to loved ones as individually wrapped treats. The grand name (pagkain para sa mga diyos in Filipino) is thought to go back to the days of Spanish rule over the archipelago, when dates and walnuts were delicacies not many could afford, making them fit only for divine consumption. While we can't vouch for the accuracy of that story, we can confirm these bars are pure buttery bliss.

1½ cups (334 grams) bourbon
1½ cups (250 grams) packed whole Medjool dates
2 cups (440 grams) firmly packed dark brown sugar
1½ cups (340 grams) unsalted butter, melted
¼ cup (50 grams) granulated sugar
3 large eggs (150 grams), room temperature
1 teaspoon (4 grams) vanilla extract

1½ cups (187 grams) all-purpose flour, divided
1½ teaspoons (7.5 grams) baking powder
¾ teaspoon (2.25 grams) kosher salt
¾ cup (85 grams) roughly chopped toasted pecans
¾ cup (85 grams) roughly chopped toasted walnuts

1. Line a baking sheet with paper towels.
2. In a large microwave-safe bowl, heat bourbon on high until an instant-read thermometer registers 180°F (82°C), about 2 minutes. (Alternatively, in a small heavy-bottomed saucepan, heat bourbon over medium heat until an instant-read thermometer registers 180°F [82°C].) Stir in dates; let stand for 20 minutes, stirring occasionally. Drain dates, reserving liquid for another use, if desired. Spread dates on prepared pan, and pat dry. Remove pits; chop dates into ¼- to ⅓-inch pieces.
3. Preheat oven to 350°F (180°C). Line a 13x9-inch baking pan with parchment paper, letting excess extend over sides of pan.

4. In a large bowl, whisk together brown sugar, melted butter, and granulated sugar until well combined. Beat in eggs and vanilla until well combined.
5. In another large bowl, whisk together 1¼ cups (156 grams) flour, baking powder, and salt. Gradually fold flour mixture into butter mixture just until combined.
6. In a medium bowl, stir together chopped dates, pecans, and walnuts; add remaining ¼ cup (31 grams) flour, stirring until well combined. Fold date mixture into batter. Spoon into prepared pan, smoothing top.
7. Bake for 10 minutes. Reduce heat to 300°F (150°C); bake until a wooden pick inserted in center comes out clean and an instant-read thermometer inserted in center registers 205°F (96°C), about 40 minutes more. Let cool completely in pan. Using excess parchment as handles, remove from pan. Using a serrated knife, cut into bars.

GINGERBREAD COOKIE CHEESECAKE BARS

Makes 12 bars

Makes 12 bars

An indulgent layer of cheesecake filling is sandwiched between chewy, delicately spiced gingerbread dough. It's a simple formula, but when that molasses-rich gingerbread meets that vanilla- scented cheesecake, you'll get flavor fireworks.

1½   cups (340 grams) unsalted butter, softened
1¼   cups (250 grams) granulated sugar
¾   cup (165 grams) firmly packed dark brown sugar
½   cup (170 grams) unsulphured molasses
2   large eggs (100 grams)
4   cups (500 grams) all-purpose flour
2   teaspoons (4 grams) ground cinnamon
2   teaspoons (4 grams) ground ginger
1½   teaspoons (4.5 grams) kosher salt
1   teaspoon (5 grams) baking powder
1   teaspoon (5 grams) baking soda
¼   teaspoon ground nutmeg
⅛   teaspoon ground allspice
⅛   teaspoon ground cloves

3   tablespoons (33 grams) minced candied ginger
Cheesecake Layer (recipe follows)

1. Preheat oven to 350°F (180°C). Line a 13x9-inch baking pan with parchment paper, letting excess extend over sides of pan.
2. In the bowl of a stand mixer fitted with the paddle attachment, beat butter and sugars at medium speed until fluffy, 3 to 4 minutes, stopping to scrape sides of bowl. Add molasses, beating until no streaks remain. Add eggs, one at a time, beating well after each addition.
3. In a large bowl, whisk together flour, cinnamon, ground ginger, salt, baking powder, baking soda, nutmeg, allspice, and cloves. With mixer on low speed, gradually add flour mixture to butter mixture, beating just until combined. Beat in candied ginger.
4. Spread 3¾ cups (about 1,000 grams) dough in prepared pan. Top with Cheesecake Layer. Crumble remaining dough (about 2 cups [563 grams]) on top.
5. Bake until edges are set, center jiggles just slightly, and an instant-read thermometer inserted in center registers

175°F (79°C) to 180°F (82°C), 45 to 55 minutes, covering with foil after 35 minutes of baking to prevent excess browning, if necessary. Let cool completely in pan. Cover and refrigerate for at least 4 hours or overnight. Using excess parchment as handles, remove from pan. Trim edges, and cut into bars.

CHEESECAKE LAYER
Makes 3⅓ cups

16   ounces (455 grams) cream cheese, softened
1   cup (200 grams) granulated sugar
1   tablespoon (8 grams) all-purpose flour
2   large eggs (100 grams)
1   tablespoon (13 grams) vanilla extract

1. In the bowl of a stand mixer fitted with the paddle attachment, beat cream cheese at medium speed until smooth. Add sugar and flour, and beat until combined, stopping to scrape sides of bowl. Add eggs, one at a time, beating well after each addition. Beat in vanilla. Use immediately.

CINNAMON ROLL BLONDIES WITH CREAM CHEESE GLAZE

Makes 12 to 15 blondies

Recipe by Elisabeth Farris

These Cinnamon Roll Blondies are everything you love about a classic cinnamon roll in one delicious, chewy bar.

1 cup (220 grams) firmly packed light brown sugar
¾ cup (170 grams) unsalted butter, melted and slightly cooled
½ cup (100 grams) granulated sugar
2 large eggs (100 grams)
1½ teaspoons (6 grams) vanilla extract
1½ cups (188 grams) all-purpose flour
1 teaspoon (5 grams) baking powder
½ teaspoon (1.5 grams) kosher salt
¼ teaspoon ground cinnamon
   Cinnamon Filling (recipe follows)
   Cream Cheese Glaze (recipe follows)

1. Preheat oven to 350°F (180°C). Line a 13x9-inch baking pan with parchment paper, letting excess extend over sides of pan.

2. In the bowl of a stand mixer fitted with the paddle attachment, beat brown sugar, melted butter, and granulated sugar at medium-high speed until mixture is light in color and fluffy, 1 to 2 minutes. Add eggs and vanilla, beating until combined.
3. In a medium bowl, whisk together flour, baking powder, salt, and cinnamon. Gently fold flour mixture into sugar mixture until combined. Spread batter in prepared pan, smoothing top. (Batter will be thick.) Spoon dollops of Cinnamon Filling onto batter, and swirl using a knife. (The filling will be thick and slightly grainy, but it will still bake beautifully.)
4. Bake until lightly golden on top, 22 to 27 minutes, rotating pan halfway through baking. (The center will still be a little gooey, but they will continue to bake even after you take them out of the oven. Do not overbake, or they will become dry.) Let cool completely.
5. Using a piping bag or spoon, drizzle Cream Cheese Glaze on top. Cut into bars, and store in an airtight container for up to 3 days.

CINNAMON FILLING
Makes about ½ cup

½ cup (110 grams) firmly packed light brown sugar
2 tablespoons (28 grams) unsalted butter, melted
2 teaspoons (4 grams) ground cinnamon

1. In a small bowl, stir together all ingredients. Use immediately.

CREAM CHEESE GLAZE
Makes about ½ cup

1 cup (120 grams) confectioners' sugar
1 tablespoon (14 grams) cream cheese, softened
1 tablespoon (14 grams) unsalted butter, softened
1 tablespoon plus 1 teaspoon (20 grams) milk

1. In a small bowl, whisk together all ingredients until smooth. Add more confectioners' sugar if glaze becomes too runny; add more milk if it becomes too thick. Use immediately.

Photo by Elisabeth Farris

MULLED SPICE BROWNIES

Makes 16 brownies

These fudgy stir-together brownies get rich, sophisticated notes from a blend of mulling spices and port-soaked orange peel.

1¾ cups (350 grams) granulated sugar
1¼ cups (284 grams) unsalted butter, melted
⅔ cup (147 grams) firmly packed light brown sugar
1 teaspoon (4 grams) vanilla extract
5 large eggs (250 grams), room temperature
1 cup (85 grams) unsweetened natural cocoa powder, sifted
¾ cup (94 grams) all-purpose flour
3¾ teaspoons (7.5 grams) Mulled Spice Mix (recipe follows)
1 teaspoon (3 grams) kosher salt
¾ teaspoon (3.75 grams) baking powder
1½ teaspoons (5 grams) finely chopped port-soaked orange peel (reserved from Spiced Port Syrup [recipe follows])
Ganache Frosting (recipe follows)
Spiced Port Syrup (recipe follows)
Garnish: Mulled Spice Mix (recipe follows)

1. Preheat oven to 350°F (180°C). Spray a 9-inch square baking pan with cooking spray; line pan with parchment paper, letting excess extend over sides of pan.
2. In a large bowl, whisk together granulated sugar, melted butter, brown sugar, and vanilla until well combined. Add eggs, one at a time, beating until well combined after each addition.
3. In a large bowl, whisk together cocoa, flour, Mulled Spice Mix, salt, and baking powder. Gradually stir cocoa mixture into sugar mixture until combined. Fold in chopped orange peel, breaking up any clumps if needed. Spoon batter into prepared pan, smoothing top.
4. Bake until a wooden pick inserted in center comes out with just a few moist crumbs, 45 to 50 minutes. Let cool completely in pan on a wire rack.
5. Spread Ganache Frosting onto cooled brownies, using a small offset spatula or the back of a spoon to create swirls. (For deeper swirls, refrigerate brownies for about 15 minutes to slightly firm up frosting before swirling.) Using excess parchment as handles, remove from pan. Cut into bars. Drizzle with Spiced Port Syrup just before serving. Garnish with Mulled Spice Mix, if desired.

MULLED SPICE MIX
Makes 7½ teaspoons

2 teaspoons (4 grams) ground cinnamon
2 teaspoons (4 grams) ground ginger
1 teaspoon (2 grams) ground nutmeg
1 teaspoon (2 grams) ground cloves
1 teaspoon (2 grams) ground allspice
½ teaspoon (1 gram) ground black pepper

1. In a small bowl, stir together all ingredients until well combined.

GANACHE FROSTING
Makes about 1¾ cups

4 ounces (115 grams) unsweetened chocolate baking bars, chopped
¼ cup (57 grams) unsalted butter, cubed and softened
1 teaspoon (5 grams) ruby port
⅔ cup (160 grams) evaporated milk
½ cup (100 grams) granulated sugar
⅓ cup (73 grams) firmly packed light brown sugar
¼ teaspoon kosher salt

1. In the container of a blender, place chocolate, butter, and port.
2. In a medium saucepan, combine evaporated milk, sugars, and salt. Cook over medium heat, stirring constantly, until sugars and salt are dissolved. Add to blender. Let stand for 5 minutes.
3. Process until thick and smooth, about 15 seconds. Using a spatula, stir mixture to check consistency. If needed, blend in additional 15-second intervals to thicken more.

SPICED PORT SYRUP
Makes about ⅓ cup

½ medium navel orange (about 100 grams)
1 cup (224 grams) ruby port
⅓ cup (67 grams) granulated sugar
1 (2½- to 3-inch) cinnamon stick
8 whole black peppercorns
⅛ teaspoon ground nutmeg
⅛ teaspoon ground allspice
⅛ teaspoon ground cloves

1. Using a Y-peeler, remove orange peel in long strips. Using a small paring knife, carefully remove any white pith from peel. Reserve remaining orange for another use.
2. In a 10-inch stainless steel skillet, stir together orange peel, port, and all remaining ingredients. Bring to a boil over medium-high heat. Reduce heat to medium, and cook, stirring occasionally, until thickened and reduced to ⅓ cup, 12 to 15 minutes.
3. Strain mixture through a fine-mesh sieve into a medium bowl. Finely chop 1½ teaspoons (5 grams) cooked orange peel; reserve for Mulled Spice Brownies. Discard remaining solids. Let syrup cool completely before using.

MISCELLANEOUS

BLOOD ORANGE AMBROSIA PAVLOVA

Makes 8 to 10 servings

Recipe by Marian Cooper Cairns

The Australian classic gets an exotic twist. The coconut milk in the pastry cream offsets the blood oranges' acidity with nutty richness. Break down the process by making the pastry cream and meringue a day ahead, and assemble right before serving.

4   large egg whites (120 grams), room
    temperature
¼   teaspoon cream of tartar
⅛   teaspoon kosher salt
1   cup (200 grams) castor sugar
1   tablespoon (8 grams) cornstarch
¼   teaspoon (1 gram) vanilla extract
4   blood oranges (524 grams)
Coconut Milk Pastry Cream (recipe follows)
¾   cup (63 grams) toasted large coconut
    flakes

1. Preheat oven to 225°F (107°C). Line a baking sheet with parchment paper.
2. In the bowl of a stand mixer fitted with the whisk attachment, beat egg whites at medium-high speed for 30 seconds. Add cream of tartar and salt, beating until combined.
3. In a small bowl, whisk together castor sugar and cornstarch. Add sugar mixture to egg white mixture, 1 tablespoon at a time, beating until glossy, stiff peaks form and sugar is dissolved. (Do not overbeat.) Beat in vanilla. Gently spread mixture into a 9- to 10-inch oval on prepared pan, making an indentation in center.
4. Bake until pale golden and outside has formed a crust, about 1 hour and 15 minutes. Turn oven off, and let meringue stand in oven with door closed for 12 hours.
5. Cut away peel and pith from blood oranges; slice and section fruit.
6. Place Pavlova on a serving platter. Spoon chilled Coconut Milk Pastry Cream over Pavlova. Arrange oranges over cream, and sprinkle with coconut. Serve immediately.

PRO TIPS

Castor sugar guarantees the sugar will dissolve when whipping your meringue, but traditional granulated sugar will work in a pinch, too.

If your pastry cream looks a little lumpy, don't fret! While it's still warm, pass it through a fine-mesh sieve to remove any bits of cooked egg.

COCONUT MILK PASTRY CREAM
Makes about 3 cups

½   cup (100 grams) granulated sugar
3   tablespoons (24 grams) cornstarch
¼   teaspoon kosher salt
4   large egg yolks (74 grams)
1   (13.5-ounce) can (405 grams) coconut
    milk
½   cup (120 grams) whole milk

1. In a medium heavy-bottomed saucepan, whisk together sugar, cornstarch, and salt. Whisk in egg yolks, coconut milk, and whole milk until well combined. Cook over medium-low heat, whisking constantly, just until mixture thickens and begins to bubble, 10 to 12 minutes. Pour into a medium bowl. Cover with a piece of plastic wrap, pressing wrap directly onto surface of pastry cream to prevent a skin from forming. Refrigerate overnight or for up to 2 days.

Photo by Matt Armendariz

VANILLA CRÈME CARAMEL

Makes 4 servings

Luxuriously silky and topped in a rich vanilla caramel, this traditional French custard dessert gets heightened warmth and complexity from Heilala's premium vanilla bean paste and vanilla syrup.

Vanilla Bean Caramel (recipe follows)
¾ cup (180 grams) whole milk
⅓ cup (80 grams) heavy whipping cream
¼ cup (50 grams) granulated sugar
⅛ teaspoon kosher salt
2 large eggs (100 grams)
1 large egg yolk (19 grams)
1 teaspoon (6 grams) vanilla bean paste*

1. Preheat oven to 325°F (170°C).
2. Divide hot Vanilla Bean Caramel among 4 (4-ounce) ramekins. Refrigerate until hardened, about 15 minutes.
3. In a medium saucepan, cook milk, cream, sugar, and salt over medium heat just until bubbles form around edges of pan. (Do not boil.) Remove from heat.
4. In a medium bowl, whisk together eggs, egg yolk, and vanilla bean paste. Slowly add hot milk mixture to egg mixture, whisking constantly. Return mixture to saucepan, and cook over medium heat, stirring constantly, until mixture is thickened, about 2 minutes. Strain mixture through a fine-mesh sieve into a heatproof measuring cup.
5. Place ramekins in a 9-inch square baking dish. Pour cream mixture over Vanilla Bean Caramel, filling almost to top of ramekins. Carefully place baking dish in oven. Pour enough hot water into dish to come about one-third of the way up sides of ramekins, being careful not to splash any water in ramekins.
6. Bake until edges are just set but centers are still jiggly, about 30 minutes, rotating pan halfway through baking (being careful not to splash water). Using a towel, carefully transfer hot ramekins to a wire rack, and let cool completely. Cover and refrigerate for 4 hours.
7. Run a sharp knife around edges of ramekins to loosen. Invert onto serving dishes, tap top of ramekins, and remove. Serve immediately.

*We used Heilala.

Vanilla Bean Caramel
Makes ½ cup

½ cup (100 grams) granulated sugar
2 tablespoons (39 grams) vanilla syrup*

1. In a medium stainless steel saucepan, cook sugar and vanilla syrup over medium heat until medium amber colored, 5 to 7 minutes. Use immediately.

*We used Heilala.

SAVORY SOUFFLÉ

Makes 6 servings

Recipe by Marjorie Taylor and Kendall Smith Franchini

This soufflé begins with a béchamel base and is inspired by Julia Child. At The Cook's Atelier, they enjoy making these as individual soufflés, but the recipe can also be adapted to one large soufflé.

5	tablespoons (30 grams) freshly grated Parmesan cheese, divided
1¼	cups (300 grams) whole milk
1	whole bay leaf
1	clove garlic (5 grams), smashed
8	whole black peppercorns
3	tablespoons (42 grams) unsalted butter, plus more for molds
¼	cup (30 grams) unbleached all-purpose flour
½	teaspoon fleur de sel
¼	teaspoon freshly ground black pepper
4	large egg yolks (74 grams)
¾	cup (85 grams) coarsely grated Comté or Gruyère cheese

Pinch freshly grated nutmeg

7	large egg whites (210 grams)

1. Set a rack in the middle of the oven and preheat the oven to 425°F (220°C). Butter the inside of a 6-cup soufflé mold or 6 (1-cup) ramekins. Sprinkle the inside of the mold(s) with some of the Parmesan, reserving any excess. Set aside.

2. In a saucepan, combine the milk, bay leaf, garlic, and peppercorns. Place over medium heat and bring to just under a boil. Remove from the heat and steep for about 15 minutes to infuse the aromatics into the milk. When ready to prepare the soufflé, bring the milk back to just under a boil, then strain out and discard the aromatics.

3. In a medium saucepan, melt the butter over medium heat. Add the flour and stir briskly with a wooden spoon until the butter and flour come together, being careful not to let the mixture brown, about 1 minute. Add the hot milk, all at once, and whisk to blend well. Add the fleur de sel and pepper, whisking continuously, until the béchamel becomes thick, about 1 to 2 minutes. Remove from the heat and add the egg yolks, one at a time, until incorporated. Add the Comté and nutmeg, and stir until fully combined. Transfer the soufflé base to a large bowl and let cool slightly.

4. In a large, very clean, preferably copper bowl, use a large balloon whisk to beat the egg whites until firm peaks form. Stir a large spoonful of the whipped egg whites into the soufflé base to begin lightening it. Using a rubber spatula, gently fold in the remaining egg whites, working quickly to keep the base light and airy.

5. Pour the finished mixture into the prepared mold(s), filling to just below the top rim. Sprinkle the top with the remaining Parmesan.

6. Bake on the middle rack of the oven until the top is golden brown and lifted about 2 inches over the edge of the mold(s), 25 to 30 minutes for the 6-cup mold or 15 to 18 minutes for the ramekins. Do not be tempted to open the oven during baking or the soufflé will fall. Serve immediately.

Photo by Joann Pai

BERRY-FILLED SOURDOUGH DISCARD DOUGHNUTS

Makes about 12 doughnuts

The secret to these fluffy, tangy doughnuts? Sourdough discard-enriched dough. Plus, we give you two indulgent fillings to mix and match—our homemade Berry Jam and our berry-scented crème fraîche—so you can choose your own doughnut experience.

¼ cup (60 grams) warm water (105°F/41°C to 110°F/43°C)
4½ teaspoons (14 grams) active dry yeast
6 cups (750 grams) all-purpose flour, divided
1 cup (240 grams) warm milk (105°F/41°C to 110°F/43°C)
¾ cup (188 grams) sourdough starter discard, room temperature
3 cups (600 grams) granulated sugar, divided
2 large eggs (100 grams)
⅓ cup (76 grams) unsalted butter, softened
1½ teaspoons (4.5 grams) kosher salt
Vegetable oil, for frying
2 cups (340 grams) Berry Crème Fraîche (recipe follows) or ½ cup (148 grams) Berry Jam (recipe follows)

1. In the bowl of a stand mixer fitted with the paddle attachment, stir together ¼ cup (60 grams) warm water and yeast by hand. Let stand until mixture is foamy, about 5 minutes.
2. Add 3 cups (375 grams) flour, warm milk, sourdough discard, ½ cup (100 grams) sugar, eggs, butter, and salt to yeast mixture, and beat at medium speed until smooth, about 3 minutes. Beat in enough remaining 3 cups (375 grams) flour, starting with about 1 cup (125 grams), until a soft dough forms. (Dough will be sticky.) Switch to the dough hook attachment. Beat at medium speed until dough is smooth and elastic, 6 to 8 minutes.
3. Lightly oil a large bowl. Place dough in bowl, turning to grease top. Cover with plastic wrap, and let rise in a warm, draft-free place (75°F/24°C) until doubled in size, about 1 hour.
4. Line baking sheets with parchment paper.
5. Lightly punch down dough, and turn out onto a lightly floured surface; roll to ½-inch thickness. Using a 3¼-inch round cutter dipped in flour, cut dough, and place 1½ inches apart on prepared pans. Loosely cover with plastic wrap, and let rise in a warm, draft-free place (75°F/24°C) until doubled in size, about 2 hours.
6. Place remaining 2½ cups (500 grams) sugar in a shallow dish. In a skillet or deep fryer, pour oil to a depth of 2 inches, and heat over medium heat until a deep-fry thermometer registers 350°F (180°C).

7. Fry doughnuts, 2 at a time, until golden brown, 1½ to 2 minutes, turning every 30 seconds. Transfer hot doughnuts to sugar, turning to coat. Let cool completely on a wire rack.
8. Using a small knife, cut a slit in the side of each doughnut. Place Berry Crème Fraîche or Berry Jam in a piping bag fitted with a round tip. Pipe filling into doughnuts. Serve immediately.

BERRY CRÈME FRAÎCHE
Makes about 2 cups

1 cup (240 grams) cold crème fraîche
⅓ cup (80 grams) cold heavy whipping cream
¼ cup (30 grams) confectioners' sugar
2 tablespoons (53 grams) Berry Jam (recipe follows)

1. In the bowl of a stand mixer fitted with the whisk attachment, beat all ingredients at high speed until thickened and mixture holds its shape, 1 to 2 minutes. Cover and refrigerate until ready to use.

BERRY JAM
Makes about 3 cups

18 ounces (510 grams) fresh blackberries (about 3½ cups)
14 ounces (400 grams) fresh blueberries (about 2⅔ cups)
2 cups (400 grams) granulated sugar
¼ cup (60 grams) almond liqueur
1 vanilla bean, split lengthwise, seeds scraped and reserved

1. In the container of a blender, process blackberries until puréed. Strain through a fine-mesh sieve into a medium bowl, discarding seeds. Place 1⅔ cups (400 grams) blackberry juice in a medium Dutch oven. Add blueberries, sugar, almond liqueur, and vanilla bean and reserved seeds, stirring to combine. Let stand for 30 minutes.
2. Bring berry mixture to a boil over medium heat. Cook, stirring frequently, until mixture is thickened and jam leaves a trace when a spoon is dragged across bottom of pot, 20 to 25 minutes. Remove from heat, and let cool for 1 hour. Transfer jam to a clean jar. Jam will keep refrigerated for up to 2 weeks.

> **PRO TIP**
> Instead of making the Berry Jam, you can also use high-quality store-bought blackberry or blueberry jam. We suggest Bonne Maman Blackberry Preserves or Bonne Maman Wild Blueberry Preserves, available at specialty food stores or online.

PERSIMMON-APPLE CRISP

Makes 8 to 10 servings

Persimmons take the traditional apple crisp to a new level of tasty. The Fuyu persimmons' delicate, sweet flavor already has undertones of apple, along with honey, vanilla, and cinnamon, so it complements the tart apples here perfectly. The fruits bake into a tender medley of warm autumn flavor piled high with a walnut and oat topping, which lends the distinct crunch for which the dessert is named.

3	Fuyu persimmons (435 grams), chopped
1	medium Honeycrisp apple (247 grams), chopped
1	medium Granny Smith apple (247 grams), chopped
¼	cup plus 1 tablespoon (39 grams) all-purpose flour
¼	cup (50 grams) granulated sugar
¼	cup (55 grams) firmly packed light brown sugar
1	tablespoon (18 grams) vanilla bean paste
1	tablespoon (3 grams) lemon zest
1	tablespoon (15 grams) fresh lemon juice
1	teaspoon (2 grams) ground cinnamon
¼	teaspoon kosher salt
¼	teaspoon ground nutmeg

Walnut Crisp Topping (recipe follows)
Crème Fraîche Caramel (recipe follows)

1. Preheat oven to 350°F (180°C).
2. In a large bowl, toss together persimmons and apples. Add flour, sugars, vanilla bean paste, lemon zest and juice, cinnamon, salt, and nutmeg, tossing to combine. Let stand for 10 minutes.
3. Place persimmon mixture in a 9-inch baking dish. Top with Walnut Crisp Topping.
4. Bake until topping is golden brown and filling is bubbly, 35 to 40 minutes. Let stand for 15 minutes. Serve with Crème Fraîche Caramel. Cover and refrigerate for up to 3 days.

WALNUT CRISP TOPPING

Makes about 3 cups

½	cup (63 grams) all-purpose flour
½	cup (100 grams) granulated sugar
½	cup (110 grams) firmly packed light brown sugar
½	cup (57 grams) chopped walnuts
½	cup (40 grams) old-fashioned oats
1½	tablespoons (4.5 grams) orange zest
1	teaspoon (3 grams) kosher salt
1	teaspoon (6 grams) vanilla bean paste
½	teaspoon (1 gram) ground cinnamon
¼	cup plus 1 tablespoon (71 grams) cold unsalted butter, cubed

1. In a small bowl, stir together flour, sugars, walnuts, oats, orange zest, salt, vanilla bean paste, and cinnamon. Using your fingertips, cut in cold butter until pea-size crumbs remain. Squeeze mixture into small and large clumps. Refrigerate until ready to use.

CRÈME FRAÎCHE CARAMEL

Makes 1¼ cups

½	cup (120 grams) crème fraîche
2	tablespoons (30 grams) heavy whipping cream
1	cup (200 grams) granulated sugar
4	tablespoons (60 grams) water, divided
3	tablespoons (42 grams) unsalted butter, softened
2	teaspoons (8 grams) vanilla extract

1. In a small microwave-safe bowl, combine crème fraîche and cream. Heat on high until an instant-read thermometer registers 100°F (38°C), about 20 seconds.
2. In a medium saucepan, heat sugar and 3 tablespoons (45 grams) water over high heat, being careful not to splash sides of pan. (Mixture should look like wet sand.) Use remaining 1 tablespoon (15 grams) water to brush down sides of pan, and gently whisk to help sugar dissolve. (Do not stir once it starts to boil.) Cook until desired light amber color is reached. Remove from heat; slowly add warm crème fraîche mixture, whisking to combine. Add butter, a few pieces at a time, whisking until combined. Stir in vanilla. Let cool completely.

VANILLA BERRY PAVLOVA

Makes 1 (12-inch) Pavlova

We're bringing this classic New Zealand dessert to our summer tables when the weather in the northern hemisphere is comparable to the Yuletide season in New Zealand. These conditions are ideal for creating crisp, billowing meringue. This Pavlova receives heightened flavor from New Zealand's own Heilala Vanilla, with their vanilla extract lending smoothness to the airy meringue base while vanilla bean paste adds a punch to the indulgent mascarpone filling.

1 cup (about 223 grams) egg whites, room temperature
1 teaspoon (4 grams) vanilla extract*
½ teaspoon (3 grams) cream of tartar
¼ teaspoon kosher salt
2 cups (400 grams) granulated sugar, divided
1 tablespoon (8 grams) cornstarch
1½ cups (200 grams) fresh strawberries, hulled and halved
1 cup (100 grams) fresh blackberries
1 cup (100 grams) fresh blueberries
1 cup (225 grams) cold mascarpone cheese
⅓ cup (80 grams) cold heavy whipping cream
2 teaspoons (12 grams) vanilla bean paste*

1. Preheat oven to 225°F (107°C). Line a large baking sheet with parchment paper. Using a pencil, draw a 10-inch circle on parchment; turn parchment over.
2. In the bowl of a stand mixer fitted with the whisk attachment, beat egg whites, vanilla extract, cream of tartar, and salt at medium-high speed until foamy, about 1 minute. Increase mixer speed to high. Add 1½ cups (300 grams) sugar in a slow, steady stream, beating until glossy, stiff peaks form, 2 to 4 minutes, depending on humidity. Add cornstarch, and beat until well combined, about 10 seconds. Spoon meringue onto circle on parchment. Using the back of a large spoon, spread meringue into a 10-inch disk, pressing in center to form a well with a raised 2-inch border. (Meringue will expand during baking.)
3. Bake until set and dry, 1½ to 2 hours. (Meringue will be very lightly colored and should feel dry to the touch, not tacky or sticky.) Turn oven off, and let meringue stand in oven with door closed for 1½ hours. Remove from oven, and let cool completely on pan.
4. In a large bowl, toss together strawberries, blackberries, blueberries, and ¼ cup (50 grams) sugar. Let stand for 15 minutes.
5. In the bowl of a stand mixer fitted with the whisk attachment, beat cold mascarpone, cold cream, vanilla bean paste, and remaining ¼ cup (50 grams) sugar at medium-high speed until soft peaks form. (Do not overbeat.)
6. Place meringue on a serving platter. Fill center with mascarpone mixture, and top with berries. Serve immediately.

*We used Heilala.

CHEESE AND CHIVE YORKSHIRE PUDDINGS

Makes 12 Yorkshire puddings

Yorkshire pudding is an English side dish made from a batter of eggs, flour, and milk or water—the Brits love a baked pudding. We gave the classic version a serious savory upgrade with fresh chives and melted cheese. These will deflate while cooling, so they are best served still warm, right out of the oven.

1½   cups (360 grams) whole milk
3   large eggs (150 grams)
¼   cup (60 grams) plus 4 teaspoons (20 grams) unsalted butter, melted and divided

1½   cups (188 grams) all-purpose flour
1   teaspoon (3 grams) kosher salt
½   cup (50 grams) freshly grated Dubliner cheese
3   tablespoons (8 grams) chopped fresh chives
Garnish: chopped fresh chives

1. Preheat oven to 425°F (220°C).
2. In the container of a blender, place milk, eggs, 4 teaspoons (20 grams) melted butter, flour, and salt; process just until smooth. Let rest for 10 minutes.
3. In a small bowl, toss together cheese and chives.

4. Place a 12-cup muffin pan in oven for 5 minutes to preheat. Remove from oven, and quickly spoon remaining ¼ cup melted butter into muffin cups (1 teaspoon [5 grams] each). Return pan to oven for 2 minutes. Remove from oven. Working quickly, spoon batter into muffin cups. Top each with 1 tablespoon (about 4 grams) cheese mixture.
5. Bake until puffed and golden brown, 15 to 18 minutes. Garnish with chives, if desired. Serve immediately.

RECIPE INDEX

index

CREDITS

Editorial
Editor-in-Chief Brian Hart Hoffman
VP/Culinary & Custom Content
Brooke Michael Bell
Group Creative Director
Deanna Rippy Gardner
Art Director Kelly Redding
Managing Editor Sophia Jones
Associate Editor Kyle Grace Mills
Assistant Editor Lillie Mermoud
Editorial Assistant Alex Kolar
Copy Editor Meg Lundberg

Cover
Photography by William Dickey
Food Styling by Elizabeth Stringer
Styling by Sidney Bragiel

***Bake from Scratch* Photographers**
Jim Bathie, William Dickey,
Nicole Du Bois, Mac Jamieson,
Stephanie Welbourne Steele

Test Kitchen Director
Irene Yeh

***Bake from Scratch* Food Stylists/
Recipe Developers**
Laura Crandall, Kathleen Kanen,
Tricia Manzanero, Vanessa Rocchio,
Elizabeth Stringer

**Assistant Food Stylist/Recipe
Developer**
Anita Simpson Spain

***Bake from Scratch* Stylists**
Courtni Bodiford, Caroline Blum,
Sidney Bragiel, Lucy Finney,
Mary Beth Jones

Contributing Photographers
Matt Armendariz **121**
Erin Clarkson **262** (top right), **264**, **343**
Amisha Gurbani **262** (bottom left)
Tessa Huff **263**
Edd Kimber **8**
Joann Pai **10** (top left), **196** (bottom
    left), **386** (bottom left)
Jason Varney **197**